D1258148

Necessity's Child

The Story of Walter Hunt

Necessity's Child

The Story of
WALTER HUNT,
America's Forgotten Inventor

by

JOSEPH NATHAN KANE

McFarland & Company, Inc., Publishers
Jefferson, North Carolina, and London

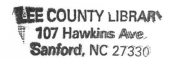

British Library Cataloguing-in-Publication data are available

Library of Congress Cataloguing-in-Publication Data

Kane, Joseph Nathan, 1899–
Necessity's child : the story of Walter Hunt,
America's forgotten inventor / by Joseph Nathan Kane.
p.   cm.
Includes bibliographical references and index.
ISBN 0-7864-0279-2 (case binding : 50# alk. paper) ♾
1. Hunt, Walter, 1796–1859.   2. Inventors—United States—Biography.
3. Inventions—United States—History—19th century.   I. Title.
T40.H8K26 1997   609.2—dc21   96-37134 CIP

FIRST EDITION

Designed by Robert Franklin

Manufactured in the United States of America

*McFarland & Company, Inc., Publishers
Box 611, Jefferson, North Carolina 28640*

Table of Contents

*List of Patent Facsimiles, Inventions
and Illustrations*   vii

Foreword   ix

Preface   xi

The Story   1

Appendix. Scientific American Editorial   297
Appendix. Walter Hunt's Patents   301
Bibliography   305
Index   307

List of Patent Facsimiles, Inventions and Illustrations

Machine for sharpening carving knives—patent granted | 51
Radiator, or globe heating stove | 61
   illustration | 64
   illustration | 65
Spiral springs for belts, pantaloons, etc.—Patent No. **649** | 94
   illustration | 95
Ice-breaking boat—Patent No. **958** | 102
   illustration | 103
Nail making machine—Patent No. **1,407** | 108–109
   illustration | 110
Nail cutting machine—Patent No. **1,853** | 112–114
   illustration | 114
Method of feeding nails into machines
   for cutting—Patent No. **3,305** | 116–117
   illustration | 118
Sole of boots and shoes—Patent No. **3,227** | 124
   illustration | 125
Inkstand (May 1845)—Patent No. **4,062** | 128
   illustration | 129
Inkstand (October 1845)—Patent No. **4,221** | 132
   illustration | 133
Inkstand (December 1845)—Patent No. **4,306** | 135
   illustration | 134

Fountain pen—Patent No. **4,927**   140
   illustration   141
   photograph   303
Method of attaching a ball
   to a wooden cartridge—Patent No. **5,699**   157
   illustration   158
Loaded ball (cartridge)—Patent No. **5,701**   159
   illustration   160
Combined piston-breech and firing-cock
   repeating gun—Patent No. **6,663**   162–164
   illustration   165
Dress pin (i.e., safety pin)—Patent No. **6,281**   168
   illustration   169
   photograph   171
Antipodean apparatus   190
Improvement in bottle stoppers—Patent No. **9,527**   197
   illustration   198
Improvement in sewing machines—Patent No. **11,161**   210–211
   illustration   212
Improvement in shirt collars (original 1854)—Patent No. **11,376**   236
Shirt collar (1856)—Patent No. **14,019**   240
   illustration   241
   Improvement in shirt collars, Reissue No. **1,828** (1864)   244
   Improvement in shirt collars, Reissue No. **1,867** (February 1865)   245
   Improvement in shirt collars, Reissue No. **1,926** (April 1865)   246
   Improvement in shirt collars, Reissue No. **1,927** (April 1865)   247
   Improvement in shirt collars, Reissue No. **2,307** (1866)   248
   illustration   249
Improvement in compound fabrics
   for shirt collars (May 1869)—Patent No. **89,768**   252–253
Improvement in compound fabrics
   for shirt collars (July 1869)—Reissue No. **3,552**   254
Life preserver, or restorative cordial   261
Heel for boots and shoes—Patent No. **24,517**   277–278
   illustration   279
Lamp—Patent No. **32,402**   282–283
   illustration   284

Foreword

This book was begun by Joseph Nathan Kane in the early 1930s. In 1935 a handsome booklet, "Walter Hunt, American Inventor," privately published by Clinton N. Hunt, great-grandson of Walter Hunt, stated that "Mr. Kane's biography of Walter Hunt, to be entitled 'Necessity's Child,' is scheduled for fall [1935] publication." The booklet listed all of Walter Hunt's patents (this list is reprinted in a slightly modified form as the appendix to the present work) and provided facsimiles of all the patent documents, specifications, and drawings, and other similar illustrative matter, that Kane could find in his exhaustive research of his chosen subject. These illustrations appear throughout the text of the present work.

A fire on December 15, 1836, destroyed the original records of the U.S. Patent Office and it is thus impossible to show specifications and drawings of the first seven patents awarded Walter Hunt. Kane has, however, unearthed the records of three of these patents, as well as the original patent document provided to Hunt for his Compound Guard and Knife Sharpener.

Despite that early optimism for the publication of *Necessity's Child* and a lifelong research fascination with Walter Hunt's life in its every recoverable detail, Joseph Nathan Kane's career moved onward. His fame became assured with the publication of *Famous First Facts*, published by the H.W. Wilson Company in 1933, a work that has to date gone through six editions, the most recent being that of 1996. This career might be said to have begun in 1913 with Kane's publication of an article, at age 14, in the *New York Hebrew Standard*; in the early 1920s he worked alongside H.G. Wells as a Washington correspondent for a newspaper syndicate.

Kane is also well known by librarians and researchers for his *Facts About the Presidents* and *Facts About the States* (both published in several editions so far by the H.W. Wilson Company), and *The American Counties* and (with Gerald L. Alexander) *Nicknames and Sobriquets of U.S. Cities, States, and Counties* (both published by the Scarecrow Press in several editions each).

ix

Were one to imitate Kane's factual style, one would write, as *Current Biography* did in November 1985, "The oldest of three living children, Joseph Nathan Kane was born at 12:15 p.m. on January 23, 1899, at 201 West 117th Street on Manhattan's Upper West Side to Albert Norman Kane, an importer of furs, and Hulda (Ascheim) Kane." A record of his accomplishments may be consulted in that and other sources; his achievements have been many. He speaks Spanish, French and German and bits of many other languages, and tells jokes in all of them. He had a radio show in the 1930s and wrote questions (and the all-important answers) for television quiz shows in the 1950s such as "The $64,000 Question."

Throughout the past six decades and more, Kane has carefully husbanded and revised and added to his manuscript on Walter Hunt. He has researched every possible detail on the man's life and inventions, his family, their exact whereabouts from year to year, the price of the food they ate, the names of those asked casually to witness documents, the number of ropewalks, sawmills and three-storey buildings in New York at the moment Hunt invented the such-and-such.

All of this is presented in the text that follows. As Kane suggests in his Preface, he has invented and supplied dialogue and other inconsequential narrative suppositions (his children staying up late to give him a hug, or the fact that missing dinner and working past eleven left him looking tired) in order to provide an appropriate flow of the enormous amount of factual details he has amassed in over seventy years of hunting.

Every fact provided herein, whether in indented extracts or in quotation marks, or merely stated, or provided in dialogue, may be accepted as certainly true and exact. In the 64 years and six editions of the 1500-page *Famous First Facts*, containing over 9,000 "firsts" (discoveries, inventions, and happenings in American history), no one, despite a standing challenge by the author that they do so, has ever found a single factual error. Any error to be found in the text that follows is the fault of the publisher. Information in square brackets has been inferred by the editors.

Author and publisher express their joyful gratitude to David Kane, the author's nephew, for his sunny execution of critical manuscript assembly and courier services around the country, and to Ann Madier, the author's sister, for her selfless, cheerful and invaluable assistance in the final stages of preparation of this work.

The Editors,
McFarland & Company, Inc., Publishers

Preface

There is a tide in the affairs of men
    Which, taken at the flood, leads on to fortune;
Omitted, all the voyage of their life
    Is bound in shallows and in miseries.
        (William Shakespeare—*Julius Caesar*, Act 4, Sc. 3)

In Green-Wood Cemetery, Brooklyn, N.Y., the two litigants in one of America's most bitter legal controversies now rest close to each other. Over the grave of Elias Howe, Jr., whose sewing machine patent earned him royalties of four thousand dollars a day, the French Legion of Honor and posthumous election to the Hall of Fame of New York University, is a huge bronze bust on a massive marble pedestal. Within the length of its shadow is the grave of Walter Hunt marked only by a small red granite shaft. Although Hunt invented his sewing machine twelve years before Howe, his invention brought him only discouragement and heartache.

The sewing machine was one of Walter Hunt's many important inventions. About thirty others, covering a wide variety of fields and subjects, are still used in the identical form in which Hunt devised them over a century ago. Equally astounding is the fact that the name of Walter Hunt is generally unknown to the succeeding generations who have profited from his many inventions.

The story of Walter Hunt is the tragedy of an inventive genius who apparently had so little acumen that he realized only the most meager living from the many inventions he devised, inventions which brought great wealth to the people to whom he sold his ideas.

Had he possessed a business insight to the same degree as he did an inventive ability, he might have been one of the richest men of his time; had he exerted a tithe of the effort of his contemporaries for recognition, he could have immortalized his name. But Hunt cared little for wealth or fame and consequently received neither.

xi

Facts in this book have been gathered from official records, original documents, newspaper stories, and advertisements, and are supplemented by data which have never before appeared in print, obtained from court records, patent files, family documents and conversations and correspondence with descendants, inventors and historians. Undocumented claims of his accomplishments—and there are many—have been ignored in this biography. Since many pertinent records have been destroyed by fire, vandalism and the ravages of time, this account does not give Walter Hunt all the credit to which he may be entitled. Nevertheless, even an incomplete record of his achievements and inventions ranks him among America's foremost inventors.

Walter Hunt, date unknown

So outstanding were his achievements that it would be superfluous to magnify them. No deviation from fact has been made, historical accuracy being adhered to in every instance. The quotations given in indented extracts are from actual documents and papers, but much dialogue has been invented to aid in revealing his story.

The author's intent is to portray honestly Walter Hunt and his inventions so that the world may judge him and his contributions wholly from facts.

Veritas simplex oratio est (Seneca).

JOSEPH NATHAN KANE
Spring 1997

Chapter 1

The impending strike in April 1828 at the flax mill was the most important event in Lowville, Lewis County, New York, since the War of 1812.

"We'll strike!" an angry workman shouted.

"Like the journeymen hatters did!" yelled a millhand.

"And the ship caulkers," a freckled thirteen year old apprentice added.

"And like—"

"You can all do what you want!" The embittered demonstrators were out-shouted by the husky voice of Willis Hoskins, proprietor and owner of the Lowville flax mill, standing on the front steps of the doorway of the mill and using a speaking-trumpet borrowed from the fire company. "If you don't want to work here, there are others who'd be glad to have your jobs!"

Boos and hisses interrupted and flax spinners surged menacingly about him as he cautiously retreated. In desperation, he shouted, "We must meet the competition of other mills, and when the price drops, your pay goes down. There's no alternative. That's the way it is."

"I don't agree with you!" shouted a dissenter.

"You know our wage is just and fair and—"

"I don't agree with you!"

"Ah, so it's you, Walter Hunt, who wants to argue!" Hoskins said with a sneer. "Come up front, here, if you have anything to say, which I doubt."

A sturdily built, ruddy complexioned worker edged forward, thirty years old, six feet three inches tall, auburn hair. He didn't look his age. The crowd made way for him.

Hoskins immediately regretted his hasty invitation. He shook his fist as Hunt approached the steps and warned, "Don't you get your steam up, Walter Hunt. Don't you start any trouble. You know just as well as I do that we're obliged to make this wage cut."

All eyes were focused on Hunt as he passed through the crowd and ascended the steps. Slowly and with great poise he mounted the steps. He towered ten

1

inches above Hoskins. Hunt weighed over two hundred pounds and seemed strong enough to pick up Hoskins with one hand and toy with him like a rag doll. The mood was tense. The crowd awaited action.

A few seconds passed and nothing happened, except Hunt fumbled with the open whittling knife in his hand. He carefully closed it and placed it in his trouser pocket and tucked the object he had been whittling inside his shirt. He was neither embarrassed nor angry. He seemed to be in no particular hurry to talk. When he began to talk, the crowd was silent, and everyone listened intently.

"Mr. Hoskins," Hunt said quietly and boldly, "you are the same as all the other mill owners. If you can't make money with your brains, you want to oppress the laborer."

"We are all paying all we can," Hoskins countered.

"'They are paying all they can'," Hunt mocked him, pitching his voice to reach the rear of the crowd. "They offer men five dollars a week, but are they hiring men? Precious few. Instead they use women because they work for less. Women who get only two twenty and children a dollar and a quarter a week. Do I have to tell you all this?"

"No! No!" The crowd roared in unison.

"And they work hard and long, eighty-four hours a week. Eighty-four hours! Fourteen hours a day! Six days a week! It isn't human! It's slavery, and now they dare to offer even less."

"I suspicion you don't know what you are talking about, Walter Hunt!" Hoskins bellowed loudly and angrily. "You're a farmer! What do you know about business? We don't tell you how to run your farm and don't you tell us what to do. We are losing money here as it is, and if there is any contrary mind, we will close the factory for good."

"A reduction in the wage scale," Hunt continued, "will affect our entire community and industry. A wage cut will not reduce the mill's losses but will create a still greater deficit."

"He doesn't know what he's talking about," Hoskins shouted.

"Let him finish!" someone yelled.

"A reduction in the wage scale will lessen the amount of money in circulation. That in turn will curtail purchases of all commodities and will not increase the sale of flax."

The crowd eagerly absorbed every word. Hunt's speech was taking root. "Low wages discourage people from working in the mill and stimulate home labor. The greater the number of homeworkers, and the more finished flax offered in the market in competition with the products of the mill, the lower the price."

"That's right. He's right!" voices called out.

"Walter Hunt is right," a woman yelled.

"Be so good as to measure your ribands, Mr. Hunt, and hold your tongue."

Attention was newly directed to Ziba Knox, one of Lowville's favorite sons. "We have no need for your advice."

Hunt knew Knox. His fists grew taut and his eyes flared. "Sarcasm can't offset facts, and it won't put wages back into your pockets." The crowd drank in every word. No one moved. Everyone listened attentively.

"Centralization of industry is not detrimental," Hunt expounded. "On the contrary, it is beneficial: The only reason your mill can't compete with home-made linen is because it is not operated efficiently. What the mill needs is a machine to spin flax in large quantities at a low cost. That's the real solution to your problems."

"You seem to know everything, Hunt. Can you tell us what to do?" Willis Hoskins taunted him.

"I should admire to," Hunt answered.

"Well, we're waiting."

"Get better machinery."

"Get better machinery?" Ziba Knox snorted. "You sound as if you are corned. Get better machinery! Huh? Where can you get it?"

"Buy it!" Hunt commanded.

"You know none can be bought."

"Then make it," Hunt ordered.

"You're a bigger greenhorn than I thought," was Knox's sarcastic retort.

The denunciation angered Hunt. He might have said that it was his mechanical ability which enabled Willis Hoskins and Ziba Knox to obtain their patent two years ago on a spinning and roping machine. But he kept quiet. His blue eyes narrowed and he dug his fingernails into the palms of his hands. He gritted his teeth.

"Go ahead, Hunt. Lace the wool-lightning out of him! You got my blessing," wheezed one workman.

"You seem to think, Mr. Knox, that there are no brains in Lowville," Hunt said angrily, "but you are wrong!"

"Am I?" Knox sneered.

"There are brains in Lowville. There's Wood, Merrill and King." He pointed them out in the crowd. (Elias Wood had received a patent on an improved flax machine; C. Merrill, C. Batchellor and S. King had jointly received a patent on a "horizontal spinner.") The three acknowledged the recognition by nodding, which Hunt interpreted as substantiating his point.

"There are brains in Lowville," Hunt repeated, "and certainly a solution to our problems can be found here. Amicably, I hope."

An enthusiastic cheer arose from the workers. Hunt's confidence and assurance seemed both inspiring and convincing.

"Walter Hunt talks for all of us," a young apprentice shouted.

"I've heard enough of this foolish stuff," Knox said with studied sarcasm.

"Let him talk! Let's hear him out," another voice roared.

"If you could make a better machine, Hunt, why haven't you?" Knox concluded.

Hiram Hunt, four years younger, rushed to his brother's support. "He can do it! When Charles Bradish and myself obtained our patent on a horizontal machine for spinning wool and cotton, who do you think did the mechanical work? Walter!"

"I suppose he can do everything," Knox retorted.

"I don't know much about flax machinery," Hunt interjected.

"Of course you don't," Knox sneered.

"No, but I'd be ashamed of myself if I couldn't build better machinery than you have in the mill."

"And how'll you do it?"

"By using a little horse sense."

"You're drunk."

"Maybe he isn't," Hoskins interrupted. "There may be something to what Hunt says. He did pretty good building that spinning and roping machine for us. I say let's give him a chance. If he can come up with something better, that'll be fine, but if he can't, there'll be no more argument about the wage cut."

Hoskins' quick reversal startled the crowd. The mood changed. The mill workers mostly muffled their discontent, their feelings of helplessness and hopelessness. Their anger subsided. But not everyone was satisfied. The militant group opposed the wait-and-see tack.

"Imagine the nerve of that fellow, saying he could build a better flax spinner!"

"You'd think no one else in the world had tried to do it."

"Well, he'll fail. Those that talk the loudest usually do."

"Hunt spends all his time tinkering in his barn. Polly Loucks sure made a mistake when she married that bum!"

"Yup, and they say every time he gets a dollar, he sends away for a newfangled fool contraption to help make them wheels turn."

"Looks like the only good thing about him is he's a Democrat. It's a wonder he ain't a Federalist with his crazy ideas."

But a more conciliatory spirit prevailed among the crowd.

"We differ on lots of things, Hunt," Hoskins countered, "but if you want to work on a new machine, I'll give you all the help I can. How'd you like me for a partner?"

"That's a right smart idea," Hunt said, eagerly pumping Hoskins' hand. "A right smart idea."

Faster than leaves in a hurricane, news of the encounter blanketed the hillside. Everyone was discussing it.

Later that day at her large stove, Walter's wife Polly tossed a seasoning of grated nutmeg, pepper, and salt mixed with a little thyme, sage, lemon peel and bread crumbs on some washed and skinned eels before sticking them on skewers. Walter's parents, Sherman and Rachel Hunt, breathlessly rushed into the cabin, asking where was Walter.

"I don't know. Is anything the matter?"

"Haven't you heard the fool thing he's done?" Sherman snapped.

"Of course, I have. And it's not foolish. If Walter says he can build a better flax spinner, he can."

"You're right, Polly," Rachel Hunt agreed. "When Walter wants to do something, he can do it. He was always a persistent one. Did I ever tell you how that trait showed itself when he was only six years of age?"

Polly did not reply. She looked in vain at her father-in-law, who fidgeted in his chair and sighed. She was resigned to hear the story. She knew that her mother-in-law liked to tell anecdotes about her firstborn and that practically nothing could stop her from her monologues.

"Walter had a great aversion to cornmeal," she began dramatically. "He wouldn't eat anything in which it was used. When we baked bread with it he would say, 'I don't want cornmeal and I won't eat it.' He'd keep insisting over and over again. Arguments and threats did no good. Sherman was afraid that Walter's health would be affected, so he formed a new plan.

"Sherman said, 'I'll make a bargain with you. When the present supply of cornmeal is gone, you'll not have to eat any more of it.' He didn't tell Walter that in the barn there were two sacks weighing about forty pounds each. Sherman always prided himself on being smooth."

Sherman Hunt cast a furtive glance at Polly. He twiddled his thumbs and winked at her.

"The following night, when it looked as if all the arguments had been settled, I returned home after a busy day in the fields. As I neared the cabin, I could hear my daughters Hannah and Almira cheering and screaming. I opened the door and saw a big blaze in the fireplace. Sparks were flying and Hiram, only two at the time, was sitting right in their path. I pulled him away. I didn't know what to make of it until I saw Walter come in with a pan heaped high with cornmeal. Before I knew what was going on, he threw the cornmeal on the fire.

"'What are you doing?' I shouted, 'Do you want to set the cabin on fire? Don't you know that it is a sin to destroy food?'

"And what do you think he answered?"

Neither Polly nor Sherman attempted to reply, although they both knew what she was going to say.

"He said he wanted to get rid of the cornmeal, so that he wouldn't have to eat it any more. 'Why didn't you stop when you saw the blaze and smoke?' I asked. 'Because I must finish what I began!' Walter replied."

"That's my husband. He's never changed." Polly commented. "Once he makes up his mind, good or bad…" She paused. "But there's a difference. He's not stubborn."

"I'm not sure about that," Sherman said. "I don't know whether he's plain stubborn, or persistent, or…"

"Whatever it is," Rachel Hunt interrupted, "it's all right. Do you remember when Walter was eight. Do you remember that day on the fields?"

"What day?"

Sherman's sarcasm did not reach Rachel. She settled herself comfortably in the straight-backed cane chair and related the tale as if it just happened.

"One morning, Sherman, after a brief inspection of the fields, came home and said he'd lost several hundred dollars on the farm. Turns out an unseasonable frost had killed the crops. I was very upset. Our farm was mortgaged and the loss was serious. We didn't pay much attention that Walter missed lunch. He often did as he played with the Indian boys in the woods. But he didn't come home for dinner either, so we set out to look for him. We found him at the far end of the farm. He was shivering, his face was blood-red and his lips were tinged with blue. His jacket was stuffed with corn husks and rushes, and his shoes bound with them to keep out the cold.

"We carried him home and gave him some hot broth. After the chill had gone, we asked him, 'What were you doing? Why weren't you home for lunch or dinner?'"

Rachel paused. "What do you think he was doing?"

"I don't know," Polly said. "I've heard many stories about Walter, but this is a new one to me."

"Walter was looking for the money that Sherman 'lost' on the farm. Poor boy. He thought that the loss was in cash. I'll never forget that day if I live to be a hundred."

A lump formed in Polly's throat.

"That happened when Walter was eight. Twenty-two years ago," Rachel added significantly. She then turned to Sherman. "Guess we won't wait until Walter returns." To Polly, she said, "Better not tell Walter we were here."

Sherman and Rachel Hunt left and walked arm and arm down the dirt path towards home. Polly resumed cooking dinner. She fixed the seasoned eels on skewers and fastened them to the spit. She roasted them until they began to crack and appeared white at the bone.

Walter came home about dusk. There was a peculiar gleam in his eye as he entered the cabin. Polly wanted to ask him about the argument at the mill but she waited for him to bring up the subject first.

"Has Hiram been around?" he asked.

"No," Polly replied. "Anything the matter?"

"No." Walter slumped into a chair. He was spinning a four-sided red lead pencil in his hands and intermittently rubbed his thumbs over the edges. He pulled a sheet of crumbled paper out of his side pocket and made a few notations on it. Some minutes passed without further conversation.

"I think I have it," he suddenly blurted out, arising from his chair.

"What?"

"Oh nothing. I'm going to the barn. First I'll say good night to the children."

In turn he kissed two year old Caroline, eight year old Walter, Jr., and thirteen year old Polly Anne. Then he went to the barn, which was fitted as a combination toolshop and workroom.

Polly was unhappy about Walter's irregular hours and his total disregard of meals. His staring into space, his absentmindedness and his inattention at times to her conversation aggravated her. But Polly had more or less became resigned to these idiosyncrasies. In fact she knew of them before they were wed. When Polly married him, [twelve] years after the death of her first husband, Dr. William Loucks, she had heard the town gossips ridicule him.

"If he spent as much time on the farm as he does reading, his crops'd be a heap sight better."

"All he thinks about is ways to do away with work. He works harder at that than any three men on the job."

"He's too shiftless. Wantin' to paint pictures of trees and people, too. If he puts that paint brush of his on the side of his barn, that Hunt farm would look better by a jugful."

"I don't see what Polly sees in him. He's always miles away in his mind."

Many times Polly had this kind of idle chatter. But it didn't turn her against him. Perhaps it was this very gossip that had stimulated her first interest in him. Anyway, time had proven the gossipers wrong.

That day's incident at the flax mill convinced her that time had not changed people's viewpoints. She knew that both praise and blame were indiscriminately applied to Walter. This time an opportunity had come to discredit or vindicate himself.

That evening Hunt began to work in the barn. He spent the entire night drawing and sketching under the flickering oil lamp suspended from the rafters. He didn't leave until daylight when he attended to his daily chores in the fields. The following day, just before dusk, he rushed over to see Willis Hoskins at the flax mill before closing time.

"Mr. Hoskins," Hunt said, "regarding the mill, I have an idea."

"There's a heap of difference between an idea and an invention," Hoskins observed as he looked up from the papers and patterns spread on his work table.

Hunt pulled some worksheets from inside his coat. He placed them on the desk and proceeded to describe his drawings. Hoskins listened intently.

When Hunt had concluded, Hoskins said, "I guess you do have something there. If it works out as well in practice as in theory."

"I'll make it work," Hunt assured him. "I know I can do it…" He corrected himself. "I mean we'll both do it together."

The days passed slowly. Then weeks, and the weeks stretched into months. Parts were designed and almost instantly redesigned. Model after model was completed and discarded as impractical. The flax spinner did not work as smoothly in actual operation as the plans indicated on paper. In a short time, the barn was littered with discarded parts and equipment. Hoskins became pessimistic, his patience taxed.

"This can't go on!" he exploded one night after several hours of work. "I can't give up my life to this fool invention. Like as not, we will never get it to work at all, let alone work efficiently."

"Just a little more time," Hunt pleaded.

"Just a little more time, just a little more time," Hoskins mimicked. "I know. Then it'll be finished. That's what you keep saying all the time."

But Hunt was right. After a few more days of minor adjustments, he was ready to test the flax machine. The completed model stood five feet long, two and a half feet high and three feet wide. And it worked. Mission accomplished. Lowville buzzed with excitement. Even the most skeptical felt optimistic. Everyone hoped that the new machine would increase production and that way the old wage scale could be maintained.

The gossip stopped and Walter Hunt was again regarded with respect. Those who had been the most vehement with their ridicule became the most vociferous with their praise. Compliments were showered on Hunt but he paid no attention to them. He knew that if the machine broke down or failed to increase production, condemnation would be conferred just as easily.

As Hoskins demonstrated the completed model to his associates and the millhands, he beamed with pride and satisfaction and boasted proudly, "I knew all the time we could do it."

Hunt smiled. He knew how near the machine had been to abandonment and the anxiety and worry its manufacture had given them.

"We'll invite the whole town to see it," Hoskins shouted. "We'll invite the whole country, we'll invite the whole world to see it."

But Hunt's enthusiasm had waned. He had reached his objective and overcome the obstacle. As far as he was concerned, the task was completed.

The townsfolk and visitors from nearby towns flocked to Hunt's barn to see the newfangled flax machine in operation. One of the most enthusiastic was the caustic Ziba Knox.

"Are you going to get a patent on it?" Knox inquired.

"That's what we're aiming to do," Hoskins replied. "We've got the application all drawn up. I was going with Walter to Doig's office to have him sign as witness."

"I'll go with you," Knox said eagerly, "and I'd like to sign also as a witness."

The trio followed the narrow winding path into town until they came to a small building which bore a neatly painted sign: "Andrew Wheeler Doig, County Clerk, Lewis County."

Doig took the patent application, wrote the date, Saturday May 20, 1826, and penned his signature with his usual flourish and embellishments below those of the inventors and the witness. He scarcely glanced at the four and a half pages of closely written descriptive matter and the instructions for operating the machine. His action was perfunctory.

"Hope they give you a patent," Doig said returning the application and pocketing the notarization fee.

Thirty-three days later, on June 22, 1826, Hoskins burst into Hunt's house at dinnertime. "Here it is," he announced jubilantly. "Here it is. All official." He proudly displayed the patent, On Spinning Flax and Hemp.*

"Look at the signatures!" Hunt said in amazement.

Hoskins read aloud: "John Quincy Adams, President of the United States; Henry Clay, Secretary of State; and William Wirt, Attorney General."

"And to think that with all their duties, they had time to examine our patent," Hunt exclaimed.

When Polly saw the beribboned patent signed by the three most illustrious persons in the United States, she was overwhelmed. She threw her arms about Walter and kissed him. Even the children realized that this was an auspicious occasion. Polly Anne jumped up and down with glee, and Walter, Jr., shouted, "My father's 'n ventor." Sensing the happiness, Caroline M., two years old, clapped her hands.

"Walter, it's a birthday present to you from the government," Polly joked, waving the patent, "For your thirtieth birthday."

"Not for a month. I won't be thirty till July 29th," Hunt corrected.

"Always exact," Polly teased. "Always technical. Some day your attention to details will make you a millionaire."

But Hunt smiled at Polly's naïveté. He knew otherwise. He knew that a patent had no value unless it was manufactured and exploited, and that it would not be easy to raise the capital to manufacture the flax spinner. He was not particularly distressed that Lowville did not see fit to finance its manufacture. He knew that new ideas were often stifled by provincialism, a viewpoint similarly shared by Hoskins.

"I don't imagine it will be difficult to raise capital in New York City," Hunt stated, "even if no one here is interested."

*See Reel #1—1790–1836; May 25, 1826, Hunt; recorded anew February 25, 1875. A fire on December 15, 1836, destroyed the records of the U.S. Patent Office. The specifications and drawings of the first seven patents awarded Walter Hunt are thus lost. The author has unearthed the records of three of these patents, and the original patent for the Compound Guard and Knife Sharpener (see page 51).

"I don't care," said Hoskins angrily. "If Lowville can't raise the capital to market the machine, then we'll go to Connecticut."

"But why Connecticut?" Hunt asked. "We don't have to go out of New York State for anything. New York is the finest of our twenty-four states, and it has five cities, New York, Albany, Troy, Hudson and Schenectady."

"I know," Hoskins interrupted. "I've heard you say it also has fifty-four counties and six hundred and sixty townships. You sound like a gazetteer sometimes. But suppose we don't want to go to a city?"

"Well, I still think New York City is the place, but if you don't want to go to a 'city,' then we can go to a town. There's Utica, Rochester, Brooklyn, Buffalo and Lockport."

Hoskins did not reply.

"There's also Lansingburgh, Canandaigua or Auburn," Hunt continued. As an afterthought he added, "And Geneva, Sacket's Harbor or Poughkeepsie."

"I guess you're right, Hunt," Hoskins agreed. "A city is better. We will have it your way."

"It's not my way," Hunt explained, "It's the best way. New York City is the ideal place for us. Why there are sixteen banks there with an eighty-three million dollars in capital."

Hoskins laughed. "Your arguments are sound. New York is the principal marketplace in the state, it's suitable for land and water transportation, and it's near both the source of supply and the sales market."

"And it's not too far from Lowville," Hunt added.

"You go to the city, Hunt. You can spare the time."

"No! I've never been out of Lowville, and I don't hanker to go. You go! You know more about business than I do. You know how to deal with businessmen. And furthermore, I'm sure Polly won't let me go."

But Walter Hunt was wrong about Polly. As soon as the decision was reached, she was eager for Walter to go to New York City. She knew that it had always been his secret dream to participate in the industrial life of a great city. And she knew that his hesitating to grasp the opportunity now offered him was only because of his dutiful reluctance to leave her and the children, especially since he had so neglected them while working on the flax spinner.

He had been so busy that Polly had refrained from telling him that there was to be a new addition to the family, afraid that the news of increased responsibilities would somehow deter him from his work. She had planned to tell him as soon as the invention was completed, but somehow in all the excitement of people rushing to the barn to see it in operation and the enthusiasm upon the receipt of the patent, she had not yet done so. Now she was glad she had said nothing for he certainly would refuse to go if he knew of her condition. Polly stoically convinced him that he owed it to himself and family to undertake the trip which, if successful, might put an end to all their financial problems.

"If you think so, I'll go," Walter agreed resignedly.

"Maybe we can make a lot of money selling this flax spinner to others. It would pay us handsomely for our time," Hoskins said.

"I'm not doing this just for the money," Hunt exclaimed. "It's the challenge. It's the fun of overcoming the odds, the joy of pioneering, the satisfaction of accomplishment and the help given to the mill and the mill workers."

"Well, I don't imagine hard-earned cash isn't just as important," Hoskins said philosophically.

Hunt's upcoming trip was the talk of the town for many days before he left. He assumed a bravado that he scarcely felt and tried to appear nonchalant although inwardly he was tense with excitement.

He took one of the smaller models of the flax machine apart and carefully packed it into a wooden case and tied a stout rope around it. The smaller parts he placed in a linen bag. The packing of Hunt's clothes presented no problem. He dumped them into a portmanteau and had space enough for some tools he tenderly laid on top.

When the day came, it seemed like eternity before the stagecoach arrived. When it stopped at the inn to pick up and discharge passengers and packages, an unusually large crowd was there to wish him bon voyage. Hunt tried hard to conceal his emotions.

"Don't let the city slickers scalp you!"

"When you make your first million, send us a letter."

"Don't get lonesome in the wicked city."

Solicitous friends and facetious neighbors filled the air with sallies as Hunt climbed into the rickety egg-shaped coach drawn by four horses which was to convey him the forty-one miles from Lowville to Utica. At Utica, he changed to another stagecoach, which bobbed like a canoe in a squall, and jolted him all the way to Albany.

Hunt did not grumble about the crowded coach, originally built to accommodate only six passengers. He marveled at the uncanny ability of the coach to sink into every rut and hit every obstruction.

"Don't complain," advised the corpulent passenger alongside him, fouling the air with pungent smoke from an evil smelling Connecticut segar, "you're lucky that there was only a slight rain yesterday. The last time I took this trip I and all the passengers had to get out to make the coach lighter. Then we had to help pull it out of a mud hole."

Another passenger commented, "And we can be lucky this coach hasn't turned over. It usually does, especially when the driver takes a turn too fast."

The coach made stops in front of the taverns at Turin, Leydon, Booneville, Remsen and Trenton where baggage and passenger changes were made. Hunt appreciated the interludes in the long and tortuous journey as it afforded him an opportunity to see the countryside and stretch his cramped limbs.

Throughout the trip, Hunt eagerly looked forward to reaching Albany, where he would have his first chance to see a steamboat.

Albany came at last, but Hunt had little opportunity to visit the city, which consisted of one street of very considerable length, parallel with the river, from which the rest of the city rose abruptly. Not many of its population of 15,000 were at the dock as the arrival and departure of steamboats was a common occurrence.

At daybreak the following morning, Hunt boarded the safety barge *Lady Clinton* and paid the fare of one dollar to Captain George E. Seymour, who also acted as purser. The barge, which left Albany on schedule on Wednesdays and Saturdays, was a flatboat with chairs and benches scattered about for use by the passengers. Spit boxes were located in the corners and at strategic points. Hunt had heard reports about these barges but was now able to observe that the much heralded "snow white awning" which served to deflect soot from the belching smokestack on the steamboat which towed the barge, bore little similarity to its advertised description. Faded by the sun and punctured with holes caused by burning cinders, spotted by oil and streaked by rain, it was no thing of beauty. However, it served as a protection from the sun and wind.

At the dock, the barge was connected by a gangplank to the steamboat *Commerce* but when the trip began it was pulled up and left in the stern of the steamboat. The barge proved to be a better form of transportation than the steamboat. It provided none of the bone-shaking vibrations and offered greater protection in case of a boiler explosion.

The blast of the steamboat startled Hunt. It was a weird penetrating sound, louder than any he had ever heard.

"What's the matter?" he inquired nervously as he saw his fellow passengers line up alongside the deck.

Two more shrill blasts in quick succession rent the air.

"What's the matter?" Hunt repeated.

"Nawthing's the matter," said an old man beside him, "that's the going signal."

With a sudden yank that strained the tow line and seemed to cause the bow to squeak in agony, the steamboat, followed by the passenger-laden barge, proceeded downstream on the one hundred and fifty-four mile trip to the metropolis, New York City.

Chapter 2

Sailing vessels with extended cotton canvas sails, cockboats loaded with fish, poultry and fruit skittered away from the Cortland Street pile-reinforced pier to make room for the churning steamboat to dock. Before the clank and roar of the machinery had subsided, a riotous crowd of begrimed attendants, vagrants and busybodies gathered near the quivering gangplank.

After the ropes and hawsers had moored the boat to the pier, the passengers disembarked. Men stood by while women descended first. Husbands, even though accompanied by their wives, were not allowed on the gangplank—not permitted off the boat—until all the women had landed.

Hucksters, peddlers, hackney coach drivers and porters intent on their wares and services noisily greeted the disembarking passengers.

"Corn piping hot! Hot corn."

"Soda. Iced soda!"

"Carriages. Carriages."

The hustle and bustle was disturbing to Hunt. He accepted it with a measure of alarm, oblivious to the fact that his appearance was also unusual to the onlookers. Very tall, sinewy, sturdy and upright, his muscular appearance bespoke an outdoor life beneath country skies. Baggy, unfashionable homespun typified him as a farmer. Obviously he was a newcomer, and was eagerly welcomed by the porters and hucksters who swooped upon him like vultures seizing prey.

A policeman approached Hunt and cautioned, "Don't let these thieves shave you."

"Of course not," Hunt replied good-humoredly, "I shave myself."

The policeman laughed and walked away. He had gone only a few steps when he again noticed Hunt besieged by more porters.

"Don't hurry me!" Hunt warned. The porters hesitated. Here was a man who apparently knew his own mind. Certainly not as easy as his country clothes indicated. His voice was low and quiet. Force and determination were in his eyes

13

and his firm-set jaw. The porters observed his physique and put his baggage down, but not without argument.

"Hey, you," the policeman said, returning to Hunt, "I thought your answer was smart, but now I know you don't know what I was talking to yez about. When I said 'Don't let them shave you' I meant don't let them overcharge you. Shave means 'cheat' here."

"I didn't know that," Hunt confessed. "I thought you were joking."

"Ye gotta be careful of these water-rats," he warned in his distinctive brogue "They'll steal your eye-balls right out of your eyes. And where did you say you wanted to go?"

"I don't really know," Hunt answered, "I'm looking for lodging. I expect to be in the city just a short time."

The policeman reached in his pockets and brought out a few soiled pages torn from Blunt's *Stranger's Guide to the Commercial Metropolis*. They were creased with innumerable folds and showed much evidence of handling.

"Well, if you got a lot of money, you can stop at the City Hotel at Thames and Cedar streets. If you stay two days or more, they'll charge a dollar fifty a day. Or ten dollars a week. You can also get board there for five fifty a week."

"That's a lot of money."

"It's worth it. The City Hotel has more than a hundred rooms, and it has two entrances, one for guests on the American plan, and one for those on the European plan."

Hunt did not understand the difference but concealed his ignorance.

"Bunker's Mansion House at 39 Broadway and the National Hotel at 112 Broadway will fit you up good for twelve dollars a week, including meals," the policeman volunteered after again looking at the list.

"That's a heap of money! Twelve dollars a week!" he said astonished. "Nothing cheaper?"

"Well, there's the Park Place House, the Franklin House and Niblo's Bank Coffee House. Seven dollars a week."

"I didn't come to the city to spend money," Hunt explained, "I came to make money. Can't you tell me a good cheap genteel place?"

The officer referred to his list. "There's lots of places. Now take Broadway. No. 5 is Mrs. M'Intyre's, No. 13 is Mrs. Baker's place. Mrs. Wood's is at No. 24, Mrs. Chapman's at No. 33. There's any number of places at two or three dollars a week."

"Can you recommend a good private place?" Hunt asked.

The officer reflected a few minutes. "Why don't you go to the Gadwin house? Well, it was Gadwin's house. Now it's the Montgomery Boarding House, owned by William Albertson. You can get a room for two dollars a week."

"Where is it?"

"At 65 Barclay Street, three doors from Greenwich Street."

"I'll go there," Hunt said. He picked up his portmanteau and a bundle with one hand and lifted the wood packing case with the other.

"And, you want to carry that stuff?" the bewildered policeman asked. "Why, man, you can't do that, this is a big city."

"It may cost too much to take a coach."

"Well, I don't know how much money you have, but I know you can't carry all that stuff. It'll only cost twenty-five cents a mile in a hackney. At least, you should load it on a handcart. They're only allowed to charge eighteen and three-quarter cents a mile. Wait a minute—put your stuff on a wheelbarrow, they'll charge twelve and a half a mile."

"I'll move it for you, mister. You walk alongside me," a black porter with a strap fastened over his shoulders and a brass plate with a number on his breast, proceeded to load the packages on his wheelbarrow.

"Give me so slick," the officer scolded, "you won't do no such thing unless this man wants to." Hunt acquiesced and the porter finished loading his effects.

"Don't walk him all through the town," the policeman warned. "Take him the shortest way."

"Mister, we go this way," the porter informed Hunt. He pointed north. "The first street is Dey, then Fulton, then Vesey, then Barclay. Four blocks north, then east to Washington and Greenwich Street."

Hunt thanked the obliging policeman and then followed the porter and the heavily loaded wheelbarrow. Leisurely they strode up West Street, dodging packing cases and merchandise on the streets at the same time avoiding the ruts and puddles which blotched the path. Hunt's blue eyes devoured the strange sights of the seething city. Its magnitude was almost inconceivable.

A startled sow dashed in front of them trying to escape stones thrown by a group of boys. Hunt bellowed at the boys and they scattered.

"Does this happen often?" Hunt inquired.

"What, sah?"

"Boys throwing stones at the porkers."

"Oh yaas, sah. Oh yaas, sah. Those pigs are no good. The city has lots of them, about twelve thousand. They smell awful."

The walk uptown was a revelation to Hunt. Lean, dirty and starving dogs rushed about chasing alley cats who were preying on well fed water rats and mice. Foul odors from dunghills and outhouses and uncollected garbage permeated the air.

"How can people tolerate all this filth?" Hunt asked.

"The city ain't all like this. It has right pretty places too," the porter answered.

Hunt made no further comment. He was busy dodging the old men and Negresses peddling apples, oysters, clams, pears, fish, buns, tea rusk, yeast and spiced gingerbread. He watched the peddlers scurry in and out of the pedestrian and vehicular traffic. Many carried their wares, shoes, hats, and other belongings tied by cord and strung on poles. He was pestered by them and their doubtful bargains.

"Aren't there any shops—any merchants—besides these?" Hunt pointed to the ship chandleries and the innumerable taverns which lined West Street.

"Oh, sah," the porter replied, "lots of them in this city. About six hundred places where a man can get a good fresh ale."

"I mean stores. Where are they?"

"Stores. Shops. Business houses." The porter repeated each word carefully, proud of his knowledge. "Why, sah, we've got more of them than you can count... Too many of them."

They turned into Barclay Street and stopped in front of No. 65. A black houseman came to the door wearing a blue damask apron which extended from his neck to below his knees, concealing his sweater and grimy pantaloons.

"You want the boss," he volunteered. "I'll go fetch him."

He returned with William Albertson, an elderly gentleman whose cravat matched his carrot colored hair. He carried a metal horn with a flexible tubing, the extremity of which he inserted in his ear. The speaking trumpet he held like a horn in front of Hunt's face.

Although Hunt had never seen anything like it before, he surmised that the horn was intended as a hearing aid and he spoke into it. He talked louder than usual and had no idea whether his words were heard. The landlord's expression was motionless.

"I have only one empty room. If you want it, it's only two dollars a week, payable in advance."

The room had a four-post bedstead covered by a crocheted blanket, a small wooden chest, a washstand and a dressing table on which stood a little mahogany framed looking glass and a thin cotton towel the size of a pocket handkerchief. There was only one window, partially covered by a muslin blind. Hunt, with a little difficulty, raised the window. At a certain angle, he had an unobstructed view of the Hudson River and could clearly see the Jersey shore in the distance.

Hunt was satisfied and took two silver dollars from his folding leather coin purse and handed them to the landlord. He then paid the porter, and the houseman carried Hunt's baggage upstairs to the room. Hunt poured some water from the hand-painted water pitcher into a ceramic bowl. After he washed, he emptied the water into the slop pail alongside and used the commode as a writing table and wrote to Polly.

He described the steamboat, the stagecoaches and his impressions of what he had seen. He concluded with, "I have not yet seen the city, and I cannot give you my estimate of it, but I am certain of one thing. I am going to succeed and soon I will be home with my loved ones. I am going to look over the city so that I will know how to proceed on the morrow."

"If you want to see the city," the landlord, Albertson, advised Hunt the following morning, "start with Broadway. It's three miles long and extends from the Battery as far north as Tenth Street. I'll go with you a few blocks and show you the sights."

Hunt noticed that the average width of Broadway was eighty feet, but the profusion of Lombardy poplars near the curb made the distance appear less. The streets were paved with cobblestones but huge gaps and holes were evident. The sidewalks, by contrast, were level and straight and their gneiss and mica slate content made them sparkle in the sun.

"Buildings on both sides of the street, as far up and down as you can see!" Hunt exclaimed in surprise, "and lots of them of brick. And look at the painted shutters!"

Old Mr. Albertson straightened up as if the observation was a compliment intended for him. He felt proud and pointed out, "There's the Merchants Exchange at Wall Street."

"That's the prettiest building I ever did see. What's that crazy fellow doing up there?" He pointed to a man in the cupola of a building constantly changing the position of two crossbars on the extremity of a pole.

"I don't know, but I heard it was something to do with boats coming up and down the river." Albertson didn't know that the two bars, or arms, adjusted to twelve different positions, were used to signal to Sandy Hook via Staten Island by means of a code which enabled the operators principally to obtain news of incoming vessels.

Hunt did not pursue his questioning. Yelling into the man's ear trumpet was too difficult just to make conversation. He found it easier to listen and wonder.

"If you want to see some pretty colored satins, bombazines, Mandarin capes, merino and cashmere shawls, you oughta look into this window." Albertson said pointing to P. L. Vandervoort's store at 111 Broadway. The show windows were piled high with Levantines, patent flannels warranted not to shrink, black Vestalines for ladies' mourning dresses and other cloths.

The walk north tired Albertson and he soon left. Hunt continued walking. Henry Suydam's show window at No. 286 Broadway flaunted blue and green cloth table and piano covers, Marseille quilts and strikingly odd Irish diapers. Across the street at Charles E. Muzzy & Company, 287 Broadway, blue and green taffetas were featured together with blue and green umbrellas with whalebone frames. At the same address, Cochran and Affoms displayed long scarlet merino shawls, and crimson, blue and scarlet cashmere shawls.

Hunt stopped in front of 321 Broadway and observed the sign, "Intelligence Office. Male and female help can be obtained by applying at this office." Other signs also commanded his attention. Coffin Warehouse. Oyster Refectory. Hollowware, Spiders and Firelogs. Flour and Feed Store. Cheap Store. Clothing Store. Cake Store and Bakery. Wine and Tea Store. Leather and Finding Store.

The sign "Undercurrent Note Store" interested him. He found out that it referred to the practice of buying notes and commercial papers of the banks located outside the city whose rates and notes were subject to constant fluctuations.

Hunt observed a crowd in front of M. D. Whitin's store at 407 Broadway which featured unbleached sheetings at 12½¢ a yard and "oxygen soap" for "making the complexion one shade clearer and ruddier than usual." A barker outside the store was shouting the virtues of "nature's remedy, the one and only oxygen soap."

An onlooker attracted by the spiel whispered to Hunt, "These new things are all fakes."

"Do you mean that just because a thing is new," Hunt answered, "it is a fake?"

"The only things that are good are those that are tried and true."

"I'm going in to buy some of that new soap," Hunt said defiantly.

"Why, the newspapers condemn these new things," the critical onlooker said authoritatively and boisterously. "Look at what they think of them." He pulled a clipping out of his pocket and handed it to Hunt, who shifted his position so that the light shone on the paper.

The city is crowded with these ridiculous and pernicious commodities. We have soap that removes every impurity of the skin, and a wash that immediately cures weak eyes; a vial of liquid remedies for all disorders of the lungs, and a cerate that turns the bald pate luxuriant, and the gray one black. There is a fellow somewhere in town who sells a panacea that is a remedy for every disease that can afflict a human being. It cures consumption and dropsy, reduces the plethoric, recovers the asthmatic, and puts the apoplectic free from danger. He gives it to one for liver complaint, to another for ague and fever, to a third for rheumatism.

"See, that article proves it," the onlooker insisted, "all those new things are frauds."

Hunt did not reply. He had made up his mind. He returned the clipping without comment and walked through the crowd into the store. He deposited twenty cents on the counter and put the cake of soap into his pocket, his first purchase in the city.

With an exalted feeling of self-confidence, he continued his exploratory trip of the city. He looked condescendingly at the side-whiskered men, wearing grey and white beaver hats and long black cloaks lined with red silk, dashing in and out of stores where lottery tickets were sold. He regarded with pity those in less pretentious garb who ambled into the lottery offices and passed their hard-earned dollars over the marble counter for pieces of printed paper courting Lady Luck.

Absorbed by the hustle and bustle of people hurriedly walking, Hunt adjusted himself to the hellish din that so short a time before had clashed on his ears.

Mechanically, he dodged the ubiquitous omnibuses, clumsy great vehicles painted red, a row of windows on each bulging side, which clattered by in the charge of yelling and cursing drivers.

"Hey, there, you fool, get out of the way!"

Hunt instinctively leaped to the side as he glanced up. The driver of a stagecoach was shouting, swerving his coach to prevent running into him.

"Out of the way, you lout! Do you want to get killed?" another Jehu yelled at him. Before Hunt had time to collect his wits, another stage jounced by, its wind almost pulling his coat into the lumbering red wheels.

A moment later Hunt was jolted by the grinding of brakes, drowning out other street noises. It was followed by a shrill cry and an agonized yell. Frightened horses plunged by despite the efforts of a startled driver to curb them. People were running after the coach and Hunt followed them. Suddenly, they stopped running, stricken by a horrified silence. The crushed body of a little girl was being removed from the roads. Her moans and cries were soul-searing.

Pity and anger moved the crowd. Some of them pounced on the driver whose coach had been brought to a jarring stop a short distance from the accident.

"String him up!" they roared. "Tear him to pieces..." "Murderer..." "It'll teach the others..." "Hang him..."

"It wasn't my fault," the scared driver whimpered and pleaded. "I done all I could! I yelled to her. She didn't hear. I didn't mean to do it!"

The crowd surged around the cringing driver held securely by a policeman. They tugged at his light green corduroy pantaloons, they ripped his short drab coat adorned with pearl buttons as large as Spanish dollars, they snatched his broad-brimmed white hat encircled by a bright ribbon. They tore these gaudy garments, as they ripped and clawed at him. Only the intervention of the policeman saved him from a serious beating.

Keeping the attackers back, the policeman mounted the retrieved coach, and with the driver under arrest, drove to the police precinct, leaving behind a sullen muttering crowd who switched their attention to a doctor who was ministering to the unfortunate child.

Hunt stared at the departing coach. Thoughts of the shrieking of the child and later the pleading voice of the driver—"It wasn't my fault! I yelled to her!"—made a deep impression. Something should be done to prevent this, Hunt thought.

Chapter 3

Walter Hunt was restless and could not fall asleep on the lumpy, straw-filled mattress protruding beyond the rudely carved wooden bed. The long trip, heightened by excitement and apprehension, combined to keep him awake. But the katydids chirping in the long grass under the trees in the back yard gave him friendly assurances. (The swarms of mosquitoes, however, were a nuisance, proof that the proud metropolis was only an overgrown country town.)

His interest was not in the surroundings. His sole thought was in completing his business assignment. Before the clerks had time to set their brooms against the dirt on office floors, Hunt was downtown soliciting business in the commercial center.

"Whom do I see to make trade?" he inquired from office to office.

Individually or collectively, quiet or bellicose, politely or rudely, the answers were generally the same. No one evinced any interest in his flax spinner. Rejection followed rejection. The response was consistently disheartening.

"We are too busy now, and it is too warm. Come back some other time."

"We are not interested in advancing money on untried inventions."

"Let us see the machine in operation, then we may be able to tell you if we are interested."

Day after day, week after week, Hunt trudged from capitalist to capitalist, from manufacturer to manufacturer, from promoter to promoter, from agent to agent. Everywhere, answers were pessimistic and negative.

A festive mood blanketed the city. On July 4th, 1826, the fiftieth anniversary of the signing of the Declaration of Independence was to be celebrated. Speeches, parades and fireworks were scheduled to thrill the city. But gloom dispelled the joy on Saturday when news was received that John Adams had died on the holiday. Delayed news also was received that in an unusual coincidence Thomas Jefferson had also passed away on the Fourth of July. Feelings of grief dominated everybody and everything. The death of the two former presidents of the United States cast a pall over the city. The members of the Common

Council voted to wear black crepe on their arms for one month. And the people worried what the future would bring.

After the grief had subsided, the city again returned to normal but Hunt's search for a capitalist was still a fruitless one. "Your story is as long as the Mississippi," one friendly clerk told him. "Why don't you set up your machine in some convenient location so that people will be able to see it working?"

No one would grant Hunt space in which to set his machine in operation. Where could he show it? South Street was crowded with chandlers and ship suppliers. Pearl Street was occupied by dry goods merchants and earthenware dealers. Curriers were located on Ferry Street and Jacob Street. Furriers predominated on Water Street. Cabinet and chair makers had the best locations on Broad Street, while Broadway was devoted almost exclusively to retail emporiums.

Searching for a possible location to set up his flax spinner, Hunt noticed a store crowded with people. He stepped inside. The bellowing singsong chant of a man standing on a raised platform gave indication of what was taking place within and the red flag hanging over the entrance had no significance for Hunt.

"What's happening?" Hunt inquired of a thin, foppishly dressed old man puffing a fat segar and blowing smoke through his nostrils.

"Nawthin'," he said lazily. "Just a sale by vendue."

"What?"

"Ah, nawthin'. An auction."

Hunt listened for awhile to the auctioneer's harangue for higher prices. His interest appeased, he walked over to the park on the east side of Broadway at City Hall and sat on the grass. The freshly cut lawn gave him a sense of communion with his family and Lowville, his home town. Earth was earth regardless of where it was located.

He extracted two letters from his pocket and reread them. One was from Willis Hoskins, "I have several people who are willing to advance further money, but it will be necessary to have some evidence that New York will take to the machine. If not, our funds are low, and you will be obliged to return."

The other letter was from his mother. It excited his courage and stimulated his fears. It disclosed the information that Polly had courageously withheld from him the news that another child was expected. As he read it, his eyes clouded and it was with difficulty that he read the closely written script.

I trust my dear son that your wife will not turn against me when she learns that I have betrayed her confidence, but I feel it my God-given duty to inform you of this serious event, and to remind you of your sacred responsibilities as a husband and a father, and to urge you to finish your business in that far-distant Godless city with all possible speed to be home with her when she gives birth.

Tears blurred his eyes and the buildings facing the park appeared hazy. Gazing intently, he could make out the sign "Tammany Hall."

"Why didn't I think of it before?" He crossed over to the east side of the park, entered the hotel on the corner of Chatham and Frankfort streets, and asked to see the proprietor. Pot-bellied, florid J. D. Smith greeted him enthusiastically, summing up with "If it's space you want, we got it! Tammany Hall is a fine place for an exhibit."

The necessary arrangements were amicably concluded and Hunt brought his flax spinner to the hotel. He unpacked it from its wooden case and assembled it. It worked perfectly and was not damaged by the trip. Then, he carefully piled up the lumber from the crate and tied the planks with heavy cord, placing the bundle out of the way in a corner.

Hunt was now ready to conquer the world. He invited everyone to see the machine. Promoters, capitalists and even the curious and the idle went to see it. He contacted a reporter from the *New York Evening Post*, who was so impressed with it that he wrote an article which appeared in 1826, in the editorial column under the heading SPINNING FLAX:

> Messrs. Hunt & Hoskins, of this state have invented a machine, for which they have taken out a patent, for the purpose of spinning flax. A small model may be seen by those who have curiosity to examine what we believe to be a very valuable invention, in the large room at Tammany Hall. As the work has already been done by fingers, one person could only attend to one spindle. By the present machinery, a woman, it is said, can attend to 80 spindles: and it is obvious that if the culture of flax be attended to in this country, with a view of its domestic manufacture, and should this invention succeed, linen goods may at no distant time become nearly as cheap as cotton.

Like a stone thrown into a pond, wave after wave of comment followed. The *New York Mirror* also rushed onto the bandwagon of recognition and printed the following notice under the heading INTERESTING TO LINEN MANUFACTURERS:

> We have taken note of the machine now being exhibited at Tammany Hall, for spinning flax and hemp. It was recently invented by Messrs. Hunt & Hoskins, of Lewis County, in this state. It is constructed on the most simple and certain principles, which are easily comprehended, even by a casual observer. It requires less power, and its graduating principles are extremely simple. The flax or hemp (as it comes from the hotchel, without any further preparation) is laid in narrow troughs, in a direct line with the flyers or bobbins, and is gently pressed down by covers, the flax is drawn out in small parcels by instruments called feeders, and the end of the staple is conducted between two rollers, from which it passes through small revolving eveners to the flyers.
>
> The office of the eveners is to draw the flax from the rollers, and pass it to

the flyers, to remove all irregularities in the thread, and to perform the same operation that the spinner does with the fingers on the common spinning wheel. The quality of the thread is regulated by turning a screw in the feeders, which throws more or less flax into the groove that forms the thread. The principle may be extended to any number of spindles, and water, steam, horse, or any other power, can be applied.

Mr. Hunt, one of the inventors, is now in the city, and is about erecting a machine on an extensive plan, for the manufacture of fine linen. As we consider the above improvement generally, we take this opportunity of directing public attention to the subject.

The crest of recognition spread to Lowville. Those who had rejected the opportunity for interesting themselves in the invention now besieged Hoskins with offers. As capital was required to maintain Hunt in the city, Hoskins accepted money from three townsmen, Phineas Cole, Jared House and Sam Ruggles.

No formal organization of a company was effected and no letters of incorporation were sought. However, to prevent the actions of an individual partner from binding the others and to forestall discussions and arguments, a legal agreement was reached. It was drawn up on October 16, 1826, by Charles Dayan, a Lowville attorney and candidate for state senator. He was given power of attorney to act

> for us and in our names from time to time at all times to receive all monies and other considerations arising from the sale of the said Improvements (the flax spinning machine) and to receipt and discharge the same, and to transact all and every part of the ordinary business.

Dayan mailed the contract to Walter Hunt, who signed it in New York City on October 26, 1826, before Charles Edward Ellis, Commissioner of Deeds. Hunt remailed the contract to Dayan who summoned Hoskins, Cole, House and Ruggles to meet at his office. They met on November 10, 1826, at which time a Lowville commissioner of deeds recorded their signatures. On the following day, Dayan filed the agreement with Andrew W. Doig, county clerk of Lowville.

Relieved of the monetary details and financial arrangements, Hunt was optimistic. He could return to Lowville and await the birth of his child; others could look after the financial matters.

Chapter 4

Eager to return to his family and feeling that he had concluded his business in New York City, Walter Hunt went back to Lowville on the day before Christmas, 1826. No one had known the date he was returning. He opened the front door of his house. The children were running about and hiding. They were playing their favorite game, I Spy. When they saw their father, they joyfully ran into his outstretched arms. With a powerful swoop, he picked them all up.

When Polly entered the hallway, he placed the children on the settee, walked over to her and kissed her, a rare occurrence in front of the children. "Why didn't you tell me?" he asked immediately. "Had I known I wouldn't have made the trip. Being father to another child makes me feel thankful. How do you feel?"

But Polly didn't have a chance to answer. The children couldn't wait. They ran over and hugged their father again, tugging at him, each individually vying for his attention, asking a myriad of questions, "Are you going to stay home now?" "Will you be going away again?" "What did you see in New York?"

"Patience!" Hunt chided. "I can't answer everything at once and I have something more important to do."

Chagrined and puzzled, the children became silent. They watched as with a grand flourish he opened both his carpet bag and portmanteau.

"This is for you, Caroline. Now you can eat like a real grown-up lady." He handed his littlest one a pewter plate, a miniature knife and fork, and a pusher, a small spoon with its shank curved back.

"And I also have something for you, Polly Anne."

"What is it?" The thirteen year old asked excitedly.

"Wait and see."

He reached into the portmanteau and pulled out a stuffed rag doll, with a china head and china arms and legs, dressed in Quaker habit. Polly Anne clasped it to her breast and began singing to it.

"And good old Saint Nicholas also sent you these for Christmas," said Hunt handing her a pair of black shoes. "Try them on and see how they fit."

Caroline rushed over to see them. Admiration, envy and other emotions appeared in turn.

"Come here, Caroline," the happy father said. "I almost forgot. I also have a pair of new shoes for you. They may be just a little bit large now, but soon you'll be big enough to wear them. Not many two year olds have shoes."

Caroline no longer felt slighted.

"And for you, Polly, the mother of these wonderful children, I have something special. I bought you this from the big city, New York City. It is a parasol. It is the latest thing in Paris, and all the elegant women in New York are using them. Don't move, I've also brought you this five-yard cutting of bombazine which is quite a favorite of the women who make their own dresses. I hope you will like it. It is also imported from Europe."

Polly threw her arms about him, a gesture which the children with their Quaker upbringing looked upon with great surprise.

As his sisters played with their gifts, and Polly fondled the parasol, Walter, Jr., shifted from foot to foot. He bounced a clumsily-made leather ball and tried to conceal his disappointment in being neglected.

"Come here, son," Walter coaxed. "You don't think for a moment that I would forget you, do you? My boy, my pride and joy. I have something for you too. But, you know, ladies first. Forgive me, young man."

Walter, Jr., smiled. His imagined disappointment disappeared. His joy was visible. Hunt reached into his carpet bag and pulled out a black slate, framed by a colored wood border, also a blank book with lined pages, a few square wooden pencils and the newly published two hundred and fifteen page textbook *Elements of Arithmetic*, by Ferdinand Hassler.

"They are all for you, Walter."

"Pretty soon you'll be able to write as well as your father," Polly said proudly.

"I admire to," the youngster said reflectively. "Papa writes very nice."

"And he wrote a good hand even when he was a little boy your age," Polly added. "I'll show you something he wrote when he was no bigger than you are." She opened the top drawer of the highboy and took out a cloth-wrapped, slightly soiled, frayed book which she showed Walter, Jr. Then she handed it to her husband.

Walter Hunt thumbed through it. It bore his name in block capital letters on the second page. On the inside cover was the date, 1806.

"Twenty years ago," he said meditatively, "I wrote those notes when I was ten years old, two years older than you are now, Walter."

Hunt examined his old copy book. It contained pages and pages of stern admonitions, written over and over again. Solemnly, he read one page aloud.

1. Let thy thoughts be divine, awful and Godly.
2. Let thy talk be little, honest and true.

3. Let thy works be profitable, holy and charitable.
4. Let thy manner be grave, courteous and cheerful.
5. Let thy diet be temperate, convenient and frugal.
6. Let thy apparel be sober, neat and comely.
7. Let thy will be compliant, obedient and ready.
8. Let thy prayers be devout, often and fervent.
9. Let thy recreations be lawful, brief and seldom.
10. Let thy meditations be of death, judgment and eternity.

Walter Hunt smiled and closed the book. He did not show the margins filled with curious designs and caricatures of old Erastus Barnes, his teacher.

"Did you like school, Daddy?" Walter, Jr., inquired.

The elder Hunt reflected. He remembered the primitive one-room schoolhouse at the brow of the hill ruled severely by the demagogue Erastus Barnes. The school was located some distance from his home and he remembered that to go to school he was generally obliged to walk, except in inclement weather. His father had a wagon with some broken wheels that he mounted on a flatrunner, making it a sled drawn by a yoke of oxen. He particularly remembered the sled. It was painted a deep orange. Buffalo and deer skins served as blankets. Colored cloths fluttered in the breeze. He remembered the brass bells that jingled in various cadences as the horses or oxen jogged along.

He remembered how his father would stop all along the road and pick up children or how he would be picked up when his father did not make the trip. Parents generally took turns in making the trip but ordinarily there was enough transportation as the older boys were trusted with the horses and carts.

Barnes taught all ages in the same class and without distinction of age or size administered the lash to stress the facts and assigned students lessons as befitted individual ability. He chastised the playful and the incompetent, but never rewarded the deserving. School was not a theater for glorification. There was only one reason for a school: "the dissemination," as Barnes put it, "of orthography, etymology, syntax and prosody." In simple language, the three R's.

Barnes was a rugged disciplinarian and demanded that all pupils bow low before entering or leaving the school, a gesture that freedom-loving Hunt always resented.

"Did you like school, Daddy?" Walter, Jr., repeated his question.

Walter Hunt did not answer his son's question. He remembered old Barnes and the treatment the teacher meted out to his pupils. They resented Barnes' severity and wasted little love on him. When his back was turned, the older boys threw spit-balls at him or annoyed the younger pupils so as to cause them to make disturbing cries. They placed burrs on the chairs of those called upon to recite or unceremoniously reached forward and pinched them. Full of mischief, the younger pupils aped the antics of the older ones with the result that proper decorum was usually obtained only after vigorous application of the birch rod.

Hunt awoke from his reverie with a start and realized that the children were eagerly awaiting his account of his experiences in the city.

"What do you think, children?" Hunt said. "When I went into the parlor of my rooming house, they had a goldfinch in a wicker cage."

"What was the matter with it?" asked his son.

"Nothing. Perhaps they just kept the bird because they wanted a pet or maybe they just wanted to save it from the cat.

"Many of the stores in the city were lit by gas, and the lamps were very pretty. In a music store, I saw a lamp in the shape of a harp!

"On Sundays, chains were stretched across the streets in front of the churches to keep people from riding in carriages."

"Is it true that ladies have to leave the table at dessert?" Polly Anne asked.

"There's no written law about it, but they do. The gentlemen keep their seats and tell stories, jokes and drink."

"Did you drink too?" Walter, Jr., piped in.

"You don't have to unless you are so minded and I didn't because I don't like liquor, and secondly because I'm a Quaker. Those city people drink a lot. On the boat they put a bottle of brandy on the table just as if was the water bottle. They also had a part of the deck roped off for the bar where they sold whiskey. They charged five cents a glass on the boat, but in the city the price was only three cents a glass.

"I'll tell you what I did drink, and it was right enjoyable too. Soda water! You never heard of that, did you? It's regular water, flavored with lemon, with carbonic gas."

"What's that?"

"Well, it's like a lot of air bubbles that tickle your throat."

"Did you eat apples?" Caroline asked.

Walter Hunt picked her up and put her on his lap. "I calculate I did. And what do you think? I also ate some pineapples."

"Do they come from pine trees?" the three children asked almost simultaneously.

"Oh no! I think they come from somewhere in the south. They cost thirty-seven cents each. They have a big heavy scaly..."

"Howdy, Walter." A greeting from the doorway interrupted him.

"Glad to see you, Lyman Graves, of all people." Hunt put his arm about the caller's shoulder.

"The city didn't do you any harm," Graves commented. "You look fine. How was it? Did you visit any Masonic lodges while you were there?"

Lyman Graves was an enthusiastic Mason. He, Peter Hoe, John P. Johnson, Consider H. Morrison, Jr., and Walter Hunt were all raised to the degree of Master Mason on August 20, 1817, in Orient Lodge No. 150 Free and Accepted Masons.

"No," said Hunt apologetically.

"Did you hear any news about William Morgan?" Graves inquired.

"William Morgan?"

"On September twelfth he was abducted from Canandaigua."

"What for?"

"Where have you been?" Graves asked. "That's all they've talked about here for months."

Hunt did not have a chance to continue the conversation: Willis Hoskins, Charles Dayan, Ziba Knox and several other friends had called to hear his tales about the city.

"How'd you like the city?" Hoskins inquired.

"It was wonderful, but at first I was not at all well. The victuals didn't settle with me. I missed Polly's home-cooked meals."

Polly smiled, her teeth flashing. Good old Walter was now a celebrity. He had been to the big city.

"I almost forgot, Polly," he said, extracting two clippings from his jacket that he had cut out of a magazine. Here is a new receipt for you." He read it aloud.

Tooth Powder. We know of no better than finely powdered charcoal; it cleans the mouth mechanically and chemically. But as alone it is dusty and not easily mixed with water, it may for this purpose be mixed with an equal weight of prepared chalk, and, if requisite, scented with a drop or two cloves."

"I use charcoal and honey now," said Polly.

"Did you get me that receipt for influenza?" asked Charles Dayan.

"All orders were faithfully executed." Hunt laughed. "Here is a clipping from the *New York Mirror*." Dayan read it aloud.

An efficacious remedy is used for the influenza, which is drinking very plentifully of barley-water sweetened with brown sugar and strongly impregnated with acid, and observing a strict diet.

"Thanks, Walter, but I hope I will never have occasion to use it."

"Did you see Castle Clinton?" Hoskins inquired anxiously, "and is it true that they have pyrotechnic displays?"

"I was there several times. It was a wonderful place, right out in the harbor overlooking the Hudson River. The gardens were beautiful. Bands played at night and the firework displays were gorgeous, unbelievable."

After the guests had departed, Polly listened to her husband's explanations of the odd and interesting things he had seen. He described the magnitude of the city, the luxurious hotels, the varied types of stores, the stagecoaches, and the crowds of people. He paused a moment and looked troubled.

"What's the matter?" Polly asked.

"Oh, nothing," Walter replied. "I was just thinking of something."

He then described the stagecoach accident he had witnessed the first day in the city and stated that since then he had heard of others.

Polly was shocked. She surveyed him coolly. "And you suggest," she said, "that we should go to New York?"

"Of course."

"Never!" Polly declared emphatically. "Do you think I want anything like that to happen to our children?"

Walter did not reply. He had no immediate prospect of going to the city again and felt no answer was necessary.

On January 29, 1827, Walter Hunt stopped pacing the floor long enough to hear a feeble cry. It thrilled him and he smiled. The midwife allowed him to enter the bedroom. He beamed with pride at the latest addition to his family.

"A boy!" he whispered to Polly holding her hand. "Now we have a quartet."

Polly smiled faintly. He always included Polly Anne as his own. He never referred to her as the daughter of Dr. William Loucks, Polly's first husband. Polly Anne had never been told that Walter had adopted her.

"What do you think we should name the baby?" Polly murmured. "Mind you, pick a good name," she added, "because some day he may be president."

"Then let's call him John Quincy Adams. He's president now."

"No, really. What do you think would be a good name for him?"

"If you want to name him for a president, why don't you call him George Washington?" Hunt said.

"Well, why not? George Washington was still living when we were young."

"Then George Washington Hunt he will be."

As the baby required considerable attention, Polly could not spend as much time with the other children. The winter was colder than usual but the children didn't seem to mind. They enjoyed huddling around the fireplace listening to their father's tales about the big city.

"Why do children get hurt in New York?" Polly Anne inquired. "They never get hurt in Lowville?"

"New York has a thousand times more people," Hunt exclaimed, "and the stages are dangerous..."

"But can't they do something about it?" Walter, Jr., asked.

"I hope they will," Hunt answered. "Someone will do something about it sometime."

When the children had gone to bed, Hunt stared into the slowly dying embers in the brick lined fireplace. Young Walter's question presented a problem. Why *were* there so many accidents in New York? Well, traffic was heavy;

the narrow thoroughfares were congested with vehicles; and the drivers were obstreperous.

Hunt knew that the city had attempted to solve the problem by restricting certain streets to one-way traffic. A seven-point code was passed for several areas and its provisions advertised in the daily newspapers by the Hon. Philip Hone, mayor of the city.

Hunt mulled the situation over. Despite laws and ordinances, accidents continued. The fault did not lie in the laws, Hunt reasoned, because they were stringent enough. The fault was due to the human element.

He was busily absorbed with the problem when Polly Anne came bounding into the room in her nightgown to kiss him goodnight. As she approached him, she tripped and fell.

Hunt picked her up, kissed her, made sure that she had not been hurt and hustled her back to bed.

The fall had given him an idea. The fault of most accidents, he reasoned, was the carelessness of pedestrians. On his first day in the city, he had almost been run over twice. But knowing the problem and finding a solution were two distinct things.

Hunt methodically analyzed the situation. The stages were equipped with warning horns the drivers could blow into but they did not use them. They generally shouted their warnings—which usually was ineffective as their voices were nearly always drowned out by the street noises around them, not least their own conveyance. They could be heard only from a short distance away, usually too late to be of any value.

The drivers objected to the horns because the narrow air-channel clogged with dust and dirt, and often didn't sound when they were needed the most. In cold and rainy weather, the cold metal touching their lips was most unpleasant. Another great disadvantage to the horn was that in dangerous or emergency situations, the drivers wanted to hold the reins with two hands, so as to better manipulate the coach horses.

If a driver could retain both hands on the reins and work some sort of a device with his feet, Hunt reasoned, a solution might be reached. But, how could one signal with his feet?

Suddenly an idea dawned. He went to his barn which he also used as a workshop, extracted some old scraps of copper and iron, and made a metallic disc formed like a soup-plate. A hammer-like knob struck the gong a resounding blow. He fastened the gong in an inverted position to the floor with a center pin. When he stepped on the knob, the hammer hit the gong causing it to clang and ring.

He made another gong and installed it on his wagon. He drove along the roads near his house and stepped on the knob as he neared pedestrians—but the gong did not perform the way he had intended. Instead of scaring people away, it attracted them to his wagon. He knew that although this was not the purpose for which the gong was intended, as soon as the novelty wore off, it would serve its purpose as a warning device.

"What's that crazy contraption for?" Willis Hoskins asked. "Something new instead of sleigh bells?"

Hunt explained that the purpose of the gong was indeed to attract attention but in such a way as to provide a coach alarm to warn pedestrians of the coach's approach.

"Did you patent it?" Hoskins asked.

"No."

"Why don't you get a patent on it, if you can?"

"Patents cost money," Hunt explained.

"The gong's no good without a patent. Anyone can copy it if they want to. If you get a patent on it, maybe you can go to New York again and sell it."

New York! The sound of the name was like music to the inventor. New York! Over the next few days Hunt drew up the necessary patent application. It was granted on July 30, 1827.

"Here is the patent for the coach alarm! It will lessen accidents all over the world." Hunt jubilantly waved it at Polly. "Now, New York will be safe for children."

"That's wonderful," Polly said excitedly.

"Now that I have the patent, when will you be ready to leave?"

"Leave?" Polly asked in amazement. "Where are we going?"

"To New York!"

"You're teasing."

"No, I am stark serious."

"We can't afford the trip," Polly argued, "and besides what would we do with the children?"

"We're taking them with us. I am going to sell the coach alarm and we'll have all the comforts of life, and we are going to move to New York."

Polly had never seen Walter so optimistic. His enthusiasm encouraged her but she hesitated about giving her approval.

"We have an acre of ground and a house. What are we going to do with them. And the cow? And the hog!" she added as an afterthought.

"We are going to sell everything. We are going to burn our bridges behind us. We are going forward. You will have all the comforts of life and you will be a lady."

"We will be away from our friends," Polly countered.

"We will be in a land of opportunity!"

The next few weeks were spent in disposing of the household goods, the farm and the livestock and the packing.

"We can't take everything with us," Walter argued. "We have packed too much already."

"But how about this?" Polly displayed a china statuette.

"We can't take any more," Walter pleaded. "We will either have to sell it or give it away."

"I didn't see you pack that box," Polly exclaimed. "What's in that box over there?"

The cover was not yet nailed down and Walter opened it. He extracted a brass chemist's scale and weights, which he handled affectionately. "That was the first gift you ever gave me. It belonged to Dr. Loucks. And I told you I'd treasure it as long as I lived," Hunt said tenderly.

Tears streamed down Polly's face but she did not cry. She walked over to Walter and pressed his hand tightly. Not a word was spoken.

"But what are the other things in the box?" Polly asked when she had regained her composure.

Walter raised the cover and Polly looked inside. The case contained the medical equipment left by her deceased husband.

Dr. William Loucks died less than a year after they were married, leaving her with a baby, Polly Anne, less than two months old. His estate consisted of $891.50 in outstanding bills and twenty-one books, Cheselden's *Anatomy*, Cooper's *Surgery*, Denman's *Midwifery*, Hooper's *Vade Mecum*, Bell on *Wounds*, Underwood on *Diseases of Children*, a book on nervous temperaments, a system of surgery, an English dictionary, a Greek grammar, a new American Latin grammar, a *Dictionary of Terms Employed in Medicine*, Blair's *Lectures*, Lee's *Botany*, Gibson's *Surveying*, *Conversations on Chemistry*, *The Botanic Garden*, *The Economy of Human Life*, Robert Burns' poems and Ovid's *Art of Love*.

In addition to the books, Dr. Loucks left a saddlebag fitted out as a medical kit, scales, sponges, syringes, pillboxes, a mortar and pestle, and a few surgical instruments, as well as some medicaments such as magnesia, white vitriol, Juniper berries, resin, aniseed, cinnamon, Peruvian bark, Burgundy pitch, gum albumin, gum aloes, sweet oil, borax, sugar of lead, dragon's blood, asafœtida, gum myrrh, Carolina pink, camphor, sulfur, snake root and castor oil.

"That's very nice, Walter," said Polly trying to conceal her emotion. "It's nice of you to do that, but we can't take all that."

"Of course we can," Walter replied sympathetically. "You remember you once told me you wished I'd study medicine."

"But that was before we were married."

"I'm thirty now and that's too old to study medicine, but maybe Walter, Jr., will become a doctor."

"I hope so, but that's a long way off," Polly replied. "Let's continue our packing."

A large group of relatives and friends were on hand when the family boarded the stagecoach on their trip. Polly carried George Washington Hunt in her arms, while Walter looked after Caroline, Polly Anne, Walter, Jr., and the baggage.

He kept tapping his coat pocket from time to time to make sure that his purse and the alarm gong patent were safe.

"Good-bye, all. Good-bye, Lowville," Hunt called out. Polly sat rigidly in the back seat. She could not make up her mind whether to be glad or sad. She wondered about the future.

Chapter 5

The pleasure and thrill Walter Hunt experienced when he viewed New York City for the first time was gone. Even the scenic boat ride down the Hudson River was not as thrilling. He was already aware of New York's magnitude, and it no longer impressed him. The problem of supporting his family was foremost in his mind.

It was dusk when the boat docked at the pier, and the children were tired and sleepy, so Hunt bundled his family into a hackney cab, filled every available space with luggage, and instructed the driver to go to 45 Washington Street, a rooming house in which he had engaged a large room.

The coach stopped in front of a two-story wood house dabbed over by a thin coating of whitewash. Its dilapidated exterior belied the inside which was neat and clean. Shingles, curled by the heat of the sun, covered the slanting roof.

The room assigned to them by the German landlady, who led the way up the creaking stairs, had two narrow windows and four large beds. The beds and mattresses were almost new and were covered with freshly ironed spreads, but the furniture showed much signs of wear. In the center of the room was a small coal-burning stove. An oil lamp was on a shelf, and gray and white glass candlesticks, with the candles almost completely burned down, were on a table near the wall.

"It's not just what I expected Polly. But, I guess it will do until we can get something better," he whispered.

"It will be all right, Walter. Everything will turn out all right. Just wait and see."

"I guess the first thing we should do is to get ready for dinner. Where is that package of fruits?"

"Oh!" Polly gasped, "I left them on the boat."

"Never mind. Sooner or later we'll have to go to market. Why not now?"

"Where's the best and cheapest store?" he inquired of the landlady who was tidying up the room.

"What do you want to buy?"

"Victuals."

"There's a nice store down the street—"

"Will they have fresh chickens?" Polly interrupted.

"No, of course not. You can't buy meat in stores here. You can get meat only at the markets."

"At the markets?"

"Yeah. There are eleven of them: Fulton Market, Franklin Market, Duane Market…"

"Which is the nearest?" Polly asked.

"The Washington Market between Fulton and Vesey streets, up the street a few blocks."

"Will you take care of the children while we go out to get a few things to eat?"

"I don't usually. I'm too busy, but seeing that you're new in the city, I'll oblige. Just this once."

Together the Hunts leisurely walked to the market. Polly was amazed at its size. It was the largest building she had ever seen.

"Why look!" she exclaimed excitedly after she had entered and regained her composure. "Look! Mutton, six to eight cents a pound. Six to eight cents a pound!"

She excitedly pointed to a sign. "Look! Beef. Fourteen cents a pound! Walter, we only got eight dollars for our cow. We can't afford to buy here."

"If everyone else does, I guess we'll have to."

"For mercy sakes," Polly gasped as she read the sign aloud, "bear, deer, raccoon, groundhog."

"'Possum, squirrel, rabbit and hare," continued Walter reading the hand-lettered sign that listed the items for sale at the meat stall.

"Got some nice birds today," the butcher's assistant suggested.

Polly stared at him, then recoiled. His hands and apron were stained with blotches of blood.

"Nice birds. Robin, lark, blue jay, woodpecker, wild goose, wild pigeon, brant, quail and partridge."

"No. No, thanks," Polly stammered.

She walked to the long, oilcloth-draped table covered with fish and flies. It displayed many items she had never seen before.

"What are those large flat things?"

"Skates!" The clerk snapped, at the same time using a feather duster to chase the flies away.

"And these?"

In turn the clerk pointed out blowfish, dogfish, angelfish, stingray and grunts. "How about some fresh lampreys or menhadens?" he asked.

Polly shook her head.

"Look at all this seafood!" Hunt pointed to a group of rattan baskets. "Oysters, lobsters, prawn and crabs."

"Crayfish, shrimps, clams, scallops, mussels and periwinkle," the clerk from an adjoining stall bellowed, taking pride in the attention paid to his wares.

The high prices for foodstuffs surprised Mrs. Hunt. In Lowville, vegetables had practically no value. A filled barrel could be purchased for a few cents. A price list on a swinging sign hung from the ceiling above the vegetable counter listed the selection. She looked at it in amazement and disbelief: Potatoes and turnips 37½¢, Indian corn 50¢ to 60¢, and white beans $1.25 to $1.38.

"A barrel?" Hunt wondered.

"No! A bushel! Can you imagine that?"

"Imagine asking up to two dollars a barrel for apples," he said.

At another stall, signs prominently displayed the items on sale: Butter 9¢ to 18¢ a pound, sugar 14¢ to 19¢ a pound, Java 13¢ to 15¢, green tea 90¢ to $1.30.

"I guess only millionaires live in New York," Polly said.

"Look at what they get for chickens," exclaimed Hunt as he passed one of the butcher stalls, "Twelve to fifteen cents a pound!"

"The folks in Lowville won't believe it when I write to them."

A clerk wearing a tight fitting blouse with a handkerchief tied around his head, paused long enough from plucking and cleaning chickens to call out, "What'll you have?"

"Do you mean you get fifteen cents a pound for chickens?" Hunt asked.

"Sometimes the price is twenty cents."

"Why I owned hundreds of them," Hunt exclaimed, "and I never got that for them!"

"Where are they?" the clerk inquired.

"In Lowville."

"Where's that?"

"Next to Martinsburg."

"Where's that?"

"About three hundred miles upstate."

"Is it worth fifteen cents to go up there to get a one-pound chicken?" the clerk asked.

"But that isn't it."

"The trouble with you countrymen," the clerk sneered, "is that you think New York is a country town. We pay rent for this stall, we pay salaries and we have expenses, and we are not in business for your health. We are here to make money."

"I understand that."

"New York is the world's food market. There isn't a day that boats don't come to New York from all over the world bringing every imaginable delicacy.

Money doesn't mean anything here. On some items we can get any price we want. You take it or leave it."

"He's not wrong, Walter," Polly said, leading him away from an argument. "This is not Lowville. This is New York, and while we're here, we'll have to do like all the others."

Despite the high prices, the Hunts left the market with their arms full.

"I don't see how people can starve here in this land of plenty," Polly remarked.

Outside, on the street as they turned the corner, they observed a large queue of shabbily dressed men waiting in line for the free meals dispensed by one of the many soup kitchens. Instinctively, Polly grasped Walter's hand and shuddered. She hoped her remark would not be prophetic.

When the Hunts returned, the landlady was regaling the children with folktales. They listened eagerly, fascinated in part by the German accent they had never heard before.

"What do you think of the city?" the landlady inquired.

"I have always been used to space and air," Polly commented as she placed her bundles on the table. "The city is like a giant octopus with crushing tentacles."

"What is it, an octopus?"

"It's something like a lot of snakes joined together at one point that swims in the water."

"I don't know what it is still," the elderly woman said. She changed the subject abruptly and said, "Did you leave your order for water?"

"Water?"

"Did you leave your order for water?" the landlady repeated.

"Water?" said Polly in amazement.

"Yes, water," the landlady said with a little impatience, "don't you know city water isn't fit to drink?"

"Where do you get your water?" Hunt asked.

"We buy it from Jacob's Well, a spring on Jacob Street, but the hotels buy it from Knapp's Springs or the Manhattan Company."

"You buy it?" Polly repeated in amazement.

"They charge a penny a gallon. Every day you will see a horse pulling a two-wheel or four-wheel cart with a barrel on top."

"They call those barrels hogsheads, the water comes out from a spigot at one end," Hunt said.

"Do you have to buy water to wash in?" Polly asked.

"No, we have a cistern which collects the rain water. When we finish with the water that we use to wash the dishes, we don't waste it. We use it for the lawns, to sprinkle the streets or wash the windows."

"I forgot to tell you, Polly, water is quite a problem here. It's not that New

York hasn't any water but that the demand is too great. Sometimes so much water is used that the fire-engines can't get enough to put out fires."

"I never saw a fire-engine," little Caroline said.

"You'll see plenty here," the landlady said. "Every day the engines are running helter-skelter. New York without its fire-engines would be just as impossible as New York without its mosquitoes."

"You'd better be getting dinner ready, Polly," Hunt suggested. "It's getting late. I'll help."

The landlady went downstairs and Polly prepared their first meal.

Time passed quickly. Days and weeks slipped by as in a dream.

"Do you like the city any better now?" Hunt inquired one day. He noticed Polly was reading a book.

"I'll never get used to the noise here," she confided. She laid aside the copy of James Fenimore Cooper's brand-new *Last of the Mohicans*. "It's like bedlam. Here is part of a letter I started to write to your parents, parts of which I copied out of a book. I'm sure it will be read by everyone in Lowville."

Walter laughed, and Polly began to read a section of the letter.

From early morn to late at night, New York is a procession of noises. Grimy chimney sweeps, followed by dirty apprentices carrying brooms, ropes and ladders, salute the dawn with their melancholy howl. Grinders plod the streets tinkling their bells before, during and after their shouting. Long rickety wagons crawl along, led by men with hands, faces and clothes of a uniform black shouting "Oh Oh" at the tops of their lungs to designate that they have charcoal for sale.

Omnibuses clatter along over the cobblestones at the crack of dawn, the iron rimmed wheels striking each stone block with the fury of a blacksmith's hammer on an anvil. The raucous shout of the drivers, accompanied by unnecessary loud blasts of horns to attract passengers, help to make sleep barely possible.

No sooner are the barefoot children on the streets playing their games which resemble Indians on the warpath, than the bells from the steeples, markets and factories commence to toll. Peripatetic vendors of fish burden the air with dolorous songs, recording the virtues of dead shad, lobsters and mackerel. Peddlers of straw lead their well loaded carts through the city to their peculiar tone of "Ay ay."

During the day, the succession of noises continues. Organ grinders, street singers and vagabond musicians add to the confusion. At the slightest provocation bands parade about the city adding their martial music to the din.

And I forgot to add that Walter has brought his flute with him. As you know, he has no regular hours, but fortunately, it is not as bad now as it was.

At night, most of the loudest noises were hushed, but they gave way to the cries of the dealers in eatables anxious to dispose of their stocks, of the sweeps eager to do a last minute cleaning, and of the straw-sellers and milkmen hoping to clean out their wares. These cries of desperation mixed with the braying of bugles from the museums, the full bursts of the bands at Vauxhall, Niblo's and Castle Garden; the loud and constant alarm of fires, the hideous noises of the firemen yelling through their speaking trumpets, the whizzing of rockets, the thunder of engines, the murmur of voices and the groaning of pianos broken only at intervals by the uproarious shouts of some late bacchanalian, or the occasional thump of the watchman's club, makes life a bedlam.

Added to all this, the howling of predatory dogs, the shrieks of whole legions of feline night walkers, and the solemn measured stroke of the waning hour, repeated again and again. Naturally, I have made no mention of the constant squabbles in which Walter, Jr. joins, or the almost constant crying of George.

Polly put the letter down and looked at Walter for his approval. "Your letter is marvelous," he said. "Now I know why you spent so long on it."

"Well, I could have written how you spend your time playing your flute or singing and humming 'The Mountain Maid' or 'Hurrah for the Bonnets of Blue'."

"And you could also tell them that I sing 'Rest, Warrior Rest'," Hunt said.

"If I told them that you, a Quaker, were singing those new songs 'Comin' Thru the Rye' and 'The Last Rose of Summer,' I don't know what they would think!"

"And imagine what they would say if you wrote that the children enjoy hearing the hurdy-gurdies and watching the antics of those cute monkeys in their fancy red coats doing their stunts at the end of a chain attached to the hand-organ."

"I'll finish the letter tomorrow. I've got some work to do now."

Polly took a large iron pot into which she melted ten ounces of mutton tallow, a quarter of an ounce of camphor, four ounces of beeswax and two ounces of alum. The tangy odor attracted Hunt.

"What are you doing?"

"Making candles."

"What for?"

Polly looked at him in surprise. "Because the stores get from twenty to twenty-two cents a pound for them."

"Well, you won't have to make them anymore," he said as he helped her steep the wicks in lime water and saltpeter. "I wanted to surprise you but now I'll tell you. I have made arrangements to move from this place to a house that has gas-light. While walking through the Arcade on Maiden Lane, I met a man who told me about a very nice house, out a little ways. I went to look at it and I think it will do us very nicely. It has gas light. But you can't blow out the gas like candles," Walter admonished, "you have to turn it off."

"Walter Hunt," Polly chided, "you know we can't afford to live in a whole house in New York."

"There are many houses in the same vicinity that rent from four hundred to six hundred dollars a year."

"Four hundred to six hundred dollars a year!" Polly was aghast.

"But I'm not taking one of those," Walter explained. "I found a very genteel house for only two hundred and ten dollars. Before I close the deal I want you to see it and if you like it, I'll rent it."

"That's a lot of money."

"It is, but it's only four dollars a week and that will be nothing when I start earning money."

"But don't you think we should wait?"

"I want my family to have the best of everything."

The house entailed considerable work and not long after they moved Polly was exhausted.

"I'm going to get a girl to help look after the children."

"A girl?" said Polly, alarmed. "Why, that's luxury."

"It won't cost too much. We can get girls between thirteen and eighteen years old for three to four dollars a month, or a maid from four to six dollars."

"I suppose the next thing you'll do will be to hire a good cook and pay her from six to eight dollars a month. Or perhaps a handyman at ten or twelve dollars."

"Some day we may do that."

"I understand that help changes so fast," Polly countered. "It is better to have no one than a new person every month."

"Well, we can join the Society for the Encouragement of Faithful Domestic Servants." Hunt suggested. "Someone gave me one of their circulars. It says the object of the society is

> to offer liberal premiums to those domestics who conduct well, and remain longest in a family; and to remedy that restlessness and love of change in them, which produces so much inconvenience to all housekeepers.

Servants who remained a year with the same employers were presented with a handsome octavo Bible or in lieu thereof $2.00. Servants who remained two years thereafter received $3.00; three years thereafter $5.00; four years thereafter $7.00; five years thereafter $10.00, and every year thereafter $10.00.

"The Society wants an annual fee of five dollars," Polly objected. "We shouldn't squander our money."

Nevertheless, a neat, tall, Negro girl was hired. She assisted in lighting the fires, as well as caring for the children, attending to the housework and cooking, and cleaning the sidewalk.

One night after the family had ensconced themselves in the new home, Walter surprised Polly by saying, "Tonight we are going to the theater."

"You're joking. You know Quakers don't go to the theater."

"That was all right in Lowville, where there were no theaters," Hunt said, "but this is New York. It's a new life for us. We are going. We're New Yorkers now."

"I don't think we should go. We don't want to get to be like New Yorkers."

"What do you mean?"

"You know," Polly hesitated, "Like... like, er... Wait a minute, like Asa Green wrote about in that book, *A Glance of New York*:

> There are others—and the number is pretty large. They attend the theater every night. They talk of the theaters every day. They criticize, they spout, they hum snatches of songs, they debate on the merits of their favorite actors or actresses, they eulogize the beauty, the grace, the tenderness of Miss Such-a-One, they proclaim aloud the vigor, the pathos, the startling force and effective points of Mr. Such-a-One. Theatricals are never out of their thoughts, and rarely out of their mouths. They seem to have found in plays what the Platonists were looking for—the *summum bonum*—the greatest good. They use them as Boniface did his ale; they eat, drink and sleep upon them. At last they dream of them when asleep, and have them constantly in their mouths when awake.

"We'll never be like that," Walter Hunt stated emphatically; "besides we haven't enough money. Tonight we'll go to the Park Theater, and maybe in the near future to the Bowery Theater or to the Chatham."

Seated in the spacious gallery of the Park Theater, Polly Hunt observed the commodious pit, three complete circles of boxes and two side tiers, in all of which blacks and whites sat together. Everything was a revelation. She wore the same simple Quaker attire that she had always worn in Lowville but now was conscious of the simplicity of her clothes. She marveled at the beautiful appearance of the women in the boxes, at their powdered faces, necks and arms, whitened by pulverized starch. The mass of hair with which they bedecked themselves shocked her.

Her life in Lowville and her Quaker creed had taught her to regard such women as Jezebels; and not entirely without similar opinion did she later read a magazine article in which a society woman of the day censured the members of her own sex for their slavery to the latest Paris mode.

> We appear to be losing consciousness of the charm of simplicity and of straight flowing lines. Beauty is made to consist in elaborate and excessive ornament; and one wonders in surveying a modern belle with her layers of flounces, puffings, sashes, fringes, ear-rings, and gew-gaws, how a creature so fearfully and wonderfully made can be put together and taken apart in the space of twenty-four hours.

But still Polly was woman enough to be conscious of her own plain old-fashioned clothes. She noticed during intermission that Walter's attention was riveted upon the exquisitely dressed and glamorous women in the boxes. But the little cloud of vague misgivings and loneliness that passed over her was dispelled when Walter said, "When I see that finery, all those jewels, I am convinced that there is plenty of capital in the city available for putting the flax machine and alarm gong across. And when my time comes, Polly, and it will come, you're going to be sitting down there in one of those boxes, more beautifully dressed than any of those women."

The pressure of her hand on Walter's hand was her reply, her assurance that her faith in him would never die, for her heart was too filled with emotion for words. But practical matters began to occupy her thoughts even though the curtain was up. She really should not have allowed him to spend so much money on amusement or entertainment the past few days. The time might come when every penny might count; she should try to live on a budget.

Of course, she knew that Walter would succeed. Her belief was unshaken. But until he did, the children couldn't be fed and clothed on dreams and hopes. She felt the money they had spent on the theater and museum would have bought one of the children a pair of shoes.

The following morning, conscience stricken, Polly brought the family's brief holiday to an end. Her mind was set to settle down to the serious business of making their way in the city that was now their home.

Chapter 6

Hunt carried one of the alarms wrapped in newspaper from office to office, from promoter to promoter, from capitalist to capitalist. None was enthusiastic about his invention nor even thought it had possibilities. Petty clerks and officious assistants bellowed their disapproval.

"What's the good of it? If people don't get out of the way of the coaches, they'll get killed anyhow."

"What can we do with it? The coachmen won't install it."

"The sales possibilities do not warrant the cost of manufacture."

"We're not in business for pleasure. Unless we see immediate prospects for profit, we're not interested."

But Hunt was not discouraged by these rebuffs. He knew the gong had possibilities.

In desperation, he finally called upon livery stable owners. As a group, they rejected it. "Why try and sell them to us? We don't use them. If you want to sell your gong, why don't you go direct to the people who could use them, the coachmen?"

Acting upon the suggestion, Hunt called upon the coachmen. The likewise were not receptive to the gong. Almost to a man they refused it.

"I wouldn't have one of those newfangled bells on my coach. They'd scare my horses to death."

"I don't need one, I can yell louder."

"Why should I spend my hard-earned money for a gong? Why don't people get out of my way? You'd think they owned the streets."

"Business is bad enough as it is. The first money I get I'll buy a new whiffle-tree."

No one appreciated Hunt's invention. He was unable to make a sale. His optimism waned and his hopes sank to a new low.

With but little enthusiasm he called on Asa Hall, proprietor of the three stagecoaches which ran from Greenwich Street to Pine and Nassau streets.

43

"Mr. Hall ain't seein' no one, and he ain't to be bothered," the stableman informed Hunt.

"I want to show him this alarm," Hunt said, removing the newspaper covering the gong.

"He don't want to see it, and he's busy. Get out!"

Hunt held the alarm gong in his hand and pulled a string causing the hammer to hit the gong. Clang! Clang! Clang!

A sandy-haired, heavy-set, tall man wearing a beaver hat that sagged over his eyes dashed from behind a partitioned section of the barn. "What's the matter?" he yelled excitedly.

"This fellow here!" the stableman shouted while trying to push Hunt out of the barn. "He did it!"

"Take your hands off him. Leave him alone!" The man commanded. The stableman obeyed.

"Who are you and what do you want? And what's that infernal contraption in your hands?"

"I came to show this alarm gong to Mr. Hall," Hunt said. "I didn't intend to cause any commotion."

"I'm Asa Hall. What do you want?"

"I think this gong I invented will be useful on your stages," Hunt said slowly, regaining his composure. "It'll cut down on traffic accidents and save lives."

"Let me see it." Hall picked it up and examined it carefully. "A very clever alarm. If I'd seen it a year ago I'd have bought it. But I don't need it now. I've been in this business for ten years and I'm tired of it. I'm selling out. I'm going to make hats. It's cleaner and there's less worry to it."

Hunt was discouraged, of course, but pleased when Hall ended the conversation by stating, "Leave your name and address with the stableman and I'll suggest to the new stage owners, Kipp and Brown, that they buy your alarm."

When Hunt returned home, he confided to Polly, "Maybe our move to the city was a mistake. Perhaps New York isn't so progressive after all. Or else it is I am wrong. Maybe my invention is not as practical as I thought."

"Everything will turn out all right," Polly reassured him. "But it may take a little time."

"But I have to do something!" Hunt exclaimed. "I can't live forever without an income."

Several months later when their funds had become all but nonexistent, Hunt received a letter from Asa Hall advising him to show the alarm gong to Kipp and Brown, the new owners of the stagecoach line.

At the appointed time, Hunt demonstrated the gong to Mr. Kipp who promptly said, "I'll buy you out, Hunt, lock, stock and barrel."

Hunt did not hesitate or haggle. Within a few minutes a deal was consummated.

Soon afterwards the gongs were installed on the Kipp and Brown stage-coaches. Eventually, the other stage owners accepted the innovation and soon most public vehicles in New York City were equipped with Hunt's invention.

The invention increased Walter Hunt's prestige but because it was another outright sale, he was again searching for new ideas for his daily bread, although the owners of his invention were making a steady profit from the gongs.

"Humanity owes you a debt of gratitude," he was told.

"Your invention of the alarm gong is a boon to mankind."

"It'll save hundreds of lives yearly."

Despite the recognition Hunt received as inventor of the alarm gong, he had great difficulty finding odd jobs to increase his income. It was not until October 30, 1827, that he did something constructive about his situation.

While attending the dedication of the Great Masonic Hall on the east side of Broadway, between Duane and Pearl streets, opposite the New York Hospital, he met Edmund Wilkes, the lawyer.

"Great building, this," Wilkes commented. "I remember when the foundation was laid; June 24th last year, St. John's Day. New York is an up-and-coming city. Everything is booming. Can't help but make money here."

"I wish I knew the secret of success," Hunt brooded.

"It's simple. Hard work if you want to make money the slow way, but if you want to get rich in a hurry, real estate is the business."

"I'm all ears. I could use a lot of money."

"Then why don't you go into the real estate business, Mr. Hunt?"

"I don't know anything about real estate. Once I owned a farm in Lowville but I sold it when I came to New York. That's all I know about real estate."

"You don't have to know anything. All you have to do is to buy something, then sell it at a higher price."

"That takes capital!"

"Not much. You work on options. Sell first, then buy and pocket the difference."

"It sounds easy."

"It is easy. Why the other day, two paupers escaped from the almshouse. They were recaptured the following morning but by that time each had made $1,800.00."

"It can't be as easy as that, otherwise everyone would be doing it."

"But everyone is doing it," Wilkes replied. "Capital is plentiful. The banks have so much money they don't know what to do with it. Everyone has money. Even counterfeits," He laughingly took out a three dollar counterfeit bill on the Merchant's Bank and showed it to Hunt. "And don't get stuck with these," he cautioned.

"How can I get in the real estate business?"

"You're in it. Mr. Hunt, I picked up a piece of property on July 31st. It is on Eighth Avenue and 19th Street on the northeast side of the street. It's an irregular size lot (seventy-eight feet one inch on Eighth Avenue and seventy-nine feet two inches on 19th Street). It was owned by Samuel Boyd and his wife Maria. It has three houses on it. Someone is bound to make money with it because on the 22nd of October we petitioned the Common Council to cut 19th Street to the river. If they do, the property will be worth a lot more to whoever owns it. You can have it for $6,500. Sell it for more and the difference is yours."

When Walter Hunt returned home, he told Polly of the offer. She was horrified! "Chelsea is a cow pasture. They raise frogs there now. I heard someone say a few days ago that two years ago they sold land in the Chelsea section for seven hundred an acre."

"But that was two years ago," Hunt argued. "Prices have gone up sky-high since then."

"I don't know anything about prices, "Polly answered, "but who do you know who has six thousand five hundred dollars?"

"I don't know," Walter answered sheepishly.

"Why don't you try some other transaction first? A smaller one to see how it works."

"Mr. Wilkes also told me about a little yellow house on Wall Street, near the Exchange, with a forty-foot front and only twenty-eight feet deep, that brought twenty thousand the other day."

"That's a lot of money," Polly commented. "But if others can sell property, I don't see why you can't do it as well. I hope that you'll be able to make money too." She placed her hand on his shoulder and smiled.

Hunt approached many people for their reaction to real estate.

"It's just as easy to have a string of properties to sell as it is to have just one," someone advised. "If you can't interest a person in one piece of property then maybe you can interest him in another."

"That sounds logical," Hunt agreed, "but who is there who has property to sell? I don't know anyone."

"Have you spoken to Professor Moore?"

"No. Who is he?"

"You don't know Professor Moore? Clement Clarke Moore? He's one of the trustees of Columbia College. He owns a farm that extends all the way from the north side of 19th Street to the south side of 24th Street, from Eighth Avenue to the Hudson River. He inherited it from his father, Bishop Benjamin Moore of Trinity Church."

"I'll go and see him."

"You'll find him a different sort of owner than the others. He's not a land speculator. He's a professor at the General Theological Seminary and he speaks Hebrew."

Hunt visited Moore and found that Moore was more interested in discussing religion, politics and city affairs than business. But finally the conversation drifted to real estate.

"I don't believe in selling land, Mr. Hunt," Professor Moore explained. "I think a man who owns land should keep it. But, I don't believe in keeping other people off the land either. I'll lease you some lots, let's say for a twenty-one year period."

With a list of Moore's property as a basis, Hunt decided to sell real estate.

On November 6, 1827, Hunt leased a plot of ground on 20th Street for a term of twenty-one years, agreeing to pay Moore $25.00 annually, in two installments, on May first and November first. The lease contained the usual restrictive clause:

Neither he, nor his executors, administrators, nor assigns shall or will, at any time during the term hereby grant, permit or suffer any distillery, brewery, livery stable, slaughter house, tallow chandlery, smith shop, forge, furnace, brass foundry, nail or other factory, nor any manufactory for the making of glue, varnish, vitriol, ink or turpentine, nor for the tanning, dressing, preparing or keeping of skins, hides or leather, nor any manufactory, trade or business whatever which may be in any wise offensive to the neighboring inhabitants, or upon any part thereof.

That same day, Hunt assigned the lease, making a profit of $30.00.

Two days later, on November 8, Hunt visited Wilkes. "I'll buy that plot on 19th Street," he told the lawyer, "if it isn't sold yet."

An indenture was effected whereby Hunt purchased the property for $6,500, paying $650 or 10 percent in cash, the balance $5,850 on mortgage at 7 percent.

With the deed to the land in his pocket, Hunt approached Shepherd Ostrom and William F. Ostrom who confirmed an offer they had made previously to Hunt. They would take two-thirds of it for $9,750, giving Hunt $3,900 in cash and leaving $5,850 on mortgage.

The following day, the deed of sale was made and Hunt was in the real estate business.

"Polly!" Walter shouted, "I did it! I sold that Wilkes property. I made three thousand two hundred and fifty dollars net on it and still own a third interest in it for nothing."

On January 28, 1828, the Common Council assembled at the City Hall, voted to open 19th and 20th streets from Sixth Avenue to the Hudson River. This made the Chelsea section more valuable and in greater demand.

Fortune began to favor Hunt. The phenomenal success encouraged him. During 1828, Hunt leased sixteen additional pieces of property from Moore for twenty-one year periods which he in turn sublet at profits ranging from $30 to $100 each.

Hunt had become a land speculator!

Chapter 7

"Can you imagine this?" Hunt shouted, waving a letter.

"What's the matter?" Polly asked.

"Here's a letter from the Common Council of the City of New York."

"Do they want you to run for mayor?" Polly teased.

"No. It's a letter stating that city has made awards for the property which it confiscated in order to open up the road through 19th and 20th streets." Hunt had been awarded $432.00.

"You mean that the city is going to pay for that little strip? Why, I thought people had to pay for making streets as it made their property more valuable."

"I'm only one of the many to whom they sent money," Hunt said. "John Jacob Astor is getting five hundred and seventy dollars. Clement Clark Moore five hundred dollars and lots of others are getting paid."

"Real estate is profitable," Hunt confided to Polly. "It pays better than inventing. I didn't get much for the flax spinning machine or the alarm gong, considering the time and effort I expended."

Polly said cheerfully, "But maybe some day you will do something that will bring in a lot of money. Not that money is everything, but it helps."

"Do what, though?"

"You're always doing something. It shouldn't be difficult for you to find a project. But when you get your idea, get one that appeals to the masses, not the limited few."

"But *what?*"

"Dinner's ready," Polly announced, ending the conversation. A thick broiled sirloin was served. Walter tucked the large red and white checkerboard-pattern napkin under his chin and proceeded to carve. He soon put his own knife down, borrowed Polly's, and began again to cut the sizzling meat. The result was the same. In turn, Hunt looked at his wife, at the knives and at the steak.

"It's not the steak," Polly said, "it's the knives. We have no grindstone here as we had back home."

3 122 1121 21121 21111

After dinner, Hunt gathered the knives and gave each several strokes on the hone and leather strop.

"If we had a grindstone here like the one we had in Lowville," Polly said, "it would be too big for our kitchen."

"That's it," Walter interrupted excitedly. "That's it! That's the idea I've been looking for. A knife sharpener. An inexpensive object with a universal use. Every home should have one."

To determine the most suitable knife-sharpener, Hunt soon began experimenting with various contraptions. He finally decided that the revolving wheel, the principle of the grindstone, was best. A large grindstone, because of its size and price, was out of the question in the city.

Hunt knew there were only two ways of sharpening knives. One was to draw the knife against the grinding surface and the other was to move the object against the knife. The latter seemed impractical. This left the alternative, move the knife against the grinder on the hone. But that was the procedure generally employed; there was nothing new to that.

But Hunt kept on. The more he experimented, the more firmly he was impressed with the grindstone principle as it could be operated with little experience or technique while a hone and strop required greater skill and presented a danger. Hunt built several wooden models, each slightly different. He increased the width on one; on another he increased the circumference. On others he decreased the width and circumference. Size made little difference. They all operated smoothly. If only some way could be found to overcome the required space and eliminate both the handle and the turning.

Hunt was pondering the situation when he was interrupted by a succession of shouts and cries from the children.

"Daddy, I fell."

"She broke my wagon."

He rushed into the bedroom where he found both Caroline and Walter, Jr., crying. They ran to him, tears streaming down their distraught faces.

Quickly Hunt surveyed the situation and found that the children were more scared than hurt. Little Walter was crying because Caroline broke his wagon, while Caroline was crying because she hurt herself when she tripped over it.

He patted the heads of both children and said reassuringly, "You're not hurt, Caroline." She stopped crying almost at once. "And Walter," he said in feigned surprise, "I don't know why you are crying. Nothing is the matter with you. Suppose your wagon is broken? I built it for you and I'll fix it for you."

The din subsided as if by magic. Hunt picked up the wagon, a miniature stagecoach made of wood painted in gay colors. Its axle was broken. The damage was comparatively slight. In a few minutes, Hunt made the necessary repairs. He held the coach upside down and spun the wheels to make sure that they would turn. He repeated the process. His mind became intently active.

Now, if the wheels were a trifle closer—if they almost touched; and, if they were made of a hard substance; and, if a knife was placed at the junction point—then a double strength sharpener could be had. The conclusion stirred him.

He had stumbled upon the new idea. Impatiently, he rummaged through his tool box. He cut two sets of thin discs, each with a different diameter, and arranged them alternately on a common axis: A disc of steel, a disc of wood, a disc of steel, etc. He made a second and duplicate set of wheels which he likewise alternated on a common axis. Then he brought the discs opposite each other. He made a few minor adjustments in spacing so that the sides of the two series of wheels would not be too far away from those on the other axis. He drew the blade of the knife across the periphery of the two wheel series. He repeated the motion and the wheels turned slightly so that new grinding surfaces were brought into play.

The results were even better than Hunt had anticipated.

"Try this, Polly," he said, demonstrating the procedure.

Polly drew a knife blade across the parallel turning wheels and instinctively knew that the blade was being sharpened. "It's wonderful, Walter. Wonderful!"

Polly continued hurriedly drawing the knife against the wheels. Then the knife slipped and almost sliced her finger. Hunt quickly ascertained that Polly had not been cut. "What the sharpener needs is a protective guard. It'll only take a few minutes to make one."

The improvement was immediately made and the danger in the knife sharpener was eliminated.

A few days later Hunt showed the improved knife sharpener to Shepherd Ostrom, who praised it highly. "Have you applied for a patent?" he inquired.

"Do you think I should? I'll try and sell the idea first."

"Better get your patent first," Ostrom advised.

Hunt took Ostrom's advice and prepared the patent application. Ostrom and S.E. Angevera, a neighbor, witnessed Hunt's affidavit on January 23, 1829, on which date it was mailed to the Patent Office.

Twenty-six days later, on February 19, 1829, the patent was granted. It bore the seal of the United States and the signatures of President John Quincy Adams, Secretary of State Henry Clay and Attorney General William Wirt.

The patent was accorded instant recognition. The staid and conservative *Journal of the Franklin Institute* of May 1829 wrote

This knife sharpener consists of two small wheels of hard steel, turning upon center pins, and so placed that their peripheries intersect each other. The knife to be sharpened is drawn across between these two discs, by which means it readily obtains a fine cutting edge. We have one of them in use, and find it to answer the intention perfectly.

The United States of America

TO ALL TO WHOM THESE Letters Patent SHALL COME;

Whereas *Walter Hunt* a citizen of the United States hath alleged that he has invented a new and useful improvement in a machine for Sharpening carving knives & other edge tools that require a rough edge denominated The Compound Guard & Knife Sharpener which improvement he states has not been known or used before his application, hath also said that he does verily believe that he is the true inventor or discoverer of the said improvement; hath paid into the treasury of the United States the sum of thirty dollars, delivered a receipt for the same and presented a petition to the Secretary of State, signifying a desire of obtaining an exclusive property in the said improvement, and praying that a patent may be granted for that purpose These are therefore to grant, according to law, to the said *Walter Hunt* his heirs, administrators or assigns, for the term of fourteen years, from the *nineteenth* day of *Feby* one thousand eight hundred and *twenty nine* the full and exclusive right and liberty of making, constructing, using and vending to others to be used, the said improvement, a description whereof is given in the words of the said *Walter Hunt* himself, in the schedule hereto annexed and is made a part of these presents.

In Testimony whereof, I have caused these Letters to be made Patent, and the Seal of the United States to be hereunto affixed.

GIVEN under my hand, at the City of Washington, this *nineteenth* day of *Feby* in the year of our Lord one thousand eight hundred and *twenty nine* and of the independence of the United States of America the *fifty third*

John Quincy Adams

BY THE PRESIDENT.

H. Clay, Secretary of State.

City of Washington, TO WIT.

I DO HEREBY CERTIFY, That the foregoing Letters Patent were delivered to me on the *nineteenth* day of *Feby* in the year of our Lord one thousand eight hundred and *twenty nine* to be examined; that I have examined the same, and find them conformable to law, and I do hereby return the same to the Secretary of State, within fifteen days from the date aforesaid, to wit: on the *nineteenth* day of *Feby* in the year aforesaid

Wm Wirt Attorney General of the United States.

But the inventor was not content to rest upon his laurels. He was looking for further fields to conquer.

Hunt was intrigued by the ropewalks in upper Manhattan, some of which were more than a quarter of a mile long, in which ropes were manufactured. They seldom consisted of more than a shed with open sides, a board flooring, and a roof supported by poles.

He noticed that rope was never produced in a continuous length and that the longest length was limited to the length of the ropewalk. He observed that individual strands of fiber were stretched between two extreme points in a quantity that accorded with the desired thickness: If yet heavier rope or cord was desired, more strands were added. One of the extremities was attached to a wheel which was turned by a crank operated by one or more men. As the wheel revolved, the twine became heavier and the length shorter. If heavier twine was desired, several strands of twisted rope would be grouped together and the same process would be applied. Boiling tar was smeared over the ropes to give them firmness. The completed ropes would then be passed between rollers or through apertures surrounded with oakum to remove the tar, and the rope hung up to dry to lessen the chances of unwinding and unraveling. The twine was allowed to remain for several days to retain its shape.

Watching these operations furnished Hunt with the germ of an idea and he set about to build a miniature twine twister. Within a short time he had satisfied himself that his idea was practical and made a model which he submitted with his application for a patent.

On June 11, 1829, the Patent Office advised Hunt that his invention had sufficient merit and that a patent had been awarded.

The *Journal of the Franklin Institute* of September 1829 recorded the granting of the patent as follows;

> For an improvement in spinning hemp, flax, cotton, wool, and other materials capable of being wrought into thread, yarn, etc. by means of a machine called the Spiral Self-Supplying Twister, Walter Hunt, New York, June 14. This is a peculiar kind of spindle with its appendages, which appears to be principally designed for the spinning of hemp or flax. We have not, from the drawings and description, obtained a very clear idea of its mode of operation, nor could this be explained without engravings. When a model is received, it may obtain further notice.

The income from small real estate transactions, combined with the money from the sale of the knife sharpener and the spiral self-supplying twister increased the Hunt family's standard of living.

"Polly," Hunt said gleefully, "I've decided that there is nothing too good for my family. We can afford it now so I've rented a house at 111 Amos Street."

"I don't think we should move," Polly protested. "Ever since we left Low-ville, we've been like Gypsies. And I don't want to go to Amos Street."

"What's the matter with Amos Street?" Hunt inquired.

"The New York State Prison is on that street. That big high stone wall is a grim oppressive sight. We don't want to live so near the prisoners."

"If that's your only objection, forget it. There are no prisoners there any-more. Last year all the men prisoners were moved to Sing Sing Prison and the early part of this year all the female prisoners were removed. I selected a good house for us and the rent is reasonable, and it is not close to the prison."

Polly acceded without further opposition, and the move was made. And it was in this house that she gave birth to Frances Augusta Hunt.

The house was an improvement over their previous habitations. They liked it. Hunt had a small room in which he worked and, with more time at his dis-posal, dabbled in painting. After visiting him, the compilers of the City Direc-tory classified him as an artist and gave him that designation in the directories of 1829 and 1830. But painting did not stop Hunt from accepting odd jobs.

"If you have time, Mr. Hunt," said Levi Kidder, who lived in the house next door at 107 Amos Street, "I would like to hire you and pay you to work with me on a new type of cistern idea I've got. For some reason or other I just can't seem to work it out completely."

Hunt worked with Kidder and they developed a new idea for cisterns. "It's mighty good," Kidder stated jubilantly when the model was completed. "Maybe I can get a patent on it if you'll help draw up the patent papers."

The application was sent to the Patent Office and on January 21, 1831, Levi Kidder was awarded a patent on a "water cistern." Hunt felt an inward satisfac-tion with this accomplishment.

"We've lived in this house two years," Walter told Polly one day. "I think we should improve our habitation."

"What are you up to now?" Polly inquired.

"I was down to Asylum Street."

"Asylum Street? Where's that and what for?"

"It's a new street running from Cornelia to Christopher Street, just opened last year. I saw a very pretty house there, number 22, to be exact. I hope you'll like it, because I just made a deal and rented it."

As arrangements had already been made, Polly knew better than to argue. And the Hunts moved to 22 Asylum Street.

Minor inconveniences irritated Polly and she was not happy with the new house. Basically, she did not like it. Hunt too was disappointed, as it did not have as much space as he imagined.

Towards the end of the year, he told Polly, "I'm doing a lot more mechan-ical work now and I need a shop of my own. I've rented a shop at 62 Bedford Street, between Commerce and Morton Streets."

"That's fine," Polly commented, "I wish *we* were moving from here too."
"We are."

Polly stared at him in amazement. She was speechless.

"Do you remember when we lived at 111 Amos Street? Remember that nice little house across the street that you always liked? Well, it's empty now, and we are going to move into it. Here's a copy of the lease."

They moved to [62] Bedford Street and he took a shop at [112] Amos Street. The year passed very quickly, and in [1832] Hunt again started on his peregrinations. He moved from [62] Bedford Street across the street to 63 Bedford, and his shop moved from [112] Amos Street across the street to 103 Amos.

"Every year we move," Polly commented. "Now I know why those English people think of us as they do."

"What English people?"

"Those writers like Darusmont. In his book *View of Society and Manners in America*." Polly picked up the book and found the passage:

On the first of May, the City of New York has the appearance of sending off a population flying from the plague, or of a town which has surrendered on condition of carrying away all their goods and chattels. Rich furniture and ragged furniture, carts, wagons and drays, ropes, canvas and straw, porters and draymen, white, yellow and black, occupy the street from east to west, from north to south, on this day.

"Not far from wrong!" Hunt interrupted.

"And here is what Mrs. Felton wrote," Polly continued, turning the pages of another book to find this passage:

This removing reminds me of the removal of furniture which annually takes place on the first of May. By an established custom, the houses are let, from this day, for the term of one year; and, as the inhabitants in general love variety, and seldom reside in the same house for two consecutive years, those who have to change, which appears to be nearly the whole city, must, consequently, be all removing together.

"Well, I guess it's easier to move than to pay rent," Polly joked.

"At least, now they can't put you in jail for nonpayment of debt. They stopped doing that in 1831."

"We'd better not joke about these things," Polly concluded. "No one can ever tell what will happen."

The following days Walter was busy moving his belongings from his shop while Polly attended to moving the household effects. Even in the new and larger house, Hunt's papers were always lying around. As usual, the task of picking them up and putting them away was greater than that of looking after all the children combined. Elusive papers slid behind sideboards and wardrobes. Her tidiness was rewarded with anger; Hunt continually warning her not to disturb his papers. Polly paid little attention to his ramblings and as a result minor disturbances were frequent.

"Hey, Polly," Walter called, "I had some papers here. Where are they?"

"I don't know," Polly replied.

"Well, they were here yesterday. They're very important."

"I picked up a bunch of notes all over the house. You don't mean those large yellow sheets?"

"No, just small pieces of paper. I'm working with Levi Kidder on a machine for sweeping the streets. It's almost completed, and he's going to apply for a patent on it."

"I wish you'd invent a machine for cleaning up this house and looking after your papers."

"Those papers were here yesterday. I distinctly remember putting them on the sideboard."

"If they're not there," suggested Polly, "maybe they fell behind the sideboard. Let's move it and see."

The sideboard was a heavy mahogany piece, huge and massive. It was too heavy for one person to move so they both pushed until it was away from the wall. The papers were found standing end up against the dusty wall!

"Look at that dust!" Polly exclaimed. "If there was only some way of moving that big heavy thing, I assure you the dust wouldn't be there."

In the process of repeated moving of their cumbersome furniture, Hunt had observed that it was impossible, once the massive lares and penates were in place, either to change their position or properly clean behind or under them. He studied the ornate Chippendale furniture, which had superseded the simpler styles in popularity. He noticed the carved legs with the dragon's claw clutching a rounded ball. An idea immediately presented itself.

"This claw and ball foot is a useless thing," Hunt commented, "They should have put a caster underneath."

"But casters wouldn't be much good," Polly answered, "They move only to the right or left, or from front to back."

"We should have something that can move in all directions," Hunt commented. "Wait, I have it. It's obvious! That ball held in the claw is useless because it's stationary. Why not place a real ball in the claw, one that can revolve in any direction?"

They pushed the sideboard back in place against the wall and Hunt turned to leave.

"Where are you going?" Polly called.

"Down to the glasshouse and have them roll me a glass ball."

About two hours later, Walter returned home with a wooden block, one side of which he had whittled into the form of a claw. In the hollow palm of the claw, he inserted the glass ball. It held solidly, but still loose enough to revolve when the furniture was moved.

Hunt then cut away the wooden ball in the leg of the furniture and inserted the glass ball in its place. Then he followed the same procedure for each of the claw extremities. They all rotated, and the furniture could be moved with much less effort.

Polly displayed Walter's handicraft to their neighbors. News of its simplicity and usefulness spread throughout the city. By word of mouth recommendation he received orders to fix the furniture in various localities throughout the city.

"Maybe if you get a patent, you might be able to sell the idea to furniture manufacturers," someone suggested.

Despite his hesitation in applying for patents, Hunt made an application for one and on April 22, 1833, it was granted. It did not receive a patent number, as the numerical system was not adapted until 1836.

Chapter 8

"Would you object, Polly, if my baby brother Adoniram comes and lives with us?" Hunt asked one day in the spring of 1833.

"Adoniram. He's the... Let's see." Polly started counting the children of Rachel and Sherman Hunt. "You were the first and the oldest. Then there was Levisa, Hannah, Almira and Hiram. That's five. Then came Harry, Enos, Philo, Rachel and Sherman, Jr. That's ten. Then Albinos—"

"No," Hunt interrupted. "Adoniram came before Albinos. He's the eleventh. Albinos was the twelfth. Angelina was the thirteenth and Elizabeth was the fourteenth."

"How old is Adoniram now? You're thirty-seven. I guess he's about twenty-four."

"No," Hunt corrected. "He just turned nineteen. Born in 1814."

"If you want him to live with us, we have room, I'm sure the children will be glad to have him. And so will I."

"I'd like it, and furthermore, I can use an apprentice. I'd like to train him and teach him a trade."

A few weeks later, early in June, Adoniram finally arrived. He went directly to Hunt's shop at [Amos Street] where Walter was forging a red hot iron bar on the anvil.

"Let me show you how to do that, Mr. Hunt," Adoniram yelled from the doorway to surprise him.

Hunt looked up from his work, shoved the iron back into the furnace, and rushed to greet his brother. After a long chat about what had transpired during the many years that they had not seen each other, Hunt confided, "I've had something in my mind for a long time, and I'd like to have you work with me and help me with it."

"I'd like to. What is it?"

"A stove. Practically all stoves are either square or oblong. They concentrate heat in one spot instead of radiating it. The reason stoves do not give out heat equally in all directions is because they are not designed to do so. Now, if the stoves were round..."

"How can you build a round stove?" Adoniram asked.

"Why not? I've got all the plans drawn up on paper!"

"But, even if you could, how do you know it will work?"

"I'll build a model."

"That'll cost a lot of money."

"But then I will be able to start manufacturing stoves for myself, or else I'll sell the idea to some stove company."

But Hunt did not anticipate the difficulties of construction. Plans on paper for a stove and a commercially manufactured stove were two different things.

While constructing the stove, he endeavored to interest numerous people in investing in it. The capitalists and promoters replied, "How can I tell from your diagram whether it will do what you claim for it? Let me see the stove in actual operation. We have no capital for untried inventions. We can use our capital to better advantage in promoting our own products."

The arguments were not new. He had heard them before. But Hunt was not unduly discouraged. He kept on looking for a manufacturer.

J. G. Pierson, owner of the firm of J. G. Pierson and Brothers, dealers in iron and cut nails, whose office was at [26] Front Street, listened carefully while Hunt outlined his plans for the stove. "It's out of my field," Pierson said. "I suggest you see Benjamin Folger."

Hunt went off to 8 William Street, to the firm of Folger and Lamb. "I'm pretty sure I'll be able to do something with it," said Benjamin Folger. "But I sure never thought of a round stove before. The, er, uh, what kind of a stove did you call it?"

"The Globe Stove."

"I don't want to manufacture them, but if you can produce them at a competitive price I'll buy a few. If they're any good, there is no reason why I can't sell them."

The slight encouragement cheered Hunt. He carefully rechecked his plans and specifications, then set out to have a model cast. None of the foundries in the city would undertake to cast it, and those who could do so demanded an exorbitant price.

The arguments against the stove were many. It was not favorably received. "We wouldn't undertake to build a round stove. It will explode the first time it is fired."

"We can't cast only one stove. Why, the cost of a mold would make it out of reach of a millionaire. Now, if you wanted a hundred stoves, or two hundred, that would bring the proportionate price of the mold within reason."

"If you want us to build it, you'll have to pay cash in advance for the whole job, without any guarantee that it will be built exactly like the specifications."

"We're not interested in your problems. We don't care what you do with the stove. Whether it's good or bad, we don't care. If you want molds cast, you got to pay for the work. Your profit or loss doesn't interest us."

Hunt told Benjamin Folsom of the rejections, and was quite discouraged. But Folsom gave him a ray of hope.

"Maybe I can help you. I'll give you a letter to John Kilby. He does a lot of casting at Waterford."

"Waterford?"

"Waterford's a little town four miles from Troy and about ten miles from Albany, on the Champlain Canal, near the junction of the Hudson and the Mohawk rivers," Folsom explained.

"I'll go and see him."

Hunt went home, arranged his plans, and then took the boat to Albany, from which he went to Waterford by stagecoach.

"Sorry," said Kilby at first, after talking to Hunt. "We're not interested. We got too much work on hand now."

After much persuasion, however, Kilby agreed to undertake making the molds and casting. Hunt felt encouraged. But his encouragement waned day by day until he finally became desperate.

On September 14, 1833, he wrote a frantic four-page letter to Adoniram F. Hunt at 62 Bedford Street which he mailed after paying the 18¾¢ fee. In a post-script, he wrote that no one but a member of the family was to see the letter:

Waterford, Sept. 14, 1833
Dear Brother,

You are probably surprised that I have not forwarded castings long before this time for a large quantity of stoves, but I have learned to *my cost* the reasons why my patents have lingered this three months without attention at this foundry, and probably would for as many more without my presence and constant attention. The fact is they work for all that come, many of whom are old customers and will not be put off although their job may not be worth one shilling. They will watch the moulders and when I am busy at some of the others their work is put in and mine crowded out. Every night since I have been here I have drawn my plans for the following day, selected patterns and have placed them before the moulders after having obtained a promise from Mr. Kilby and the foreman that they would positively be attended to, and as I have above described, whilst I was attending to one moulder to see one pattern put in the other moulders would leave a dozen out, and in this manner when night came, among five moulders I could not obtain the entire parts for one stove until at length I became discouraged and have told Mr. Kilby that I should go home and give the whole project up entirely. This has extorted a new promise which has been followed by a new disappointment. I have concluded to stay one day more on the condition that I am to have the entire use and control of five moulders and am resolved to use my powers arbitrarily and dash the first pattern across the foundry that I find upon their flasks that does not belong to me. I shall probably forward about one dozen or more of stoves on Monday. I have made a material alteration in the plan of the grates which is better and cheaper as there is no labor in putting them together after they are cast. I shall use the same plan in all of the stoves. It is composed of a lever entering the side as usual but to move horizontally in the end of which is a hole through which the stem of the grate passes, and the whole is told. I have consequently dispensed with the linke rod or bolt, and have substituted columns from plain patterns made here, of a triangular form with a similar formed base and cap[.] [A]s you will perceive the rods are to pass perpendicularly through these columns in the proper place to accommodate the feet and fasten the whole stove together except the arch which will stand midway between the columns and are fastened in a manner which you understand. The stoves which I send on Wednesday are plain ones without the arch, I shall send or bring some home with the arch pattern in order to facilitate business. I have made caps and bases for the Globe stove of cast iron to fit upon columns of sheet iron, for the center cylinder also, although I should prefer cast, but if I depend on casting the whole I cannot get stoves enough up this season for samples. It will therefore be absolutely necessary for me to return here again if I come home. I therefore want you to take hold as though my life was at stake (and I feel that it is) and drive the work with all the care and perseverance in your power and the instant that it will do for me to leave here I shall do so. I want you to go to Messrs. Folger and Pierson, and see if they will let me, or you have means on some conditions, to pay the shop expenses for one week to come, except to pay you and Mr. Highit. Do take hold and do the best you can for me and I will see you rewarded if ever in my power. I have my hands full here, to keep the patterns in order, as fast as they are broken by the careless workmen whenever they use them, that are at all tender. I wish you would ask Mr. Pierson, if Mr. Highit had not best make the model as soon as possible. If he would copy the Globe Stove except the grate, which may be made after my improved plan which I will send you immediately. Make the model as small as you please of mahogany varnished and blacked. I want you to write the state of affairs precisely by the first mail that I may know whether it is necessary to come home or not immediately. Ask Mr. Kidder to write if he is at home. Call on the family and learn their wishes and write accordingly.

Respectfully yours
Walter Hunt

W. F. Hunt
Do not let any except one of the family see this letter for fear of unfavorable constructions. Mr. Kilby was very kind to me and I presume does the best in his power, but where there is custom work done these stoves cannot be carried on with success.

W. HUNT'S PATENT RADIATOR, OR GLOBE STOVE,

DESIGNED FOR THE BURNING OF ANTHRACITE COAL.

The proprietors of this valuable invention have, after a series of experiments testing its comparative utility, and thorough investigation of its principles, become fully convinced of its decided superiority over all other plans heretofore adopted, in the economy of producing and diffusing heat by the combustion of Anthracite Coal.

The Globe or Sphere is evidently nature's favorite form for all bodies adapted to the generating, transmitting, or diffusing of light or heat ; which important fact alone speaks volumes in favor of our principle, and should not be overlooked by an enlightened and scientific community, whose interests are so deeply concerned, without an impartial and thorough investigation.

The following are among the peculiar advantages of the Radiator, or Globe Stove.

First. The whole amount of heat produced by the combustion of the fuel, is radiated equally in every possible direction, *leaving no cold corners or overheated sides* ; consequently, although more heat may be produced, the temperature of the atmosphere is lower at a near given distance, and less injurious in its effects upon furniture, or whatever may be near it.

Secondly. As much heat is radiated *downward as upward*, by which means the whole floor, in every supposable point, is acted upon by direct rays of heat, escaping from the under section of the globe, and the lower region of atmosphere, which is always cold in a room heated by a cylindrical or angular Stove, is kept perfectly warm ; and the universal objection against Stoves, namely, their deficiency in conveying warmth to the feet, is here perfectly obviated. For Public Houses, Offices, Stores, &c. this one item in the character of the Globe Stove, is of vast importance, and cannot fail to be appreciated by those who examine them in operation.

Thirdly. The perfect adaptation of the form of the Globe Stove to the free and equal ignition of fuel, as well as transmission of heat, preserves it at the same time from becoming burned or fractured, by contraction and expansion, which is invariably the case with the Angular Stove. The Globe Stove combines, in a high degree, the requisite advantages of neatness with that of economy. With proper care no dust is created in kindling, charging, or discharging, and it may be kept ignited and tended with less difficulty and labor than any other Stove now in use.

The Globe Stove will be varied in its style and dimensions, to suit the taste and wants of the community, without departing in any one respect from its original principles.

In tending the Globe Stove there are a few simple facts to be understood, and rules to be observed.

In kindling. When a quantity of half burned extinguished coal remains in the Stove, care should be taken to thoroughly shake out the ashes, by vibrating the pendulus handle below ; then make a small opening centrally, on the top of the coal, where burning coals should be deposited, and a sufficient quantity of fine broken charcoal permitted to ignite, observing always to put small anthracite coal upon the kindled charcoal : in this manner the Stove may be readily kindled *upon the top* when nearly full of coal, or it may be emptied and kindled in a similar manner at the bottom.

As cinders are seldom formed from good coal in these Stoves, it is not often necessary to discharge the unconsumed coal, which may be rekindled as above stated ; but when necessary, the pendulum, which is only vibrated to dislodge the ashes, may be passed several times round, operating upon the principles of a rack and pinion, by which means the grate is raised into the centre of the Stove, and the coal permitted to fall into the pan beneath, at which time the ventilator should be closed, to prevent the escape of dust.

By a slight movement of the ventilating ring, which will be understood at sight, the combustion may be increased, diminished, or wholly extinguished, at pleasure.

Orders directed to the Globe Stove Office, No. 8 William street, will be attended to in the order in which they are received, and correct advices given as to the time when they can be executed.

Patterns may be seen at the office, No. 8 William street.

New York, November, 1833.

BENJ'N H. FOLGER.

Adoniram was unable to raise any money. Folger, learning of the desperate financial situation, came to the rescue. For his assistance, however, he demanded a major interest in the patent rights of the stove.

Folger's cash spurred the foundry to action and within a short time they completed the molds and had cast several stoves. Hunt returned to New York with one of the stoves and with the aid of his brother installed it in Folger's office. It was equipped with an ashpit, below which was a drawer for the removal of ashes. The draft was controlled by a perforated collar. The shaking of the grate was accomplished by moving the grate up and down by means of a ratchet.

Anthracite coal was placed in the stove and eager eyes watched the flame spread. Gradually, the heat began to circulate. It radiated equally in all directions and performed exactly as Hunt had anticipated. Everyone was happy.

Folger was enthusiastic. In November 1833 he prepared a one page circular which, when printed, was hand delivered by a gangly freckled boy to business houses and homes.

George A. Arrowsmith approached Hunt and said, "I hear you got your patent?"

"I haven't applied for a patent yet."

"Don't try to fool me Hunt, I know. It was awarded on September 20, 1833. I remember the date very distinctly. It was my wife's birthday."

"Oh, that! That was not for the stove. It was for the street sweeping machine."

"Well, then, congratulations on that."

"That's the machine I worked on, but the patent was granted not to me, but to Levi Kidder. I helped him with the mechanical part."

"Well, I also hear tell that your stove's quite a success. Folger is elated with it. And the circulars showed that people were interested in it. And now Folger is willing to advertise it in the newspapers."

The *New York Commercial* ran a descriptive advertisement for the stove from November 8 to November 29, 1833. On the 30th Folger omitted the description of the method of operating the stove, greatly lessening the amount of space used. This later advertisement announced that the patterns could not only be seen at Folger's, 8 William Street, but also at the Lackawanna Coal Office, 256 Broadway, New York City.

To protect his investment and to discourage infringers, Folsom insisted that Hunt apply for a patent. Hunt worked all day December 5, 1833, Thanksgiving Day, on the specifications. On December 11, Hunt's signature and affirmations were witnessed by [A. Loucks] and D. E. Wheeler, a lawyer of 23 Nassau Street.

The patent was speedily processed by the Patent Office and was granted on February 8, 1834. In his eight pages of handwritten specifications, Hunt made the following claims for his invention of the stove, all of which were allowed by the Patent Office.

The improvement claimed in my invention are as follows;

First, I claim the style, general arrangement and fashion of the above described Radiator or Globe Stove believing the peculiar advantages of said arrangement in the generating and equal diffusion of heat exclusively confined to the globe or spheroid form as a reservoir of fuel for the following reason, viz, it is the only form from which heat can be equally radiated and consequently, it has the peculiar advantage of imparting one half of its heat downwards warming the floor and lower regions of atmosphere which cannot be effected by the regular or cylindrical stove.

Secondly, I claim the spheroid or hollow globe, or inverted hollow cone for the bottom section in particular as a reservoir of fuel and radiator of heat, in combination with the vibrating and [h]oisting grate as before specified together with the said centre hollow column which prevents the escape of ashes into the room in its descent from the globe to the ash pan.

Thirdly, and lastly, I claim as my improvement, separately, and as a part, the rack or pinion or vibrating and hoisting grate as before specified.

The technical magazines, on the search for current inventions, took cognizance of it and made their reports. The *Mechanics Magazine* of 1834 (volume 2, page 216) stated,

Patent Radiator, or Globe Stove.—A stove with the above name, has recently been invented by Mr. Walter Hunt, of this city, one of which was in operation a short time since at the Exchange. The main part of the stove where the coal is deposited is of a globular form, and from its peculiar construction, produces a greater quantity of heat from a given quantity of fuel than any other stove now in use. After repeated trials, the inventor informs us that it requires a very little quantity of fuel in comparison with many others now in use, and from what we witnessed we are disposed to entertain the same opinion. This article is well calculated for halls, churches, courting rooms, etc., and when once provided, will no doubt be generally sought after.

The *Journal of the Franklin Institute*, September 1834 (page 177), printed the claims allowed, followed by the comment,

The appearance of this stove is peculiar, the body of it being a hollow globe, supported by a column, and having two columns, one on each side of it, which support an arch passing over the body of the stove. The fuel is to be put in at top, an urn that surmounts a cylindrical opening, which stands in the place of the key-stone of the arch, being removed for that purpose. The grate is placed at the bottom of the globe, and consists of bars which are convex upward, and is supported by a centre shaft that descends through the column under the globe; this shaft has on it a rack, which, by means of a pinion, may cause the grate to vibrate up and down for the discharge of ashes, which fall through the column into the ash pit below.

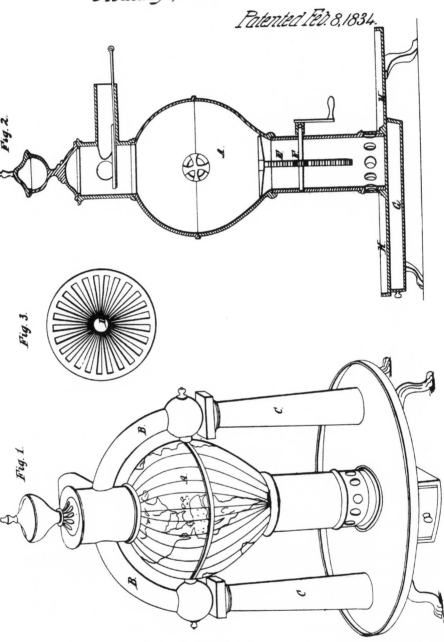

W. Hunt.

Heating Stove.

Sheet 1-2 Sheets.

Patented Feb. 8, 1834.

Fig. 2.

Fig. 3.

Fig. 1.

W. Hunt.

Heating Stove.

Sheet 2-2 Sheets.

Patented Feb. 8, 1834.

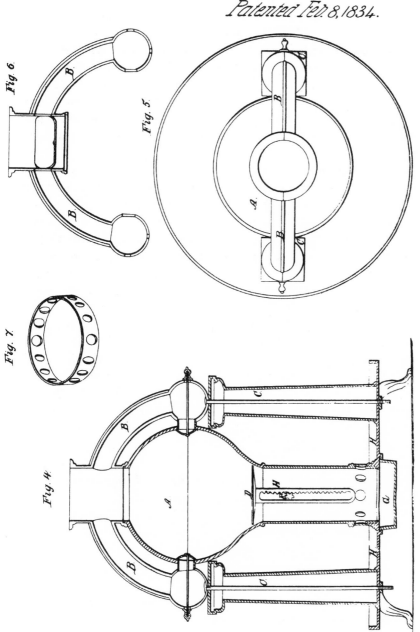

Fig. 6.

Fig. 5.

Fig. 7.

Fig. 4.

The stove was well received and Hunt's reputation as an inventor was enhanced. The designation "artist," which was applied to him in the city directories from 1829 to 1833, inclusive, was changed to "stovemaker" in the 1834 directory.

The initial added income enabled Hunt to seek better living accommodations. He moved his family to 182 Bleecker Street but retained his shop at 103 Amos Street.

On July 29, 1834, Walter Hunt assigned "all his right, title and interest in the within specified letters patent for the rest of the term," to Benjamin H. Folger. The assignment was witnessed by Daniel Ullman, attorney, and T. G. Smith, Commissioner of Deeds.

At the eighth annual fair of the American Institute, the Globe Stove was displayed by Doyle and Patterson of 213 Water Street together with two cooking stoves. Great crowds flocked to see it and marveled at the way it distributed its heat.

"Great stove you have, Mr. Hunt," said James E. Doyle, the junior member of the firm. "We have already received a few orders for them. I also want to congratulate you on the award the Institute granted you for the stove."

Hunt smiled. He was too modest to state that the Institute also saw fit to award him diplomas for his invention of the forest saw, for a japanned steam table to keep foodstuffs warm and a silver medal for his machine for cutting brads.

"A man as versatile as you should be making a lot of money now," Doyle added joyfully.

"I just make out to live," Hunt replied with little enthusiasm.

Folger continued making and selling the stove until ill health forced his retirement from business. Two years later he contacted Doyle, who continued selling the stoves.

"Some time ago," Folger began, "you told me that if I ever wanted to sell my interest in the Globe Stove that you would like to buy it. If you still want to buy the patent on the Globe Stove, I'll give it to you now at a good price."

"How much?"

"Two thousand dollars."

"I'll give you a thousand."

"For one thousand and seventy dollars, the seventy dollars for drawing up the papers," he countered, "and you can have it."

On December 14, 1836, Folger assigned James E. Doyle and Abijah Patterson "all the Letters Patent and full and exclusive liberty of making and using and vending said invention for the residue of the term." It was witnessed by George Cooper, an attorney, and Henry Taylor.*

It was on the following day that the devastating fire in the U.S. Patent Office destroyed all of its original patent application and registration documents.

On December 20, 1836, the Patent Office recorded Folger's assignment to Doyle and Patterson, as well as Hunt's previous assignment to Folger which had not been filed.

The patent assignment to Doyle and Patterson was acquired by James E. Doyle, who became the sole owner. It was witnessed by John McClelland and George E. Baldwin, a notary public. It was not sent to the Patent Office until February 24, 1837, on which date it was recorded. Thus Doyle, one of the first purchasers of the stove, became the owner of the Globe Stove.

Doyle took over the sale of the Globe Stoves, which were well received. On August 7, 1837, he published the first of a series of advertisements in the *New York Morning Herald* under the heading LOOK AT THIS BEFORE THE COLD WEATHER SETS IN. After an account of its advantages, testimonials were printed.

Townsend Harris, who later became the first American envoy to Japan, wrote on March 28, 1837

In the autumn of 1833, I placed a No. 1 Nott Stove in my house (which is a three story basement) and passed the pipe through the floors up to the attic, and thence across into a chimney. On an average I burned ten tons of coal and found I had but two difficulties—1st I could not warm the lower surface of the atmosphere on the first or basement floor, consequently, we all had cold feet—2nd. the great difficulty in getting servants to manage so complex a piece of machinery as the stove. The expense of repairs on this stove were [a] full $10 per annum.

Last Autumn I was induced to try the Globe Stove on the simplest plan, and I find it to answer the purpose admirably.—From its shape the heat is radiated downward in so perfect a manner, that the best place to warm the feet is to place them on the zinc, within a yard or so of the fire.

I cannot sufficiently praise your stove, its simplicity of management—the ease with which a fire is made—the small expense of repairs—the perfect manner in which heat is thrown out, render it worthy of great public attention.

Dr. Jonathan Dodge, who became known in the profession of dentistry for his method of setting artificial teeth, was another Globe Stove booster. (It was now being promoted also as a cooking stove.) He wrote, on March 20, 1837,

This certifies that Messrs. Doyle & Patterson's Globe Cooking Stove has been used in my kitchen the past season and I am happy to state, with much pleasure to the cook and gratification of all the family. I therefore do cordially recommend its superiority over others, in its easiness to light, its utility, compactness, radiation, and though last, not least, *economy.*

Dr. Alexander Abbott added, "From my own observation, I fully coincide with the above recommendation of Dr. Dodge in favor Messrs. Doyle & Patterson's Globe Cooking Stove."

A joint testimonial letter was signed by Thomas S. Stevens, Superintendent of Almhouse; John Phillips, Keeper Blackwell's Island and Henry Van Stoutenburgh, resident physician,

> In answer to inquiries respect the Globe Stove in use at Blackwell's Island, and the Almhouse at Bellevue, since October 1835, it affords us pleasure to have it in our power to say, that they have fully sustained the recommendations given them, and with perfect confidence can recommend them for their simplicity of management, economy of fuel, diffusions of heat, and perfect safety in preference to any other stove heretofore used in these establishments.

Many additional testimonial letters with the names and addresses of users of the stove were given.

"The way your stoves have been selling" said James S. Baillie, an artist, at 105 West Broadway, "you should have made a lot of money."

"People don't understand," Hunt explained; "they don't see under the surface. Suppose, for example, the stove brought me four hundred dollars. It didn't. Just suppose. That's quite some money. But suppose I worked twenty weeks to build it, that means I only got twenty dollars a week.

"No one knows how many times a casting mold had to be made. Some had to be made over and over and over again. All this cost money. And the old molds have no value. It's like painting fifty different pictures before you get the right composition."

"If it doesn't pay," Baillie asked, "why do you work on it?"

"You don't understand," Hunt replied. "Inventing is like a disease. It's a gamble. It gets into your blood. When you work on a new idea, you never know how long it will take. You judge you can finish the job in two weeks. Two weeks pass and you are not finished. There is only one thing you can do, put in a few more days, a few more weeks, a month, if necessary, until you finish."

"Then you make a million," Baillie joked.

"No, then you try and sell your invention so that you can get some money to pay your bills for parts, and some money to pay you for your time. And if you don't get enough money, then you have to worry how to make ends meet. That's my situation at the present time."

"I guess there's no fun in being an inventor."

"There's lots of fun in it, but not much money. You work and work, always hoping that the next invention, or the one after that, will be the one to make money."

"Why don't you quit?" Baillie asked. "Seems like it's a vicious circle. You work to make money to pay your debts so you can work to make more debts."

"I think I am going to quit," Hunt said in a low tone that was scarcely audible.

"What did you say?" Baillie asked.

"Nothing," said Hunt. "Nothing."

Chapter 9

"It's queer," Hunt remarked one day in [1833] as he placed Benjamin Henry Day's successful penny newspaper *The Sun* on the parlor table.

"The editorial?" Polly questioned.

"No," Hunt responded, "you. Rocking in that chair. One minute you are up, the next you're down. Seems to parallel our lives."

"But, somehow or other, despite bad breaks, we always come up again," Polly answered reassuringly.

Hunt did not reply. His brow wrinkled. He was deep in thought, looking off in the distance.

"Walter, I want to show you something," Polly said placing a decorative tidy on his lap.

"What is it? What's it for?" he asked.

"An antimacassar. I'm going to put it over the armpiece on the big parlor chair."

"It's pretty. Where did you get it?"

"A fine observant husband, I have," Polly commented in feigned disdain, "after you've seen me sewing it."

"Sewing it? Did you sew it?"

"Why, of course. It's very easy if you have time. Here, look." Polly took a needle and thread and began to stitch the unfinished part.

"How do you make those stitches?" he asked.

Polly showed him. Then she handed him a small swatch of cloth and a threaded needle. He held them, uncertain what to do with them. "It's simple," Polly explained. She guided his hand while he attempted to make several stitches.

As with most men whose hands were accustomed to rough tools, minute intricate work was difficult for Hunt. He found that the needle was harder to manipulate than the lathe. Sewing was not as easy as it looked. His first attempt at sewing was a failure. Uneven stitches, pulled cloth, loose ends, unpulled loops and knots resulted.

"You'll never be able to sew, father." Caroline chided. "Better give it up as a bad job."

"I never give up, Caroline," he said determinedly. "I'm going to learn to sew just to prove that I can do it. But personally, I have no interest in it."

Polly Hunt beamed. She knew the relaxation would benefit him and take his mind off immediate problems. Her contention proved correct. In the evening, he would sit near the gas burner practicing with the needle. In a short time, he had learned how to make regular and even stitches with great proficiency.

Watching his father sew irritated young George, now six years old. He felt ashamed, and hoped his friends would never observe his father doing a woman's task.

"I don't understand," George told his father. "Why do you want to sew? You're not going to be a tailor."

Walter Hunt made no comment. He looked at his son and smiled. Like an automaton, he kept turning the cloth over and over, stitching the reverse as well as the face side. Then with the same fervor he used in sewing he ripped out the stitches. Sometimes he used two needles at the same time working them in tandem; at other times he used two needles in opposite directions, one from the front side, the other from the reverse.

"What are you doing?" Polly asked as she observed him using two needles. "One needle is all anyone uses. You can't sew anything like that!"

"Why can't I?" he inquired. "If I want to use two needles, there is no law, written or otherwise, which says I cannot."

"But you can't sew that way!" Caroline insisted, adding her voice to the argument. She was now seven years old and had great skill herself with the needle.

But Hunt continued using two needles. Every once in a while, the needles, going through the cloth, pricked his fingers and the stillness of the evening was frequently punctuated by his muffled oaths. A few stitches and many specks of blood appeared on the cloth when he put it away that first night.

"Didn't I tell you?" Caroline chided. "You'll never learn how to sew."

"The cloth looks like it had the measles," Walter, Jr., teased. (He was now thirteen.)

Polly Hunt could not fathom why her husband sewed and then just as meticulously ripped the stitches out. His progress was marked and he demonstrated proficiency. Within a short time, he was very skilled with the needle.

"That's wonderful," Polly praised. "You can sew almost as well as I can. Now you can help me."

"I don't like to sew." Walter answered. But, he continued sewing, ripping and sewing.

"Then tell me what are you doing?" Polly asked bewildered. "One would think you are creating a masterpiece, then, all of a sudden, all the stitches are gone. What are you doing?"

"Just thinking," he replied dreamily.

Hunt's interest in sewing stopped almost as quickly as it developed. In the evenings, he hunched over the oak table on which he kept his papers, drawing patterns and designs. Odd bits of paper of all sizes and shapes were covered with pencil notations. Some were on wrapping paper, some on pages torn from magazines, and others on plain writing paper.

"You are neglecting the children again, Walter." Polly scolded. "Just like you did when you worked on the stove. You have no interest in anything but your work."

Hunt peered at her from behind his desk. He wanted to reply that the reason he worked so hard was for his family but he said nothing. Polly sensed his unspoken words and then said softly, "What are you spending so much time on? What are you doing?"

"Just thinking."

Night after night, the same procedure took place. He concentrated upon his work and was oblivious to almost everything that went on about him. The presence of guests did not alter his routine. He continued working at his desk. There was no deviation for more than a month.

One night Walter Hunt did not come home for supper. This was usual when he had to work late at the shop but now things were slow and Polly was worried.

"Should I go to the shop and see if everything is all right?" Walter, Jr., inquired.

"Yes," said Polly eagerly, then— "no, no, don't go!" she said nervously. "Father wouldn't like that. Remember what he always says: 'I don't work by the clock. If I'm not home in time for supper, eat without me. And never worry'."

"No!" Polly cautioned. "It will only anger him."

About eleven o'clock, the key clicked in the latch on the front door. Hunt entered the foyer, looking tired.

"Anything wrong?" Polly asked, a trace of uneasiness in her voice.

"No," Hunt answered. "Am I too late for dinner?"

"It's eleven o'clock," Caroline explained.

"Then what are you doing up so late, young lady? It's way past your bedtime."

"I'll have supper ready in a few minutes, Walter." Polly said. "Caroline, it's your turn to help."

Caroline put her school books away and served the meal.

After Hunt had concluded his meal, he reached into his pocket and pulled out a piece of cloth which he gave to Polly. It had been carefully sewn with fine parallel lines less than half an inch apart. The lines were straight as if made by a ruler. The stitches were even and identical.

"What is this?" Polly asked.

"The reason I was late for supper tonight," he explained, "was because I sewed it."

"You sewed this? You?" said Polly laughingly. "Not you. Only an expert could have sewn this cloth!"

"You never sewed that," said Caroline knowingly.

Polly Anne came into the kitchen to hear what the conversation was about. (She was now eighteen.) "Why, it's perfect!" she exclaimed in amazement.

"Who would want to make a lot of stitches like that on an old piece of cloth anyway?" said young Walter in disdain.

"Where did you really get it?" Polly inquired.

"I told you I sewed it!" Hunt replied firmly.

"Not you!" the family chorused in unison.

"I did it this evening down in my shop at Amos Street," Hunt said indignantly. "I did it this evening on a machine."

Polly Hunt was speechless. She looked at her husband, then at the cloth. The sewing was as exact as if it had been accomplished by the most skilled seamstress. It seemed preposterous. She held the cloth to the light. She examined the stitches with the greatest of care. She pulled at the threads to test their strength. She was too amazed to say anything. It was completely unbelievable. "And where did you get the machine?"

Polly did not realize that all the time she had been teaching her husband to sew, his interest had not been in sewing but in creating a machine to dispense with the labor of hand-sewing.

News of the invention spread and friends came to see the sewing machine. They wanted to see the impossible.

One of the first to see it in operation was George A. Arrowsmith. It was built almost entirely of wood. Each and every part, regardless of its size, was accurately constructed and built to synchronize with all others. Levers, wheels and cogs were infinitesimally exact. The teeth on one gear meshed with those on others. The slightest variation would have impeded the harmonious operation of the machine. The speed of the shuttle passing through the thread to form the lockstitch was accurately timed to coincide with the movements of the needle. Otherwise the machine would perform unevenly and would be useless.

"The machine is a wonder, Mr. Hunt," said Arrowsmith sincerely.

And indeed it was. The machine which Hunt constructed in 1833 was a masterpiece. With nothing to serve as a basis or model, with no other machine from which parts could be obtained, he evolved a plan for mechanical sewing which was so revolutionary that had he even dared to suggest it before completion of his model he would have been scoffed at and regarded as insane.

"The machine is a wonder," Arrowsmith repeated, enraptured.

It performed perfectly at times but once in a while little defects hampered its operation. Rough and splintery parts had to be sandpapered and resandpapered.

Again and again, sandpaper had to be used to smooth the surface. Frequent handling and operation of the sewing machine caused the wood to splinter and catch the cloth.

Hunt's machine was set up at the Globe Stove Company and men and women both flocked to see it in operation. The curious and the scoffers inspected it. Their comments and praise were very enthusiastic.

"No machine can sew, but *it* does!"

"It's the greatest invention since the printing press."

"It will do the work of ten people."

And also: "It will throw thousands of people out of work."

The sewing machine was a sensation. Its performance thrilled and amazed all who saw it in operation. But it had one obvious serious drawback: It was made of wood.

"The model is all right, but the machine should be built of something solid, perhaps iron."

"It will take a lot of time and money before the machine can be marketed."

Money. Money. Money. Hunt had none and was disinclined to raise the necessary amount. The experiences he had undergone to build the Globe Stove scared him. Only by stint and scrape had he managed to pay off his obligations. To attempt another similar venture where capital was required was beyond him.

"I can't raise the money," Hunt explained to Arrowsmith. "I went through fire and water to build the stove, and up to now it hasn't paid off."

"Give me a half interest in the sewing machine," Arrowsmith proposed, "and I'll handle its manufacture and sale."

Time had worked wonders for Arrowsmith. Five years before he was unable to pay city taxes and interest of $20.46 due on his farm at No. 68 Cherry Street, between Montgomery and Gouverneur streets. Consequently the city sold his property to S. Vanduzer on September 23, 1829, for back taxes. Arrowsmith had lived on this site for many years. It was the address he gave on his application when he had applied for membership in Fire Engine Company No. 33 in which he served from April 8, 1816, to September 7, 1818.

After Arrowsmith lost his property, his fortune changed. He obtained the rights from Walter Hunt for a machine to manufacture pill boxes and a machine to manufacture nails. He profited handsomely from the deal, which netted him several thousand dollars.

"Give me a half interest in the sewing machine," Arrowsmith repeated. "I'll manufacture it and sell it."

"But I need money now," Hunt countered. "I have to make up for the time I spent making it. It took so much time and money to make everything by hand that I couldn't do much else to make any money."

"I'll also return my interest in your brad machine and the pill box process," Arrowsmith bargained.

"Agreed. It's a deal." Hunt consented.

No legal papers were drawn up for the transaction. The swap was made without legal formality.

Having obtained the rights to the sewing machine, Arrowsmith endeavored to profit from it. He showed the machine to his friends and to prospective purchasers for their opinions. They reacted differently.

"The model certainly is a wonderful machine, but maybe it won't operate as well after you begin building them."

"You can't make them of wood. That's out of the question. They'd be too expensive and, if you made them of iron, it would cost a lot of money to make molds."

"The point is how much will it cost to make them? Their acceptance will depend upon the selling price."

Arrowsmith appreciated the wisdom of the arguments against the machine and summoned Walter Hunt's brother, Adoniram, to his office.

"Adoniram," he said, "I've just acquired the rights to Walter's sewing machine."

"Yes. I know."

"I want you to build me one just like it, but a duplicate made of iron."

"Why don't you get Walter to do it? He built the machine."

"I spoke to him about it, but he doesn't want to. I offered him two dollars a day, the same amount I'll pay you, but he says he can't work for that."

"Of course not. He's married and has a family to support. Two dollars a day doesn't pay his expenses."

"Well, you can do it. Two dollars a day is more than enough for a single man."

"I'd rather have Walter do it. I don't know anything about a sewing machine."

"Walter said that you can duplicate it. You won't have to do anything but duplicate it. Just copy it. That's all."

Adoniram, being a skilled mechanic, built a duplicate machine made of iron. It was scaled true to the plans and model and performed as well as the original model. In fact, it operated better than the original because no splinters of slivers or wood impeded the passage of the cloth.

The iron sewing machine attracted as much attention as the wooden model and people came from far away to see it operate. Much praise were bestowed upon its inventor and great predictions made for it.

"It's a great machine," one of the spectators said to Arrowsmith, "but do you think it will make money?"

"The machine will make all the money I want," Arrowsmith said emphatically.

"Have you got a patent on it?" he was asked.

"There's no hurry," Arrowsmith replied confidently. "We can get a patent on it any time we want. The life of a patent is only fourteen years. If I patent it now, it doesn't mean that I'll have fourteen years to manufacture it. The life of a patent is fourteen years from the date of issuance. Suppose that it takes me two or three years to raise the money and get into production, than all that time is lost and the only protection I'll get will be the remaining period. Maybe only eleven years."

"But you can get a seven year renewal," Adoniram suggested.

"That's right," Arrowsmith agreed. "But there is no certainty that a renewal will be granted. If they give me a patent now, the patent and the model will be on file in Washington. Everyone will be able to see it and get a copy of it. Hundreds and thousands of inventors will get ideas from it. It may stimulate them. Maybe someone will be able to get the necessary capital before me and even may start manufacturing first. Then where do I come in? Why should I give everyone the opportunity to beat us to it?"

"Maybe you're right," Adoniram said.

"I know I'm right," Arrowsmith insisted. "I'm going to raise the capital first and then if I get enough I'll start manufacturing the machines."

But Arrowsmith's optimistic plan did not become an actuality. A money crisis developed in January 1834 and capital became more difficult to snare. The system of United States coinage was changed on June 28, 1834, and uncertainty prevailed.

Not only financial conditions, but social conditions were unfavorable. During the election of April 8, 1834, for instance, gangs roamed the streets intimidating citizens. A protest meeting met at the Masonic hall "to protect the sacred rights of suffrage." Merchants were afraid. They closed their stores. Commerce was at a standstill. Panic reigned. Pitched battles in the streets were commonplace. The police were routed and the mayor and hundreds of citizens were wounded in confrontations.

Slowly the outlaw gangs were dispersed. Conditions had not entirely returned to normal before an epidemic of cholera, attributed by many to "invisible vapors" from the earth, broke out in the city. People saturated themselves and their homes with vinegar. Tar was burned on the streets to purify the atmosphere. Every man, woman and child who could do so fled to the country. A heat wave sent thermometers to 100°. Simultaneously the epidemic took on renewed vigor.

The seriousness of the epidemic was reported in William Dunlap's diary:

July 7, 1834. The cases of cholera increased on the 4th, 5th and 6th. On the 6th of July, 37 cases were reported and 19 deaths. The assumption was that the sufferers were imprudent or intemperate persons. [Tuesday, July 17.] Sunday the cholera stood 133 new cases, 84 deaths. Monday, 163 new cases, 94 deaths. Of course, More Panic. Wednesday, July 18th, cholera account stands 118 new cases, 58 deaths.

In July, 2,467 cholera deaths were recorded and in August, 2,206. The epidemic finally abated and the *Niles Register*, of September 6, 1834, reported

In New York last week [ending August 30] there were 448 deaths, of these 193 were by cholera, being an average of 27 a day. The reports for the last three or four days, we are gratified to add, show that the disease is evidently on the decline.

Business stagnated. Everything was at a standstill.

To add to the confusion, race violence flared. On July 7, 1834, a group of Negroes went to the Chatham Street Chapel to hear a sermon. The New York Sacred Music Society claimed the same meeting place at the same time. Both groups argued and insisted on their rights. Name calling degenerated into fighting. A pitched battle ensued. A riot followed and the entire military force of the city was called out. For four days, the troops remained on duty to prevent further bloodshed.

The progress in promoting the sewing machine was still further aggravated by the rising tide of organized labor, whose power was manifesting itself both locally and nationally. On August 20, 1834, the mechanics of Utica, New York, held a convention and protested against the competition of prison labor which was offered at 40 percent to 60 percent less than the ordinary wage scale. Three days later, August 23, 1834, workers in New York City organized and formed the General Trades Union of New York, culminating in a great convention on December 2, 1834, at the Chatham Street Chapel attended by delegates from Philadelphia, Boston, Brooklyn, Newark and Poughkeepsie.

The stonecutters rioted and construction work on New York University was interrupted in August and the 27th Regiment was called out to preserve order.

The time was not propitious for introducing a sewing machine. One calamity followed another. Arrowsmith's plans to market the sewing machine seemed further and further from fruition.

Arrowsmith approached Caroline Hunt with a plan.

"Caroline," he said, "as of this moment I haven't been able to manufacture the sewing machine, but in the meantime if you want, I'll let you use the model built by Adoniram. You can sew corsets with it and make more money than hand-sewing."

But, Caroline declined the offer. "All my friends told me," she said sadly, "that women won't buy corsets made by machine. They want hand-sewing. And they told me that a machine which sews will make conditions worse for the country, and that no one should use it."

"I can't understand it," said Arrowsmith to a group of friends at the Adelphi Hotel, an imposing six-story stuccoed edifice at the corner of Beaver and Broadway. "I don't know why it is so difficult to get capital to manufacture the sewing machine."

"There's nothing wrong with the sewing machine," one of the group explained. "The trouble is with the people. They are afraid of improvements which they think might replace labor."

And they continued to relate real or imaginary instances, one after another. Elsewhere Amos Whittemore's invention of a shoe pegging machine that successfully pegged 150 pairs of shoes a day was abandoned because the women binders refused to put bindings on machine-pegged shoes and because of sinister threats to burn down the factory.

John Waterman's improved spinner was also rejected because "its labor saving features threw men out of work...."

Thomas Davenport's invention of the electric motor was frowned upon and George Stevenson's railway locomotive was received with disfavor.

"Well, they objected to horsecars, too," said Arrowsmith, "and you can see how much better they are than the stagecoaches."

"The question is not how much benefit there is in a thing," one of the group volunteered. "That's not the consideration. Anything mechanical, no matter how progressive, which can do work better than a workman will be rejected by the people. Labor is asserting itself. Its power is really beginning to be felt."

Arrowsmith was not satisfied with the opinions of his luncheon friends and consulted David Everett Wheeler, the attorney.

"You'd better drop the whole thing," Wheeler advised. "Eighteen thirty-four isn't a good year to do anything original. If you had the machine a few years ago when labor wasn't so strong, you might have done something with it. In fact it may even be a good idea to wait a few years until conditions get better."

"People tell me I'd better patent it to protect it."

"I'll bet you couldn't get a patent on the sewing machine, even if you wanted it. I was reading the other night about Sir Edward Coke [1562–1634]. He was the first to be called Lord Chief Justice of England. He said 'a patent is not grantable for an invention that is not generally convenient'."

"But the sewing machine *is* convenient!" Arrowsmith argued. "It will do the work of a sempstress better and quicker."

"But that is what is meant by convenient," Wheeler explained. "A patent that may make workers idle is deemed an inconvenience."

"Well, he doesn't know what he is talking about," Arrowsmith said angrily. "The United States Patent Office recognizes inventions. It is not a social agency. I can get a patent any time I want to."

Wheeler reflected a few moments. "Possibly you are right. If you want to apply for a patent, I guess we can get one."

"But I don't want to go to any further expense now," Arrowsmith hedged. "Possibly things will get better and the situation will change."

Conditions did not improve and the bad luck swing of the pendulum remained fixed. On January 29, 1835, an attempt was made upon the life of President Andrew Jackson by Richard Lawrence. The misguided attack was unsuccessful, but it reflected dissatisfaction in government affairs.

The Five Points riot in New York City started June 22, 1835. The militant spirit was rampant and hostility and bloodshed again ruled the metropolis. Turmoil and fear were in the ascendancy.

In July 1835, the laborers of Paterson went on strike. Two thousand people employed in twenty mills demanded an eleven hour day, refusing to work thirteen and a half hours. After a strike of two weeks, a compromise was effected and the hours of labor were reduced to twelve hours a day for five days and for nine hours on Saturday.

"Conditions are terrible," Arrowsmith confided to Adoniram, "I don't know what's going to happen."

"Something usually does," Adoniram replied airily.

"I don't know about that," Arrowsmith said, "but I know that now is not the time to attempt to market sewing machines. This year is no better than last. A man is lucky these days if he manages to keep the little money he has without trying to make more."

"Did you ever get the sewing machine patent?" Adoniram inquired.

"No. And I'm not going to apply for one just yet, I don't want to spend the money, and furthermore, I can't see what good it will be right now."

"Someone else may get the idea," Adoniram protested. "Many have seen the machine, and someone may try and copy it."

"Don't be afraid," Arrowsmith answered reassuringly.

Had Arrowsmith known that Barthelemy Thimmonier of France, Thomas Saint of England and Josef Madresberger of Germany had been at work on sewing machines, he might have rushed the patent application but he was oblivious to the efforts and experiments of others in foreign countries and even in the United States.

In fact Arrowsmith had no knowledge that others in the United States were seeking a method to sew by machinery. Had he read the *Rochester Daily Democrat* of December 10, 1835, he might have changed his mind.

The second page of the newspaper contained an article with the heading "Sewing by Machinery."

It seems there is no end to human ingenuity—Whoever anticipated that sewing and stitching broadcloth—making garments, etc. would be done by machinery. And yet, such we believe will be the case in a very short time, and that too by an invention of a young Rochester mechanic.

We were yesterday permitted to witness the operation of a very simple machine, which has been constructed within a few months in this city, and which demonstrates the fact that tailoring will not always be done by fingers and thimbles. In its present imperfect state, it takes from three to four stitches a second, and the inventor thinks one may be constructed with improvements which have suggested themselves to his mind, which will more than double this number. But he finds difficulties in the way—similar to those which cramped the genius of Fulton before he found a patron in Livingston:—he has expended his little means in bringing it thus far forward, and must delay further progress for the present, unless he can find assistance, by one or more becoming interested with him, who can furnish funds for constructing a machine as near perfection as possible.

Should he fail in finding such assistance here, he designs visiting New York or Boston to effect that object:—but this would not tell well for the enterprise of Rochester, when the sum required is so trifling.

The operation of the machine may be witnessed anytime this afternoon by calling one door west of J. E. Lee's shop, west end of Market Bridge upstairs. We are authorized to invite those who feel interested in mechanical improvements to call.

Had Arrowsmith seen this notice he might have been inspired to action. Had he seen the article which appeared in the *Albany Evening Journal* of December 14, 1835, and the *New York Evening Post* of December 16, 1835, his fears might have been allayed.

SEWING BY MACHINERY: The Rochester Daily Democrat says a Mechanic of that city has invented a machine for making clothes which will "hereafter take the place of fingers and thimbles." If such be the case, we hope that machine will find its way to the bottom of Lake Ontario, and its inventor be handed over to the disposal of a Jury of Females, each of whom has a family of destitute children depending upon her "fingers and thimbles" for support.

But Arrowsmith evidently never read these reports. "Possibly we'll be able to do something with the sewing machine later on. Things will change in the city," was his comment to Adoniram. And the matter was temporarily dropped.

Chapter 10

Time passed quickly, Adoniram again visited his brother, as usual offering his advice. "It's about two years since you turned your sewing machine over to Arrowsmith," Adoniram told Walter Hunt. "Too bad that he didn't do anything with it."

"The fate of the sewing machine isn't as important as my fate," Hunt replied. "I spent a lot of time and money to make that machine, and much more on the stove. As of this moment I have practically no money at all."

"Why, I heard you received some money last week."

"You're right, I did get some for my forest saw, but I used most of it to pay my bills."

"Your forest saw?" Adoniram inquired. "You mean the one you displayed at the American Institute Fair last year? The one that got you that diploma of merit?"

"Yeah," said Hunt pensively, "but I can't eat the diploma. Now I've got to do something else to make money."

"What?"

"Remember those leases I spoke to you about? The ones I got about seven years ago from Professor Clement Clark Moore."

"Vaguely."

"Well, originally, each sale brought me about thirty dollars. Since then those leases have been sold and resold, each time at a much higher price, and now every single one of them is worth several thousand dollars."

"But they don't bring you in any money anymore."

"No, not those leases, but others will. I'm sure of it. I'm going back into the real estate business and have just rented an office at 20 Wall Street."

"Not 20 Wall Street!" said Adoniram, aghast.

"Why not? That's a good building."

"A good building!" Adoniram laughed. "Don't you read the newspapers? Haven't you seen the scandalous articles in the *New York Herald*? Don't you

know that James Gordon Bennett is denying landowners any land speculation?"

"I got a good office at a very low rental…"

"A low rental?" Adoniram interrupted. "Why, I wouldn't take space in that
building if they gave me offices for nothing."

"Why not?"

"Can't you read? Didn't you see yesterday's paper?"

He rummaged through a batch of newspapers on the table until he located
the *New York* [*Morning*] *Herald* of May 21, 1835, a newspaper published in the
basement of 26 Wall Street. He turned to the editorial on page two in the first
column entitled LAND SPECULATIONS:

Not long since a well educated polished intellectual person, a branch of one
of the earliest emigrants, came to this city to reside and spend his time agree-
ably. He was in possession of a fortune, snug, not large, probably $60,000 or
thereabouts. For some time he passed life in agreeable society, he mixed in
company, and moved about like a person at leisure. One morning a friend of
his, au fait, in the value of real estate, the fall or rise of every rock or heap of
rubbish on the Island, asked him; "Would you like to make a small speculation
in land?" "I don't know," replied the other. "I am quite ignorant of the value of
land." "Never mind," said the friend, "purchase this lot. It is in the market.
Keep it a few months and see how it will come out." The gentleman did so. It
was what is called Commodore Chancey's property. It is situated on the eastern
shore of the Island, near Yorkville, about fifteen acres, and cost $60,000. It was
the same which sold the other day for $120,000.

This is one of the numerous specimens of the large sums of money recently
made in speculations in landed property.

The spirit or mania is rising still higher. From the hours of twelve to two the
public sale room in the Exchange is crowded to suffocation with buyers and
sellers. Three or four auctioneers, one in each corner, are sometimes busy at the
same moment—lands, lakes, swamps, meadows, alluvial, are selling and
reselling as if the people were mad. Such is the eagerness of the purchasers, that
like ladies at furniture auctions, they almost bid on their own bids. The most
beautiful lithographs of the articles are handed about. Who can resist the fine
arts? The auctioneers and some of the dealers are making rapid fortunes. Of
one, it is said he will clear $60,000 this year out of his commissions, another
$40,000, another $25,000, etc.

It is now high tide, full moon, but take care for the turn. The cholera breaking out in the city—a certain vote in the Chamber of Deputies—or any other
unforeseen contingency would change the scene in a couple of days. This lati-
tude is variable. The real estate in Maiden Lane, Water Street, up town, down
town, has varied three or four times from two to eighty percent on its value
during the last twelve or fifteen years. Be cautious, be prudent.

Hunt read the entire article but was not deeply moved by it. He returned the newspaper to Adoniram.

"Don't you realize," said Adoniram excitedly, "that James Gordon Bennett and the *Herald* have their offices in 20 Wall Street? Taking an office in that building is worse than walking into the lion's den. You are either more daring or more foolish than Daniel!"

"But Daniel came out all right," Hunt answered.

"But you're not a Daniel," Adoniram protested. "If anyone ever gets stuck in a business proposition, it's you."

"I agree that there is real estate speculation in New York," said Hunt after deliberation, "but this is a growing city. It is not only a residential center, but a commercial metropolis as well. It is a city of change. A city of constant change."

Walter Hunt knew whereof he spoke. He had recently signed yet another new lease for his family to move to 56 Hammond Street.

"Well, I hope you're right," Adoniram said resignedly, "but if I had my way I'd prefer to live in a smaller city."

"You can live in a smaller city if you want to, but as far as I am concerned, I have faith in New York. And I am going to live in the city as long as I am able to."

"I hope you succeed, but I doubt it. I don't think you are cut out for it. You are too trusting to compete."

In the real estate field, promoters and land operators worked prospects into a frenzy. The universal desire for easy money induced thousands to use their life savings to dabble in real estate. Profits on paper were large and earnings were exaggerated. The land rush was on and the public was easy prey. Optimism flourished and even the ultracautious succumbed to the lure of quick and easy profits. Leases turned over so fast that often they were resold before they were recorded.

Easy credit and surplus money helped to encourage wild speculation. Desirable sites were gobbled up at increasing values. Frequent changes of ownership, supplemented by intensive building, brought about neighborhood transformations and even farmlands were converted into dwellings.

Outlying properties in New York City as far north as Yorkville and Harlem also profited from the speculation. What had previously been regarded as useless land was converted into farmland and then into residential properties shortly thereafter.

About six months later, Adoniram came to his older brother for advice but wound up instead the one giving it.

"Why don't you give up real estate, Walter? I've told you before," he pleaded, "you're really not equipped to deal with these sharpers."

Hunt looked at his brother in surprise. He said nothing but resented the interference.

"I know you made some money in real estate, but that doesn't happen every day. Sooner or later, you will lose whatever you made. Get out while the going is good. The boom in New York real estate is over. I'm your brother. I'm saying this to help you, not hurt you."

Hunt pulled a newspaper clipping from his wallet. "Does this look like the boom is over?" Hunt countered as he read him an article in a newspaper. "In eighteen twenty-five, the assessed value of city property was $101,160,046. Now in only ten years, it is $218,723,703. It more than doubled itself in ten years. Does this look like the boom is over?"

"But—"

"Let me continue reading. There are ten breweries, nine distilleries, fourteen ironworks, ten ropewalks, six sawmills, five tanneries, two grist mills, one paper mill, one woolen factory and the annual payroll is about one hundred thousand dollars a year."

"I know," Adoniram conceded.

"The value of the raw materials produced was $1,778,612 and the value of the manufactured articles was $2,788,347," Hunt continued.

"That may all be true," Adoniram agreed.

"Then why put water on the fire?" Hunt protested, "New York is getting bigger all the time. You don't have to believe me but you can't argue with statistics. Listen to this. In eighteen thirty-two, 1,810 ships brought 48,589 arrivals to the city; in eighteen thirty-three, 1,926 ships brought 41,752 people, and in eighteen thirty-four, 48,111 immigrants arrived on 1,933 ships. So far this year more than two thousand ships have already put into port [1835: 2,049 ships and 35,303 immigrants]. I know what they are talking about. I'm reading these figures, not guessing at them."

"But what good are these foreigners? They haven't any money. The first thing they do is look for charity," Adoniram argued.

"And jobs!" his brother said. "When they work they increase production. And with their income they need food and rooms."

"Real estate!" said Adoniram with scorn. "They all crowd together in one room."

"Here's a survey of the situation. Let me continue reading." Hunt revealed that more than 1,250 buildings had been put up in the city that year, 1835—380 of which were brick dwellings of two stories, 122 were three-story houses, and two of them were five stories high.

"You're right," Adoniram acknowledged, "the city is growing but so are its expenses. I read too. I read an article that said that now they've got about six hundred watchmen, three hundred for day and three hundred for night duty. The city will go bankrupt. They're paying eighty-seven cents a day while captains of the night receive an additional dollar a night! I tell you the expenses will bankrupt the city."

"You're wrong," Hunt countered.

"We never needed so many policemen before these foreigners came," Adoniram protested. "And the fire force has grown beyond belief. The city now has thirteen hundred firemen, fifty-six engines, and twelve thousand feet of hose. There are also six hook and ladder companies with a complement of a hundred and thirty-six men, and five hose carts with ten men each, and six hundred feet of hose to each cart. Also there is a company with twenty men to take charge of hydrants in time of fire—that's fifteen hundred firemen in all. I know. I was a volunteer for a while."

"But this protection is needed," Hunt argued, "in case of fire…" He stopped, and looked at his watch. "We're going to have steak for supper tonight, and I promised Polly I'd be home by six. If we don't hurry, it'll be burned to a crisp, and we'll need the fire department."

Adoniram and Walter arrived home just as Polly placed the steak on the table. She apologized: "You said serve the steak the minute of six, not one minute before or one minute after. I would have waited but I had a special reason for doing so tonight. Walter, Jr., is eating with us tonight and he has to go back to work."

Hunt's eldest son had been working a year at 141 Macdougal Street as a helper in a drug store.

A discussion of real estate and the development of the city took place at the conclusion of the meal. Adoniram and Walter continued airing their viewpoints.

Polly did not interrupt until the discussion seemed to be drawing to a close. "I should imagine," she said, almost apologetically, "that if there is such a great development of real estate, even in the country, that there should be a greater demand for your forest saw."

"That's right," Adoniram agreed. "I understand that they are clearing land everywhere. Labor is scarce. It's hard to get men to work and there should be a demand for the saw."

"That's funny," Hunt said philosophically. "I'm right on the scene and I never think of the saw anymore. But how can I reach those who could be potential customers?"

"Why don't you advertise?" Adoniram suggested.

"Why don't you put an ad in the *Evening Post*?" Polly suggested. "It can't cost much."

"That's a good idea," Hunt agreed. On December 5, 1835, this advertisement appeared in the *New York Evening Post*:

IMPORTANT TO OWNERS OF VALUABLE TIMBER LANDS: THE FOREST SAW, a simple and effective machine, invented by Walter Hunt, of this city, designed for felling forest trees, &c is now offered for sale, with Patent Rights for States,

Counties, &c by the inventor, at 20 Wall St., up stairs. This machine, which was exhibited in perfect operation at the recent Fair of the American Institute, where its important utility was established to the entire satisfaction of hundreds who witnessed its performance, is not only adapted to the felling [of] timber of every size and description, but also to the cross cutting [of] the same into logs, blocks, &c for the various purposes required. It is likewise adapted to all seasons and situations, as it can be carried and operated by one man even amidst the snows of our northern winters, in swamps or hill sides, its weight being only about 30 pounds. Another important advantage arising from the introduction of the Forest Saw is that thousands of able-bodied foreigners and others, who remain in our cities unemployed, or at low wages, and who are unskilled in the use of the axe, can, with this machine, in the forests of our interior, compete with the most experienced axemen.

The facility of operation, and the saving of timber in the use of the Forest Saw over the axe, is another important item in its favor; of this fact, the public can judge for themselves by an examination of the machine in operation, at the place above mentioned.

An establishment for the manufacture of the Forest Saw on an extensive scale, is now in operation at Westport, Conn. which will enable the Proprietor not only to supply orders from purchasers of territory in the United States, but also for the South American trade, where its importance in the mahogany and dyewood districts cannot fail to be appreciated.

The advertisement brought a few inquiries. One prospect was sincerely interested in acquiring Hunt's invention.

"Have you got a patent on it?" he inquired.

"No, I haven't applied for one."

"Do so, and I'll buy it from you now. Here is some money for your expenses just to show my good faith."

Hunt proudly handed a roll of bills to Polly. She asked, "Did you put over another deal?"

"Yes."

"Which property did you sell?"

"I sold all my rights to the forest saw."

Polly's attitude changed from joy to anger. "How do you expect to make money when you sell your ideas for a song? You always made a few dollars each time they sold a saw in Westport. Now you've given away all your interest and that's the end."

Hunt listened calmly, but made no retort. That evening he busied himself with preparing the patent papers.

On January 6, 1836, before a month had elapsed, the Patent Office awarded him a patent, recognizing the originality and utility of the invention. The *Mechanics Magazine* (volume 6, page 266), described the invention as follows.

Walter Hunt—Patent Forest Saw—We cannot better describe this article than in the inventor's own words "A simple effective Machine designed for felling trees and cross-cutting their trunks for lumber and also, for the purpose of clearing wild lands." We consider this an article of peculiar value for the following reasons: First, are confidant trees may be felled with it as fast, and we think faster than with the axe. Second. It may easily be carried by one man—its weight being only 30 lbs. Third. It will cut nearer the ground than can conveniently be cut with the axe, and of course leave the stumps lower. Fourth. By felling trees with the axe, the trunks are often split near the ground, and valuable timber spoiled, which will not be the case in sawing. Fifth. Its cheapness is within the reach of every man engaged in lumber.

On page 269 of the same magazine, another article referred to the Hunt Forest Saw:

This article stood in the Fair by the side of, and of course in competition with that of Hunt, and we noticed the preference alternately given to each, by the multitude who examined them. But these opinions weighed nothing with us. We assume the right to judge for ourselves. There were some strong points respectively in favor of each. Cheapness and portableness were in favor of Mr. Hunt's machine.

The *Journal of the American Institute* for October 1836 (volume 2) listed Hunt's invention of the saw under the column devoted to recent patent awards, but made no comment about it.

An opinion contrary to that expressed in the *Mechanics Magazine* was published in the *Journal of the Franklin Institute*, August 1836, page 112. The report is as follows.

FOR A FOREST OR TREE SAW. Walter Hunt. City of New York, Jan. 6.

Considerable ingenuity has been developed in the arrangement of the apparatus described and figured by the patentee, who has made his invention fully known. The apparatus consists of a grabble by which the whole is to be attached to the tree to be felled, by means of a screw, spike, etc; the lever, to which one end of the saw is to be attached, and which, by being moved backward and forward horizontally, operates on the saw; the saw and a spiral spring by which the latter is to be kept up to its cutting bearing. The particular construction of these parts, we shall not attempt to describe.

The patentee claims "the style of construction, combination, and arrangement of the forest tree saw, as above specified, etc." We shall not, as we have said, attempt a particular description of the proposed arrangement of the parts of the machine, but predict that it will share the fate of other saw machines for felling trees, and be found by far less efficient than the axe of the woodsman. We apprehend that the patentee has not had much experience in clearing land, or he would have known that his wedges and other contrivances would not enable him to determine the direction in which trees should fall, and that the experienced axesman is sometimes at a fault in this particular, an event which would be fatal to the whole apparatus before us.

When Hunt showed this particular review to Polly, he commented, "Can't always be right and please everyone."

Chapter 11

About two weeks before Christmas, Adoniram visited Arrowsmith and they engaged in a serious business discussion.

"Of course, Adoniram, I could be wrong," Arrowsmith replied, "but I think people will appreciate sewing by machine. Sooner or later, they will."

When Arrowsmith made that prophecy, he had no idea that two days later, on December 17, 1835, fate would play a hand.

The fire warden stationed in the cupola of the City Hall shouted through his speaking trumpet, "Hurry! Hurry! On! Haste! Turn south near Wall Street." Then he fastened a lantern to the end of a long pole and pointed it towards the south. Firemen ran towards the fire.

A hand-pumped fire-engine rattled towards the fire. It was supposed to be manned by a crew of twenty-six, but since many of the volunteer firemen had joined solely to obtain exemption from jury duty and military service, and not because they liked their job, full complements were rare. Mongrels, street urchins, idlers and thrill seekers trailed after the engine, adding confusion to the congested streets.

Within minutes, what had been a small fire spread into a full-sized blaze. By the time the firemen had located the source, it had become a conflagration. Frozen fire hydrants prevented the inadequate water supply from passing through the debris-filled pipes. Quickly smoke blanketed the city. The wind, howling, sweeping and blustering, carried blazing embers across the East River and set afire the roof of a house in Brooklyn. The lower tip of Manhattan soon glowed like a torch. Pandemonium was everywhere.

Six hundred and seventy-four buildings were reduced to ashes. Business was thoroughly demoralized. Merchants found themselves burned out and bankrupt. Affluent merchants became instant paupers. Very little of the damage was covered by insurance. Insurers could not collect their losses. Ten of the twenty-six insurance companies became insolvent, while the others found they could not pay the damage losses as their assets were not liquid.

Financial institutions did not know how or where to turn. Even the Stock Exchange suspended operations. Temporary headquarters were set up a week later in Howard's Hotel at 8 Broad Street.

Merchants, store owners, and those with money who had always paid their bills promptly could not meet their daily obligations. Others who could pay took advantage of the situation and demanded heavy premiums for cash.

Those whose property had been dynamited by the city to prevent the spread of the flames to the rest of the city brought suit against the municipality for damages. To offset these claims, an emergency appropriation of six hundred thousand dollars was made. To relieve those who had suffered losses, the city government authorized a stock issue of four million dollars by advancing upon the transfer of bonds and mortgages.

The December 17-18, 1835, *New York Courier and Examiner* reported:

> The fire burned four days and nights, destroying everything in its devastating march. People fled from the stricken area. Martial law was declared. The Navy and the Marines dynamited buildings to prevent the fire from spreading. Looters and thieves preyed upon the unfortunates and the militia patrolled the streets with orders to shoot to kill.

When the last smoldering embers had become charcoal or graying ashes, New York planned its readjustment and rehabilitation. Capital and labor cooperated to salvage what had been damaged. Banks recalled outstanding loans and restricted new loans to reconstruction enterprises. Interest rates soared. Bonuses and premiums were offered for money. Office workers left sedentary positions and took jobs as bricklayers, masons, carpenters and mechanics because wages were higher.

Readjustment was the main subject under consideration. Lumber, cement, bricks, shovels, brooms, necessities, foodstuffs, beds, blankets, rugs, and kitchen utensils were in terrific demand. Novelties, luxuries, and nonessentials languished on the shelves.

New projects were nil. No one anywhere had any interest in promoting a sewing machine or anything else. And if they did have the vision, the shortage of capital destroyed any hope.

No one anywhere had any interest in anything other than a quick return to normality. All projects were stifled in favor of immediate readjustment.

Arrowsmith confided to Hunt's brother the difficulty and impossibility of obtaining a loan to manufacture or market the sewing machine.

"I guess that means that you've given up your plans for the sewing machine," Adoniram said.

"Not at all."

"I suppose it means then that our association is ended."

"Of course not, Adoniram, you're too good a mechanic to lose. I'll need you and I'm taking you with me to Baltimore."

"Me? To Baltimore?"

"I've got a job to do there."

"And will we take the sewing machine with us?"

"Of course. Make your plans to leave because we are going in a fortnight."

In Baltimore, George A. Arrowsmith and Adoniram Hunt boarded at the home of Joel Johnson, owner of the Canton Iron Works.

When Adoniram showed Johnson the sewing machine model, Johnson asked, "Got a patent on it?"

"No. Arrowsmith's got some sort of a notion that you don't need a patent until you're in production as all the time in production shortens the selling time of the patent."

"Yeah," Johnson nodded understandingly. "He's not too far wrong. Patents are not much good anyhow and are really only of value if the courts sustain them. And who has the time to win a lawsuit?"

Arrowsmith and Adoniram remained in Baltimore a year to fulfill the contract and then returned to New York City. Any effort they made to promote the sewing machine was unproductive.

Back in New York City, Adoniram remembered he had forgotten to bring back all his possessions and on May 17, 1836, he wrote a letter to Joel Johnson,

Dear Sir;

Mr. Arrowsmith informs me that a friend of his is going to Baltimore tomorrow and is to return shortly, and as I have some few articles at your house and at the mill, I should be much obliged to you if you will be so good as to send them on with Mr. Arrowsmith's things—there is some articles of clothing at your house and at the mill—there is my little engine which sits behind the first saw, and in the desk is a small vise which I should like you to send—and now I suppose you would like to know what I have been doing this winter that has kept me so still, well, I will tell you. I have been to work at my sewing machine and some other little machinery. I made that little sewing machine that I had at your house work to a charm but the wood work was not strong enough and therefore I have commenced building one all iron which I think will be a very pretty machine—I suppose you thought that I had forgotten that I owe you a little debt but I have not, and I should have paid it long before this but money has been pretty scarce here this winter, but times are getting better now and I am in hopes that I shall be able to pay you in a short time. I have got no time to write more. Please to excuse me for the present and I will again write shortly. Please to remember me to Mrs. Johnson, Angeline, Eleazer, Mr. & Mrs. Abbott and all inquiring friends.

Adoniram T. Hunt

to Joel Johnson,
Baltimore, Md.

The passage of time helped to ease the hectic situation. In the United States in general business improved considerably. Speculation increased and commerce flourished. Money became more plentiful and credit became free and easy. Production spurted, out-producing consumption.

The Congress, however, refused to extend the charter of the Bank of the United States, and forced its withdrawal from business. Public deposits were placed in "pet banks," thus enabling them freely to dispense funds. Surplus revenues accumulated and the government refunded them to the states, which tended to make money still freer.

The so-called prosperity proved disastrous, however. The structural value of legitimate credit was completely undermined and political winds swayed the situation. Too rapid development of new banks on an unsound structure, lack of a stable currency, and mismanagement of speculative banks inevitably led to a catastrophe.

The presidential election of 1836 was not held on the same day in all the states. On November 4, Pennsylvania and Ohio voted, and not until November 23 did Rhode Island vote. No one knew who was elected. Politicians and the public were kept in suspense. It was not until the first week in December that the Democrats were able to rejoice in the certainty of their victory and they looked forward to the inauguration of Martin Van Buren.

Public opinion was divided. In New York City an undercurrent of dissatisfaction prevailed. In January 1837, rioters stormed the warehouse of Eli Hart & Company and destroyed five hundred barrels of flour and a thousand bushels of wheat. People could not or would not pay their bills. On April 8, only one month after the inauguration on March 4, there had been ninety-eight failures in the city with liabilities of over sixty million dollars. By April 15, there were a hundred and sixty-eight failures. Gloom prevailed. The future looked bleak.

On May 10, 1837, every bank in New York City suspended payments. The crisis of 1837, also known as the Panic of 1837, was on. The value of real estate in New York City depreciated forty million dollars. Thirty-three thousand business houses failed, entailing financial losses of $440,000,000 and paralyzing the country. Many who had believed themselves rich found their status to be no better than a pauper's. More than 30 percent of the gainfully employed were thrown out of work. Jobs were at a premium. The almshouses were filled. Hundreds, unable to obtain admittance or too proud to beg for charity, died of cold and starvation.

Suspension of specie payment by the banks was followed by the disappearance of coins as a circulating medium. Specie was hoarded. Merchants gave change in shin plasters and coupons redeemable only in merchandise.

Life droned on precariously and slowly. The city, like others in the United States, strove to recover. The American Institute held its tenth annual fair on

October 16, 1837, at Niblo's Garden. It drew crowds of the general public but speculators and capitalists were not interested in their new exhibits. They were too occupied with salvaging whatever they could from their investments.

Arrowsmith's doubts about his ability to market Walter Hunt's sewing machine were fully substantiated by both local and national conditions. The panic had closed every door on it as well as on every other new or speculative endeavor.

Even depressions do not prosper, and times eventually change. The cycle of misfortune had run its course and new conditions presented a new vista. Just as the development of the Western Territory helped the United States to ease out of the panic of 1789, so did the growth of the Midwest alleviate the Panic of 1837. Improved transportation facilities brought about a migration of settlers westward and a more hopeful spirit prevailed.

Gradually the trend of population moved westward. New communities sprang into existence like mushrooms. The territories developed into prosperous agricultural centers. Worthless land again commanded value and real estate made a valiant effort to revitalize itself. Speculation and boom times returned. Increased values enticed the money interests and the conservatives adopted a more liberal attitude. The nation's fortunes began to turn.

"The future of America lies in the West," Adoniram declared to Arrowsmith, "and I'm going west to build a steam engine for the Hydraulic Flour Mills at Chillicothe or maybe the one at Warren, Ohio."

Arrowsmith found construction work paid handsomely. He was too busy making easy money to think of promoting the unproductive sewing machine. He relied on his earlier sentiments, that the sewing machine would keep. It could be introduced later.

Chapter 12

Like most of New York, Walter Hunt felt the repercussions from the fire of 1835 and then the Panic of 1837. No one was interested in buying property. Forced to give up real estate, which was in a horrible slump, he sought employment as a mechanic. The market for labor was severely depressed and jobs were scarce. Few paid workers more than a living wage. His capital dwindling rapidly, Hunt was forced to economize. He moved to 56 Hammond Street, and lived there in 1836 and 1837.

"Life is like a rocker," said Hunt. "One minute you're up, and the next you're down."

"Depressions don't last," Polly said. "Better times are coming and prosperity will return."

"If you live long enough. I hope you're right. It's no fun now."

Polly changed the subject. "Enough of worry. Have you forgotten, we were going for a walk this afternoon."

"All right, I'll go."

"But, you're not going the way you are! Why don't you wear your good clothes? You'll feel better and, besides, have you no respect for the Sabbath?"

"Is today Sunday? It doesn't seem any different to me than any other day of the week."

"You heathen," Polly teased. "You know it's Sunday. You haven't changed your arguments about getting dressed one iota in the last twenty years."

Reluctantly Walter put on his Sunday suit and announced that he was ready.

"You ready?" Polly laughed. "Where do you think you are going? Look at your pantaloons. They are about a mile about your boots. Why don't you tie the strap under them?"

"The strap is broken."

"Put your foot up on the chair and I'll sew it."

"Do you know why the straps always break?" Walter asked.

UNITED STATES PATENT OFFICE.

WALTER HUNT, OF NEW YORK, N. Y.

MODE OF MAKING SPIRAL SPRINGS FOR BELTS, PANTALOONS, VESTS, &c.

Specification of Letters Patent No. 649, dated March 21, 1838.

To all whom it may concern:

Be it known that I, WALTER HUNT, of the city, county, and State of New York, have invented a new and useful mode of con-
5 structing or forming flat, coiled, or spiral wire springs, adapted to various purposes of dress, such as pantaloon-straps, vest-backs, suspenders, belts, &c., and that the following is a faithful description thereof.
10 In forming springs for the above purposes I use about No. 20 steel wire (other metals may be used) which by hand in a turning lathe or otherwise I wind spirally around a flat steel arbor or blade of suitable dimen-
15 sions, (a piece of thin, inch hoop iron may answer the purpose) upon this the wire is wound, the turns about ¼ inch apart, see Figure No. 1 in the annexed drawing—arbor A, spring B. Thus far there is no novelty
20 in the spring or mode of forming it; I next proceed to withdraw the arbor or mandrel, and with pliers or otherwise, I form hooks or tongues of and upon the projecting ends of the wire of which the spring is composed.
25 See Fig. 2, C C. In this last forming of the tongues upon the opposite ends of the spring, consists the novelty and utility of

my invention in as much as it affords the most simple and advantageous means of attaching the spring to straps, &c., in such 30 manner that it may act by extension and perform the twofold office of spring and buckle as exhibited in Figs. 3 and 4 which represent an inner and outside view of a strap for the bottom of pantaloons com- 35 posed of one long and two short straps see D and E E. The ends of which pass through two springs Fig. 2, and receive the tongues or hooks C C in graduating holes punched in the ends of the long center strap 40 D at F F F F. The same mode of attaching is applicable to belts, suspenders, &c.

What I claim and desire to secure by Letters Patent is—

The forming of hooks or tongues upon the 45 ends of flat spiral spring designed to act by extension and to be attached in the manner and for all, and especially the purposes herein above set forth.

New York Jany 20th 1838

            WALTER HUNT.

Witnesses:
HENRY PRAY,
D. E. WHEELER.

"Because you put your pantaloons on like a kicking mule, I suppose."

"No. The reason is because there is no give or stretch to the strap. I just got an idea. You know at the Eighth American Institute Fair, the time I won an award, well, there was another exhibit there by a Charles Goodyear of New Haven."*

"Well?"

"It was for some kind of a new discovery in India rubber."

"Now tell me, what's that got to do with your pantaloons?"

"Rubber is elastic and it has spring." Walter paused. "Spring! That's it! That's what pantaloons need. Springs."

"Let's go out," Polly remonstrated, "before it gets winter."

"For a new discovery in India rubber rendering it applicable to a variety of new important purposes—a silver medal," page 87 Annual Journal of the American Institute *[1837?]*.

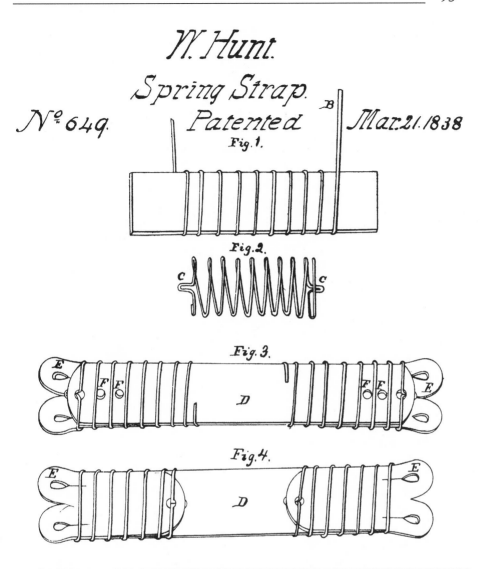

W. Hunt.
Spring Strap.
N⁰ 649.   Patented   Mar. 21. 1838
Fig. 1.

Fig. 2.

Fig. 3.

Fig. 4.

But Walter was thinking.

"Are you ready?" she asked.

Walter left the room and a few minutes later returned with a coil of wire and a small flat bar and a hammer.

"Now what are you going to do? I thought we were going out for a walk."

"Just watch." He wound the thin wire tightly around the bar, tapped the wire slightly with the hammer, then slid the wire off. He pulled the ends of the wire and stretched it. It expanded. Hunt beamed with satisfaction as he glanced at the flat coil contracting.

"It'll work," he announced excitedly. "Get a needle and thread."

Polly watched Walter tear off the cloth strap she had just sewed on the pantaloon. Before she had a chance to protest, Walter said, "Now sew this spring on in place of the strap."

Skeptical, but silent, Polly complied.

"You see," Walter beamed. "There's the solution. Now there is give and stretch to the pantaloons. Instead of a fixed strap of cloth, we now have a spring which will give and stretch, and it will eliminate the tension at the knees. Now, let's go for our walk."

In the park, they met David Everett Wheeler, who introduced them to Lewis B. Morrison. After the formalities of introduction were over, Hunt demonstrated the operation of his flat coiled spring idea.

"It's a fine idea," Wheeler said enthusiastically. "And, it's so simple too. It's a wonder no one thought of it a hundred years ago."

"A hundred years ago," Polly said, "men didn't wear pantaloons."

"Anyhow," Wheeler interrupted. "I think the strap is a good idea."

"But it's not a commercial idea." Morrison argued. "Anyone can copy the idea. You can't protect it. It's nothing but an ordinary spring."

"I don't know," Wheeler answered. "But people won't take the trouble to make them and furthermore they haven't the equipment or know how. Now, if the springs were made in commercial quantities, they could be produced at such a low price that it wouldn't pay anyone to go to the trouble of making them. They can be made so cheaply that the tailors and drapers will put them on all new garments they produce."

"You could use the spring for belts, suspenders and other purposes," Hunt added.

"I'll tell you what I'll do, Mr. Hunt," Morrison countered. "If you can protect the idea with a patent, I'll buy the idea from you and I'll have one of my factories manufacture the spring."

"It's a deal," Hunt said. "Even though no price has been agreed upon."

"It's no contract," Polly reminded them; "today is Sunday."

Walter nodded his head. Production problems were already absorbing his attention. When he and Polly returned home, he went to his desk and drew up the patent application.

On January 20, 1838, he entered Wheeler's office at 128 Nassau Street and said, "Here's the patent application on the spring. As commissioner of deeds and as a friend, will you please witness my affidavit?"

Henry Pray, a butcher, who happened to be in the office at the time on another matter, acted as the second witness.

Nothing was heard about the patent application until March 21, 1838, when the United States Patent Office granted U.S. Patent No. 649 on a "mode for making spiral springs for belts, pantaloons, vests, etc."

This was not the 649th patent issued by the United States but the 649th issued since the Patent Office's consecutive numbering system went into effect on July 13, 1836. Prior to the commencement of the numbering system, the Patent Office had issued 9,957 patents, designated solely by date and classification.

Chapter 13

Hunt was twisting and untwisting a piece of copper wire when Levi Kidder entered his shop. Kidder, who had recently become Collector of City Revenue, was accompanied by a distinguished gentleman in an elegantly tailored frock coat.

"Mr. Hunt," Kidder said austerely, "I want you to meet a friend of mine, Mr. Jacob Townsend."

"You're both in the wrong place if you think you can collect any money from me," Hunt joked.

"Mr. Townsend doesn't need money, and I guess the city can run a few days longer without yours," said Kidder. "I told Townsend about your many inventions. What are you working on now?"

"Grab hold of these two metal cylinders," Hunt directed, "and I'll show you."

"As you say."

"Hold them tight," Hunt commanded. He turned a crank protruding through the front end of a small oak box.

"I'm doing it."

"Do you feel anything?" Hunt asked.

"No, nothing except that the tubes feel cold."

Hunt tightened the copper wires attached to the end of the tubes, adjusted a small endless belt in the box, and then turned the crank. He kept turning faster and faster until the box emitted a low hum.

"Stop! Stop!" yelled Townsend, still gripping the tubes.

Hunt stopped turning the crank. Townsend let the metal cylinders drop and gave out a long breath.

"Why, it felt like needles and pins sticking into me. What is it, a torture machine?"

"I'm not sure yet," Hunt laughed, "but this magnetic box which I call a galvanic current machine may be a good cure for certain illnesses."

"Well, if it doesn't kill, it might cure," Townsend joked.

"When I am completely satisfied with it, I'll show it to a few doctors and get their opinion on it," Hunt continued.

"If you can put that contraption aside long enough, Mr. Hunt," said Kidder gravely, "Mr. Townsend has a proposition for you which might bring you in some money."

"I'd like to iron out a few of the rough spots," Hunt answered, "but if you have anything that will bring in money, tell me quickly, because I certainly can use ready cash now."

"It won't bring in money right now," Townsend countered, "but eventually it will. There should be quite a demand for it."

"What is the proposition?" Hunt asked.

"I want you to help me build an iceboat," Townsend confided. "It's a difficult problem. If you work with me, we will be partners."

"An iceboat?" Hunt inquired. "What in heaven's name is an iceboat?"

"To keep the water open," Kidder said.

"What water and what for?"

Jacob Townsend continued. "As you know, Mr. Hunt, ice jams prevent the boats from operating. When the boats stop, river traffic is paralyzed. This means that hundreds of seamen are thrown out of work. Thousands of dollars are tied up in idle boats and millions of dollars of business are at a standstill.

"If we can build some sort of attachment to fasten on the bow of a boat to break up the ice so that other boats can follow in the wake, we can sell them on every ice-bound river or lake or we can even build a boat especially for crushing ice jams."

"The idea seems fine," Hunt answered, "but aren't there any boats now that keep the rivers open?"

"Well, they are using heavily constructed boats to plow through the ice, but their hulls get damaged by the ice and generally they get so hemmed in that they can't move. Then the ice crushes their sides. Now, my idea is this: If we can attach something like a spar or a saw, then the boats can cut their way through the ice."

Hunt was toying with his knife-sharpener while Townsend was talking. His fingers idly turned the concentric wheels, giving the impression he wasn't listening and was bored.

"Are you listening to me?" asked Townsend, who felt slighted.

Hunt did not answer. If he heard the question he paid no attention. He continued spinning the discs on the knife sharpener.

"Is something the matter, Mr. Hunt?" Kidder asked.

Hunt looked up in surprise. "Why, no."

"But you haven't been paying any attention to what Mr. Townsend has been saying. You've just been sitting there playing with that thing."

"I'm sorry," Hunt apologized. "Go on with what you were saying."

"There is a real big market for a device of this kind," Townsend continued. "Here is a newspaper article which says that the citizens of Philadelphia have gone so far as to petition for an appropriation to keep their river open: 'The closing of the River Delaware by ice is universally considered as a calamity; it locks up not only the great avenue of our commerce, but the capital invested in our shipping feels it to an extent that is almost incalculable'."

Hunt continued looking at the knife sharpener. He was intently absorbed in thought.

"Now, take New York," Townsend continued. "There are—"

"That's it!" Hunt interrupted.

"What?" Kidder asked in surprise.

"It's simple!"

"I don't understand you, Mr. Hunt," Townsend exclaimed. "You seemed so polite when I came in and now you don't seem to be paying the slightest attention to anything I've been saying."

Both Kidder and Townsend were staring in mild annoyance at Hunt. They found it difficult to understand his attitude.

Hunt appreciated their situation and laughed. Kidder and Townsend were nonplussed.

"It's simple!" Hunt exclaimed. "Do you see this knife-sharpener? See these turning discs? That's all there is to it. If we made a giant-size wheel, like a grindstone, but out of iron, of course, and put knives or blades on it, then it could be used to chop up the ice. The principle is sound, but whether it will actually work is something else."

"That's even better than what I had in mind!" Townsend shouted, jumping up out of his chair. "Something like that might work. What do you say we work together on it, Mr. Hunt?"

"I think this problem will be fun," Hunt replied. "Let's start at once."

Townsend and Hunt continued discussing it and soon agreed on the general plan of construction. They drew rough sketches and more sketches. Night after night, they worked together, an oil lamp glaring in addition to the gas light. They felt very optimistic.

When Polly returned home late one night, she asked Walter, "Who is that Mr. Townsend, and why do you have to work with him so late every night?"

"We're working on something."

"Well, I hope it will bring you some money. Your work usually brings a fortune only to others."

"We are partners on an idea, and if we can do what we have in mind, it will make us both independently rich."

"I hope so," Polly said, but inwardly doubt outshadowed hope.

Walter hardly noticed her almost forlorn intonation but maintained his enthusiasm. Days passed, then weeks and months slipped by.

"Everything looks fine on paper," Townsend gleefully told Hunt one day. "Everything checks perfectly. We'll start and build a lifesize model, then we can test the machine in actual operation. But, if we start building a machine, others might see it and copy it."

Townsend saw their idea being appropriated by others, but Hunt did not seem worried.

"Isn't there any way we can protect the idea while we are working on it?" Townsend asked.

"Well, we could get a caveat," Hunt answered.

"Well then, get one, whatever it is."

Townsend and Hunt prepared a caveat, an intention to invent, which was witnessed June 24, 1837, by Abraham Corl and Levi Kidder. The document was immediately mailed to the United States Patent Office with the required twenty dollar application fee. Townsend paid the fee and the receipt was mailed to him at 257 Rivington Street, New York City.

Secure in the knowledge that they had some protection, the two partners continued their labors. The plan did not materialize as fast as expected. The machine failed to work smoothly. It was necessary continually to replace parts. The strength of the materials used and their weights played an important part.

Blades cracked and chipped. They had to be made shorter and heavier and the spacing between them had to be altered for maximum results. The speed of the revolving drum varied with the diameter. Other obstacles were confronted. Their persistence was, however, achieving results.

Finally a contrivance was made which answered the purpose. It was a portable attachment that could be affixed to the bow of a ship. It consisted of a huge cylinder extended and supported in front of the ship's bow by means of stirrups, or yokes.

Attached to the periphery and ends of the cylinder were a series of irregularly placed iron teeth about one foot in height and depth at the base and about two inches in thickness. As the cylinder revolved, the extension blades cut into the ice. The action was similar to that of a circular saw, but instead of cutting evenly and regularly like a saw, the blades were placed irregularly so that the ice was broken into odd-shaped pieces.

The cylinder was revolved by power obtained from the boat's steam engine. To insure a greater effect, as many cylinders could be placed on the iceboat as it had power to turn. Similar cylinders could be attached to different parts of the boat—the sides and the stern, if desired—the amount of ice thereby chopped being regulated by the number of cylinders in use.

"I certainly had no idea what a big job this would be when we started," Townsend confided. "Theory and practicality are far apart."

"That's the trouble with new ideas. They're fun to work out but it is impossible to foretell with much degree of accuracy what will happen," Hunt replied.

UNITED STATES PATENT OFFICE.

W. HUNT AND J. TOWNSEND, OF NEW YORK, N. Y.

ICE BOAT FOR BREAKING ICE AND FACILITATING NAVIGATION IN THE WINTER SEASON.

Specification of Letters Patent No. 958, dated October 3, 1838.

To all whom it may concern:

Be it known that we, WALTER HUNT and JACOB TOWNSEND, both of the city, county, and State of New York, have invented a
5 new and Improved plan of machinery to be applied to boats and vessels and designed for breaking ice and facilitating the navigation of rivers, lakes, bays, &c., in the winter season; and we do hereby declare, that the
10 following is a full and exact description.

The first and principal machine in the above plan is a cylinder (see letter A Figure 2 in the annexed drawing), with its periphery and ends, armed with strong iron hooked
15 and wedged shaped teeth, about one foot in height and depth upon the base, and some two inches in thickness (see letters D, D, D, D, Fig. 2). The cylinder, which may be made of wood in the usual manner, and the
20 teeth fastened on the periphery by means of strong hoops binding over flanges cast upon the base of the same (see letters F, F, F, F,) or it may be formed entirely of iron, cast in rings or zones, and united in a similar man-
25 ner to iron water pipes or otherwise, is to be suspended horizontally in front, and supported upon end gudgeons, revolving in strong iron arms affixed to the sides of the same at their back end, by means of heavy
30 iron bolts passing through brackets into the boat's side timbers in the strongest manner. These arms are further supported at the forward ends near the bearings of the cylinder by means of stirrups or yokes, that fall down
35 astride the ends of a strong beam situated across the bows of the boat (see G Fig. 1). The arms H H passing through the slots in said yokes are raised and depressed by means of upright screws or otherwise working
40 through the tops of said yokes, with their feet resting in steps on the ends of the beam G.

Though not essential to our plan, we have in our model adopted the twin boat, with a
45 paddle wheel in the center, the outside rim of which is cogged at I Fig. 1, into which gears pinion P on the shaft of the fly wheel, by which means the power is communicated to the paddle wheel I, and from thence to
50 the cylinder A, by a chain band or bands passing over spurs upon the same at K, or otherwise the power may be communicated from the engine as usual by means of cranks upon the shaft of the paddle wheel.

To prevent the accumulation of ice upon 55 the paddle wheel and cylinder, they can be housed upon their upper sections into which the exhaust steam and smoke may be discharged. The periphery of the cylinder in its rotation may travel somewhat faster 60 than the paddle wheel in order that the boat may not be forced upon the ice any faster than its path may be cleared.

If necessary, stern and side cylinders may be added, and the whole or part moved by 65 gearing bands or otherwise.

The teeth D, D, D, D, should range spirally around the cylinder in the manner of a right and left hand screw from the center (see Letter A) in order that they may 70 take alternate effect upon the ice, their sharp ends striking first in the manner of an adze upon the edge of the broken ice, chipping it off in fragments without allowing the body of the cylinder to come in contact with the 75 solid ice; by this arrangement it will be seen that the principal force of the engine may be exerted upon each tooth singly at the moment of contact, and the resistance of the ice will in a measure aid in propelling the 80 boat in case the cylinder is not immersed to its center, in which case it may not be necessary to put extra heads upon the journals of the cylinder on the outside of the arms as represented in figure. 85

In this invention we confine our claims to the use and application of revolving cylinders with teeth or spurs upon their outer surfaces to be attached to boats and vessels; said cylinder being suspended upon arms, 90 and the whole constructed substantially in the manner and for the purposes as hereinabove set forth.

New York September 18th 1838.

WALTER HUNT.
JACOB TOWNSEND.

Witnesses:
S. O. BENNETT,
WM. L. MORRIS.

Hunt & Townsend.

Ice Boat.

Nº 958.

Patented Oct. 3, 1838.

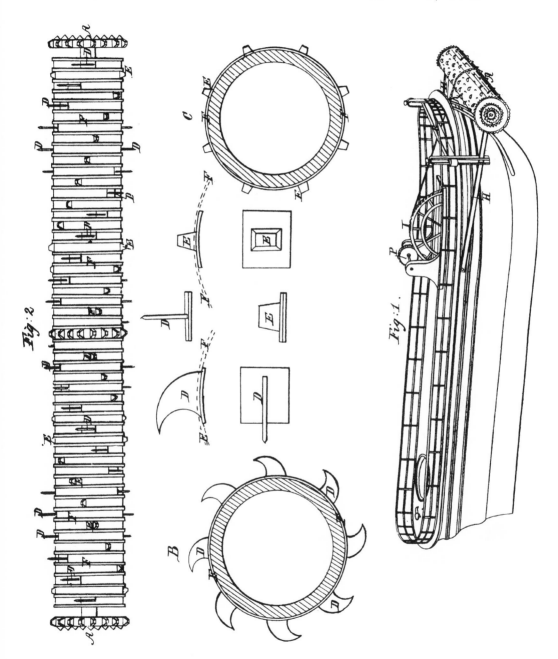

Fig: 2

Fig: 1.

"Well, I'll say this," Townsend continued. "I've certainly spent more time and money on it than I anticipated."

"And so have I," Hunt replied. "I need immediate cash. I have another idea I'd like to work out. Something I hope will bring me in some real money."

"What is it?"

"Well, you know how much trouble we had getting those teeth for the cylinders."

"We didn't get them. You had to make them all yourself."

"Well, I've thought the matter over, and it's not much more difficult than making nails."

"We couldn't have used nails. They're not strong enough."

"I didn't mean nails for the iceboat, I meant nails for building. I think I can manufacture them more uniformly and more cheaply than they are made now."

"Then why don't you do it?"

"It takes money. I'll need at least a hundred dollars for parts, and I don't know where to get the money," Hunt confessed.

"Do you want to sell your share in the iceboat?"

"If you'll give me a hundred dollars, I'll sell you all my interest, and at the same time, I'll work on it with you to perfect it so that we can get a patent."

"Agreed. I'll get you the money this week, Mr. Hunt."

On July 13, 1838, an agreement was signed. "In consideration of one hundred dollars ... the full and exclusive right to all the improvements made by me ... and I hereby authorize and request the Commissioner of Patents to issue Letters Patent to Jacob Townsend as the assignee of my whole right and title thereto."

The summer passed quickly. Early in September, the final touches were made on the iceboat.

Further tests had demonstrated the value of the iceboat. After fifteen months of experimenting, Hunt and Townsend made their application to the Patent Office. On September 8, 1838, S. O. Bennett and William L. Morris, acting as Commissioner of Deeds, witnessed the patent application.

The Patent Office realized the importance and the utility of this invention and awarded Hunt and Townsend, the joint inventors, U.S. Patent No. 958 on October 3, 1838, granting their claims on "the use and application of revolving cylinders with teeth or spurs upon their outer surfaces to be attached to boats and vessels; said cylinders being suspended upon arms, and the whole constructed substantially in the manner and for the purpose as hereinabove set forth."

Friends and visitors congratulated Hunt on the award of the iceboat patent.

Polly Hunt witnessed the demonstration. "Now let's wait until winter when the river freezes for a real test. I hope that your expectations are justified, and that this will be the machine that makes your fortune for you."

"Well, I...," Walter stammered.

"Now what is it?" Polly asked suspiciously.

Walter rummaged through a pile of papers and handed Polly a copy of the assignment. She read it. Tears clouded her eyes. The signatures of the witnesses appeared blurred. She handed the paper back.

"Oh, Walter," she sobbed, and left the room.

Walter followed her and found her stretched out on the bed. "Don't cry, Polly," he pleaded. "Don't cry. I have another invention that is still better. One that really will make a fortune for us."

"It is always the same. Always. You have fortunes in your hands and you let them slip away like grains of sand. You're a genius—a genius in making bad deals!"

"Don't worry," Hunt confided. "Everything will turn out all right. I hope."

Chapter 14

"I guess Townsend is finding it difficult to get enough capital to manufacture the ice-breakers," Hunt remarked to Polly as they were eating breakfast.

"Capital or no capital, I still think you were foolish to sell your interest for a hundred dollars."

"But a hundred dollars is a lot of money when you don't have it and when you need it."

"Well, you could have waited," she chided.

"The butcher, the baker and the candlestick maker won't wait for us! When their bills are due, they want to be paid."

"That's true," Polly admitted. "But you jumped at the hundred dollars, whereas if you held out, he might have given you five hundred."

"But Townsend didn't have five hundred dollars."

"You'll never change," Polly said.

"I guess you're right," Walter conceded.

"But I love you just the same," Polly added.

"Jobs are starting to come to the shop now, " Hunt said, "and I'll be able to afford to work on another new plan."

"Another new plan?" Polly queried.

"A nail-making machine."

"A nail-making machine? Why, you made one! Didn't the American Institute give you a silver medal for it?"

"But I figured out a way to improve it."

"Did you ever get your patent on the other nail machine?"

"No. Not yet."

"Not yet! Do you want to wait until it gets stolen like the others?"

"Well, you see…"

"What is it?" Polly asked, fearing the worst.

"Well, I needed some money, and I borrowed some from George A. Arrowsmith."

"And you turned the patent rights over to him?"

"No. Not really." Hunt explained. "I gave him the machine as a sort of security. He has a mortgage on it."

"Well, pay him back!" Polly ordered.

"I wish I could."

"You can!" Polly exclaimed emphatically. "The money I saved for that cloth coat, and the money for—"

"No!" Hunt insisted. "No. Not that. That money is yours. I'll pay my bills with my earnings, not your savings. I'll repay him somehow."

Early the next morning Hunt arrived at his shop and thumbed through the mail.* One of the letters informed him that his father had died on March 30th. It contained a newspaper clipping dated April 4, 1839, from the *Northern Journal*: "In this village on the 30th ult. Mr. Sherman Hunt, age 65 years. He was one of the early settlers of the town of Lowville." Hunt had not seen his father since he left home thirteen years earlier and corresponded with the family only at rare intervals. His grief was not pronounced.

Walter Hunt had saved his coppers, nickels and dollars. Small jobs brought in some money. Eventually he had accumulated enough to pay off Arrowsmith and reclaim his nail-making machine. On August 26, 1839, Arrowsmith reassigned to Hunt "all the right, title and patent interest, claimed or owned by him by said Hunt as set forth in said specification and by him transferred to me."

When Walter showed Polly the reassignment from Arrowsmith, she was extremely happy. "Now take out patent papers on it," she said.

"Not yet..."

"Not yet!" Polly argued. "Why? Do you want someone else to get ahead of you?"

"No. But there are just a few minor improvements I have in mind which will make it worth much more money."

"And then you'll sell it for a hundred dollars," Polly chided.

"No," Hunt said emphatically; "it'll be worth more."

The improvements were in fact subsequently made, and on October 14, 1839, Hunt applied for a patent. Eight days later, he dashed home excitedly. "Polly! I've just sold the nail machine."

"What did you get for it? A hundred dollars?"

"No. More than that."

"A hundred and ten dollars?"

"No. More than that. Much more."

"I don't know whether to believe you, Walter Hunt," Polly answered. "What did you get for it?"

*The mail was prepaid and did not yet bear stamps, as adhesive postage stamps were not issued until July 1, 1847.

UNITED STATES PATENT OFFICE.

WALTER HUNT, OF NEW YORK, N. Y.

NAIL AND MACHINE FOR MAKING THE SAME.

Specification of Letters Patent No. 1,407, dated November 12, 1839.

To all whom it may concern:

Be it known that I, WALTER HUNT, of the city, county, and State of New York, have invented a new and useful Improvement in
5 the Shape or Form of and Mode of Manufacturing Cut Nails, Brads, &c., and that the following is a full, true, and accurate description of the form of said nails, &c., and also of the machine for and mode of manu-
10 facturing the same.

The improvement in the form of said nails, brads, &c., consists in their being cut (from hoops or plates of iron) with blunt wedge-shaped points and dove tail, or wedge
15 shaped heads, as shown in Figure 4, in the annexed drawings which also exhibits the nail plate, from which they are cut, alternately head, and point; see Nos. 1, 2, 3, 4, each intervening point being cut from be-
20 tween the projections which form one half of each head of the adjoining nails, which heads are separated on a line with the center, or edge, of the point of said intermediate nail.

25 The machine for the above purpose of cutting said nails, is constructed as follows: See the annexed drawings which are marked with the scale of dimensions over each. Fig. 1, letter A, is a strong cast iron frame, in
30 the form of a right-angled oblong box, with a metal shaft B made to revolve in bearings C C upon the top of said frame A at right angles with, and near the center of the same. In the center of said shaft B midway be-
35 tween its said bearings, are inserted the two rotary cutters D D which are shown in Figs. 1 and 2, but more perfectly exhibited in an enlarged sectional view Fig. 5 D D. Said cutters are square blocks of steel, except their
40 outer surfaces, and are fitted into mortises, cut into opposite sides of the said shaft, each about one-third of the way through the same, and are regulated and secured in their places by a strong screw E, which passes
45 through the center of each into said shaft at B. Said screws are formed with a collar or ring made solid on the shaft of the same, at F which fits into a countersink, under the bottom of said cutters, while the upper
50 end of the screw, or bolt, passes up through the center of the same, and receives a nut G upon the upper surface of the cutter, which is then let into a corresponding countersink in the top and somewhat below the sur-
55 face of the same, as shown in said Fig. 5, letters G G which nut binds the cutters down

upon the collar F as aforesaid, and by turning the screw F F in, or out, the cutters are raised, or depressed, and secured firm, by turning down the nuts G G as aforesaid. 60

Horizontally opposite to the shaft B are placed two bed-cutters H H arranged side by side upon a carriage I, which is made to vibrate laterally with the shaft B upon a platform, or bed V (see Figs. 6, 1 and 2,) 65 which is cast solid with the frame A somewhat below, and forming about one third portion of its upper surface. On the back end of said carriage, it is extended into two arms J J, which are nicely fitted in corre- 70 sponding slots in the sides of the frame A and which serve as guides to keep the said carriage steady in its vibrations. The aforesaid bed-cutters are fastened down to the carriage I by central screws K K and are adjusted by 75 means of tail-screws L L, which are formed with indented or female collars, fitted into corresponding slots in the back of said carriage I as shown at L L Figs. 1 and 6 so that the cutters H H may be raised out by 80 unscrewing K K and without altering or turning the said tail-screws, which are only moved, in the horizontal adjustment of the said bed-cutters. Near the outside of said bed-cutters are two steel guides M M the 85 back ends of which are secured by screws or otherwise; firm in the carriage while the forward ends project and fit into zig-zag grooves or slots N N made around the shaft B turning alternately to the right, and left, 90 on two opposite sides of the same, and upon the outsides of the rotary cutters D D aforesaid. By this arrangement, the vibrating motion of the carriage I and bed-cutters H H is produced; the impulse being given 95 by the rotation of the shaft B so that the bed-cutters are alternately brought opposite to their respective mates, the rotary cutters D D as shown in Fig. 1. Over the carriage I is placed a top, or guide plate O as shown 100 in the sectional drawings Figs. 2 and 3, the latter of which is detached from the frame A, upon which it is to be bolted through the holes 1, 2, 3, 4. Under the bottom of said guide-plate at P is a gage-slot through 105 which the nail-plate Z is introduced directly on a line with the rotary cutters D D and upon a horizontal line with the surface of the bed cutters H H, which are flush and even with that of the said carriage I, to and 110 in which the latter are secured.

Centrally upon the top-plate are two ears,

2   1,407

or flanges Q Q between which is secured the end of a tilt-bar R, secured by a center bolt passing through the same, which tilt-bar R is forked at its acting end and passes length-
5 wise over the frame A and rotary cutters D D leaving room in the opening of the forks for said cutters to revolve in, free of contact with the same. Near the acting joint of said tilt-bar between the forks of the
10 same hangs a pawl, or gate, upon a pin, or bolt, which passes through the forks of the said tilt-bar and upper end of said gate at S the bottom end of which passes down through a corresponding slot in the top-
15 plate O. The object of this gate is to hold down the nail-plate (from which the nails are to be cut,) firm upon the bed-cutters H H at the times that the nails are being cut off by the rotary-cutters D D, (see Figs.
20 1, 2, 5,) which exhibits a profile view of this arrangement, showing at T T portions of the shaft which are left to operate as cams upon the under side of the tilt-bar at X and which raises the same a sufficient length of
25 time for the nail plate Z to be forced forward by the hand of the operator, or otherwise, and is brought down again by its own or additional weight, (as the shaft B presents in its revolution, its indented portions
30 at Y) and confines the nail-plate as aforesaid.

The form of my bed-cutters, which is shown in Figs. 6, 1, and 2, letters H H is a right angled, six sided slab of steel corre-
35 sponding in width, with the length of the nail to be cut, about double, in length and one half of the same in its thickness. The outer ends of my rotary-cutters, are convex, nearly on the same curve with that which
40 is described by the limits of their revolution, though somewhat raised at their cutting corners, as shown in Fig. 5 letters E E, which is an end view, of the shaft B cut off through their centers. The edges or cutting corners of
45 both rotary and bed-cutters, are formed precisely similar to the lines of separation as shown between the nails 5, 6, 7, 8, in Fig. 7 and are made to match, in pairs, in the same manner as said nails are represented by said

lines of separation, and alternately, a rotary 50 cutter on one side of the shaft B, to one of the reciprocating cutters, and the opposite rotary, to the adjoining reciprocating cutter, H, successively.

The width of the nails, is regulated by the 55 projection of the rotary cutters above the surface or periphery of the shaft B. Consequently the mode of using is confined simply to the rotation of the shaft B and the introduction of the nail-plate Z as before 60 described.

The nature of motion, and of effect having been fully explained in the above, I deem a recapitulation thereof, entirely superfluous, neither do I consider it pertinent to my 65 specification, or claims, to attempt a description of the various modes of manufacturing, or forms in which nails, and brads, have been wrought, or cut; although I am aware that brads have been cut from hoop, or plate 70 iron; so as to make the head of one out of the metal left beyond the point of another, alternately, on opposite sides, and that the same have been made, by both rotary, and reciprocating machines, and that nails and 75 spikes have been made with wedge shaped points and with pyramidal, or square counter-sunk heads, neither of which brads, spikes, nails, or machines for making the same are included in my claims; but   80

What I do claim and desire to secure by Letters Patent, is—

1. The making of the two sides of the head of one nail out of the metal left by cutting the wedge shaped points of the nails 85 on each side, as herein above described, and this I claim whether effected by the above described machine, or any other.

2. Also in the machine above described, I claim the shifting of the bed cutters, for the 90 purpose, and in the manner therein set forth.

In testimony whereof I have hereunto subscribed my hand, this 14th day of Oct. 1839.

WALTER HUNT.

Witnesses:
    JOHN EBBITT,
    D. E. WHEELER.

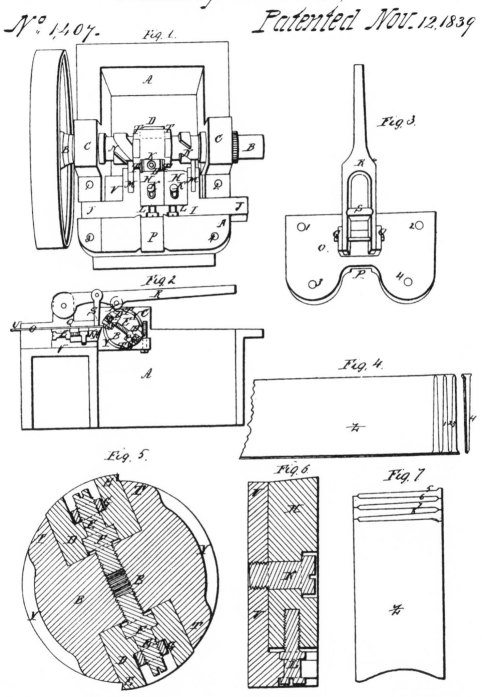

W. Hunt,

Making Cut Nails,

Patented Nov. 12, 1839

Nº 1,407.

Fig. 1.

Fig. 2.

Fig. 3.

Fig. 4.

Fig. 5.

Fig. 6.

Fig. 7.

Walter stood erect. His hands were on his hips. He paused a few seconds. His smile was devilish. His eyes sparkled. It was difficult to conceal his joy.

"How much did you get?" Polly said eagerly.

"Two thousand dollars!"

"Two thousand dollars," Polly gasped. "You mean two hundred."

Hunt smiled. He pulled a folded sheet of white paper from his pocket and handed it to her. James Thompson of Milton County of Saratoga, New York, contracted to pay Hunt $2000. It was dated October 22, 1839, and witnessed by John Sergeant and David Van Pell.

"Real money again," Polly said eagerly. She trembled. Her voice was choked with emotion. Tears ran down her cheeks. "It's like the old real estate days, except this is cash instead of paper profits."

"And it's only the beginning," Hunt said gleefully.

The Patent Office recognized the originality of the patent application, and on November 12, 1839, less than a month from the filing date, he was granted U.S. Patent No. 1,407.

As nine-tenths of the nails used in the United States were at that time imported, the nail industry eagerly welcomed Hunt's nail-making machine. There were no standard sizes in the industry and uniformity of production did not exist. No batch proved identical with others. There was no standard size, as each nail was separately forged from a thin rod of iron and there was always some slight deviation.

Thompson believed that the Hunt machine would standardize American production, but a serious illness overtook him and on September 22, 1842, he sold out all his interest in Hunt's patent to George D. Strong and Jonathan Dodge for $2,000. The two exhibited the nail machine at the 14th annual fair of the American Institute held in October 1840, and it received a silver medal.

The *Journal of the Franklin Institute* gave the invention considerable attention in its columns, summing up with:

> So far as we can judge from the model, and from the nails and brads cut by the machine, its operation appears to be perfect, whilst its construction and arrangement are such as to promise durability.

Although everyone was satisfied with its operation and its uniformity of production, Hunt was determined to strive for something superior. He designed and built a new machine with a completely different principle. It had two cutting blades instead of one, one blade cutting while the other receded. This double action greatly increased production. Justifying his fondest hopes and expectations, the new machine worked satisfactorily after final adjustments had been made.

"This new machine will double production," Hunt exclaimed to Polly. "It is twice as good as the old one."

UNITED STATES PATENT OFFICE.

WALTER HUNT, OF NEW YORK, N. Y., ASSIGNOR TO GEO. D. STRONG AND JONATHAN DODGE, OF NEW YORK, N. Y.

MACHINE FOR CUTTING NAILS, BRADS, &c.

Specification of Letters Patent No. 1,853, dated November 13, 1840.

To all whom it may concern:

Be it known that I, WALTER HUNT, of the city and county and State of New York, have invented a new and useful Improve-
5 ment in Machines for Cutting Nails, Brads, &c., and that the following is a a full and accurate description of said machine.

Figure 1 in the annexed drawings, gives a perspective, general view of said machine.
10 The frame A which is an oblong square may be made of wood, or of cast iron; upon said frame is firmly secured by bolts or otherwise, a cast iron form B, made in one piece with enlargements upon the side rails
15 which form two standards, one upon each of the same at C C, which standards are placed opposite to each other. Through these standards, are four perforations, two in each, one over the other, ranging in parallel
20 lines, at right angles across said form. In these perforations are inserted four mandrels or centers, two of which are shown in Fig. 1 at D D, and which are forced out, and in, by the regulating screws E the heads
25 of which run in cross slots in said centers, which centers are secured, by two, or four wedges entered between the same, upon the outsides and insides of said standards; one of which is shown at F in Fig. 1. Upon said
30 centers D are suspended the head levers G G which are partially shown in Fig. 1 and more fully exhibited in the sectional drawings Fig. 2. These levers are made of wrought or cast metal and correspond in
35 length with the opening in the standard form in which, they reciprocate upon said centers, similar to the walking beam of a steam engine, the motion being given by the crank H upon the horizontal shaft of the
40 fly-wheel I which shaft runs in a box, or boxes, 9 in the frame A. From said crank, the motion is communicated to said levers by the pitman K the upper end of which has a strap joint upon the pin or bolt which
45 connects the ends of the bottom lever, or levers, at L. These said levers may be made in two pieces, cast entire or in four slabs united in pairs as in Fig. 2 by bolts *h h h h* Fig. 3 which pass into, or through studs or
50 spreaders at M, M, M, M, two in each pair of levers, placed equi-distant from the centers, upon which said centers, the levers re-

ciprocate. These spreaders are turned square upon their ends, which fit into circular mortises, countersunk in the inner 55 faces of said levers, as shown in the sectional drawing Fig. 2 letters N, N, N, N.

In the inside faces of said levers are circular grooves in which are inserted the tennons of the cutters, which are four in num- 60 ber, an end view of which is given in drawing 2 at O, P, Q, R where two of said levers are removed in order to show the position, and manner of securing said cutters, which is effected by check-screws S, S, S, S which 65 pass through studs T T T T the ends of which studs, are inserted in said levers nearly opposite to the back of said cutters and parallel with the same, at T T T T. These cutters are formed in the first place 70 into cast steel zones or thimbles see Figs. 5, 6, 7, which are nicely turned in a lathe with tennons upon the ends *k*, *k*. The surface or peripheries of these thimbles, are made tapering in three grades or elevations with 75 two declivities or angles near each end which angles, form the heads and points of the brads, &c., in the process of cutting the same, and when the butts, or largest ends of two of these thimbles are placed together 80 (the centers being parallel) the space left in consequence of the taper and angles between said cutters will precisely describe the form of the nail or brad, which they are designed to cut. For example, if a wedge head 85 and pointed nail is required, as shown at O Fig. 8 the thimble is made with obtuse angles as in Fig. 7, and for a curved T head and round or bead point as in Fig. 9, letter P, the angles are reverse curved, as in 90 Fig. 6; and for a square T head and square point, as in Fig. 10 letter Q the angles on said thimbles are made right angles as in Fig. 5.

The Figs. 8, 9, 10, exhibit pieces of nail 95 plates with three different forms of nails or brads adjoining as above described, and also the lines in which the same are separated from said plates.

In order to form the above described 100 thimbles into cutters, they are sawed lengthwise into four sections, or staves, each pair of which, being reversed, forms one set of cutters, see Fig. 11, letters Q, P, and the other two quarters form the other set; these cutters are inserted, two in each pair of levers, through openings cut for the purpose, opposite to the circular grooves at r, r, and are situated as follows, (see sectional drawing Fig. 2, letters O, P, Q, R,). P in the upper lever at the right hand is mate to Q, the left hand cutter on the bottom lever; and R, the right hand cutter, in the bottom lever, is mate to O, in the upper lever, at the left hand. Thus it will be seen that the up and down motion of the pitman end of these levers, will alternately bring the cutting edges of Q, and P, and of O, and R; in close contact past each other, operating as cylindrical shears between which, the nail plate V, (which is shown in the drawing Fig. 2,) would be separated in lines corresponding with those of the cutting edges of said cutters, and consequently if the nail, plate V, is inserted precisely the depth of the taper of the cutter, or depth of the nail to be cut, at each vibration of the levers, upon the centers D, D, D, D, aforesaid; a perfect nail, or brad, will be produced.

The nail plate may be introduced by hand, with tongs, or by a regulating screw (or otherwise) through the plate-guide W, which is secured to a standard placed vertically upon the form B, at C, directly opposite to the cutters, before described. Said plate-guide is a gutter of sheet, or plate iron, standing directly over and the bottom end of which enters between the two upper cutters, as seen at V, V, Fig. 2.

The introduction of the nail plate, or the width of the nail, is regulated by a nail-gage, the end of which is seen in Fig. 2 at Z, but more fully exhibited in Fig. 3, letter Z. It is formed of a long flat spring secured at one end by the nut X, upon the end of the pitman bolt, and at the other end is bent at right angles, and passes between the two bottom cutters, a sufficient distance to catch the corner of the nail plate as it is pressed down in the process of cutting; this constitutes the nail gage and which is thrown back in time to let the nail drop between the reciprocation of the levers, by means of a spur Y which projects upward, from near the gage end of said spring which spur fits into a notch or depression cut in the lower edge of the upper opposite lever, at J, J, the limits or banks of which depression, operate as combs upon said spur in throwing back said spring at every reciprocation of the levers as aforesaid.

The two bottom centers, upon which are suspended the lower levers, are inserted in movable head-blocks, fitted in openings in said standards at M, Fig. 1, and are raised, or depressed by check-screws, underneath each one of which is seen at Q Q. These head blocks are cast with flanches upon the insides, by which they are secured to said standards by bolts and nuts, I I which pass horizontally through each, and by which means the cutters may be adjusted with required accuracy. The pitman ends of said levers are connected by means of two stirrups or links, N, N, and their motions when in operation are similar to that of a parallel rule, supposing one of the straps to be held firm in a vertical position and a reciprocating motion given to the other end of the rule.

As before mentioned, I have anticipated casting these levers in two pieces, instead of four as herein above described in which case openings will be cast for inserting the cutters, and directly back of which, they will be contracted each to one arm, tapering to the pitman ends which may be connected similar to those above described. I have also anticipated the casting of the frame and standards in one piece similar to the standing head of a large lathe, in the standard of which, my centers may be inserted and between which my levers may be suspended similar to the plan above specified and in which case an opening may be cast in the base which may project from the feet of said standards which opening makes room for the play of the crank, upon the shaft of the fly-wheel, which shaft may run in boxes or plummer blocks, cast on or bolted to said base.

Either of the two arrangements of this plan of a machine may be made to operate in a horizontal, vertical or in an inclined position, and the nail plate introduced by hand with tongs, or by means of a gage screw, feeding rollers, or otherwise.

In the above specified machine, my claims as inventor, are as follows, and not otherwise:

1. I claim the plan of forming the cutters for cutting nails, brads, &c., from staves, or longitudinal sections of metal zones or thimbles, in the form, or forms above specified, whether the same are first made or turned in entire pieces and afterward cut. or sawed into sections, or whether said sections are fitted up separate, or made of cast steel, or other metal.

2. I also claim in connection with said above described cutters or those of any other form, having similar shaped cutting surfaces, or edges, the mode of arranging the same, in such manner as to operate upon the same principle of motion, (that is to say,) arranged in two opposite pairs, fitted in levers, or other fastenings, by the vibrating motion of which levers, two opposite cutters, one from each pair, is made to approximate, and pass each other, operating as cylindrical shears, in cutting off one nail, and as these cutters recede, the other pair operate in a similar manner in cutting the next nail alternately.

3. And I further claim the combination, and general arrangement of the head-levers, cutters, and spring-gage constructed and arranged as above set forth and described, 5 without reference to the particular form of the cutting edges of the cutters; for the purpose of cutting nails, brads, tacks, &c., without regard to the particular form or shape of the same.

WALTER HUNT.

Witnesses:
  B. H. MORSELL,
  EDMUND MAHER.

W. HUNT.
NAIL MACHINE.

No. 1,853.   Patented Nov. 13, 1840.

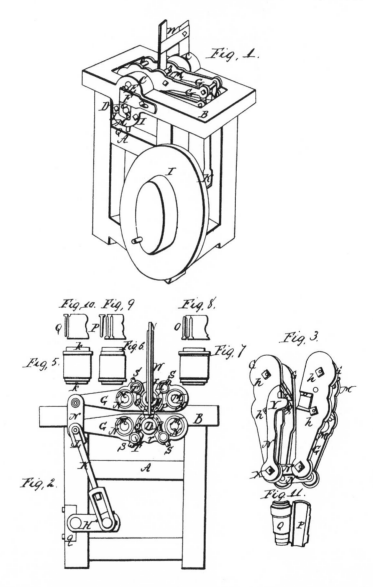

Fig. 1.
Fig. 10. Fig. 9. Fig. 8.
Fig. 5. Fig. 6. Fig. 7.
Fig. 3.
Fig. 2.
Fig. 11.

"Have you shown it to anyone yet?" Polly asked.

"No," Hunt replied. "I'll show it to Strong and Dodge first. I guess they'd like to see it."

"See it? They'll have to buy it. They'll need the new machine to protect their investment from others getting it. But don't sell it to them unless you can keep a share in the profit."

On October 7, 1840, Hunt agreed to sell George D. Strong and Jonathan Dodge each "one equal undivided third part of the whole of said patent." Hunt retained the third part for himself. But, less than three weeks later, on October 27, Hunt sold his one-third interest to George D. Strong.

The Patent Office approved the application on November 13, 1840, and Hunt was awarded U.S. Patent No. 1,853 on a "machine for cutting nails, brads, etc."

Two weeks later, after the grant of the patent, new assignment agreements were prepared to establish the title and obviate any future controversy. An agreement was signed by Hunt, Strong and Dodge assigning the rights of the patent to Strong and Dodge. A further agreement was signed by Walter Hunt assigning his interest to Strong and Dodge.

The money Hunt had received for the sale of the nail machines enabled him to wipe out obligations and set up a cash reserve. Feeling more secure, he moved across the street to a newer and better house at 256 Bleecker Street.

On New Year's Day, 1841, friends of the Hunts paid them the customary New Year visits.

"This place is quite an improvement over your last one," Jonathan [i.e., Jno.] Chapin commented, "I'm glad, Polly, for your sake. You deserve it."

"We have a lot to be thankful for," Polly said.

"I agree with her. A lot to be thankful for," Hunt added.

"What are you working on now, Hunt?" Kipp asked.

"Walter Junior is going to be twenty-three. For many years, he has worked hard as a drug clerk, too hard in fact. On his birthday, May 8th, I'm going to give him five hundred dollars so that he can open a drug store of his own. I would have liked to have given it to him on his twenty-first birthday but I didn't have that much money then."

But fortune decided otherwise. About the middle of February, Walter, Jr., became ill. A doctor was summoned. He diagnosed the illness as influenza and advised Hunt to "Take an ounce of extract of liquorice, place it in a pint of water, then simmer it down to half a pint. When it is cold, add one ounce paregoric and one ounce antimonial wine." He added, "Let him take a swallow whenever his cough is troublesome."

The remedy did not prove efficacious. It did not cure nor relieve young Walter of his short hacking cough. Another doctor was called in for his opinion. "Consumption," he said laconically. On April 14, 1841, Walter, Jr., died, 25 days short of his twenty-third birthday.

UNITED STATES PATENT OFFICE.

WALTER HUNT, OF NEW YORK, N. Y., ASSIGNOR TO JAMES THOMPSON AND HALSEY ROGERS.

METHOD OF FEEDING NAIL AND TACK PLATES, &c., INTO MACHINES FOR CUTTING NAILS, TACKS, &c.

Specification of Letters Patent No. 3,305, dated October 12; 1843.

To all whom it may concern:

Be it known that I, WALTER HUNT, of the city, county, and State of New York, have invented a new and useful Improvement in
5 Machines for Introducing Nail-Plates, Tack-Plates, &c., into Machines for Cutting the Same into Nails, Tacks, &c., but which is more particularly designed to be connected with my improved double-acting nail-en-
10 gine, for which Letters Patent were granted to George D. Strong, Jonathan Dodge and Richard W. Redfield, as assignees of my whole patent dated November 13, 1840, and that the following is an accurate and faith-
15 ful description of my said above-named improvement.

The subjoined drawing, Plate 1, Fig. 1, exhibits a general view of the said entire feeding machine.
20 A, is a stanchion-post, to which the whole machinery is attached. To the upper end of the said post is secured a cap B, screw C, and plate D, which are arranged to secure said stanchion in a vertical position between
25 a beam or other fixture, and the top of the nail engine to which it is to be attached. Upon the side and near the upper end of said post is attached the gear box E in which is arranged the feeding rollers F, F, Figs. 1
30 and 2; placed horizontally within and parallel across said box, with journals or bearings in the opposite sides of the said gear box, and which rollers are connected by the pinions G, G, fixed upon the ends of the shafts
35 of the same.

Upon the opposite end of the shaft of one of said rollers is fixed a worm-wheel H, into which gears the endless screw, or worm I, which screw is placed upon the worm shaft
40 J, and which shaft is supported by, and revolves upon its end journals in two flanges K, K, formed upon elevated portions of the feeder-box E, before mentioned. Upon the opposite end to the worm on said shaft is
45 secured the driving pulley L, around which the driving band M, from the nail engine, or an intermediate pulley passes, and gives motion to the feeding rollers aforesaid. One of said feeding rollers F, is suspended in a
50 bracket N within said gear box, which bracket is supported by two fulcrum centers O, O, which are inserted horizontally through the opposite sides of the said feeder box. See Figs. 2 and 3. Upon the back of

the said bracket is secured a lever P, which 55 projects downward in an inclined position to the corner of said stanchion post where the bottom end of said lever rests upon a screw cam Q, which is perforated centrally and secured upon the upper portion of a square 60 metal rod R, which rod is placed vertically in a niche cut out of the corner of said stanchion post, and is supported in a step at the bottom end, and a journal in the feeding box at the upper end. Around said shaft R, 65 is placed a sliding thimble S, with a projecting ring T secured around the center of the same, which ring forms the hub of the handle U, the whole of which is made to traverse up and down upon said shaft by the 70 hand of the operator as the case may require. In addition to which motion said handle is moved to the right or left horizontally, by which movement (the rod, thimble and screw cam, receives the same motion, and by 75 which motion) the incline upon the screw-cam Q, operates similar to a quick screw, in raising and depressing the end of the lever aforesaid, which lever in connection with the bracket N, operates as one general 80 lever upon the fulcrum centers aforesaid, in closing and separating the feeding rollers F, F, one of which rollers being supported in said lever bracket as before described. Between said feeding rollers (which are 85 fluted similar to common cotton rollers) is placed the feeding rod, or shaft of the feeding tongs V. The bottom end of said rod (near to where the tongs or pliers W, are attached) is secured to, and guided by a 90 curved arm X, which arm is screwed upon the side of a slide box Y. Into the side of said slide box is cut a small notch Z, in which notch the horizontal circular projection or hub T from the handle as aforesaid 95 is made to reciprocate freely, in order to allow of the horizontal motion of said handle and rod R as before described. Another and important object of the connection of said handle (by means of said hub in said 100 notch) is for the purpose of raising and depressing the slide box Y upon the slide plate, and, which slide plate is secured laterally upon the front side of the stanchion post A, and is of corresponding length with the rod 105 or tail of said feeding tongs before mentioned. Said feeding tongs are formed principally of two pieces and are a kind of grad-

uated hook, the mouth of which may be lessened or enlarged by moving the hook, *a*, which has a slot in its upper end, through which the screw *c*, enters and secures it firm
5 to the gage *b*, the mouth being set to the thickness of the plate &c., to be cut, similar to a hand saw set. That portion of the said tongs which forms the gage &c., extends upward, and laps upon a corresponding flat-
10 tened portion at the bottom of the feeding rod V, through which a slot is cut lengthwise inclosing a dovetail slide, into which (through the end of said gage) the screws *d*, *d*, are inserted, securing the two pieces
15 (slide and hook) firmly together, the slide being shorter than the slot in which it reciprocates allows said tongs to have a partial vertical, or endwise play in said slot. In the space between the flattened bottom
20 end of the rod V, and the upper end of the hook, *a*, a spiral spring *e'* is wound around about the middle of the gage *b*, which spring acts by extension upon said tongs, but yields to a slight pressure upon their bottom ends,
25 which play permits of a momentary check of the downward motion of said tongs, without arresting that of the rod V, which rod is forced regularly downward, by the rotation of the feeding rollers, between which it is
30 held as before specified. Supported upon the two flanges, or studs *f*, *f*, (which are bolted to the side of the stanchion post aforesaid) is secured by screws or otherwise the feeding trough *g*, perpendicularly in
35 which trough, the tongs W, and rod V, are elevated or depressed at pleasure when the machine is in operation. Said trough is made of sheet metal of about two thirds of the length of said tongs and rod V. The
40 width of the back of said trough is made to correspond with that of the nail plate to be used, and its depth, say one half less than its width. At the bottom end of said trough, is placed a small spring *h*, having a spur
45 upon its lower end which is let through one of the sides of the trough, and which is designed to bear upon, and keep the nail plate against the opposite side of said trough as it is forced down by the tongs, and which plate
50 is kept against the back of the said trough, by means of side stops *i*, *i*, which stops are fastened upon the side flanges of the said trough. There is an opening through the back of said trough near its upper end at *k*
55 through which two side springs *j*, *j*, enter from the back side of the same, pointing downward, and curve partially above the inside of the said back, leaving space be-

tween said springs for the tongs W, to pass up and down, but which springs are so 60 placed that as the tongs ascend, with a short portion or remnant of the nail plate in the hook aforesaid, the same will be caught by the said springs and forced from the tongs through the opening *k*, as before named, and 65 thereby thrown from the machine all being produced by one and the same motion of the handle U by which it is raised to receive the next nail plate, a short flange being turned up, upon the upper end of the same, which 70 flange is inserted in the hook of said tongs, which tongs are next brought down to enter the nail plate between the cutters below; the handle is then moved horizontally to the left, which raises the lever P, by means of 75 the screw-cam Q and closes the rollers F, F, upon the shaft (or feeding rod of the tongs V, which rollers being kept in motion by the worm or endless screw I aforesaid: consequently the nail plate is gradually 80 forced into the cutters of the nail-engine with perfect regularity and at any required graduation. The bottom section of said feeding machine as connected with, and attached to, my improved double acting nail 85 engine is exhibited in plate 2 Fig. 1, by means of a circular or crescent shaped flange *m*, upon the bottom of the said stanchion post A, which flange is secured upon the top of one of the standards of said engine, 90 through the bolt holes *l*, *l*, and is so placed that the mouth of the feeding trough *g*, stands directly over and midway between the cutters of said engine.

What I claim as new and useful in the 95 above described machine is—

1. The pliers or feeding tongs W, constructed as above described, in connection with the spring *c* and the feeding rod V as forming a new and useful instrument for the 100 purposes above set forth.

2. I also claim the plan of gripping, and disengaging, the feeding rod V, between the rollers F F by means of the combined arrangement of the crank or lever U, the cam 105 shaft R, the screw cam Q, the lever P, and the bracket N, constructed and combined in the manner above set forth or similar thereto, for the above and all other purposes to which the same may be usefully applied.

New York Oct. 2d 1843.

WALTER HUNT.

Witnesses present:
W. T. Thompson,
Com. Jno. De Witt

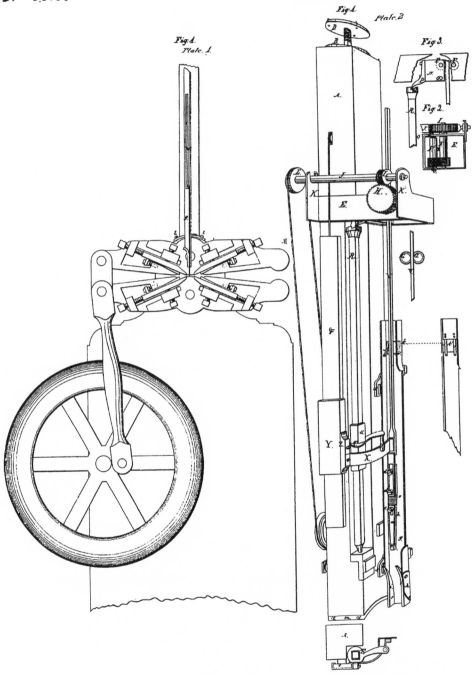

Fig. 4.
Plate. 1.

Fig. 1.
Plate. 2.

Fig. 3.

Fig. 2.

The death of his eldest son had a marked effect upon Hunt. He brooded. His shop no longer held an attraction for him and he neglected his work. He could not think of anything but the tragedy. His interest in fixing things disappeared. Plans on which he had been eagerly engaged lost their glamour. Nothing mattered.

Polly Hunt concealed her grief and busied herself with household tasks. She also worried about her husband. To keep him from brooding and to distract him, she encouraged their friends to visit as often as possible.

Despite her strenuous efforts to lessen the gloom, a chill and stillness blanketed the house. Polly was contemplating moving to another location when she was interrupted by the ringing of the doorbell.

"Will you please tell Mr. Hunt that Mr. Graham is here and would like to see him?" a tall stately gentleman wearing a gray beaver hat announced.

"Won't you come inside?" Polly ushered him into the parlor and then sought out her husband.

"I don't know any Mr. Graham, and I don't want to see anyone," Hunt brusquely told Polly.

"He said it's important. He said it is about the New York Patent Nail Company."

"Oh yeah, I remember Graham. Tell him I don't want to talk business."

"Better go in and see him," Polly insisted.

Listlessly Hunt shuffled into the parlor. Mr. Graham arose and put his arm over Hunt's shoulder. "Mr. Hunt, I know that you don't want to be disturbed, so I'll make my mission as brief as possible. I have been down to your shop several times, but I have never found you in. You are the inventor of a nail machine?"

Hunt nodded.

"You received two patents on them. My company, the New York Patent Nail Company, is prepared to offer you $24,000 for the rights to them."

Polly gulped.

"I'm sorry, but I have nothing to do with the patents," Hunt said after a few minutes of silence. "I sold them to Strong and Dodge. I suppose they are the people you should see."

"Maybe you can buy your rights back from Strong and Dodge?" Polly suggested.

"Not a chance. A few weeks ago they said they'd never part with them."

On the April 22, 1841, the New York company raised the offer to $27,000 which Strong and Dodge accepted, assigning the two patents to them.

A few days later, the New York Patent Nail Company offered Hunt employment in their factory at 60 Gold Street. Hunt accepted, with the provision that he could still carry on his own work if he wanted to do so. The official title given him was "actuary."

This appointment assured him a steady income and justified his removal to a better house at 45 Jones Street, on the right hand side, next to the corner of Bleecker Street. The Hunts lived in this house during 1842 and 1843.

The nail machine that was originally exhibited at the American Institute fair in 1840 was a great attraction and by popular demand, it was again exhibited in 1841 at the 15th annual fair, where it received a diploma.

In the latter half of 1843, Hunt decided to open a mechanic's shop of his own and rented space at 42 Gold Street (on the righthand side) between Ryder's Alley and Fulton Street. The designation "mechanical designer" appeared in the 1842-1843 city directory.

R. Hoe & Company's plant was located across the street. Hunt came in frequent contact with the mechanics and printers and learned they were having difficulty with the ink balls on the presses. He looked at the presses and suggested that rubber rollers replace the ink balls. The idea was a good one and revolutionized the printing industry, but it brought Hunt no returns.

In his shop he worked on a new nail machine, an improved method of feeding the nail and tack plates into the machine.

Halsey Rogers, owner of the building in which Hunt had his shop, called to collect the rent. He looked at the machine in operation.

"Fine machine, Hunt," he commented. "Made any plans for it?"

"The New York Patent Nail Company thought they might buy it, but they decided their equipment is good enough."

"I'll make you an offer on it," Rogers volunteered, "but first I want to speak to James Thompson, my partner." Thompson approved the expenditure and on May 10, 1843, Hunt assigned his machine to them.

"We'll wait a few months before we apply for a patent," Thompson suggested. "No sense in telling the world about the new invention until we are ready to use it."

On October 2, 1843, Commissioner John De Witt and W. T. Thompson witnessed Hunt's application for a patent. On the 12th, it was announced that the Patent Office had awarded Hunt U.S. Patent No. 3,305, which was assigned to James Thompson and Halsey Rogers.

The machine cut more than six hundred ten-penny nails a minute.

"If you get patents as fast as that," Rogers declared, "you'll be a millionaire in no time."

"Don't let that fool you, Mr. Rogers," Hunt stated quietly, "it's not the inventor who makes money from patents, it's the manufacturer. Few patents immediately command a big price. It's only after they have established themselves that they are worth any money, and then the inventor has already disposed of his rights."

"What's money mean to you, anyhow?" said Rogers jokingly. "Any time you need money all you have to do is to come out with a new idea."

"I hope you are right," said Hunt. The humor did not appeal to him.

Chapter 15

It was the custom of the workmen employed by the New York Patent Nail Company to sit on the wooden benches outside the factory during the lunch hour and play practical jokes on each other.

One of their pastimes was teasing Pierre Leroux, a French immigrant, who constantly boasted of the superiority of his countrymen. He was a likeable chap even though he was highly excitable. The day was a success only when he poured forth a string of expletives in his native language.

"You Americans," he said. "You think you have everything. I'll show you something we have in France that you Americans never even heard of."

"I'll bet it is a skinless onion."

"Maybe it is a noiseless horn."

"No!" Leroux snorted, "it's something you haven't in your country." He raised his foot displaying the sole of his boot. It was studded with small square iron discs inserted in grooves hollowed out at strategic points.

"Who wants to wear those things anyhow?"

"Only a crazy Frenchman is dumb enough to stick nails in his shoes."

Hunt joined the group during the harangue and approached the annoyed Frenchman.

"Let me look at it," Hunt requested.

"Sure, Mr. Hunt," he agreed, taking off his boot.

"Make him put his shoe back on again."

"We can't stand the odor."

Hunt ignored the workmen's sallies. He was interested in the shoe.

"Those nails make the sole last twice as long and prevents slipping in wet places," the French workman explained.

Hunt nodded. He held the shoe in his hand and applied a little pressure while bending the sole. One of the pegs fell out. He bent the boot a little further. Another peg fell out.

"Don't do that," Leroux said angrily. "You're ruining my boot."

121

Hunt was absorbed. He paid no attention and bent the boot again.

"What are you doing!" Leroux shouted, fearing that Hunt was not only ruining his boot but making him the butt of a joke.

The workmen laughed heartily.

"You're spoiling my boot. I'll have to send to France to get a new one, and I'll make you pay for it."

Hunt raised his hand to quiet the excited workman. "No, you won't have to do that. I'm going to make you a new pair, but not like the kind you have on. A better kind."

"A horseshoe," one of the workmen called out.

"This is no joke. I'm in earnest. I'm going to give him a better boot."

"There isn't any better kind," the workman protested. "They don't use this kind of boot in America."

"These nails have given me an idea," Hunt exclaimed.

The workmen gathered about Hunt, eager to hear his explanation. "Instead of using a square peg, a round one should be used. To keep it from falling out, the peg should be threaded and inserted through the leather. Not into it. This will give it a greater binding and clinging surface."

"But won't they fall out just as the other did?" Leroux asked.

"No," Hunt explained, "you see, your pegs go only half way into the outer sole. My idea is to make the pegs go all the way through."

"Then they'll hurt the feet."

"No, the pegs you have are inserted after the shoe has been made up. My plan is to screw the pegs into the outer soles only. To prevent them from falling out, I'll flatten the inner end with a blunt center punch, then put the outer sole over the insole."

"Do you think it will work?" The workmen were as interested as if they were confronted with a serious design problem.

"Of course it will work," Hunt insisted. "The idea is as simple as the A, B, C's."

When Hunt went home he took an old pair of shoes out of a closet. He detached the outer sole and studded it from the inside with screws, the points of which protruded through the surface side. Then he went to Joseph Clark, a shoemaker at 252 Delancey Street, and requested him to sew the studded outer sole to the inner sole.

"What are you trying to do, Mr. Hunt?" the shoemaker asked. "Are you going to tear up someone's carpets?"

Hunt laughed. "I hope not. As soon as you have the outer sole sewed on, I'm going to file the points off the screws so that just a little flat stub will be exposed."

"Then what are you going to do?"

"I don't know yet, but if the idea is sound, then I'll make a special kind of stud."

The shoemaker hand-sewed each outer sole to the inner sole. Using a heavy file he borrowed from the shoemaker, Hunt then filed the studs to his own satisfaction. He took off his shoes and then put on the shoes with the studs. Then he walked home. After he was convinced the idea was practical, he walked to the New York Patent Nail Company where he met Leroux and his fellow workmen enjoying their lunch.

Hunt showed them the shoe with the studs. "That's better than they have in France. Isn't that so?"

"Will you fix my shoes like that, Mr. Hunt?" one of the workmen asked.

Within a short time, Hunt had obtained several orders for the studded sole shoes, but the production of studs by hand was slow and tedious and costly. To increase the output and decrease the cost, Hunt built a cutter for stamping the holes in the soles and a riveting machine to insert the pegs. As a result, it was easier to supply the demand, which was steadily increasing. Orders came in from dairymen, from iron foundries, riveters and other workmen.

Shoemaker Joseph Clark displayed a pair of the studded shoes in his shop. Robert B. Ruggles, a gold beater, noticed them and inquired about them.

"Mighty clever." Ruggles said, "Is this your idea?"

"I wish it was," Clark answered. "There's an inventor named Walter Hunt who had the idea. He has a shop at 42 Gold Street."

"Do you sell many of the studs?"

"Doing a nice business with them but he doesn't give much attention to them. He's too busy. Working on some other kind of invention."

"I wonder whether he'd like a partner?" Ruggles said. "I'm tired of gold beating and would like to get into some kind of business for myself."

"Go and see him," Joseph Clark advised. "Chances are you can buy the whole thing at a price. I think he has a patent on it."

Ruggles visited Hunt at his Gold Street shop on June 7, 1843. They came to an agreement. Ruggles wanted to buy and Hunt was willing to sell.

Hunt sold Ruggles "one rolling press, one stamping press with six cutters for stamping out soles together with a lot of lettering and numbering stamps, and all the appurtenances used, including patterns and dies, also the riveting engine invented" for $1,000.

Several days later Clark and Ruggles went with Hunt to the office of Sparhawk Parsons, a lawyer and commissioner of deeds, where the assignment was recorded.

Clark was happy. There was a steady and increasing demand for the pegged shoes and business was good.

A few days after the transaction had been terminated, Ruggles called on Hunt. "In the bill of sale," he said, "you made no mention of the patent, Mr. Hunt. Didn't you intend to assign that to me?"

"I didn't assign any patent to you," Hunt replied, "because I haven't any patent."

UNITED STATES PATENT OFFICE.

WALTER HUNT, OF NEW YORK, N. Y., ASSIGNOR TO ROBERT B. RUGGLES.

SOLE OF BOOTS AND SHOES.

Specification of Letters Patent No. 3,227, dated August 17, 1843.

To all whom it may concern:

Be it known that I, WALTER HUNT, of the city, county, and State of New York, have invented and made a new and useful im-
5 provement in preparing the soles, heels, &c., of boots and shoes by studding or inserting into the same metallic screw or jagged rivets or plugs and that the following is an accurate and faithful description of said
10 improvement separately and compared with other plans now in use.

The advantages of the plan long in use, of studding the soles, &c., of boots and shoes with the common hob nails, has fully estab-
15 lished the utility of the introduction of iron in some form, connected with leather, for the above purpose; with a view of securing the advantages and avoiding the objections of the hob nail in the above plan, a new ar-
20 rangement has been invented by a Mr. Jurisch in Paris, which consists in the inserting of square metallic plugs or cubes into boot soles, &c., a, a, a, (see Figure 1.) Fig. 2 shows a tap, or half sole, with the
25 cubes inserted, which are set in rows near the edge of the half soles or taps of boots, &c., previous to making up the same, which taps have blank holes left between said plugs through which they are screwed upon
30 the outsoles of the boots, &c., with some 10 or 12 short screws B, B, &c. (see Fig. 2) with a half sole C attached as described. The principal objection to this plan is that a portion of the cubes frequently fall out
35 before the sole is half worn, especially if made of thin leather. In order to obviate this defect, I have substituted as an improvement upon the above plan a round, or cylindrical rivet, to which it is obvious that
40 the leather (closing upon the principle of a hoop) will bind more closely on all sides, than upon a square, or any other form. In addition to this advantage, I prepare my rods or wire, from which said rivets are
45 made, by passing the same through a screw plate, or dies, thereby forming them into a fine cut screw (see Fig. 3) or otherwise I pass them under a swage, the grooves in which are cut in such manner as to produce
50 a spiral or transverse thread upon said wire, which when driven into the soles, &c., answers the same purpose of holding in the leather as that of a screw. The wire thus prepared, I coat with india rubber varnish,
55 and when dried, I cut into plugs with common rivet shears, or otherwise, the lengths of which plugs correspond with the thickness of the soles to be filled, into which they are

inserted by means of a small punch and hammer in one or more rows near the edge 60 of the sole, or as the case may require, (see Figs. 4 and 5) which exhibits a sole D, and tap E, prepared to sew or peg on. In order to bind the rivet more firmly, the inner ends of the same are expanded by means of a 65 blunt center punch, and are then closed down even with the surface of the sole, with the hammer as before mentioned, which effectually forces the leather into the threads or jags upon the surface of the rivets as 70 before described. Rods for making the square plugs on the French plan, may be jagged by means of a swage as above mentioned, and thereby materially improved for the above purpose. The cylindrical plug 75 will however be preferred, for the reasons before stated. The soles, taps, heels, &c., thus prepared, being coated with india rubber varnish on the inside, (if designed to be water proof,) are adapted to the manu- 80 facture or repairing of boots and shoes of all descriptions; a margin being left outside of the rivets for sewing, nailing, pegging or screwing on, as the case may require.

What I claim in the above specified inven- 85 tion, is,

An improvement upon the French plan or the plain plugs, as before described; which improvement consists in preparing the soles, heels, &c., of boots and shoes pre- 90 vious to manufacturing the same into said shoes, &c., by inserting in said soles, &c., in manner above described metallic screw rivets or plugs made from rods or wire, which is tapped with a screw plate or dies, 95 or otherwise stamped, cut, indented, or made with spiral, diagonal, or transverse threads, grooves, or indentations, in such manner as to hold more firmly when driven into said soles, by means of said screw, stamped, cut 100 or indented plugs, or rivets; which improvement renders the soles, &c., thus prepared, more durable and useful, in consequence of their retaining the screw or indented plugs more firmly than the plain or smooth plugs 105 before described, and for which said improvement, in the combination of said screw rivets and soles, prepared as hereinabove described, I do hereby solicit Letters Patent of the United States.

New York, July 20th, 1843.

WALTER HUNT. [L. S.]

Witnesses:
  S. PARSONS,
  EDMD. ELMENDORF, JR.

W. Hunt,

Shoe Peg,

Nᵒ 3,227.   *Patented Aug. 17, 1843*

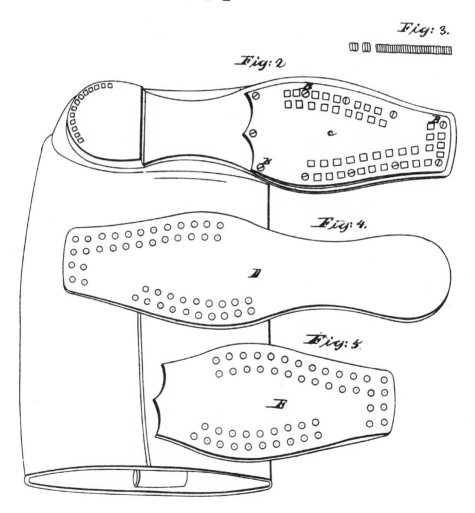

"I thought you had one." Ruggles faltered. "Clark told me that you had one."

"No. I never had a patent. I never applied for one."

"Will you apply for it?" Ruggles asked. "I'll pay you for your time and expense."

"If you want a patent, I'll apply for one," Hunt agreed. "I won't charge you for my time and I'll give you the patent if they issue one, but you'll have to pay the application fee."

"I'd appreciate that very much," Ruggles beamed.

On July 20, 1843, Hunt applied to the Patent Office for a patent. The application was witnessed by Sparhawk Parsons and Edmund Elmendorf. In Hunt's application, he stated the principle of using hobnails was known and that his invention was an improvement of the French invention.

The Patent Office recognized the patentability and utility of the improvement and granted Hunt U.S. Patent No. 3,227 on August 17, 1843, less than a month after his application.

The money that Hunt received from the sale was more important to him than the possibility of the value of the patent. The cash enabled him to pay off a few of his obligations and reestablish his credit.

With the money, Hunt was able to devote more time to the completion of several other inventions, one of which was the third nail-making machine.

Chapter 16

I'm surprised at you, Mr. Hunt," Jonathan Chapin jested. "A year has passed and you haven't received a patent. I guess you're getting old."

"I'm not fifty yet," Hunt snapped.

"Forty-nine isn't far away," Chapin teased.

"I'm not interested in accumulating patents. I'm interested only in making things."

"You may be right, Mr. Hunt, but I'm a firm believer in patents. They are the inventor's only protection."

"If you've got a million dollars to go to court to defend them."

"Million dollars or no million dollars, anytime I can get a patent, you can bet I'll try and get one."

Chapin was sprawled on Hunt's desk. While making himself comfortable, he upset an inkwell which spilled its contents over some papers.

"Never mind. Those papers have no importance anyway," Hunt assured him as he mopped up the ink.

"I must have an inkwell phobia. Every time I get near an inkwell, I seem to upset it. I guess I have a perfect mania for doing it. You'll do me a great favor, Mr. Hunt, if you will invent an inkwell that doesn't leak…"

Hunt immediately mused over this new challenge.

"I'll be your best customer for them," Chapin called out as he was leaving.

No sooner had Chapin left the office than Hunt went over to the fireplace and selected a small log. He trimmed the ends so that the log was about twelve inches long. Then he sawed it lengthwise to form a flat base. He went to a closet and picked a glass square inkwell from among the varied objects strewn on an upper shelf. He chiseled a square opening in the upper surface of the log, taking care not to split the surrounding bark, and then fitted the inkwell into the empty space. The following day he carried the inkwell stand to Chapin's office and set it upon Chapin's desk. "Let's see whether you can spill this," he said in triumph.

UNITED STATES PATENT OFFICE.

WALTER HUNT, OF NEW YORK, N. Y., ASSIGNOR TO AUGUSTUS T. ARROWSMITH.

INKSTAND.

Specification of Letters Patent No. 4,062, dated May 29, 1845.

To all whom it may concern:

Be it known that I, WALTER HUNT, of the city, county, and State of New York, have made a new and useful Improvement in the
5 Construction of Inkstands, and that the following is a full and accurate description of the same.

My said improvement consists in the introduction of a float upon the surface of, or
10 submerged in the ink, which float, I make of cork, see Figure 2, letter A, in the annexed drawings, which figure exhibits a cut vertical section of my ink-stand made in two parts, viz., the glass cup, or reservoir B, and
15 the metallic cap C, in which cap, or top, are the ordinary pen sockets D, D, and ink tube E, against the bottom of which tube, the float A is buoyed up by the ink F, contained in the glass cup B, thereby wholly closing
20 the bottom of said tube, and excluding the passage of the external atmosphere through the same.

When the stand is newly filled, the ink will flow to the line H, over the base of the
25 float, (which is in the form of a truncated cone, with a cylindrical base) in which base, a considerable portion of the ink would be exposed to the action of the atmosphere, through the ink-tube E, were it not excluded
30 by means of the float A, as before described. It will be seen that the said float will retain its position and operate as a stopper to the ink-tube, until the ink is reduced below the conical part of the float, to the upper line
35 of its base at I, at which elevation the float covers the whole surface of the ink, wholly protecting it from the atmosphere until it is exhausted by use. One other important advantage of this arrangement is, that at
40 each introduction of the pen, the float is forced down and operates as a loose plunger in removing the sediment, which is ordinarily deposited in the bottom of the stand, and forces it upward and remingles it with
45 the fluid, thereby preventing the separating and consequent deterioration of the ink; the point of the pen is also kept constantly clean, when in use, in consequence of it penetrating the upper surface of the cork, whenever it is
50 filled with ink. Although other materials may be substituted for cork, in forming said float, I have adopted this article as preferable in consequence of its lightness, cleanliness and durability. An elastic arch K, made of a fillet of sheet india rubber, may 55 be placed across the center of, and nearly spanning the upper surface of said float A, into which, the feet of said arch are inserted. (See Fig. 7.) By this arrangement the crown of said arch will, at all times, (except 60 when forced down by the pen) bear against and cover the bottom of the tube E, instead of the cork A, which will remain submerged, when the stand is full, and nearly so, until it is exhausted. 65

The body or reservoir of the stand, may be made of metal, best calculated to resist the action of the ink, or coated with cement for that purpose, but I consider glass preferable in every respect, which may be made in 70 the form of a plain cylindrical cup in the inside, with such external form as fancy may suggest, see Fig. 1, which presents a profile view of a form which I shall adopt for one style of stand, which is here exhibit- 75 ed entire in its external form, with the metallic cap C, complete, which cap is cemented with shellac, caoutchouc or other proper luting, by means of a flange to the upper rim of the reservoir as shown in Fig. 2, as 80 before mentioned.

Fig. 3 is an elevated view of the float A. Fig. 4 gives a similar view of the ink-stand and the cap C. Fig. 5 also presents a top view of the glass reservoir B, and Fig. 6, 85 a vertical cut section of the same.

What I claim as new, and my own invention in the within above described ink stand, is—

The introduction of a float with a soft 90 yielding or elastic upper surface, and so formed as to operate at all times either as a stopper to the ink tube, or a floating cover to, and upon the surface of the ink in said stand, arranged substantially in the man- 95 ner, and for the purposes, herein above set forth and described.

New York, July 12th, 1844.

WALTER HUNT.

Witnesses:
C. NAGLE,
JACOB DE BOIS.

W. Hunt,

Inkstand.

No 4062   Patented May 29 1845.

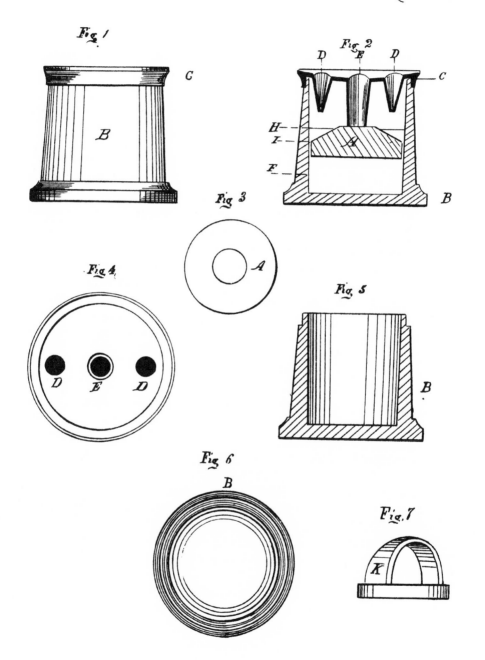

Fig 1

Fig 2

Fig 3

Fig 4

Fig 5

Fig 6

Fig 7

"But I don't spill ink on my own desk," Chapin jested. "You'd better keep it as protection, or did you make one like it for yourself?"

"No, I didn't. But I've an idea. I'm going to make an inkwell—a practical one—one that doesn't let the ink spill. It will always be covered, yet will open easily so you can dip your pen into it."

"I suppose you mean an inkwell with a lid?"

"No. Of course not. There's nothing new about a lid. My idea is to have an inkwell that will always be covered, yet always open to receive your pen."

"Sounds like a tall order."

"Actually, I think it's simple," Hunt answered. "I'm going to put a float with a soft yielding surface on top of an ordinary inkwell, and I'm going to—" Hunt paused. "No sense now in telling you what I'm going to do. I'll show it to you when it's finished."

A few days later Chapin met Augustus Arrowsmith, George Arrowsmith's brother, who was buying a newspaper headlining the story about the mob which broke into the jail at Carthage, Illinois, and murdered Joseph and Hiram Smith, the Mormon leaders. After discussing the happenings of the moment, such as Henry Clay's opposition to the annexation of Texas, and the July 3, 1844, peace treaty with China that opened that territory to trade with the United States, the conversation drifted to discussion of mutual acquaintances.

"I haven't seen Hunt lately," Arrowsmith remarked. "What's he doing now?"

"I'm not sure, but he's working on something. He told me about it but I don't know whether he's really serious or whether he is ribbing me," Chapin replied.

"What is it?"

"He's got some kind of an inkwell that won't tip or spill or leak or something or the other."

"Well, at least it's something that won't cost a fortune to manufacture like his stove or the sewing machine. I'll drop in and see him, and if it's any good, maybe I'll buy it. And if Hunt is as broke as he usually is, I guess he'll be glad to get some money and will sell it for a song."

A few days later, true to his word, Augustus Arrowsmith visited Hunt at his shop. He asked, "Where is that inkwell you were working on?"

"Oh, that?" Hunt answered casually. "It's around here somewhere. I've finished it. I'm working on a couple of other things now."

"Let's see it."

"It's up there somewhere on the shelf."

"Let me see it."

Hunt walked over to the closet, reached behind some tools and supplies on the shelf, and handed it to Arrowsmith.

Arrowsmith examined it. The mouth of the inkwell was closed by a floating cork plunger, but when the plunger was pressed down by the insertion of a pen, a limited supply of ink floated over the surface of the plunger and wet the pen. When the pen was withdrawn, a spring floated the plunger upwards to the top of the inkwell, closing the opening so that the ink would not evaporate, nor spill if the inkwell was upset.

"Looks good," Augustus commented. "Have you patented it?"

"No."

"Why not?"

"The application costs thirty dollars."

"That's not much."

"No, not if you have the money, but I haven't the money and furthermore I haven't got either the time or the money now to start making them."

"I'll buy it from you," Augustus said, "if you'll draw up the patent papers."

"Come back on Friday and we'll close the deal."

On Friday, July 12, 1844, Arrowsmith came to Hunt's shop with Jacob de Bois and Cornelius Nagle, a lawyer. Hunt had prepared the patent application making the claim on "the introduction of a float with a soft yielding or elastic upper surface, and so formed as to operate at all times either as a stopper to the ink tube, or a floating cover to, and upon the surface of the ink in said stand."

An assignment was made to Augustus Arrowsmith "for and in consideration of one dollar" (not of course the actual amount).

Arrowsmith waited until November 26, 1844, before he forwarded the application to the Patent Office as he was busy with other interests and with his plans to manufacture and market the inkwell.

On May 26, 1845, Arrowsmith finally filed Hunt's assignment at the Patent Office, and three days later, Hunt was awarded the patent, which bore U.S. Patent No. 4,062.

"I've made quite a few of those inkwells," Arrowsmith told Hunt a few days later. "They're the best things on the market. They can't be beaten!"

"Why not?" Hunt inquired.

Arrowsmith was startled. It took him a few seconds to reply. "They can't be beaten because they're the best on the market."

"Well, here's an improvement, a better type of inkwell," Hunt said, pointing to the rough model on his desk. "It has a flat top containing an aperture covered by a clapper which is held in place by a spring. The pen will push the cover lid down, or cover at an angle so that the pen may be inserted and withdrawn easily. When the pen is withdrawn, the spring will force the top closed."

"In one way, it may not be as good," Arrowsmith drawled. "But, in another way it may be better. If you draw up the patent papers on the new inkwell, I'll buy it. I'm buying it of course to protect myself. In other words, to kill any competition."

On June 21, 1845, only 23 days after the grant of the first inkwell patent,

UNITED STATES PATENT OFFICE.

WALTER HUNT, OF NEW YORK, N. Y., ASSIGNOR TO AUGS. T. ARROWSMITH.

INKSTAND.

Specification of Letters Patent No. 4,221, dated October 7, 1845.

To all whom it may concern:

Be it known that I, WALTER HUNT, of the city, county, and State of New York, have made certain Improvements in the Con-
5 struction of Inkstands, which I term the "Inclined-Valve Inkstand"; and I do hereby declare that the following is a full and accurate description of my said improvement.
10 The nature of my invention consists in the application of an inclined valve or clapper A. See the vertical cut section in the annexed drawings, Figure 1. Said clapper is made of plate glass, (or other material
15 with a hard smooth surface) with a bracket hinge B, made of copper or silver plate, cemented upon its under surface. Said bracket projects partially beyond one of its sides, and is formed into a thimble C from
20 which the plate is bent back to, and is clamped over the edge of the upper surface of said clapper, as shown at D. Through the said thimble C, is inserted a corresponding wire E, with its ends project-
25 ing say ⅜ of an inch. These ends are let up into gaps cut into two studs F, F, which are cast entire with the inkstand top G. Before being secured in this position, there are two coiled silver wire springs H, H,
30 placed on each end of said hinge wire E: said springs being wound right and left, the two ends of the wire nearest the bracket are projected forward, and bear upon the under surface of said bracket about the cen-
35 ter of said clapper A, at I, I, while the outer back ends of said springs project back about ¼ of an inch, and bear upward upon the under surface of the top G at J, J. The ends of said hinge wire being now let up into the
40 gaps aforesaid, are there secured by closing the chaps of said studs together, by means of pinchers or otherwise. By means of said coiled springs it will be seen that the valve A, is forced upward against the bottom of
45 the ink-tube K, which is in the form of a funnel or cone, cut at an angle of 45° which cut section forms a seat for the said clapper, it being closely fitted upon the same, as shown in said Fig. 1. (See letters of refer-
50 ence, which designate similar parts in all the drawings.)

Fig. 2 exhibits a horizontal, bottom view of said inkstand top G, with the valve or clapper A, bracket B, thimble C, hinge wire E, studs F, F, coiled springs H, H, the
55 bearing ends of the same I, I, and back ends of the same J, J.

Fig. 3 gives a top horizontal view of said top G, and of the ink tube K, a partial view of the clapper A, and the plug tube L,
60 into which is fitted a cork or other stopper to be removed for cleansing the inkstand, &c.

Fig. 4 shows an elevated view of the inkstand, with the top G, and reservoir M, as ready for use.
65 The objects gained by the above arrangement are, the exclusion of the atmosphere from the ink, and security from spilling the same in the upsetting of the inkstand, and also of cleaning the point of the pen on
70 the edge of the valve, which is an inevitable result at each time the pen is inserted or withdrawn in using.

What I claim as my invention in the above described improvement, and desire to secure
75 by Letters Patent, is—

The application of an inclined valve or clapper A, having a surface of glass or other hard, smooth material, in combination with said inclined valve; and ink tube which
80 valve is forced upward by means of springs or otherwise upon the bottom of the ink tube K, and arranged substantially in the manner and for the purposes above set forth and described.

Dated New York, Sep., 1845.

WALTER HUNT.

Witnesses:
    T. JAMES GLOVER,
    A. T. ARROWSMITH.

W. HUNT, Ass'or to

A. T. Arrowsmith,

Inkstand.

No 4221.   Patented Oct. 7. 1845.

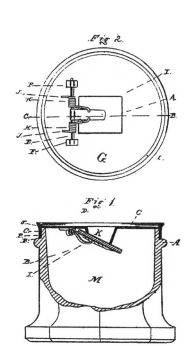

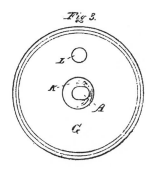

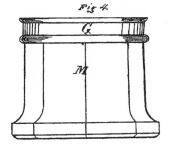

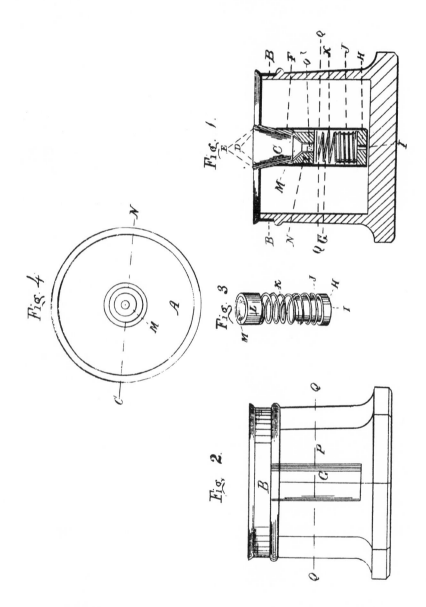

W. Hunt,

Inkstand.

No 4306.

Patented Dec. 11. 1845.

Fig. 1.

Fig. 4.

Fig. 3.

Fig. 2.

UNITED STATES PATENT OFFICE.

WALTER HUNT, OF NEW YORK, N. Y., ASSIGNOR TO GEORGE ARROWSMITH.

INKSTAND.

Specification of Letters Patent No. 4,306, dated December 11, 1845.

To all whom it may concern:

Be it known, that I, WALTER HUNT, of the city, county, and State of New York, have invented a new Improvement in the
5 Construction of Filtering-Tubes to be Used and Connected with the Tops of Ordinary Inkstands, and that the following is a faithful description of the same.

Figure 1, in the annexed drawing, gives
10 an entire vertical cut section view of said top, ink-tube, and its appurtenances, as embraced in my plan with letters of reference to every material part thereof, as follows.

The metal top, or cover of the ink-stand
15 A, which is made with a circular flange B, to fit over the top rim of the ink reservoir in the usual manner.

The ink-tube C, which is funnel shaped, is screwed into said top at D, up against a
20 shoulder or projecting collar E, which is elevated above said top sufficiently to be controlled by the thumb and finger, as required. Said ink-tube projects down below said top about one-half of one inch,
25 upon which projection is fitted by a ferrule joint at F, the filter-tube G. In said filter-tube is contained at the bottom, a cork or stopper H with a small aperture I through it for the admission of the ink. Above said
30 stopper is inserted a piece of soft sponge or spongy substance J, but similar in form to a common cork, and which fills the caliber of said filter-tube about one-fourth of its length. Upon the top of said sponge, or
35 upon the said bottom H, rests a spiral spring K, (which should be made of silver or other material not affected by the ink) and of sufficient length when expanded, to extend from the bottom H, up to the ink-tube
40 C, and corresponding in its diameter across the coils with the inside of the filter-tube. Upon the top of said spring K, is fitted a plunger L, (made of cork or otherwise) and which can be moved up and down freely
45 in said filter tube. The upper surface of said plunger is covered with a conical, or conical shaped cop M, firmly secured by cement, (or otherwise) upon the same. Said cop has a small opening N in its center
50 (see Fig. 4, top view) precisely similar to the common funnel, with the tube removed, which is only large enough to admit the nib of the pen in using. Concentric with said opening, is one of similar diameter through
55 said plunger, in which is inserted a small

piece of sponge as shown at O, which prevents a sudden jet of the ink when the pen is introduced, and also allows the ink to subside gently, when the pen is withdrawn, while at the same time it excludes the at- 60 mosphere from the ink in the filter-tube below.

Fig. 2, exhibits an elevated view of the ink-stand entire, with the filter-tube G, as seen through the glass stand or reservoir P. 65

Fig. 3, gives an elevated perspective view of the contents of the filter-tube G, viz: the bottom H, with the aperture I; the coiled spring K, the sponge J, the funnel-top M, and the plunger L.
70

The operation, mode of using, and advantages of the above described arrangement are obvious. Suppose the stand to be filled with ink as usual, say to the line Q Fig. 2, it would find a similar level through 75 the orifice I, in the filter-tube bottom, or if it was far below said line, provided it reach the bottom of the sponge J, said sponge would continue saturated to its upper extremity; consequently when the spring is 80 forced down by the pen pressing upon the funnel M, (the orifice I being very small) the ink would be forced up around, and through the orifice in the plunger L, and flow into the funnel above, and around the point of 85 the pen, which being filled and withdrawn, would allow the plunger, &c., to rise with the spring, pressing the funnel against the bottom of the ink-tube, and the ink to recede below as before described. The advantages 90 of this plan, in the exclusion of the atmosphere and security in upsetting. &c., are equal to, if not greater than in other plans previously invented by myself, and others. The facility of cleaning both the stand and 95 the contents of the filter-tube, by unscrewing the ink-tube, I think, renders the use and management of this plan simple and effective.

My claims in the above described inven- 100 tion, are confined to the filter-tube in combination with the funnel, plunger, spring, sponge, and perforated bottom, arranged substantially in the manner, and for the purposes, hereinabove described.

New York Sept. 12th, 1845.

WALTER HUNT.

Witnesses:
T. JAMES GLOVER,
JNO. R. CHAPIN.

Hunt had completed his specifications for his second inkwell. Thomas James Glover, a lawyer and friend of Hunt, and Augustus T. Arrowsmith witnessed the application.

An assignment was made to Arrowsmith, who paid half the patent application fee. On July 10, 1845, he forwarded the balance of fifteen dollars to the Patent Office. In the patent application, Hunt stated

the objects gained by the above arrangements are, the exclusion of the atmosphere from the ink, and security from spilling the same in the upsetting of the ink stand, and also of cleaning the point of the pen on the edge of the valve, which is an inevitable result at each time the pen is inserted or withdrawn, in using.

The application did not completely conform to Patent Office requirements and the patent was returned for correction. On September 26, 1845, Arrowsmith wrote the Patent Office:

I herewith transmit you my papers returned by you for amendments in lieu of which I now make application for a patent, hoping Mr. Hunt's letter which accompanies the papers will explain the full merit of his claim to the inclined valve.

The letter and documents proved satisfactory. On October 7, 1845, U.S. Patent No. 4,221 was granted to Walter Hunt who assigned it to Augustus T. Arrowsmith.

Even before the granting of this patent, Hunt had conceived yet a newer type of inkwell.

The third inkwell differed in the center shaft and floater. It consisted of a flat top with a cylindrical tube into which was placed a spring-like attachment which pressed against the cover from the base, keeping the inkwell closed unless pressure was applied against it. Operating on the principle of physics that water seeks its own level, the amount of ink in the center tube, it was demonstrated, would be equal to the amount held in the side wall reservoir. When the spring of the cylindrical tube center was depressed, the orifice being very small, the ink would be forced up around it, and through the orifice into the plunger to rise with the spring.

He built a model and then drew up a patent application. On September 12, 1845, it was witnessed by Jno. R. Chapin, who was himself a designer, and Thomas James Glover, a lawyer and commissioner of deeds.

On December 11, 1845, Hunt was granted U.S. Patent No. 4,306 and his claim was "confined to the filter-tube, in combination with the funnel, plunger, spring, sponge and perforated bottom."

Hunt had now put three new inkwells on the market. One might imagine that his thoughts would have been on ways to improve their sales or create still better models, but Hunt's mind conceived a new plan. His new interest was to make inkwells unnecessary.

Chapter 17

"Another new invention, Mr. Hunt?" James Glover inquired, as he and Jonathan Chapin were visiting.

"Yes, a couple of months ago, I had an idea and I mentioned it to the Alexanders. You know them. I. and G. C. Alexander. They liked it so much they made me file a caveat with the Patent Office. Here is the receipt for the thirty dollar fee."

Glover looked at it. It bore the date April 29, 1845, with the caveat April 28. "It doesn't say what it's for, Mr. Hunt."

"That's just a receipt," Chapin explained. He turned to Hunt. "Why don't you tell us something about it, or is it a great secret?"

"It's a combination inkwell and pen. When you write, it feeds ink to the pen point."

"Must be a clumsy thing," Chapin remarked.

"No. It's not much larger than a pencil, but it's a trifle wider at the holding end."

"What do you mean when you say it feeds ink?" Glover asked.

"It has a well or reservoir that holds ink. It's what I call a reservoir pen."

"But how does it feed ink? And why does it?" Chapin asked.

"Here is one of the pens." Hunt demonstrated: "You press the knob here, and when you start to write, ink comes out like a fountain from the reservoir. That's it! I'll call it a fountain pen."

The pen consisted of a barrel-shaped reservoir gradually tapering into a thin shaft. One extremity was a slip loop to hold a pen. The loop was slid forward, so that the pen extended from the holder when the pen was in use. When the pen was not in use, the loop was pushed in the opposite direction, and the pen point retracted. A ridge on the extremity protected the point when it was not in use. When the pen point was extended, ready to be used, the plunger at the top of the pen was drawn back to release ink to be supplied to the point.

"Does it really work?" Glover asked.

138

"Try it and see for yourself," Hunt said. "Might as well put it to a practical use right away. Why don't you both use it when you sign my patent application?"

Hunt picked up the completed patent application and signed his name and the date, September 12, 1845. Then Glover and Chapin, who served as witnesses to his signature, took the pen and recorded their names.

"Gone are the days of the old quill," Chapin sighed.

Glover stood erect and dramatically recited:

Nature's noblest gift, my greygoose quill!
Slave of my thoughts, obedient to my will,
Torn from thy parent bird to form a pen,
That mighty instrument of little men!

"Now, what is that?" Chapin asked.

"That's Lord Byron."

"I didn't think that law and poetry mixed," Hunt added.

There was a defect in the oath and the patent application of September 12, 1845, was returned to Hunt for corrections. A new affidavit was signed and mailed on October 18, 1845, in the presence of Glover.

The application was again returned to Hunt for him to make a further correction in the text. Instead of completing it at once, Hunt put it aside. Other problems required his priority.

On January 29, 1846, the family gathered for supper to celebrate the nineteenth birthday of George Washington Hunt. Two days before, he had been advanced to the position of draftsman in the shop at 82 Nassau Street. Everyone was happy.

After the table had been cleared and the dishes washed, the conversation drifted to the tense situation with Mexico. War with Mexico actually existed, although no formal declaration had been made. Congress had appropriated the money for troops to assure the safety of those living near the border. Rumors of conflicts and atrocities had inflamed the citizens to fever heat.

"We Americans should do something," George Washington Hunt declaimed, "And I'm going to do my part. I'm going to enlist in the Army."

Polly Hunt shook with dismay. Her eyes flashed and her cheeks flushed.

"I do not want a son of mine to be a soldier!" she cried. "What has happened to you? Have you forgotten the Sermon on the Mount? 'Ye have heard that it hath been said "Thou shalt love thy neighbors and hate thy enemy." But I say unto you, "Love your enemies." Ye have heard that it hath been said "an eye for an eye and a tooth for a tooth"; but I say unto you, that ye resist not evil'."

"But this is a patriotic duty," George protested.

"Quakers," Walter said calmly, "have always declared against wars. We are not fighters!"

UNITED STATES PATENT OFFICE.

WALTER HUNT, OF NEW YORK, N. Y.

FOUNTAIN-PEN.

Specification of Letters Patent No. 4,927, dated January 13, 1847.

To all whom it may concern:

Be it known that I, WALTER HUNT, of the city, county, and State of New York, have made a new and useful Improvement in a 5 Fountain-Pen, and that the following is a full and accurate description of the same.

The objects aimed at by me in the construction of said pen, is the combination of all in one of inkstand, pen, shaft, and pen 10 holder, so arranged as to be convenient for the pocket, and adapted to the common steel pen, to be changed at pleasure, to be supplied from the combined fountain or from the common inkstand. Its construction is 15 as follows. See the longitudinal cut section Figure 1 in the annexed drawings—A, is the shaft, which is a small tube about $2\frac{1}{2}$ inches long and $\frac{1}{4}$ inch in diameter. B, the fountain or reservoir for the ink, which is 20 a bulb or an enlarged tube forming the upper portion of said shaft, say $1\frac{1}{4}$ inch long and $\frac{1}{2}$ inch in diameter, more or less. C is the stuffing box fitted into the top of said reservoir by a screw joint. D, is a nut screwed 25 upon the upper end of said small wire piston-rod E, which passes through the packing F, made of india-rubber fitted into the stuffing-box aforesaid. Upon the bottom end of said piston-rod, on which a screw is 30 cut, is fitted a plunger G, made also of india rubber punched out for the purpose: (Leather saturated with india rubber paste, answers the purpose well.) The caliber of the bottom end of the shaft A, is lessened 35 for about $\frac{4}{8}$ of an inch in length, say to about $\frac{3}{16}$ in diameter, and forms what I term "The filling tube" H, into which tube, the plunger G, is fitted as shown in Fig. 1. In the bottom end of said filling 40 tube, is inserted a sponge or spongy stopper I, say $\frac{3}{8}$ of an inch long, and from one side of said tube; at the extreme bottom end, is a small downward inclined opening K, from the sponge, to the hollow of the pen 45 L, which pen is inserted, (through a crescent shape opening M, in the bead, or band which surrounds the extreme bottom end of the shaft, an end view of which is given in Fig. 5,) into the penholder N. See Figs. 3 50 and 4 and a separate end view the same, in Fig. 6.

In Figs. 1, 2 and 3, the pen holder and pen is slided down in the position for filling and writing. In Fig. 4 the holder is drawn back against the stop P, and the point of 55 the pen is placed underneath, and shielded by, the band O, before mentioned, as it is carried in the pocket.

The manner of filling and using, is as follows: when the pen is to be filled, the plun- 60 ger is drawn back by the thumb and finger, hold of the nut D, which allows the ink to fall from the reservoir B, into the filling tube H. The plunger is then suddenly returned, which forces the ink in said tube 65 into the barrel of the pen, through the aperture K, said plunger forming a perfect stopper in said tube which prevents the escape of the ink until another supply for the pen is required. 70

Felting, or woolen cloth, will probably answer in the room of sponge, for the purpose of the stopper, as its office is to check the flow of the ink through the aperture K, except under the pressure of the piston as 75 before stated. I have given a fair trial to a fountain pen on this plan, and have found it to work well, and free from the difficulties that have rendered all other plans that have come to my knowledge, utterly useless. It 80 is well adapted to the steel pens now in common use. It never dries up, nor leaks, and is certain to throw out the requisite quantity of ink, as long as there is a pen-full in the fountain. The capacity of the filling-tube 85 being made to hold a due quantity, no more can be injected into the pen at one action of the piston.

What I claim, as my own invention and desire to secure by Letters Patent of the 90 United States, in the above described "fountain pen," is—

The filling tube of a graduated capacity for filling the pin, combined with the fountain pen, as above set forth and specified, or 95 arranged in any manner which is substantially the same.

New York Septr. 12th 1845.

WALTER HUNT.

Witnesses:
T. JAMES GLOVER,
JNO. R. CHAPIN.

W. Hunt,

Fountain Pen.

№ 4927

Patented. Jan 13 1847

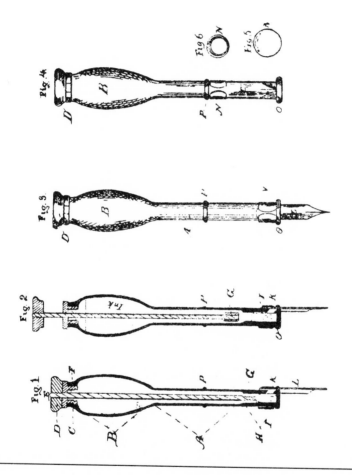

"But that is not the American way," George argued.

"I said we are not fighters, but I did not say we won't help the government. Our family has always been proud of our loyalty, but not at fighting."

"When the Almighty took little Walter away five years ago," Polly sobbed, "that was an act of God. It was beyond our control. But to throw your life away in the cause of snuffing out other lives is of no use to anyone."

"War has not been declared yet," Walter argued. "The government has not made any call for men. George, why go out of your way looking for a fight? Maybe everything will be settled peacefully by the commissioners and you won't have to go." Walter explained to George that there was more to war than the beating of drums and the blowing of trumpets, the marching of military bands and the cheers of the multitude.

"I won't enlist now," George promised, "but that doesn't mean I won't later." He had begun courting a young woman named Sarah Torboss.

The conversation terminated peacefully, but Polly was worried nevertheless. Polly Anne, Caroline and Frances Augusta comforted her. Finally, she smiled and became her cheerful self again.

Not three months later the ticklish international situation with Mexico reached an abrupt climax. A Captain Thornton, in charge of a reconnoitering party on the Texas side of the Rio Grande, was ambushed on April 25, 1846. This was the spark that set off the smoldering conflict. The populace flared and on May 11, President James Knox Polk sent his war message to Congress. "The Mexican Government," he said, "at last invaded our territory, and shed the blood of our fellow citizens on our soil."

Within two days, Congress declared that "by the act of the Republic of Mexico, a state of war exists between that government and the United States."

But the sentiment for war in the nation was not unanimous. Massachusetts, Vermont, New York, Michigan and other states proclaimed their utter and eternal opposition in plain unvarnished words. Popular opinion was divided and the war issue degenerated into a political conflict rather than a national problem. Incendiary orators, glory-seeking youths and medal-bedecked dragoons incited patriotic passions. Rabid fireside patriots, sensational newspapers, profiteers and opportunists fanned the embers while martial music echoed throughout the music halls.

The expansionists advocated war because in their opinion it was the quickest way to obtain their objective. The conservatives decried the needless sacrifice of lives to win territory. The Southerners and the Democrats favored annexation of Texas as it meant an increase in the number of slave states, and a firmer balance of power between slave and free states.

War with Mexico was the principal topic of conversation in the Hunt household as it was everywhere. Constant pressure from his parents and others influenced George, whose desire to enlist changed from rabid to passive.

"I am against war!" Walter Hunt declared to a few friends who were visiting him.

"That's because you are a Republican," Chapin said.

"If you lived in the South, you would have different views," [George] Arrowsmith argued.

"That proves that this is not a national conflict," Hunt insisted. "Furthermore,

I have studied the situation carefully and I have come to the conclusion that Christians do not fight with sword and arquebus but with suffering and the cross."

"Those views are out of date, Mr. Hunt," Arrowsmith said. "A war will settle matters once and for all. We can use the Mexican territory and civilize those savages. A good war will help business."

"Wars have no benefits," Hunt protested vehemently. "Nothing can compensate for the loss of human life. The increased taxation, either direct or indirect, is intolerable. Moral depravity follows war, win, lose or draw."

"You're still too much of a Quaker and pacifist to tolerate war," Arrowsmith added angrily.

"Wars lower the standard of honesty. Those who plunder cannot maintain an honest equilibrium. And the bondage of one man to another can never be justified."

"I guess we agree with you in principle at least," Arrowsmith acquiesced. "None of us really want war, provided the same results can be accomplished by peace."

They discussed the pros and cons of war at length, Chapin and Arrowsmith loudly propounding their views. The argument seemed endless. The women excused themselves, leaving the men embroiled.

"I've listened to both of you a long time," Hunt said. "You are my best friends and you both know my views against war. Come to my shop tomorrow morning and I'm certain that you'll both be surprised."

As they departed, George questioned his father. "Why do you want them to come to your shop tomorrow?"

Walter ignored the question. After a slight pause, he said, "George, do you still want to do something for the government?"

"You mean you'll let me enlist?" he inquired eagerly.

"No." Hunt replied curtly. "But, if you want to do something that will help this country, something that is dangerous, something which may have no glory, then be ready to go with me early tomorrow morning. But don't say anything to anybody."

"I won't say a word," George pledged.

"I've got some work to do now," said his father. "See you at breakfast."

George could hardly sleep. He tossed and fidgeted all night. At four o'clock, he awoke and observed the flickering of the lamp in the adjoining room. Walter Hunt was evidently still working. At seven o'clock, George dressed and entered his father's room.

"I'm ready to go to the shop with you," George said, "but I suppose you're too tired and, furthermore, it's raining."

"Let's eat breakfast, and then we'll go."

Chapter 18

Despite the light rain, Walter Hunt and his son George left the house. They walked briskly for several blocks and joined the crowds reading the bulletins pasted outside the entrance to the newspaper office. There was a subdued uneasiness in the crowd. The cheers that had previously hailed the news of American victories were not as loud as they had been and the enthusiasm of the news-seekers was not as keen. Anxious relatives stood in silence. They did not cheer. They scanned the casualty lists. Opposition to the war, a sentiment that had been regarded before as treasonable, was now outspoken. A no-war attitude prevailed.

"It is needless slaughter to sacrifice our men."

"The trouble with this war is not that the Americans are inferior fighters or that the Mexicans are better fighters, but that our guns are outmoded. Flintlocks have outlived their usefulness."

"Our soldiers haven't a chance against the Mexican army."

"If our Army had a better gun, the war would have ended in no time."

Small groups vociferously expressed their sentiments. Little American patriotism was evident. Hunt turned to George and said, "What's your opinion?"

"There seems to be much dissension."

"No, George, that's not what I mean. What else?"

"The enemy have better guns."

"Right!" Hunt thundered. "And that is just what I am going to correct."

"Correct? How?"

"I'm building a better gun."

"But," George protested, "a gun is a murderous weapon. You know how queer mother is about certain things. Remember how both you and she objected when I wanted to join the army."

Hunt explained. "We Quakers object to war. But I believe that if we had a better gun, the war may end sooner. And the sooner it ends, the less the casualties and fewer deaths."

"But, you don't know anything about guns."

"That's where you're wrong, George," Hunt confided. "I've been working on one for some time. Now let me tell you something about guns. Guns are of two kinds. They are either rifles or muskets. The army uses muskets because they can attach bayonets on them. The muskets are quickly and loosely loaded with round balls. This is why they are better than rifles. However, their faults exceed their benefits. They use a lot of black powder which makes a lot of smoke. This is very bad because it reveals the location of the soldier who fired the gun. The smoke also mars his vision for the next shot. And, furthermore, in wet weather, muskets are practically useless."

"I know that the rifle is better than the musket," George stated.

Hunt paid no attention to the interruption and continued. "Rifles are far more accurate, but they take more time to load and in war this is very important. Another thing that is bad about rifles is that you can't attach a bayonet to them. But I have studied the matter and have gone into everything, and luckily I have come up with a new idea."

"What?"

"It's so revolutionary and so superior to anything in use that I feel like I must be dreaming. You'll see what I have been doing when we get to my shop."

"I'm sure it will be a success if you're working on it," George said with filial pride.

They walked in silence the rest of the way to Hunt's shop at 42 Gold Street. Hunt selected a key from his key ring and unlocked the door. He used another key and opened a padlock inserted between two iron eyes. He handed both keys to George and said, "From now on, you're in on the secret and you can keep this extra set of keys."

Hunt crossed the room to the wooden built-in wall closet and unbolted the latch. He reached inside, pulled out an unpolished gun and handed it to George.

"Here it is," he said proudly. "It's a working model."

George looked at it very carefully for several moments, then asked, "What is this thing here?"

"This gun," Hunt explained, "differs from others, because—"

There was a knocking at the front door. It grew louder.

"Who is it?" Hunt called.

"It's me! George."

"Who?" Hunt again asked.

"Me! George!"

"George who?"

"Arrowsmith! George Arrowsmith."

Hunt opened the door, which was bolted from the inside, and Arrowsmith entered the shop.

"What's the matter with you?" Arrowsmith scolded. "Why do you always keep your shop locked? I knew you were inside because I saw you go in. And since when do I have to announce myself as if I was calling on the president of a bank?"

"Put that segar away," Hunt yelled excitedly.

"What's the matter with it?" Arrowsmith asked.

Hunt pulled it out of Arrowsmith's hand and threw it into the brass cuspidor. "What do you want to do? Blow us all into kingdom come?"

"What's the matter with you?" Arrowsmith bellowed. "Are you crazy?"

Hunt pointed to the glass jars on the shelf. They were labeled saltpetre, sulphur, gunpowder, alcohol, flints, etc. Then he pointed to his workbench. On it were gun stocks, gun barrels, triggers, ramrods, powder horns and assorted tools.

"What are you doing? Going hunting?" Arrowsmith looked around. "Why, this place looks like an arsenal! What are you going to do? Start a war of your own?"

"I know you can keep a secret and so I'll tell you. But it's a secret. I'm working on a new type of gun using a new kind of bullet."

"On a gun?" Arrowsmith laughed. "Why, you old hypocrite. And you a pacifist, a Quaker?"

"Yes, a gun," Hunt replied, ignoring the comment.

"Of all things, what do you know about a gun?"

"You'll see, but it's an expensive idea. Alcohol costs fifty cents a pound. Commercial gun-cotton a dollar an ounce, while everything else seems more expensive than gold. Have you any idea what they're asking for sulphur, potassium nitrate, and even charcoal?"

"Are you really working on a gun?" said Arrowsmith in surprise. He picked up a cylindrical object and examined it. "What's this?"

"It's a bullet." Walter explained.

"If I didn't know you, Hunt, I'd think you were crazy, but I'll tell you what I'll do. I've got faith in you and if it's money you need for anything, let me know."

Arrowsmith left and Hunt quickly locked and barricaded the door after him.

George spent the next several weeks following the instructions given him. Both labored far into the night. By the end of [August], their task was completed. Arrowsmith was informed and he called at the shop to inspect the completed gun.

"What kind of gun is it?" he inquired.

"A volition repeater," Hunt replied.

"A what?"

"A volition repeater."

"I don't know what you're talking about. Let me see it." Arrowsmith picked up the gun which Hunt had handed him and looked at it in bewilderment.

"It looks different from the guns I've seen but I don't understand it."

"This gun," Hunt beamed, "will win our war with Mexico and put a quick end to the struggle."

"But what's so different about it?" Arrowsmith questioned.

"Why, there's all the difference in the world. The guns we now have fire only one shot at a time, then you have to stop to reload it, then you fire another shot, then you have to reload."

"I know that." Arrowsmith argued.

"Well, this gun will fire at least twelve shots in succession without reloading."

"Without reloading after each shot?"

"Without reloading!"

"It's hard to believe."

"Yes. And there's another thing. No two successive shots of any gun travel exactly the same distance, as every load has a different amount of powder. But, in my gun, all the shots will be equal because each shot takes the same amount of powder, all of which is measured in advance, and ready for immediate use whenever required. And another thing, there are no globs or pieces of cloth that adhere to the sides of the barrel to affect the next shot."

"Why this gun is phenomenal!" Arrowsmith exclaimed excitedly. "It is the most wonderful thing I've seen."

Hunt was happy.

"You should earn a thousand dollars as soon as the gun gets into production, if you can get someone to manufacture it."

"A thousand dollars," Hunt mused. "Why, I invented that gun without intending to make a penny from it. I thought I could help the United States and save the lives of thousands of our boys."

"But, you can still get paid for your work!"

"Life is funny. This gun I invented to help our country might turn out to bring me money."

"This time you have an invention for which there should be an immediate demand."

"I showed it to some army officers," said Hunt, "and they said it was the most wonderful gun they had ever seen, and that it would make me rich for the rest of my life."

"Of course, they have no idea of the expense of marketing and selling an invention," Arrowsmith countered. "First you will have to get someone to market it. I'll tell you what I'll do. I'll handle the invention for you and we can both make money from it. Have you made any plans for it?"

"The American Institute will hold their nineteenth annual fair month after next. I think I'll exhibit it there, along with my mincing machine."

The fair was held in October 1846 at Niblo's Garden. The American Institute

Fair accorded Hunt recognition. He received a silver medal for his invention of the mincing machine. At the same exhibit, Arrowsmith received a diploma from the exhibition committee for his display of Hunt's improved inkstands on which he had acquired the patent rights.

But Hunt did not exhibit his gun. Military officials had asked him as a patriotic gesture not to make his invention public until army authorities had the opportunity to pass upon its value.

As no immediate recognition had been accorded by the army, and because he was busy as usual with his various inventions, Hunt agreed with little persuasion to allow Arrowsmith to promote the gun. Arrowsmith forwarded the patent application with the thirty dollar fee on September 6, 1846. It covered twelve pages of closely written text and was witnessed by George C. Sickles, lawyer and commissioner of deeds, and Elisha Bloomer, a hatter, both of whom maintained offices at 79 Nassau Street.

Arrowsmith knew nothing about guns. He had no means to expedite the application in the Patent Office. He did not have any influence with politicians and governmental officials to promote recognition. He had no contracts with the military purchasing board. He did not realize that the army was actually too busy prosecuting a military action, especially one that was unsuccessful and lacked complete national support, to take an immediate interest. He had never encountered governmental "red tape." He knew none of the gun manufacturers and no one with sufficient capital to promote the manufacturing. He was not aware of the many issues thath could crop up to hamper prompt decisions.

Time slipped by and Arrowsmith's enthusiasm waned. The instantaneous success he anticipated did not materialize. Progress on the gun lagged and Hunt again felt the curse of being ahead of his time.

On January 2, 1847, Jonathan Chapin walked into Hunt's shop to wish him a happy New Year. As usual, Chapin sat on the desk even as Hunt motioned him to sit on the new chair which his family had given him for Christmas.

"I'm not so worried anymore," Chapin joked. "I'm not afraid the place will blow up anymore, and I'm not afraid to sit on the desk since your nonspillable inkwell."

Hunt smiled.

The conversation turned to the Mexican War. After the latest war news had been discussed and analyzed, Chapin inquired, "By the way, did you get your patent on the gun and cartridge?"

"No," said Hunt, "the application is still on file."

"I guess they think a pacifist like you shouldn't get a patent on a gun," Chapin joked, "you who always maintained that the pen is mightier than the sword." There was a brief pause. "Incidentally," Chapin continued, "did you ever get that patent on your reservoir pen?"

"Oh, you mean the fountain pen?"

"Did you get your patent?"

"The patent!" Hunt snapped his fingers. "The patent!" A bewildered expression crept across his face. He opened one of the doors in his desk and fumbled through the papers in the top drawer. He slammed it shut and opened the drawer below. "Oh," he said relieved.

Chapin observed the actions without any comment.

"It slipped my mind," Hunt exclaimed. "The patent application was returned to me for amendment, and where is it? In a drawer with a lot of old papers. I forgot all about it. I'm glad you reminded me. I'll make the necessary changes in a day or two."

On January 7, 1847, Hunt used his fountain pen and wrote to the Commissioner of Patents.

Hon. Edmund Burke,
Commissioner of Patents,
Dear Sir;
I herewith forward my specifications for my fountain pen which has been twice returned to me for amendments, first, in the claim, and second, in the oath, and respectfully request that my patent will be granted in its turn, said amendments having been made as directed by the office.
WALTER HUNT
P.S. Application for the above was made about the first of May 1845, and has been overlooked among the mass of applications which I now have pending at the office.

Hunt sealed the letter and gave it to his son George to take to the post office. The postmaster marked "Paid" on the upper right corner with his pen (it would be another six months before adhesive stamps were available).

Several hours later, John Rogers walked into Hunt's shop. "Mr. Chapin told me about your fountain pen," he said. "May I see it?"

Hunt showed him the pen and Rogers scribbled his name and drew a few wavy lines on a sheet of white paper.

"Did you get your patent on it?" Rogers asked.

Hunt explained that the patent had not yet been granted. "Here is what I wrote in the application for the patent." He read,

I have given a fair trial to a fountain pen on this plan, and have found it to work well, and free from the difficulties that have rendered all other plans that have come to my knowledge, utterly useless. It is well adapted to the steel pens now in common use. It never dries up, nor leaks, and is certain to throw out the requisite quantity of ink, as long as there is a penfull in the fountain. The capacity of the filling-tube being made to hold a due quantity, no more can be ejected into the pen at one action of the piston.

"Everything you've stated is correct, "Rogers agreed. "I'd like to acquire the rights to the pen if it is for sale."

Four days later, on January 11, 1847, Hunt assigned the rights to the fountain pen to Rogers. No delay was experienced in the granting of the patent. Two days later, on January 13, 1847, Hunt's application was accepted by the Patent Office and he was granted U.S. Patent No. 4,927 [see pages 140–141].

News that the patent had been granted appeared in the technical magazines devoted to patents. Visitors and friends came to Hunt's office to wish him well.

"Congratulations," Chapin said admiringly. "Another patent. Another invention finished. Now what are you going to tackle, Mr. Hunt?"

Chapter 19

Hunt had divided his time on his various inventions. Although he felt perfectly satisfied, the gun was of little value without bullets. His problem was to select which of his many cartridges was the most suitable for use, most practical, and the easiest and cheapest to manufacture in commercial quantities.

"I don't care what they say," George Arrowsmith argued. "Walter, now is the time to perfect your cartridge. Even though I haven't done anything with the gun, the future still looks bright. The Army needs guns. They need them badly. Perhaps at this very moment General Santa Anna is attacking Zachary Taylor. And thousands of Americans may be killed. They say the Mexican army is four times larger than ours. You'll have to drop your other work if you want to get the gun in time."

Hunt did not accept the advice graciously. "I'm working day and night. To listen to you, one would think that I started this war. I hardly know what my bed looks like anymore. No matter how good my gun may be, we've got to have the right kind of ammunition for it. I know it and I'm working on that too."

"I don't know why it is taking so long. You don't have to do it. You can get any of the shot towers to make bullets," Arrowsmith argued.

"I've tried to tell you: The spherical ball can be used only in muzzle-loading guns. They will not operate in a breech-loader."

"They must be made to operate," Arrowsmith insisted.

The discussion stopped when George Washington Hunt excitedly burst into the shop. "News just came over the telegraph. It's on the bulletin boards. I copied it down. It says the Mexicans retreated, leaving over two thousand dead. The American loss was two hundred and sixty-seven killed, four hundred and fifty-six injured, and twenty-three missing."

"Thank God for General Taylor," Hunt murmured.

"But we still need guns," Arrowsmith added.

Other favorable war reports buoyed the nation. A month later, General

Winfield Scott captured the impregnable fortress at Vera Cruz. On April 18, he captured Cerro Gordo, Jaiapa on the 19th and Perote on the 22nd.

"If you don't hurry," Arrowsmith warned Hunt, "the war will be over."

"I hope so," Hunt snapped. "I hope they never have to use my gun. I hope no one will have to use it to kill people."

Toward the end of May 1847, Hunt worked on his patent application. In it, he said:

> it will be readily perceived that this plan of a combined ball and cartridge is well adapted to fire-arms made to be charged at the breech, with its head or disc pressed firmly against the breech-plug, and its rim or flange forced outward against the inner periphery of the calibre of the barrel, forming an airtight stopper, which effectually prevents all backward escape of the powder, notwithstanding the breech-plug may be loosely fitted in the breech of the barrel behind the charge, which must necessarily be the case in all reciprocating breech-pins in order to prevent their binding from the heat, deposits, etc., in rapid firing. It is always obvious that in guns made with piston breech-pins the cap would be carried out forward of each succeeding ball, operating as an effectual wiper to the barrel at each discharge of the piece.

He took the patent application to Edmund Elmendorf, Jr., a lawyer at 14½ Pine Street who witnessed it and also acted as commissioner of deeds. Charles E. Grim, an attorney of 15 Nassau Street, served as the second witness.

When Hunt returned to his shop, he found Arrowsmith waiting for him.

"Everything's perfect," Hunt said jubilantly. "I've finally drawn up the patent application and am making claim on the 'construction of a ball for firearms, with a cavity to contain the charge of powder for propelling the ball, in which cavity the powder is secured by means of a cap enclosing the back end of the same'."

"In other words," Arrowsmith said, "you're asking for a patent on your cartridge."

"I'm going to hold up the application for a few days to make sure that everything in it is correct," Hunt replied.

On June 5, 1847, Hunt assigned the patent to Arrowsmith.

Two weeks later, on June 19, 1847, Hunt filed his application for the patent.

The army's need of a better gun gave the application no priority in the Patent Office. Months passed. No action was taken by the Patent Office and so none of the plans to manufacture either the gun or the cartridge progressed in any way. Hunt had not heard from either the army or the Patent Office and was dejected.

In early October 1847, George Washington Hunt happily told his father, "I'm going to marry Sarah on the twentieth. Everything is set now."

"Fine." Hunt beamed. "She'll make you a wonderful wife. I like her and you can tell her I'll give her a fine wedding present. Five hundred dollars. But what I don't understand is why didn't you marry her a long time ago."

George grinned from ear to ear. He had expected parental blessing, but the promised gift was greater than his most optimistic expectation.

When Polly heard about Walter's generosity she scolded. "I know it's for George and Sarah. And I know he is our son. But you know you can't afford to give five hundred dollars. A hundred dollars would have been more than enough and more than they could expect."

"He's been a good son," Hunt countered. "And I'd like to give him even more. I only wish I could have given Walter the same."

"I know it," Polly sympathized. "I'm really not objecting to the amount but to the way you handle money. However, I'm glad you're giving it to your own son. You give it away to strangers. You can't resist a sad story. Heaven knows how much you give away in a year that I know nothing about."

George Washington Hunt married Sarah Arnetta Torboss on October 20, 1847, in the Dutch Reformed Church. They set up housekeeping at 156 Laurens Street. He obtained a position as a trunk frame manufacturer at a shop at 48-50 Duane Street. His responsibilities occupied all his time and he was consequently unable to offer any further assistance to his father.

As the patent had not been granted by the U.S. Patent Office, Arrowsmith made an application for a patent from England. The application was granted a patent on December 10, 1847. Hunt assigned the English rights to Stephen Taylor, who prosecuted the application.

It was described in the London *Journal of Arts, Sciences and Manufacturers and Repertory of Patent Inventions.**

To Stephen Taylor, of Ludgate-hill, in the City of London, Gent., for an invention of certain improvements in the construction of fire-arms, and in cartridges for charging the same—being a communication. (Sealed 10th December 1847) Inrolled June, 1848. Patent No. 11,994.

Obstacles hampered the granting of the United States patent. To expedite action, Arrowsmith hired Charles M. Keller, a Washington patent attorney, to represent him and sent him the assignments he had received from Hunt.

On December 7, 1847, Arrowsmith wrote to the Honorable Edmund Burke, Commissioner of Patents, as follows:

I hereby constitute and appoint Charles M. Keller, my attorney, and agent, to act for me and in my name in the prosecution of two applications for Letters Patent filed in your office by me as assignee of Walter Hunt of this city. The inventions so assigned to me are, one for Improvements in Fire Arms, and the

W. Newton, London, 1850. Vol. XXXVI, conjoined series, page 12.

other for Improvements in Metallic Cartridges. In the prosecution of these two applications, amending the papers, procuring copies of them, and doing all other matters in relation thereto which the rules of your office would permit me as assignee of the said Walter Hunt to do, you will please recognize the said Charles M. Keller as my substitute to act in my name and for my interest.

Yours very respectfully,
George A. Arrowsmith.

War or no war, the Patent Office did not expedite applications on ordinances. But that did not decrease Hunt's interests in ballistics. During the first fifteen months the gun application was on file at the Patent Office, Hunt had made a further improvement in cartridges.

On December 21, 1847, he went to the office of the Assistant Treasurer of the United States and paid twenty dollars for a caveat covering a new type of cartridge, superior to the one whose title he had conveyed to Arrowsmith. Then he mailed the application to the Patent Office.

News of Hunt's improvement became known and the merits of both types of cartridges were discussed. The improved cartridge was considerably superior to the one assigned previously to Arrowsmith. Repeated tests had demonstrated its superiority.

Hearing that the application for an improved bullet was at the Patent Office, Arrowsmith went to Hunt's shop and indignantly demanded an assignment of the rights.

"I'll assign it to you," Hunt said, "if you pay for it."

"I'll not give you a penny for it. It belongs to me."

"There is no reason why I should assign this patent," Hunt argued. "It did not and does not enter into our previous contract. It was not conceived until after our deal was consummated and was not a part of our original transaction. In fact, it didn't develop until much later."

"Every patent and every improvement you make on a gun and cartridge belongs to me," Arrowsmith bellowed, "and I won't be forced into paying you extra for them."

"Mr. Arrowsmith," Hunt replied calmly, "when I sold you my patents all I sold you were those patents that were in existence. I never sold you all my productivity and there is no law, rhyme or reason that states that I should be eternally bound to you. You can buy the rights to my new application in an open market at the same price that others will pay for them. Preference, however, will be given to you."

"That patent belongs to me," Arrowsmith threatened, "and if you don't assign it to me I'll see that it is never granted."

"I am fifty-two years old, Mr. Arrowsmith," Hunt answered indignantly. "I have never been accused of unfair dealing by anyone, and I have never done a dishonorable thing in my life. I insist that the improvement does not belong to you. Suppose that five years from now, I should invent a new gun. Would you demand that too? You didn't buy a mortgage on my life or my inventions. No one can."

"Are you going to assign that patent to me, or are you not?" Arrowsmith stormed.

"No, I am not," Hunt replied laconically.

"You'll be sorry," Arrowsmith warned as he stormed out of Hunt's shop.

Arrowsmith immediately notified his attorney, Charles M. Keller, who dashed off a letter to the Commissioner of Patents on April 24, 1848, as follows:

> Application for letters patent was filed in your office by Walter Hunt during the year 1847 for improvements in the construction of metallic cartridges, and the said application was accompanied with an assignment of the whole invention to me for a valuable consideration, containing a request that the letters patent might be granted to me as his assignee. I have reason to believe that the said Walter Hunt has or is about to make application for the same invention slightly changed in form, I therefore enter this my protest against the grant of letters patent to the said Hunt for any more variations of form of the invention assigned to me as will appear from the files of your office.
> CHARLES M. KELLER

As Hunt had not yet filed any application for a patent on the improvement, the Patent Office could take no action. They had no knowledge that Hunt would ever complete his application nor of what claims he would make.

It was not until July 1848 that Hunt acted. He completed payment of the patent fee and filed his application for a patent which was witnessed by Jon. R. Chapin and John M. Kent, a carman. Hunt described his invention as follows:

> The advantage of the wooden cartridge over any other material used for loading at the breech are, first, when the piece is discharged the expansive force and heat of the powder fractures or splits the thin portion of the cylinder down to near the bottom into four equal and uniform staves, which are separated at the middle of piece by the atmospheric resistance, leaving the ball to pass undisturbed in its course between them; second, while in the barrel the wooden cartridge retains its form without adhering to the barrel, however foul, the piece may be, and in passing out separates like a wiper, in consequence of its soft texture, without injuring the cut of the smoothest rifle; third, it retains a uniform shape, and when introduced is not liable to become distorted, and hang in the tube, especially if previously saturated with tallow, in which case it is rendered waterproof.

Chapin read the patent application and remarked, "I can't understand Arrowsmith's attitude. He knows that his demand is unjust. Furthermore, there is no similarity of any kind between the two bullets. He bought a metallic cartridge. This cartridge has a wooden cover or case and there is no resemblance between the two, other than that both are cartridges. I'm certain the Patent Office will not be influenced by his personal wishes."

"I'm sorry the difference of opinion arose," Hunt confided, "but you know me well enough to know that I cannot be intimidated."

"Arrowsmith is no great loss," Chapin commented. "Whatever you obtained from him was much less than others would have given you. If you had never met him, you might have been a happier and a richer man. It's also too bad that you showed him your sewing machine."

The Patent Office had three of Hunt's applications on file, the gun and the metallic cartridge, both of which were assigned to Arrowsmith, and the wooden cartridge, the rights of which were still retained by Hunt.

On July 12, 1848, Arrowsmith wrote to Commissioner Burke urging him to hasten the decision of the interference controversy. He repeated his protest the following day with another letter again protesting granting a patent to Hunt "for what he terms his improvements on the original invention."

At the same time, Arrowsmith wrote another letter to Commissioner Burke;

> The pending application which I now have in the patent office for an improved cartridge was enrolled in England on the tenth day of June 1848 under a patent dated six months previous. I have therefore to request that my said application may receive the earliest examination consistent with the rules and practices of your office.
>
> G. A. Arrowsmith
> (Witnessed by Commissioner of Deeds)

On July 19, 1848, the Patent Office returned the patent application on the metallic cartridge for modification and amendment. Two days later, Keller returned the application with a letter to the Commissioner of Patents, again protesting about Hunt being given a patent on his latest cartridge, urging the importance of Arrowsmith's rights, and calling Walter Hunt an infringer on the patents for his own original cartridge. He maintained that the substitution of wood for metal in the cartridge cap was merely a subterfuge and that Hunt's latest invention was not essentially different from the patent assigned to Arrowsmith.

The Patent Commissioner decided that the second cartridge was different and that both applications were novel and original, and qualified for patents. Accordingly, he issued U.S. Patent No. 5,699 to Walter Hunt and U.S. Patent No. 5,701 on assignment to Arrowsmith on August 10, 1848. (The patent which Hunt assigned to Arrowsmith was filed first, but was granted a higher number than that of the wooden cartridge. The lower number Hunt received did not signify priority.)

The award of both patents was published in the June 1849 issue of the *Journal of the Franklin Institute*.

UNITED STATES PATENT OFFICE.

WALTER HUNT, OF NEW YORK, N. Y.

IMPROVED METHOD OF ATTACHING A BALL TO A WOODEN CARTRIDGE.

Specification forming part of Letters Patent No. 5,699, dated August 10, 1848.

To all whom it may concern:

Be it known that I, WALTER HUNT, of the city, county, and State of New York, have invented a new and useful Plan of Making Wooden Cartridges for Fire-Arms, and also a new method of connecting the same with the ball to be used therewith, and that the following is a faithful description of said invention:

In the manufacture of said cartridges I use wood of a soft texture—the American basswood I find preferable. I make them externally (see Fig. 1 in the annexed drawings) in the form of a cylindrical ferrule or cup, having a similar formed internal cavity, A, with a thick bottom, B, formed all of the same piece. Through the center of said bottom is a small perforation, C, through which the charge is ignited by the priming. (See horizontal cut section, Fig. 2, rear end view, Fig. 3, and front end view, Fig. 4.) The front or open end of said cartridge is formed into a circular tenon, D, having a shoulder at E, which tenon is made to fit into a corresponding mortise or circular recess cut or otherwise formed in the rear end of the ball F. (See Fig. 5, which shows a longitudinal cut section of the same as separated from the cartridge, and Fig. 6 a rear end view.)

In the process of filling these cartridges a small wad or pledget of gun-cotton being first introduced into the perforation C, the cartridge in a vertical position is then filled with powder, when the rear end of the ball is forced down upon the powder into the end of the cartridge, while the tenon D enters the cavity or mortise F in the end of the ball, by which means the powder is properly compressed and the ball and cartridge become firmly united together, which may be done with facility in a mold or tube fitted to the size of the cartridge by hand, machinery, or otherwise.

It will be observed that this plan of a cartridge is exclusively designed for loading at the breech, for the reason that the wooden cartridge is always left in the breech of the barrel and fired out in front of each succeeding ball.

The advantages of the wooden cartridge over any other material used for loading at the breech are, first, when the piece is discharged the expansive force and heat of the powder fractures or splits the thin portion of the cylinder down to near the bottom into four equal and uniform staves, which are separated at the muzzle of piece by the atmospheric resistance, leaving the ball to pass undisturbed in its course between them; second, while in the barrel the wooden cartridge retains its form without adhering to the barrel, however foul the piece may be, and in passing out operates like a wiper, in consequence of its soft texture, without injuring the cut of the smoothest rifle; third, it retains a uniform shape, and when introduced is not liable to become distorted and hang in the tube, especially if previously saturated with tallow, in which case it is rendered water-proof.

In the above described ball and cartridge I do not claim or use a loaded ball, or a ball that contains any portion of the charge; neither do I use or claim a metallic cartridge or a cartridge any portion of which is formed of metal; but

What I do claim, and desire to secure by Letters Patent, is—

The mode or plan of connecting the said cartridge to said ball—that is, by means of an annular flange and recess on and in the rear end of said ball, which recess receives, and which flange incloses the ferrule or circular tenon which forms the open end of said cartridge, thereby forming, combining, and uniting said ball and cartridge, substantially as above set forth and described.

WALTER HUNT.

Witnesses:
  JOHN M. KENT,
  JNO. W. CHAPIN.

W. HUNT.

Cartridge.

No. 5,699   Patented Aug. 10, 1848.

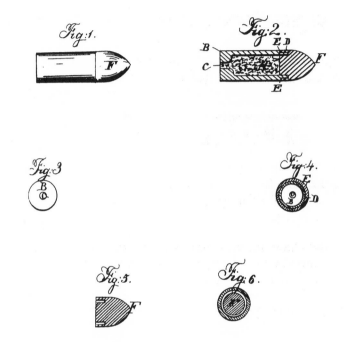

Although patents had been granted on the two cartridges, the Patent Office had not yet made a decision on the volition repeater which was filed earlier. Its application was held in abeyance.

The Patent Office insisted that Hunt's gun application was in interference with one filed by Christian W. Buchel of New York, whose application was witnessed by John James Greenough, Hunt's attorney in the fountain pen application. As customary in issues of dispute, interference proceedings were held and the various points of similarity were discussed. In July 1848, the Commissioner of Patents decided that there was no similarity and the Patent Office dropped the interference proceedings.

To obviate any misunderstanding and to clarify the patent claims, the Patent Office returned Hunt's application to Arrowsmith for technical correction and a revision of claims. On September 21, 1848, Arrowsmith wrote to the Honorable Edmund Burke, Commissioner of Patents, as follows:

UNITED STATES PATENT OFFICE.

WALTER HUNT, OF NEW YORK, N. Y., ASSIGNOR TO GEO. A. ARROWSMITH.

LOADED BALL.

Specification forming part of Letters Patent No. 5,701, dated August 10, 1848.

To all whom it may concern:

Be it known that I, WALTER HUNT, of the city, county, and State of New York, have invented a new and useful Improvement in the Construction of a Metallic Cartridge, made entire with the ball, for fire-arms, which I term a "rocket-ball;" and I do hereby declare that the following is a true and faithful description of the same.

Figure 1 in the annexed drawings is an external longitudinal view of said rocket-ball, which is charged, ready for use. Upon the open end of the cartridge is fitted a thin sheet-metal cap, A. Upon the opposite front end of B (the cartridge) projects one-half of the ball C, which, all together, resembles the ordinary top thimble.

Fig. 2 gives a longitudinal cut-sectional view of the same, showing the internal structure of the cap A, cavity D in the cartridge B, and its junction with the ball C.

The dissected longitudinal cut-section, Fig. 3, shows the cap A separated from the flange or neck formed by the shoulder, at the dotted line E, upon the rear end of B.

Fig. 4 is an end or face view of A, which in form resembles the Chinese gong, with a central perforation, F, in its discous head, which is the point of ignition from the priming. Over this perforation, upon the inside face of said cap, is placed a thin water-proof tissue or seal. (See Fig. 2, at the dotted line G, and face view, Fig. 6.) This seal may be made of any thin material through which the fire from the priming may penetrate, and which will at the same time secure the powder in the cartridge from escape or accidental injury.

This ball and thimble should be formed in molds by pressure. The powder being well packed in the cavity D, the cap A, lined with the seal G, being fixed upon the flange, and pressed up to the shoulder E, should then be subjected to a second pressure, in order to fix the cap firmly and produce a uniformity in the size of the cartridges.

It will be readily perceived that this plan of a combined ball and cartridge is well adapted to fire-arms made to be charged at the breech, from the fact that in firing this ball the cap A is left in the breech, with its head or disk pressed firmly against the breech-plug, and its rim or flange forced outward against the inner periphery of the caliber of the barrel, forming an air tight stopper, which effectually prevents all backward escape of the powder, notwithstanding the breech-plug may be loosely fitted in the breech of the barrel behind the charge, which must necessarily be the case in all reciprocating breech-pins in order to prevent their binding from heat, deposits, &c., in rapid firing. It is also obvious that, in guns made with piston breech-pins, the cap A in my plan would be carried out forward of each succeeding ball, operating as an effectual wiper to the barrel at each discharge of the piece.

What I claim in the above-described invention, and desire to secure by Letters Patent, is—

The construction of a ball for fire-arms, with a cavity to contain the charge of powder for propelling said ball, in which cavity the powder is secured by means of a cap inclosing the back end of the same, substantially as described.

WALTER HUNT.

Witnesses:
EDMD. ELMENDORF, Jr.,
CHAS. E. GRIM.

W. HUNT.

Cartridge.

No. 5,701.

Patented Aug. 10. 1848.

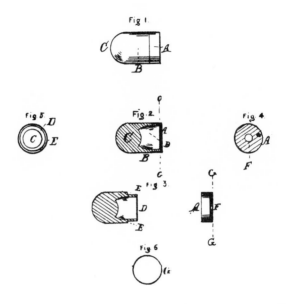

Yours of the 4th inst covering the papers and drawings of G. A. Arrowsmith (assignee of W. Hunt) applicant for patent improvement in fire-arms was duly received.

The amendments have all been made and the claim restricted as required, and the papers and drawings are herewith returned.

The pencil marks are not erased in order that you may see that his corrections have all been attended to.

Trouble rarely travels by itself. The Hunt application was again delayed as an application for a gun patent was also filed by Von Schmidt. This required another interference hearing. On January 2, 1849, Commissioner Edmund Burke ruled in favor of Hunt. He declared;

In the matter of the interference between the claims of the above named parties, it appears that the application of George A. Arrowsmith was completed on the 8th day of November 1847 and that the application of said Von Schmidt was completed on the 23rd day of September 1848.

In testimony as to the dates of their respective inventions furnished by either party, the evidence furnished by the files and records of the office is therefore the only proof upon which to found a decision, and such evidence is decidedly in favor of G. A. Arrowsmith.

Priority of invention is therefore decided in favor of said G. A. Arrowsmith

Arrowsmith was happy that the Von Schmidt application was disregarded. But his joy was lessened when he learned that on February 20, 1849, Buchel had been awarded U.S. Patent No. 6,136 on "an improved cartridge-tube forming a conveyor fire-arm." Although this patent was for a different kind of gun, Arrowsmith was worried that something might happen to Hunt's application.

The uncertainty was dispelled on August 21, 1849, when the Patent Office granted Arrowsmith U.S. Patent No. 6,663 on Hunt's application for a "combined piston-breech and firing-cock gun," the same gun which Arrowsmith had previously patented in England.

Arrowsmith had not been overly worried, as he had entered the gun in the twenty-first annual fair of the American Institute even before the patent had been granted. It was awarded a silver medal.

Despite the facts that Hunt's gun patent had been received, and that the superiority of the gun and cartridge had been acknowledged by all who had seen it, Arrowsmith could not interest anyone in promoting it or advancing capital for its manufacture.

Consequently, he decided to attempt to manufacture the gun in his shop on Gold Street, on a limited scale, in the hope that somebody would appear to expand the operation, but lack of machinery made production a slow and cumbersome task. Uniformity of production was impossible on custom work. Trained workmen were unobtainable, except at exorbitant salaries, and untrained workmen were not able to produce precision work.

Arrowsmith did, however, obtain the services of Lewis Jennings, a skilled mechanic. During his employment he became more and more proficient. He recognized the minor defects in the gun and suggested possible improvements. Arrowsmith agreed to make the changes.

Jennings substituted a standard side hammer lock for the bolt action, and by combining the firing and loading mechanism, each movement of the ring-trigger withdrew the piston and thus raised a ball from the magazine. The rear movement of the same trigger pushed the ball into the chamber, capped the gun with a pellet, locked the breech and fired the charge.

Jennings applied for a patent in his own name on the improvement and was awarded U.S. Patent No. 6,973 on December 25, 1849, which he assigned to Arrowsmith.

Arrowsmith learned from experience that guns had to be manufactured in large quantities to show a profit and that a limited production was both costly and unprofitable. As he had neither the skill nor the capital to properly finance the manufacture of guns, he finally sold his interests in the patents to one of New

United States Patent Office.

GEO. A. ARROWSMITH, OF NEW YORK, N. Y., ASSIGNEE OF WALTER HUNT.

COMBINED PISTON-BREECH AND FIRING-COCK REPEATING-GUN.

Specification forming part of Letters Patent No. **6,663,** dated August 21, 1849; patented in England, December 10, 1847.

To all whom it may concern:

Be it known that I, WALTER HUNT, of the city, county, and State of New York, have invented a new and useful Improvement in the Construction of Fire-Arms, which I denominate "The Volition Repeater;" and that the following is a full and faithful description of the same.

In the annexed drawings, which are on a scale of six inches to the foot, I have given in Figure 1 an external side view of my said improved gun, which, in length, weight, and caliber nearly corresponds to the United States rifle. Fig. 2 exhibits a vertical longitudinal cut section of the action or lock ready for pulling trigger, together with a portion of the ball-magazine and barrel, with a ball inserted at the breech. Fig. 3 exhibits a similar view of the whole gun, showing a correct profile of every part and member, external and internal, of which the same is composed, and arranged in their proper position, which I will now proceed to describe, with similar letters of reference to similar parts throughout all of the figures.

In the following description I have selected Fig. 3 as the most perfect exposé of the internal arrangement of said gun, which is externally composed of the following principal parts, as shown in Fig. 1, viz: the butt A, lock-case B, barrel C, ball-tube or magazine D, spring or rod case E, bolster F, transfer-trigger G, loading-trigger H, guard I, transfer-trigger pin J, spring end of guard K, thimble-strap L, fixed thimbles b'', c'', and P, sliding thimbles M N, fastening-spring O, head of ramrod Q, front sight, R, back sight, S, middle sight, U, priming-magazine T, fastening-back bolt V, set-screw W, discharging-trigger Y, and guard-screw Z'.

The lock-case and butt are screwed together at e'', and the barrel and lock-case at d''.

The internal arrangements of the lock, &c., are as follows. (See Figs. 3, 13, and 14, which latter is a dissected or detached side view of said lock, beginning with the charging-trigger H and the firing-trigger Y, which are suspended upon the pin u.) In Fig. 3 is shown the bottom end of said trigger H thrown forward. The upper end is hooked downward and connected by a rule-joint at a'' to the rear end of the connecting-link Z, the front end of which

link is connected by a similar joint to the back end of the breech-piston a at t. Said piston is composed externally of three parts—viz., the tail a, the cylinder or spring-case a', and breech-plug c'—which are screwed together at i'' and j'', (see Fig. 14, five dissected side views, Figs. 16, 17, 18, and 19, with top and bottom views, Figs. 20, 21, 22, and 23.) Upon the surface of a', near the front end, a notch is filed out, making a flattened surface at b', upon which is placed a slider, j, made of sheet-steel, with the front and back ends bent upward the depth of the notch aforesaid, with a spring-tongue, h'', projecting forward. (See Fig. 14½.) The end of the tongue is bent in the shape of a U, which end, as the slider is moved back and forth, falls into the priming-hole i', (see Fig. 2,) and forces the kernels of priming, which might otherwise remain in said hole, into the cavity below. The horizontal motion of said slider is restricted in its vibrations by the bottom of the priming-chamber T, which catches upon the flanges f'' and g''.

The central part of said breech-piston a' contains the helical or coiled mainspring i, wound around the firing-punch f, one end of which spring bears against a collar on said punch at k'. Upon the bottom end of said collar is attached the detent-spring e by means of the flange on the same at k''. The back end of said mainspring bears against the forward end of the tail-pin a. (See Figs. 2 and 3, 24 and 25.) Along on the under side of said main-spring-case a' it is cut through to the internal cavity, in which longitudinal slot h' is an enlargement, at g', (see Fig. 23,) through which the firing-punch f is inserted, and through which slot h' the flange k' is allowed to reciprocate, being acted upon by the attaching and detaching of the detent e to and from the detent-pin g, which motions are effected by the back-and-forth action of the trigger H and the breech-piston a', as shown by their contrasted positions in cut sections, Figs. 2 and 3, and by pulling the firing-trigger Y, which, bearing down on the back end of the lever b at o'', lifts the end of said detent at p'' from the detent-pin g, which pin is inserted up through a corresponding hole in the back part of said detent, thereby releasing the firing-punch f, which is impelled forward by the mainspring i through the tube into the rear end of the breech plug or pin c' at q'', which is the firing-chamber of the priming.

In Fig. 3 a kernel of percussion-powder is shown as having dropped into the priming-hole i from the magazine T, which in Fig. 2 is brought forward past the end of the firing-punch f and deposited in the firing-chamber of the priming at q'', as aforesaid.

Fig. 31, letter c, gives a side view of an intermediate detent in said lock, which I call the "lock-lever," which is shown in the cut-section views, Figs. 2 and 3, and also in the detached view, Fig. 34, and combined view, Fig. 33. Its object is to fasten the breech-pin secure in the end of the barrel at the time of firing, which is effected by the impingement of the hooked upper end of the charging-trigger H upon the end of said lever at n''. It being centrally suspended upon the pin r the forward hook upon the end m'' is forced up into the notch j', cut in the under side of the tail-pin of the piston breech-pin a, (see Fig. 33,) thereby securing the same firmly in its place, as aforesaid.

I would remark that this is the only position in which the priming or gun can be discharged, because the flange m'' on the front end of the lock-lever c prevents the front end of the lever b from raising the detent e from the pin g until the said flange is let up into the notch j', as before described. (See Figs. 2, 3, 14, and 33.)

Figs. 10, 11, and 12 give a top, bottom, and side view of the lock-frame X, which is cast in one piece, and in which is placed the whole action of the lock, as shown in Fig. 13, side view, the whole of which is placed in the lock-case B. (See detached side and top views, Figs. 8 and 9, end view, Fig. $9\frac{1}{2}$, and cut sections 2 and 3.)

Upon the front bottom side of said lock-case B is an enlargement or bolster, which supports the transfer-trigger G upon the pin J, and up through an opening in which, at is front end, is inserted the transfer-tube k, (see top, side, and end views of said tube in Figs. 27, 28, and 29, and vertical side cut sections of the same, Figs. 2 and 3,) where the connection of said trigger G and tube k is shown at l, which connection is made by the T-hook fixed in the front end of said trigger G, and made to swivel through an opening in the bottom of said tube k, by which it is thereby loosely connected by a swivel-joint, as aforesaid.

The office of said trigger and tube is to transfer the cartridges from the ball-magazine D (see cut section, Fig. 3) to a line in front of the breech-pin at c', in order that by pulling the charging-trigger H it may be forced into the breech of the barrel ready for discharging, as shown in cut section, Fig. 2, at r''.

The motion of said tube and trigger is effected by the left hand, which supports the gun at F G, where, by a slight upward pressure of the ball of the hand upon the bow of the trigger, at w, it is placed in the position to receive the cartridge, as in Fig. 3, when, by pressing the palm upward at G, the tube is raised and the ball carried in front of the breech-pin, as before described, and shown in Fig. 2, in which position said trigger ordinarily remains at rest, being partially held by the pressure of the guard-spring upon the heel of said transfer-trigger at K.

I will now proceed to describe the ball tube or magazine D and spring-case E, which are supported in the thimbles b'', c'', and P in the ordinary place of the ramrod. By drawing the thimble N toward the muzzle of the gun till both it and thimble M have passed the joint s' the spring r catches and holds thimble N, and as that is attached through a slot made the length of its play in the side of the tube D next the barrel C to the follower t'', on which the lower end of the spring O bears, said spring is also drawn back and held and the end of the tube D' released, as shown in Fig. 4. The ball-tube D is then separated from the spring-case E at s'', and thrown outward by the spring v'' ready for filling with cartridges from cases prepared for the purpose containing, say, twelve, more or less. The magazine being filled is returned in a line with the spring and ramrod-tube, where it bears upon the check-spring r and releases the thimble N, attached to the follower t'', which last, being operated upon by the coil-spring o, is forced down upon the cartridges, driving the bottom one into the transferring-tube k whenever it is brought into a straight line, as before described, and shown in Fig. 3. Said ball-tube is held in its position by sliding the thimble M over the joint s'' after the thimble N has been let down, as aforesaid. (See Figs. 1 and 3.)

$O^{\times}$ is a small spring in the upper end of the spring-tube E, designed to fasten the same by means of a hook fitted into a gap in the thimble P at u''.

Fig. 26, letter d, is a spring secured to the under side of the lock-frame by means of the detent screw or pin g, (see Fig. 11, at t',) which spring bears upward upon the lock and lifting levers b and c, keeping them in their positions for the action of the triggers H and Y.

The priming-magazine is a small thimble or cup with a hinged cap, T, having a slot cut through its bottom at y'. (See Figs. 6 and 7, which are side and bottom views in Figs. 2 and 3, cut-section views.) Said magazine is shown as screwed down through the lock-case and frame, directly over the priming-hole i' in the breech-pin a', when the same is drawn back ready for charging, as in Fig. 3.

The cartridges designed to be used in this gun are those recently invented by me, for which an application for Letters Patent has been made at the United States Patent Office.

Having given a full description of my said improved gun, I will now proceed to describe its mode of using and the action of its parts when in operation.

The ball or cartridge magazine being charged as before described, and the gun brought to a firing position, the left hand clasping the gun around the transferring-lever and bolster at F G, the transfer-tube *k* is brought down by the ball of the same hand bearing on the bow at *w*, as before stated, and as shown in Fig. 3. A cartridge having been forced into the transfer-tube by the spring O is thus carried up in a range with the breech-pin *a'*, which is now thrown forward by drawing back the charging-trigger H with the second finger of the right hand, which at the same time clasps the waist of the gun at A, (see Fig. 2,) by which means the cartridge-ball is forced home into the breech of the barrel. At the same time a kernel of priming is carried from the bottom of the primer T and dropped in the cavity in front of the firing-punch *f*. Simultaneously the lock-lever *c* enters the notch *j'*, being forced up by the point of the trigger H, which presses down its back end, as before described, and shown in Fig. 2.

The gun being now loaded, primed, and cocked, is fired by pulling the trigger Y, which forces down the back end of the lifting or detaching lever at *o''*, the front end of which lifts the rear of the detent-spring *e* from the pin *g*, when the firing-punch is suddenly thrown forward by the coil-spring *i*, which explodes the percussion in the chamber aforesaid, the flame from which passes through the central hole, *y*, in the breech-plug *c'*, perforating the tissue in the center of the cartridge, and discharges the gun, when the triggers H and G are again returned to their former position, as in Fig. 3,

and the operation is repeated until the magazine is exhausted, when it is replenished, as before described, and shown in Fig. 4.

The priming-magazine may safely contain from fifty to one hundred primings, and the ball-magazine may extend the whole length of the barrel and contain some two dozen cartridges, in which case it would be necessary to force them down by hand or some other arrangement; but by separating and charging the lower half of the spring-case on my plan it is advantageously charged with twelve balls from a case before mentioned, which I consider of sufficient length for convenience or utility.

What I specifically claim as new in the above-described gun, and desire to secure by Letters Patent, is—

1. The construction of a hollow sliding or piston breech-pin, which is operated by a lever in loading and securing the charge in the breech of the gun, which breech-pin, in addition to the above characteristic, contains or has attached to it the mainspring, firing cock or punch, and firing-chamber of the priming.

2. I also claim the plan of transferring the priming from the fixed magazine to the firing-chamber in or by means of the said sliding breech-pin, as above set forth and described.

WALTER HUNT.

Witnesses:
    GEO. G. SICKLES,
    ELISHA BLOOMER.

York's leading hardware merchants, Courtland C. Palmer, a promoter and industrialist, later president of the Stonington and Providence Railroad.

As owner of the patents, Palmer contracted with the Robbins & Lawrence Company of Windsor, Vermont, to manufacture five thousand of the Hunt-Jennings type guns. C. P. Dixon acted as general agent for their distribution.

Inventions generate other inventions and in the course of time many minor improvements were made on Hunt's original gun. B. Tyler Henry received a patent on August 26, 1851, and on the same day E. Smith also obtained an improvement patent. Slight changes to broaden the patent coverages were drawn up.

Reissues were requested on Hunt's patents and on February 26, 1850, Hunt received U.S. reissue No. 163 and No. 164.

D. B. Wesson, a workman in the Robbins and Lawrence factory, saw the possibilities in Hunt's gun before the improvement patents were obtained. He acquired Palmer's interest and then contacted Horace Smith, and jointly formed the firm of Smith & Wesson. They began manufacturing the improved versions

W. HUNT.
COMBINED PISTON BREECH AND FIRING COCK REPEATING GUN.

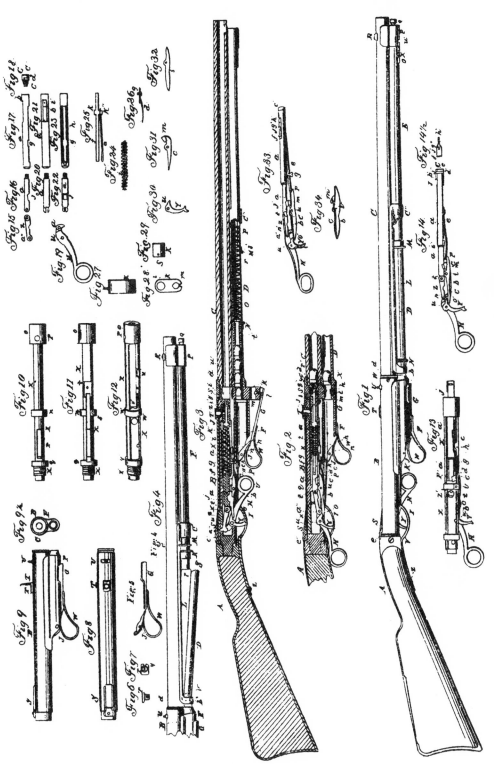

in Norwich, Connecticut. On February 14, 1854, and on August 8, 1854, the firm of Smith & Wesson received U.S. Patents No. 10,535 and No. 11,496 for improvements on the gun.

D. B. Wesson severed his connections with his concern in 1854 and assigned to the Volcanic Arms Company of New Haven, Connecticut, all rights to the manufacture of Hunt's gun. Lack of capital and business experience had exacted its toll. This concern ultimately encountered financial difficulty and its business and patents were acquired by the New Haven Arms Company, controlled by O. F. Winchester, a member of the firms of Winchester & Davis, shirt manufacturers of New Haven.

The New Haven Arms Company was later reorganized and the company and patents were acquired by the Winchester Repeating Arms Company.

If Walter Hunt's original gun had revolutionized the ammunition industry when it first appeared, the new repeating gun completed the job.

The years of expense and labor in developing the gun and cartridge had brought Hunt little revenue. As each improvement was made, the worth of the original proportionately decreased. This was the natural procedure and did not discourage Hunt as much as the fact that he and George Arrowsmith developed a dislike for each other. They were bitter and resented each other. They avoided each other and if by chance one confronted the other, he refused to talk to him.

Chapter 20

"It finally happened," Hunt moaned, "I've used up all our money, everything I had on the gun, and am in debt again. We'll have to move and spend less for rent and cut expenses."

"I'd hate to leave Jones Street," Polly admitted ruefully. "But I think perhaps we might be happier in the suburbs. I imagine there are a lot of nice places that don't cost much."

The Hunts moved into a less expensive house at 174 West 17th Street and he moved his shop to 42 Gold Street. But he then discovered that even these modest quarters were more than he could afford.

He was disheartened when he walked into Jonathan Chapin's Nassau Street shop. He sank into the faded and worn plush armchair near the door. He covered his face with his hands and slumped forward. Chapin rushed to him.

"What's the matter, Mr. Hunt?"

"I owe you fifteen dollars, don't I?"

"That's all right. I'm not worried."

"But I am. I haven't a cent in the world, and don't know where to get one."

"Don't worry about me," Chapin said consolingly. "I'm in no hurry for the money. You can pay me back anytime you want."

"Yes, I know," Hunt faltered. "But I don't even know where to get a meal of victuals."

"I've a few dollars, I have no use for," Chapin volunteered.

"I don't want a loan," Hunt said. "I want to earn money. My family has to live." He paused and thrust his clenched fists into his empty pants pocket. "I'm sorry," he apologized. "I appreciate your kindness."

"Have you any plans?" Chapin asked.

"No. That is why I am so mad." Hunt got out of the chair and paced the floor. In his hands was a piece of wire he kept nervously twisting.

At first the action was haphazard, without apparent reason. Then his movements became slower and slower. He seemed to be in deep concentration. The

167

UNITED STATES PATENT OFFICE.

WALTER HUNT, OF NEW YORK, N. Y., ASSIGNOR TO WM. RICHARDSON AND JNO. RICHARDSON.

DRESS-PIN.

Specification of Letters Patent No. 6,281, dated April 10, 1849.

To all whom it may concern:

Be it known that I, WALTER HUNT, of the city, county, and State of New York, have invented a new and useful Improvement in
5 the Make or Form of Dress-Pins, of which the following is a faithful and accurate description.

The distinguishing features of this invention consist in the construction of a pin made
10 of one piece of wire or metal combining a spring, and clasp or catch, in which catch, the point of said pin is forced and by its own spring securely retained. They may be made of common pin wire, or of the precious
15 metals.

See Figure 1 in the annexed drawings (which are drawn upon a full scale, and in which the same letters refer to similar parts,) which figure presents a side view of said pin,
20 and in which is shown the three distinct mechanical features, viz: the pin A, the coiled spring B, and the catch D, which is made at the extreme end of the wire bar C, extended from B. Fig. 2 is a similar view
25 of a pin with an elliptical coiled spring, the pin being detached from the catch D and thrown open by the spring B. Fig. 3 gives a top view of the same. Fig. 4 is a top view of the spring made in a flat spiral coil.
30 Fig. 5 is a side view of the same.

Any ornamental design may be attached to the bar C, (see Figs. 6, 7 and 8,) which combined with the advantages of the spring and catch, renders it equally ornamental, and at the same time more secure and durable 35 than any other plan of a clasp pin, heretofore in use, there being no joint to break or pivot to wear or get loose as in other plans. Another great advantages unknown in other plans is found in the perfect convenience of 40 inserting these into the dress, without danger of bending the pin, or wounding the fingers, which renders them equally adapted to either ornamental, common dress, or nursery uses. The same principle is applicable 45 to hair-pins.

My claims in the above described invention, for which I desire to secure Letters Patent are confined to the construction of dress-pins, hair-pins, &c., made from one 50 entire piece of wire or metal, (without a joint or hinge, or any additional metal except for ornament,) forming said pin and combining with it in one and the same piece of wire, a coiled or curved spring, and a 55 clasp or catch, constructed substantially as above set forth and described.

WALTER HUNT.

Witnesses:
JOHN M. KNOX,
JNO. R. CHAPIN.

---

twists and turns, instead of aimless, were made with studied concentration. He carefully bent the wire, then with equal care undid what he twisted until the wire was straight. Then he bent it back again into its previous shape. He bent the wire around his finger, making a loop spring so that the two ends of the wire had a tendency to spring outward. Then he bent one of the ends, the long one, into a sort of hook or catch, and then brought the other end to it, the hooked section constantly preventing the other end from springing open. Then he used the file on his jackknife and filed the short blunt end to a point.

He looked at the shaped wire, then stared off into space. Hunt thrust it into his bulging coat pocket and said calmly, "Chapin, I have it! I'll be back later this afternoon and pay you." He rushed out of the shop without closing the door.

Chapin was too astonished to stop him. He paused a second, collected his senses, and dashed after Hunt, but Hunt had disappeared.

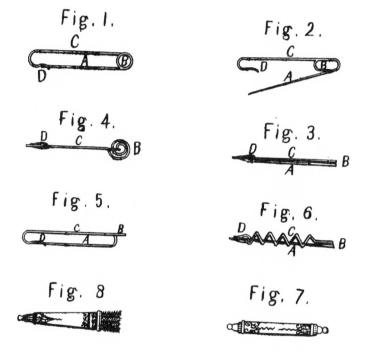

W. Hunt.

Pin.

Nº 6281.   *Patented Apr. 10. 1849.*

Hunt rushed to Jonathan Richardson, a manufacturer with a shop in Little Green Street. He showed him the bent wire.

"What's this?"

"It's a fastener. A pin that won't cut you. It's a dress pin."

Richardson looked at it. He opened it and closed it several times without comment.

"I'll give you a hundred dollars cash for it," he offered.

"One hundred dollars," Hunt sighed.

"One hundred dollars cash this minute."

"All right."

"And, of course, you'll assign the rights, and I'll apply for the patent," Richardson stated.

"One hundred dollars," Hunt repeated.

Hunt pocketed the money which was paid in bills of small denominations. He rushed back to Chapin's shop. Out of breath, the perspiration pouring from him, he dashed inside.

"What is it, Mr. Hunt? What is the matter?"

"Matter? Nothing is the matter?" He said with a studied nonchalant air, "Here is the money I borrowed from you. Help me make out the patent papers for this."

Hunt dropped the pin on Chapin's table and together they drew up the patent application. When they had completed the specifications, Hunt rushed home. It was only five o'clock. Polly was unsettled when she saw him as he seldom came home until it was dark.

"Here, Polly," he said, his voice choking with emotion as he handed her $85. "Now you can buy things again."

Polly did not have a chance to question him. She might have had an inkling that the hundred dollars he had received for his invention would eventually net hundreds of thousands of dollars for others.

The next day, August 10, 1848, Hunt brought the patent application to Jonathan Richardson. He assigned his rights to Jonathan Richardson and William Richardson. His signature was witnessed by both Chapin and John M. Knox, a lawyer. This was Hunt's fourth patent application which Chapin had witnessed: the inkstand, the fountain pen, the metallic cartridge and the dress pin. Chapin had seen others make fortunes from them. Compassionately, he did not make a comparison nor predict the outcome. It would be throwing oil on the fire.

Hunt originally did not call his invention a "safety pin" but a dress pin. One of the illustrations in his patent drawing showed an ornate and decorated pin. His pin differed from those of the ancients who used bone, copper or gold in that it was made of one piece, and that a clasp prevented it from opening. Millions of babies since that time have appreciated this significant factor.

The Patent Office recognized its utility and importance, but a Jesse Rabbeth of Hampton, Connecticut, also had a patent application on file for a pin. As two or more applications on a related object constituted interference, both applications were held up until the patent examiner could decide the merits of each and whether there was any overlapping of claims.

Hunt's application finally reached the examiner on January 5, 1849, and he appointed the third Monday of February 1849 as the date for hearing both claims.

The Richardsons hired P. H. Watson, an attorney of Washington, D.C., to prosecute Hunt's claim. He wrote Commissioner Burke:

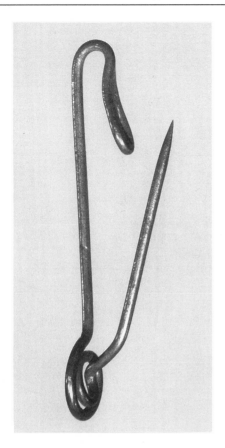
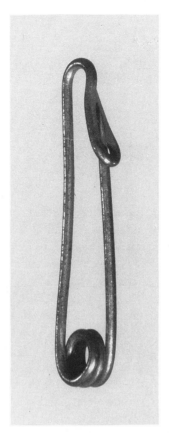

These are the models of the safety pin made by Hunt that were sent with the original patent application.

I have to request that you will postpone your decision in the matter of the interfering applications of Walter Hunt and Jesse Rabbeth for letters patent on an Improved Dress Pin, for the purpose of enabling the parties to send in their testimony in accordance with the form prescribed by the Office in such cases, both parties having failed to have the certificates of the Magistrate taking the evidence written upon the envelope in which it was enclosed to you, in compliance with the 6th rule "for taking and transmitting evidence, etc."

In the event of your not deeming the foregoing fact sufficient cause for postponement, I would request that you receive the testimony of both parties as presented, notwithstanding the informality in the manner of its transmission to you.

Hunt was awarded U.S. Patent No. 6,281 dated April 10, 1849.

Chapter 21

The industrial revolution was rapidly gaining ground. Labor's objection to improvements was becoming stronger and stronger and the public's antipathy towards machinery increased simultaneously.

While [George] Arrowsmith fatuously had believed that there was no need to hurry to present Hunt's sewing machine to the world, the inevitable happened. Machinery had invaded the needlework industry.

The press was quick to respond to the innovation. The *Edinburgh Encyclopedia*, under the heading of "chainwork," devoted twenty-two pages to a detailed description of tambouring, the weaving loom and the stocking frame. The *American Magazine of Useful and Entertaining Knowledge* praised John Duncan of Glasgow, the inventor of the tambour machine who "conceived the idea of bringing into action a great number of needles at the same time in order to shorten the process by manual labor."

Within a comparatively short time, the cycle of inventive genius embraced mechanical sewing. The United States Patent Office was flooded with applications. Many of them were impractical and worthless. Only a few showed the necessary originality and merit. As a result, patents were sparingly granted, and practically none were ever put into practice or tested.

John James Greenough, the attorney who represented Buchel in the gun interference proceedings and who was a witness to Hunt's fountain pen application, applied for a patent on a "machine for sewing or stitching all kinds of straight seams." Let us give him the benefit of the doubt and presume that Hunt had made a sewing machine eight years previously. As this was the first sewing machine application accepted by the Patent Office, Greenough received the first such patent in the United States, No. 2,466 dated February 21, 1846.

His machine was designed primarily for sewing leather and other hard material held by clamps. The stitch was formed by an awl which pierced a hole through which two threaded needles were pulled by pincers in advance of the needle. The machine was provided with a rack which moved back and forth, alternately to produce a back stitch, or continuously forward to make the shoe-maker's stitch.

As each invention generates others, other sewing machines were patented the following year; one by Benjamin W. Bean of New York City who received U.S. Patent No. 2,982 on March 4, 1843, on a "machine for sewing cloth of all kinds with a running stitch" and the other by George Henry Corliss of Green-wich, New York, who obtained U.S. Patent No. 3,389 on December 27, 1843, on an "improvement in machines for sewing with a running stitch."

The fourth sewing machine patent, U.S. Patent No. 3,672, was granted to James Rodgers of New York on July 22, 1844, for an "improvement in machines for sewing with a running stitch."

These four sewing machines were far from perfect but inasmuch as each introduced some new principle and idea, the Patent Office was obliged to grant the patents. Practicality and importance of the invention were not considered in patent granting. In fact, it was not always necessary to submit a model with the application to demonstrate the effectiveness of the invention.

On September 12, 1845, George Fisher, a coal and wood dealer in Cam-bridge, Massachusetts, loaned Elias Howe, Jr., a twenty-six year old mechanic of Cambridge, $500 and boarded him in his home, while Howe was building a machine for sewing for which he filed a caveat with the Patent Office. In return, Fisher acquired a half interest in the invention.

A year later, on May 27, 1846, Howe completed his application and received U.S. Patent No. 4,750 on September 10, 1846, on an "improvement in sewing machines," and thereby obtaining the fifth United States patent on a sewing machine.

Like Hunt, none of the five patentees could obtain the capital to manu-facture their machines. Capitalists realized that the models lacked the smooth-ness and simplicity of operation necessary for practicality and feared that the machines were novelties rather than commercial devices.

Despite numerous attempts to sell his patent or even an interest in it, nobody could be found to invest capital to promote Howe's machine. Dis-couragement greeted him at every turn. The only person who had evinced any interest was Joseph P. Martin of Nile, Berrien County, Michigan, who had bought a one-sixteenth interest out of Fisher's half interest on October 24, 1846, for $417.50.*

"You can't sell machinery in the United States," a friend told Howe. "Why don't you go to England? England has always been first to recognize industrial machinery."

The idea merited consideration. Elias Howe for various reasons was unable to make the trip, but induced his brother, Amasa, to represent him in England.

*Data are unclear: 1/16 of a half (i.e., 1/32) or possibly 1/16 overall—editors.

To finance Amasa's trip, and pay his living expenses and debts, Elias had borrowed $1,000 from his father on September 21, 1846, and had given him his half interest in the patent rights as security. Amasa traveled by steerage and arrived in October 1846.

Amasa Howe found England equally unreceptive to the invention. After repeated efforts, he interested William Thomas, a corset manufacturer of Cheapside, who agreed to test the sewing machine in his factory.

Thomas was a successful and progressive merchant who visualized the possibilities of the sewing machine. He purchased the English rights for £250, agreed to pay £3 a week for the services of Elias Howe, and pay a royalty of £3 to Howe on each machine [that Thomas] sold to others.

When Amasa conveyed the good news to Elias Howe, there was much joy. On February 5, 1847, Elias Howe, Jr., left for London, accompanied by his wife and their three children, the oldest of which was five and the youngest one year old.

Major and minor difficulties presented themselves in endless succession. Instead of decreasing with time and effort, they accumulated and finally the employment with Thomas was terminated. Without funds and without a job, Howe's situation was precarious. Through the kindness of a ship captain, he obtained for his family return passage to the United States.

But Elias Howe did not accompany them. He remained in England hoping to promote the sewing machine. His expectations did not materialize. Failure greeted him. He was obliged to pawn his clothes and belongings. He borrowed money and signed promissory notes. The inevitable occurred and his debts caught up with him. He could not meet his obligations and was arrested for debt. In desperation, he took the "poor debtor's oath."

In a deposition taken June 22, 1850, Anson Burlingame, who graduated from the law department of Harvard University in 1846 and practiced in Boston, stated;

> I know the complainant Howe, and have known him since last summer. I know that he has been much embarrassed in pecuniary matters for some time past, that some time during last summer while on a trip to England, I redeemed certain property pledged by the complainant consisting of the wearing apparel and other personal effects of said Howe and his family which said Howe had pledged in London.

Howe remained in England twenty-six months and finally returned in steerage. He was a discouraged and disheartened man when he set foot on American soil in April 1849. On the last day of that month his wife of eight years and two months died age thirty-one years eight months.

Sewing machines did not stagnate while Howe was in England. Other inventors had turned their talents to the sewing machine. J. A. Bradshaw was granted U.S. Patent No. 5,942 on November 28, 1848. In 1849, patents were awarded on February 6 to Charles Morey and Joseph B. Johnson of Boston, Massachusetts, for a single thread machine making a stitch by a hook acting in combination with a needle (U.S. Patent No. 6,099); on May 8 to J. S. Conant (U.S. Patent No. 6,437) and J. [B]achelder (U.S. Patent No. 6,439) and on October 2 to S. C. Blodgett and J. A. Lerow on a machine the peculiar feature of which was that the shuttle was driven entirely around a circle at each stitch (U.S. Patent No. 6,766). Six additional patents were granted on sewing machines in 1850 making a total of sixteen patents granted through that year.

Eventually the populace heard about sewing by machinery, saw machines in operation and began to show an interest in them. To capitalize on the surge of inquiries, many manufacturers jumped to the fore to supply the demand. Instead of a wild dream, sewing by machine proved an actuality, more exact and less tiring than hand sewing.

Refinements and improvements had converted the crude attempts of pioneers into practical contrivances. As a result, sales leaped locally and nationally. In 1851, in New York City there were about two hundred sewing machines in operation. The sewing machine industry began to show large profits.

Although Howe had been back in the United States about a year and a half, he still had been unsuccessful in obtaining capital to manufacture his sewing machine. The industry disregarded his crude machine in favor of the superior models. But Howe was not dethroned. He resorted to the courts for vindication.

No sooner had the sewing machine industry begun to feel its importance, than Elias Howe, Jr. exploded a bomb in the midst of the pleased and complacent manufacturers and users. He righteously and indignantly waved his 1846 patent of September 10, 1846, shouting that his rights were being infringed. Furthermore he demanded a royalty on each and every sewing machine made.

The manufacturers blithely ignored Howe's claims and continued producing sewing machines. They doubted the validity of his claims and had no intentions of sharing their profits with him. But Howe had no intention of letting them get rich from what he thought of as his creation. He talked it over with George Fisher.

"They are all infringing upon my patent," Howe complained. "We are entitled to royalties on each and every machine. I think we should sue the whole bunch of them."

"You might be right," Fisher replied. "But as I see it, a patent only gives a person the right to spend his life in court trying to defend it. Four years ago, I gave you five hundred dollars for a half-interest in the machine. I sold a sixteenth interest [see footnote, page 173] to Martin, and bought it back from him, paying him eighty-two fifty more than he paid. My investment stands at $582.50. It is four years old. And it hasn't brought me one red cent. And now, you want more money for lawsuits. It's like throwing good money after bad. I'm not sure whether it's worth it."

"But, we can stop them from manufacturing," Howe insisted.

"What is the good of stopping them? If we can't manufacture the machines, what good is the patent?"

"We can collect a royalty on every machine made!"

"I'll think about it," Fisher replied.

Infringers were warned to stop but the field was too lucrative to lose without a struggle. The sewing machine manufacturers ignored the warning and continued operations. Plans were made by Howe's attorney for a battle with no quarter given or expected to be taken.

Those who believed that Elias Howe, Jr., had invented a workable sewing machine looked upon him as a sort of benefactor. However, his threats to force out of business those who did not accede to his demands brought a feeling of "heaven save us from our benefactors."

As Howe's insistence upon collecting a royalty became stronger, manufacturers genuinely began to feel alarmed. Some reluctantly acceded to his demands, but others contended that he was exceeding his rights, that his machines were workable only because of the improvements of others and that Howe was not justified in his demands, and furthermore would not dare bring his case to court.

Howe affected to be unconcerned over the belligerent attitude of those whom he threatened. He maintained that the patent was *prima facie* evidence of his rights and he was determined to uphold his position.

In March 1850, Howe served a summons and complaint and brought action in equity in the United States Circuit Court, Massachusetts District, against Orson C. Phelps for infringing his patent.

Phelps girded his loins to withstand the attack. He hired Albert Brewster Ely, an attorney of Boston, to represent him. Ely was 33 years of age and had been admitted to the bar on May 22, 1844.

"If we can prove that Howe's patent was too broad," Ely explained to the defendants, "and that the claims embraced in them are greater than those covered in his patents, then we have a good basis for our defense."

"Can't you prove that Howe never made a sewing machine, and even if he did make one, it would never operate according to his patent specifications?" one of the Phelps operators inquired.

"Mr. Ely," Phelps interrupted, "if you can establish that another sewing machine antedated the Howe machine, you can knock Howe's claims higher than a cocked hat."

"There was such a machine," the operator argued. "I remember reading and hearing about it. A man named Hunt, Walter Hunt, I think, made a machine in New York about 1834 or 1835."

"I'll investigate," Ely assured them.

Ely returned to his office and undertook a diligent search to ascertain the facts. He was able to locate three witnesses to substantiate the fact that Walter Hunt constructed a lock-stitch sewing machine. They were Walter Hunt, the inventor, of 270 West 19th Street, New York City, Adoniram Hunt, his brother, who had constructed an iron model of it, and George A. Arrowsmith, its producer and promoter.

Ely wrote to the three interested parties. Walter Hunt and George A. Arrowsmith agreed to sign depositions. A letter sent to Adoniram brought no reply. A second letter followed. Would Adoniram agree to have his deposition taken? Would he come to Boston to testify, if necessary? Adoniram Hunt had moved to Chillicothe, Ohio, a town with a population of about 7000. His last known address was Warren, Ohio, where he and James S. Bradish had obtained U.S. Patent No. 6,006 on January 9, 1849, on a mechanical musical playing attachment. Ely was impatient and wrote a third letter to him which was forwarded to Chillicothe.

After a delay he received a reply. He opened the letter. It contained a death notice from the *Scioto Gazette* of April 10, 1850:

In this city, this afternoon, of consumption, Mr. Adoniram F. Hunt, age 33 years, late of Warren, Trumbull County. Mr. Hunt formerly resided in this city and was a son-in-law of E. P. Pratt. He leaves a large circle of friends and acquaintances to mourn his loss. His funeral will take place tomorrow afternoon at four o'clock from the residence of E. P. Pratt, on Paint Street. Friends and acquaintances of the family are respectfully invited to attend.

The news spread. The May 1, 1850, issue of the *Northern Journal* of Lowville, New York, reported the death:

In Chillicothe, Ohio on the 10th of April of consumption, after a painful illness of three months, at the residence of Mr. E. P. Pratt (his father-in-law) Mr. Adoniram F. Hunt, formerly of this village, in the 36th year of his age.

There was much speculation in the sewing machine industry as to what effect Adoniram's death might have on the outcome of the Howe-Phelps lawsuit. His death was opportune for the plaintiffs as it removed a vital witness from testifying.

The passage of time was especially favorable for Howe. Sixteen years had erased the memory of many who had seen Hunt's machine in operation and their knowledge of its construction and performance was hazy. Witnesses who had seen Hunt's machine in operation were difficult to locate while many had since died.

Although these circumstances were favorable to Howe, his defense did not rely upon these fortuitous chain of events. He had a bonafide patent, and he believed that it was strong enough in itself to win a favorable decision in the courts.

Ely began to prepare the defense. He obtained the required legal forms and notified the plaintiff's lawyers that he intended taking depositions before Commissioner D. Gould of New York City on August 28, 1851.

On the appointed day, Walter Hunt appeared before the Commissioner and made a deposition.

> To the best of my knowledge and belief, I was born on the 29th day of July 1795, and consequently am fifty-six years of age. Most of my time for the last twenty years has been devoted to mechanical inventions and preparing papers, etc. for patents for myself and others.
>
> Between the years 1832 and 1834, I invented, built and put into full and effective operation a machine for sewing, stitching and seaming cloth, etc. The first machine for said purpose was built on my own account and principally by my own hands in my work shop in Amos Street, between Hudson and Bleecker Streets, in the City of New York. I occupied both sides of the street at the same time in 1832 and removed from the south to the north side in said year where I remained until 1834, late in the year. The latter establishment was known as Hunt's Patent Globe Stove Factory. While in this establishment, the exact date I do not remember, I disposed of my interest in said sewing machine to Mr. George A. Arrowsmith, who subsequently employed my brother Adoniram F. Hunt, in the building of said machine.

All of Hunt's testimony was recorded. The twenty-first question put to him was whether he had any of his old sewing machines. He answered;

> I do not know where all of said machines are. Two of them and parts of others were in my possession at 42 Gold Street in the City, where, how or by whom they were removed is unknown to me. They were badly injured by a fire in said building. I had supposed they were removed with my other machinery but it turns out they were not. I have since found some of the parts of one of them (which I think was made by my brother except the needle) in the possession of Mr. George A. Arrowsmith which are now before me, and which including the needle and shuttle are in the hands of the Commissioner Gould...

Ely's twenty-fifth question to Hunt was whether he knew Elias Howe, Jr.

> I know Elias Howe, Jr. He has frequently requested me to see his attorney and agent which I have always declined. We have conversed freely on the subject of our respective inventions in the sewing machines in which he has admitted my priority of invention, but opposed my priority of right on the ground of my delay in applying for letters patent and consequent abandonment of my right.

Howe's attorney, Joshua D. Ball, objected and moved that the answer to the twenty-fifth Interrogatory "be stricken out as irresponsive."

Two more questions, twenty-seven in all, were put to Hunt by Phelps' attorney.

The plaintiffs naturally were interested in discrediting the importance of Hunt's testimony about his own invention. Attempts were made to find instances of his unreliability but none could be found. Neither could any evidence be found which reflected against Hunt's character. The only attack that could be made against Hunt's character was that he refused to swear and would only make an affirmation. Instead of accepting this as a Quaker custom, the plaintiffs claimed that Hunt was an atheist.

Joshua D. Ball started the cross examination. "Do you believe in the existence of a God who will punish perjury?"

Hunt replied loudly and clearly so that everyone could hear:

I believe in the existence of a Supreme Omnipresent power, which inflicts suffering upon every rational being who commits perjury or any other conscious wrong, be it in thoughts, words or deeds.

Ball then asked Hunt whether or not his testimony had been rejected in a previous law case because he had refused to admit the existence of a hell.

Hunt was indignant. He replied:

I did not so state to Elias Howe nor any one else or any words to that purport. I have said to Mr. Howe and many others for such was the fact that in an important suit in Boston my testimony which I believe would have saved the case was withheld (because as I was informed it would be inadmissible unless I would swear or affirm to my belief in a Hell or hereafter), when I objected and consequently was not called upon the stand. I also stated that I would not have sworn to my belief in a Hell to become a witness in or to save the best case in the world, or language to that effect.

Twenty other questions were put to Hunt about his sewing machine, all of which were answered and signed by Hunt as correct. His signature was witnessed by Commissioner Gould on August 28, 1851.

The case progressed in orderly fashion. On October 4, 1851, the deposition of George A. Arrowsmith was taken before Commissioner D. Gould. Commissioner Gould read Arrowsmith the questions submitted by A. B. Ely, the defendant's lawyer, and the cross examination prepared by J. Giles and J. D. Ball, Howe's attorneys.

Arrowsmith stated that he was born in June 1793, that he was a blacksmith and for the last twenty years had been engaged in mechanics of various kinds.

He described the machine built by Walter Hunt of wood, and the duplicate made by Adoniram Hunt in iron:

The machine was constructed as nearly as I can describe it as follows: First, there was a clamp for holding the cloth to be seamed or stitched. Second, there was an axis from which projected a short limb or lever in and near the end of which was secured a curved needle with the eye near the point. Third, there was a spool containing the sewing thread supported upon a vertical shaft fixed in the frame of the machine. Fourth, a shuttle containing a spool which played horizontally through a shuttle tube or trough nearby and laterally with the jaws of the clamp in which the cloth was held. The sewing process in said machine was as follows: by the turning of a crank, motion was given to the needle which was forced through the cloth beyond the eye when the shuttle on the other side of the cloth passed along forming a loop as the needle was drawn back again.

Attorneys questioned him,

Did said machine or machines invented by said Walter Hunt operate usefully and successfully and to any advantage, or did they or it prove a failure and not able to be worked? Did not one part of the machinery in these machines or this machine clog or obstruct or impede the operation of some other part? Can you swear positively that you ever saw said machines or machine operate? How much work could be performed by them, and was the work firm, regular and strong or how otherwise, and how do you know it? And why were said machines or why was said machine abandoned and never patented? State particularly.

The attorneys asked him,

How do you know that Adoniram F. Hunt ever constructed a sewing machine? Did you ever see it and examine it and see it work and when and where and why and for what purpose and how often did you examine it and to what extent did you see it work? Did it sew regularly and was the stitch made by it strong and regular or how otherwise? Did you notice said machine so minutely that you can swear to its construction and operation? Can you tell its distinct parts? If so, state them. How long ago and when and where was said machine made? How do you remember these facts? Do you speak of your own knowledge or from what others have told you? Was said machine ever abandoned and if yes, why?

To these questions Arrowsmith replied,

I employed and paid him. I did see it work and examined it. I examined it and saw it work in the city in 1834 or 1835 because I chose to. It was my property. It did sew regularly and the stitch it made was strong and regular. I did so notice it. I have stated the parts in my answer to the eighth direct interrogatory. It was made in 1834 or 1835 in Amos Street in this city. I remember because my money paid for them, I do speak of my own knowledge. It was not abandoned.

The cross examination inquired as to whether the machines were able to operate, and Arrowsmith answered,

> They operated to produce complete seams as I have stated, but have not put into practical use in the shops. They did not prove a failure or not able to be worked. One part did not clog or obstruct or impede the operation of another part. I can swear positively that I saw them operate. I think it did about four or five hundred stitches a minute. It was firm, regular and strong. I know it because I saw it. The reason why it was not patented was principally of a pecuniary nature. It never was abandoned for I always intended to take out a patent.

The twenty-third cross question was a surprise to Arrowsmith. It had nothing to do with the case and referred to Mr. Hunt. The commissioner carefully read it:

> Did Walter Hunt ever state to you or any of you or in your presence or hearing that he did not believe in a God who would punish perjury or anything to that effect, and, if yes, when and where and to whom, or did he ever state to you or in your presence or hearing that he did not believe in the existence of God and in future state of rewards and punishments? If yes, when and where and to whom?

Arrowsmith reflected a few minutes. Then he replied,

> I never heard him express an opinion that he did not believe in a God who would punish perjury or any thing to that effect; that is I never heard him say that he did not believe in the existence of God, that is, the God of the Bible, or God as the Bible declares it, and also that he did not believe in a future state of reward and punishment as declared by the scripture. I cannot state when I have heard him so state. It was in the City. My impression is that he so stated to myself.*

Commissioner Gould handed Arrowsmith his deposition of twenty-three pages. Arrowsmith signed it and the Commissioner then affixed his signature to the testimony.

At various times other depositions were taken. Smith Gardiner, fifty years and upwards, a manufacturer of oxide of zinc, and also a sugar refiner, testified on November 6 he knew Hunt and with regard to his beliefs stated,

> In a conversation which I had with said Hunt at Dunlap's Hotel in the city some months ago he spoke of his expecting to be called on as a witness in this suit and he mentioned that in a case in Massachusetts in which he had been called as a witness he was not permitted to testify because he would not

---

Apparent contradiction in the original—editors.

acknowledge that he believed in Hell-fire; and he added that he never should believe in any such damned nonsense as that to please any of the blue skins.

John W. Cochran, forty years old, a civil engineer of Williamsburg, Kings County, New York, testified on November 11 before the Commissioner:

I am a Civil Engineer. Nobody employed me to see said Hunt. I think I have said at some time that his testimony might do a pecuniary damage to Howe and put him to trouble and expense. I never asked said Hunt if $1,000 would not induce him to go away and not testify, nor anything to that effect, nor said anything to him about $1,000 or any sums of money in connection with that subject; nor did I ever while conversing with him on that subject show him what purported to be a draft for $1,000 or for any sum of money. I never took anyone with me when I conversed with said Hunt.

On November 22, 1851, before William Emerson, Commissioner of Deeds, Frederick Smith, twenty-eight years of age, a bookkeeper at Dunlap's Hotel, 135 Fulton Street, New York City testified:

I have some six or eight times heard said Hunt make statements in my presence about the existence of a God, and about a future state. On one occasion, some one asked him if he believed in the existence of a God to which Hunt answered, "There is no God. To talk about a Supreme Being is all damned nonsense!" The last time that I heard him make any statement on such a subject was during the last summer as nearly as I can recollect. A future state was the subject of conversation and I asked said Hunt what he thought would become of us a thousand years hence. To this he answered, "We shall be as well off as we were a thousand years ago!" He then added, "Man's life is like the flame of a candle, blow it out and nothing is known of it after." All the conversations in which said Hunt has taken part, at which I have been present occurred at Dunlap's Hotel.

On December 1, 1851, Mrs. Polly Hunt and her daughter, Caroline M. Van Buren, were also called upon to testify before Commissioner D. Gould. They both confirmed that Walter Hunt had made a workable sewing machine and that it operated satisfactorily.

Amasa B. Howe, age thirty-four, the brother of Elias Howe was another one of those called upon for a deposition. He stated,

Hunt said that he went to Boston to testify in a pistol case and was not allowed to testify because he did not believe in a God or in a future state of existence. He said he did not believe in any such nonsense, and he would not believe in it. He became a good deal excited about the refusal to let him testify and expressed a good deal of indignation at the lawyers and others. I do not remember any more about the first conversation particularly enough to state the same. On a subsequent occasion, he said the life of man ceases like the burning out of a candle, and that he did not believe in any future state of existence because he had no recollection of anything before his present life. I have heard him express himself to the effect of the above statements repeatedly.

The Howe-Phelps lawsuit had not passed the deposition stage before Elias Howe, Jr., brought similar proceedings against another infringer, William Bradford of New Bedford, Massachusetts. Howe maintained that Bradford used an average of three Lerow and Blodgett sewing machines for one year previous to the date of the writ, like his rotary sewing machine, and that Bradford unlawfully and wrongfully and without the consent or allowance and against the will of the plaintiff used the said improvement patented as aforesaid in violation and infringement of the exclusive right so secured to the plaintiffs by the said letters patent.

As had Phelps, Bradford, supported by the manufacturers, entered a denial of Howe's accusations.

Howe petitioned the court for protection of his patent rights and an injunction against Bradford's use of the machines. Judge Roger Brooke Taney of the United States Supreme Court, who was sitting as Circuit Court Judge in Massachusetts, agreed to the injunction proceedings, ordered the Massachusetts Marshal to attach the goods and estate of William Bradford to the value of $1,000 and set the case for trial on October 15th.

Both the Phelps and the Bradford cases dragged on in the court calendar. They were constantly postponed by one side or the other for one or another legal reason.

As no decision had been reached in the Phelps and Bradford cases, it was not mandatory for the recalcitrant manufacturers to capitulate. They continued using sewing machines regardless of whether they had acceded to Howe's terms. One of these who defied Howe was William E. Whiting.

Howe advertised in the *New York Daily Tribune* of February 12, 1852.

Caution. The public are cautioned against purchasing Sewing Machines or rights of William E. Whiting, No. 124 Pearl Street, under my patent, as all powers of attorney, granted to him by me, are revoked, as well as those of persons acting by authority from him; and all such are forbid paying him any money on account of my patent, and they are required to call at my office and have their powers renewed and confirmed by me.

ELIAS HOWE, JR. Patentee
of the original Sewing Machine. No. 201 Broadway.

The industry was furious. Howe's threats were curtailing business. The public was afraid to buy machines for fear of becoming involved in an infringement proceeding. Howe threatened to sue everyone. His threats of reprisals were ridiculed by the opposition, but the situation remained tense. A legal decision, one way of the other, was eagerly awaited by both sides.

Both the Phelps and Bradford cases were equity suits brought in the Circuit Court of the United States, Massachusetts District. Although the Phelps suit was instituted first, Howe's attorneys on March 8, 1852, requested prior trial of the Bradford case. The plaintiff's motion was granted and an action for damages for infringement of patent rights was scheduled for the May 1852 term of the Circuit Court. The case was scheduled for trial on June 9, 1852, but the lawyers mutually consented to delay trial until Tuesday, June 22. The Presiding Justice was Judge Peleg Sprague, former Massachusetts congressman and senator. Elias Howe's attorney was the Hon. Rufus Choate, also one of the ablest members of the American bar. He was also a congressman and senator and had been tendered an appointment to the Supreme Court of the United States to succeed Justice Levi Woodbury. He refused the offer in order to remain in legal practice.

Rufus Choate selected Joshua D. Ball to assist him as Howe's attorney.

The defendants were again represented by Albert Brewster Ely. By 1852 he had had less than nine years of legal experience and found the trail to clients difficult. On December 12, 1851, he had advertised in the *Scientific American*:

A. B. Ely—Counsellor at Law—46 Washington Street, Boston. Will give particular attention to Patent Cases. Refers to Munn & Co.

Ely's notice of defense covered eight points.

1. That plaintiff's claim is defective; because it is too broad and covers more than his pretended invention as described in his specification; because some parts of said pretended invention are described in said specification which are not embraced in his said claim.
2. Because there is a variance between the patent granted and the patent claimed because said claim is for a function, an effect or a result.
3. That plaintiff's specification and description contains more than is necessary to produce the desired effect as provided in said statute of [July 4,] 1836.
4. That the plaintiff was not the original and first inventor or discoverer of the thing by him claimed to be patented or of a substantial and material part thereof claimed as new, and that the following are the names and places of residence of those whom the defendant intends to prove have possessed a prior knowledge thereof: [witnesses for defendants] Walter Hunt, George A. Arrowsmith, Alexander M. Alling, William K. Ashland, William Carlock, George Cole, [---] Pierce, [and---] Lafetia, all of the city and state of New York and to the defendant unknown, and Adoniram F. Hunt of Cincinnati, State of Ohio, and that the same was used in said city of New York and in said Cincinnati and in other places in the states of New York and Ohio to the defendant now unknown.

5. That essential and material parts of plaintiff's machine have been for many years prior to plaintiff's patent in common use by weavers, upholsterers, seamstresses, card makers and others, and that the stitch claimed by the plaintiff's machine to be made has been in like manner commonly known among bookbinders, shoe makers, sail makers, web makers, carpet weavers and in the construction of mail bags.

6. That no machine capable of being usefully or successfully operated has ever been constructed in accordance with plaintiff's said description and specifications and drawings and that no machine can be constructed according to plaintiff's said specifications, description and drawings so as to operate practically, successfully or usefully; and that attempts made by persons interested in said patent or others to manufacture machines and according to said specifications, descriptions and drawings were after great expense abandoned as impractical.

7. That defendant had permission or license from some of his assignees to use and make said plaintiff's machine.

8. That defendant hath not made, used or tended to be used the machine claimed by plaintiff to have been invented and patented and which is described in plaintiff's specification and drawings.

The plaintiffs allowed the deposition of Walter Hunt to be read in court. At a subsequent stage of the case, Walter Hunt was offered in person as a witness by the defendants to a matter not inquired of in his deposition. The plaintiffs then objected to his competency on the ground that he was an atheist, and the court allowed the inquiry to be gone into. The defendants excepted to this ruling of the court.

Testimony was then produced in court regarding the religious belief of said Hunt. The court, upon the evidence, found that Walter Hunt did not believe in the existence of a God who would punish perjury—and he was rejected. The defendants also objected to this.

Mrs. Caroline M. Van Buren, Walter's daughter, was brought to the stand by the defense. She could not testify to the exact date of her father's invention but produced the letter written by Adoniram Hunt to Joel Johnson on May 17, 1836, asking for the return of the sewing machine. The handwriting was identified by George A. Arrowsmith, but the plaintiffs objected to its presentation and it was not admitted to the records.

When Howe was called to the stand, A. B. Ely asked him questions for the purpose of testing his credibility, and stated that he wished to do the same with the other witnesses. The court ruled that the defendant might ask the witness whether he considered the oath which he had taken binding upon his conscience and also whether he believed in the existence of a God who would punish perjury, that these questions may be divided, if desired, and that these were the only questions that could be put. Ely objected.

Ely offered evidence to show the good moral character of Hunt and also to show his good character for truth and veracity, but the court rejected the evidence in each case. To this ruling, Ely vehemently protested.

On the general question of utility in an invention, the court instructed the jury that "useful" in the statute does not require the highest degree of utility or even a great degree of utility. It does not require that it should be more useful than others or as useful as others. "If, on the whole, you find that it is in any degree useful that is sufficient to satisfy the law and render it patentable," the judge instructed the jury.

Ely objected to this interpretation of the law. Other technicalities and questions of patent law were introduced. To many of these the defendants offered exception.

After both sides had presented all their evidence, the summation was made and the case was turned over to the jury. On July 12, 1852, Cheney Hatch, foreman of the jury handed in his verdict, "Elias Howe, Jr. et al vs William Bradford. The jury find the defendant is guilty in manner and form as the plaintiff hath declared against him, and assess damages in the sum of $150."

Bradford was declared guilty on the first, third and fifth counts. Elias Howe was awarded damages of $150 and costs. The costs amounted to $467.56 as figured by Joshua D. Ball, Howe's attorney. The correctness of the figures were attested by A. B. Ely on October 7, 1852, on which date it was filed with the court.

The *Scientific American* of July 25, 1852, took notice of the controversy and reported:

> Interesting Patent Case. Sewing Machines. U.S. Circuit Court. Judge Sprague presiding. The plaintiff was Elias Howe, Jr. of Cambridge, Mass. The defendant was William Bradford of New Bedford, Mass., the machine of the defendant was Lerow and Blodgett's rotary, which has been illustrated in our columns; it was asserted to be an infringement of Howe's Patent. The trial lasted for three weeks and was decided on the 12th inst, in favor of Howe, and on the point claimed of using two threads, a needle and a shuttle. The case was very closely contested. For the plaintiff, Hon. Rufus Choate, Joel Giles and J. D. Ball. For the defendant Ambrose L. Jordan and Keller of New York and A. B. Ely of Boston.

Ely filed a thirty-two page bill of exceptions. The first blood had been shed and Howe had emerged victorious.

Although the success of this lawsuit pleased George Fisher, now a resident of Worcester, Massachusetts, his faith in the future and the wisdom of his investment was not so pronounced. When he received an offer of $2,325 on November 18, 1852, for his half-interest in Howe's machine, he jumped at the chance of recouping his losses and sold his interest to George W. Bliss.

Chapter 22

The decision of the Boston courts embittered Hunt. Whenever Howe's name was mentioned, Hunt fumed and ranted and accused Howe of concealing the truth and not letting the facts become public knowledge. He gnashed his teeth whenever he thought of the charges of atheism brought against him. He developed a hatred and resentfulness against legal technicalities and conniving barristers who practiced them. For the first time in his life, his faith in his fellow man had been shaken. His good humor deserted him. A scowl took the place of his friendly smile. He became morose. He walked as if in a daze.

"What's the matter there, Hunt?" yelled Charles T. Kipp, proprietor of the porterhouse at 535 Hudson Street, as he stood in his doorway. "You're walking the street like a scavenger with your head hanging down. Lose something?"

"Yeah," the disappointed inventor groaned.

"What was it?"

"My case at Boston."

"Forget it. What you need is a drink."

Hunt looked at him quizzingly.

"I know you don't drink," Kipp apologized, "but a drink won't hurt you. Come in and have a snack and tell me all about it."

They sat down at a marble-top table and Hunt unburdened himself. At first, he spoke very calmly, but in a few minutes, he became vehement. He pounded the table with his clenched fist.

"Take it easy, Hunt," Kipp cautioned. "All right, so you don't make money from one invention, you'll make it on another."

"But the humiliation, the aggravation, the perjury..."

"I know. But you'll get over it. I know you of old, Hunt, you'll forget your resentment."

"Maybe, but right now, I feel as if the whole world is wrong. I feel like I'm walking upside down."

"Now, that's a good idea," Kipp countered.

"What are you talking about?"

"You, walking upside down."

Hunt looked bewildered. Kipp had downed a few glasses of ale during the conversation, but not enough to make him irrational. His eyes flashed, and a big grin covered his face.

"You just hit on a great idea. I know many people in show business. They come in here regularly. I'll tell you what. If you make something so that a man can walk upside down, I'll manufacture it. We'll make a fortune!"

"How can a man walk upside down?" Hunt asked.

"Well, if a fly can do it, there's no reason a man can't," Kipp joked.

"I'll think about it," Hunt said as he left the porterhouse.

About a month later, Hunt walked to Kipp's saloon carrying a package.

"What you got there, Hunt?" Kipp asked.

"What you ordered, the fly walker."

"The fly walker?"

"The fly walker. For the circus."

Kipp grinned. "You've got some sense of humor. Come back some other time when I'm not so busy."

"Don't you want to see it?"

"See what?"

"The Antipodean Performer. The only contraption in the world where man can defy the laws of gravity."

"What?"

"The Antipodean Performer. A device that can be attached to your shoes. A person can walk upside down on the ceiling almost as easily as he can walk on the ground."

"Can you do it?"

"Yes."

"Let me see you do it."

"It'll work better on a smooth surface but I'll show you anyway."

Hunt proceeded to demonstrate it and Kipp stared in amazement.

"It's remarkable. I'll back you," Kipp said gleefully.

No expensive machinery was necessary to manufacture it. It could be built in Hunt's shop. The capital required was small.

Kipp was astute enough to realize that the antipodean walker would never become a household necessity, but would be restricted to theatrical purposes. He contacted Richard Sands, proprietor and chief performer at the Circus at the New York Amphitheater, 37 Bowery. Sands inspected the invention, learned how it operated, and immediately ordered one for the Circus.

John McCormick, an acrobat, was taught the secret of how to defy gravity. To add glamour to his performance, he was billed as "Professor McCormick, the Great Philosophical Pedestrian."

Space was taken in the newspapers to advertise the feat. The "wonderful experiment" was advertised in the *New York Daily Tribune* and the *New York Herald* on February 16, 1852.

CIRCUS. NEW YORK AMPHITHEATER — 37 BOWERY — Wonderful experiment. A man walking head downward on the ceiling — On Monday evening, February 16, 1852, the great philosophical Antipodean Pedestrian, John McCormick, of Ohio, the successful inventor of the only antipodean apparatus ever completed, will exhibit his astonishing performance of inverted locomotion, in which he will walk uppermost, upon a marble slab, nine feet in length, at an elevation of 18 feet from the ground. The marble upon which the performance is made is so smoothly polished that a fly can scarcely maintain its foot hold. The managers having exhibited a private exhibition of this extraordinary performance, pledge themselves to the public that its accomplishment is based strictly upon scientific and philosophical principles and entirely without the agency of trickery, deception or humbug, of any description. The experiment has never been made by any other man, and the success attained by it (by means discovered by the exhibitor alone) must strike all with astonishment. Besides the above unparalleled novelty, the following new features of the circle will be introduced by the members of the troupe; Mr. J. J. Nathan and Mr. J. Hankins will appear together in an unrivalled act of double horsemanship, after the manner of the famous Grecian game, known as the ancient Numidae Desultores, with splendid evolutions, changes, positions, tableaux, etc. Miss Emma Nathan in an elegant Pas Seul. Great feats of horsemanship by the Rivers Family. Messrs. Sands, Smith, Masters Rivers, Sands, Deriogs, etc. To conclude with St. George and the Dragon. Boxes 25¢. Pit 12½¢."

The *New York Herald* of February 17, 1852, reported the performance in its news columns:

Bowery Circus — The wonderful performance of John McCormick last evening in walking on the ceiling of the Amphitheater with his head downward, excited the greatest surprise. He will repeat it again this evening when, no doubt, the Amphitheater will be crowded. It is the most wonderful act ever performed within the walls of a circus.

With plenty of advertising, the daring performance quickly became the talk of the town. Many contended that the act was too dangerous, and the performer should not be allowed to court death for the benefit of thrill lovers. Others feared that an accident might result in a panic, and pressure was brought on the management to curb the daredevil. But as the opposition to the performance increased, so did the demand for tickets.

Everyone was eager to see the professor perform—or fail. People fought to buy tickets. Hundreds were turned away. The theater was jammed to capacity.

Richard Sands,

THE GREAT

ANTIPODEAN PERFORMER,

Who is now Exhibiting in London with splendid success, his apparently miraculous feat of Promenading upon a **Polished Ceiling** with his **HEAD DOWNWARD**, was trained by

PROFESSOR HUNT,

Of this city, who invented and made the astonishing Apparatus for that purpose. For this admirable invention Letters Patent will soon be granted as an improvement in philosophical mechanism, by which may be demonstrated, with a perfection and elegance never before attempted, one of the most interesting phenomena in nature.

The performance of Mr. Sands during the last season, was every where admitted to be the original and most attractive feature of the company with which he was connected, and henceforth no such exhibition can be considered complete without it.

The undersigned desires to inform all those who may wish to purchase, and to be instructed in the use of the

☞ ANTIPODEAN APPARATUS, ☜

that he is able to supply all things required for its public exhibition, of improved construction and highest possible mechanical finish. Also that he has convenient and retired Rooms, where purchasers of the Apparatus, or those whom they intend to have perform, can be trained and instructed under the direction of the Inventor, Professor Hunt.

Terms made known on application at

535 Hudson-st., corner of Charles, N.Y., to

CHARLES T. KIPP.

All kinds of theories were advanced as to the principle involved in the "antipodean" device, and no one had solved the puzzle when, after two performances, the authorities did step in. Life and limb were in danger they declared, and precaution had to be taken against accidents.

It was; and was so announced to the public, who were assured that arrangements had been made so that the operator of the device would be received safely, should he fall from his inverted platform.

Although the danger was lessened, the Circus continued to play to capacity crowds, with thousands turned away. So successful was the Antipodean Pedestrian in the New York Amphitheater that P. T. Barnum engaged McCormick for his American Museum. Barnum was too fine a showman to fail to book this act.

McCormick's appearance at Barnum's American Museum was advertised in the *New York Herald* of February 23, 1852:

BARNUM'S AMERICAN MUSEUM. P. T. Barnum, manager and proprietor; John Greenwood, Jr., Assistant Manager, Admission to the entire Museum and performances 25¢. Children under ten 12½¢. Parquet 12½¢ extra. Professor McCormick, who, having learned the philosophical secret, walks a slab of polished marble, suspended from the ceiling, with his feet up against the marble, and his head downwards like a fly, thus overcoming the attraction of gravitation. Monday and Tuesday, February 23rd and 24th, afternoons at 3 o'clock, dancing, singing, Grand philosophical feat of Professor McCormick of walking head downwards.

McCormick successfully exhibited the act in various parts of the country, receiving the acclaim of the populace. In London, Richard Sands was featured at the Drury Lane Theater in 1852, as "walking across the polished surface of an inverted platform with feet up and head down, at an elevation of twenty-five feet from the ground."

Nerve was the only requirement necessary to perform with an Antipodean. It was a simple device and little skill was required to operate it, but its mystery and manipulation was carefully guarded for many years, until finally its secret was exposed in an article about Richard Sands in the *New York Clipper* of May 22, 1875:

From two lofty draped supports was placed a temporary ceiling, twenty feet in length, and consisting of a stout timber framing, with a smooth surface; at each end was a slung seat, and beneath the ceiling was a net, provided in case of accident. Mr. Sands prepared himself by lacing sandals over his boots, to which were attached brass loops; and these were connected by springs with a pair of platterlike soles in which lay the secret, as they were brought to the theater in a locked box, and conveyed away with similar caution at the close of the performance. Mr. Sands commenced by ascending a ladder to one of the slung seats, and, lying upon his back by aid of ropes, placed his platter-shod feet upon the ceiling, then gently detached himself, and very slowly walked across the platform, occasionally poising himself on one leg. Thus he reached the seat at the opposite end and descended by the ladder.

He subsequently succeeded in walking upon a large slab of polished marble. The platter-like soles above described were made of soft leather and moistened with water. These, when pressed firmly by the feet, so as to expel the air, enabled the performer to maintain his hold upon the slab, and by a movement of the foot [to progress]....

At spasmodic intervals, the Antipodean act was again resurrected. In 1863 Signor Bliss advertised that he was "the only performer who is at present walking the ceiling head downward." Every generation or so, the act had its featured performers. Mademoiselle Aimee, of the Austin Sisters, performed "her thrilling act of walking on the ceiling, head downward" at the Eighth Avenue Theater for the week commencing March 7, 1887. As late as 1937, the Antipodean was still featured in this country and abroad by circus performers.

Even Hunt's least important invention has withstood the acid test of time!

This was Kipp's first sortie into the promoting game. And he liked it. "But there's no profit in making things to order," he complained to Hunt. "Money can only be made by interesting everybody. Invent something that people need, something that will make work easier. That's the way. Everybody's lazy." He grinned, then amended himself: "I mean everybody but you, Hunt. You're always busy."

Hunt toyed with the cameo suspended from his watch chain, tapping it nervously, waiting for Kipp to get to the point. The man had something on his mind, Hunt was sure.

"Why not invent something—" Kipp stopped short and yelled at the bartender: "Didn't I tell you to keep that bottle corked?"

"Cork's lost," the barkeep muttered.

"You'd lose your head if it wasn't tied on," Kipp snapped, then half apologetically explained to Hunt: "That fellow won't ever keep the bottles corked. I'm half a mind to—" He suddenly jumped to his feet and snapped his fingers. "That's it, Hunt! That's it! A bottle stopper! You invent one that's good, and our fortunes are made. I've tried every one on the market, and there's *not* a good one. There you are! Make one. I'll patent it!"

Finally assured that such a demand actually existed, with an almost unlimited market, Hunt once more enthusiastically set to work. Intention and accomplishment were closely related with him. In only a short time he had conceived a new bottle stopper and brought the model to Kipp.

On January 10, 1852, Kipp applied for a patent. The specifications and application were witnessed by Alexander Donaldson, a clerk at 179 Broadway, and E. M. Dunham, whose signatures were in turn witnessed by M. I. Cole, Commissioner of Deeds.

Inventions travel in cycles. Inventors appear to be curiously susceptible to telepathy. No sooner is one seized with an idea, than similar ideas bob up in widely separated places. An application for a somewhat similar bottle-stopper reached the Patent Office at about the time Hunt's was filed. The application was made by Messrs. E. and D. Kinsey, of Cincinnati, Ohio.

Because of the similarity of the inventions, the patent commissioner advised Hunt, on March 12, 1852, that interference proceedings would be required to settle the matter.

Patent interference cases generally took time, and a lawyer was needed. On April 12, 1852, Walter Hunt wrote to the Commissioner of Patents that he had appointed Edward Clark, of 61 Chambers Street, New York City, to represent him. The letter of appointment was witnessed by Charles T. Kipp and John C. Wilson. (Edward Clark later was the attorney associated with Isaac Merritt Singer, thus in time becoming Walter Hunt's bitter antagonist in the cases involving Howe's priority claims to the sewing machine.)

In the bottle-stopper interference case, Clark wrote Commissioner Thomas Eubanks, on May 29, 1852, in detail. He assured the commissioner of patents that his client, Hunt, believed a mistake must have been made in examination of his own bottle-stopper and that of the Messrs. Kinsey, for in fact there was *no* similarity. The Hunt device was new and novel, while the Kinsey invention was nothing more or less than the old poppet valve which had been universally known and used for years. As attorney, Clark wrote the commissioner:

> Mr. Hunt has no objection to the issuing of a patent to Messrs. Kinsey for the thing described in their specification, but he respectfully submits that the circumstance of their employing the very *old device* of the poppet valve, to answer the purpose of a bottle stopper ought not to prevent him from receiving a patent for the *new contrivance* which he has invented. The Messrs. Kinseys have not in their specification *claimed* or *described* and doubtless never conceived anything really like Mr. Hunt's invention.
>
> Their bottle stopper *opens on all sides alike* while Hunt's opens only on the *under side.* When *stopper* is fixed upon the central stem, his is *loose* and plays with a *swivel* or gimble joint, which produces the downward opening in whatever direction the bottle may be canted.
>
> The *stem* in their stopper is *movable* and supported in guides, in the same manner as other poppet valves, whereas in Hunt's the *stem* is *fixed to* and cast entire with the stopper tube. In short, the two plans are substantially different, both in principle of construction and mode of operation, and would, I believe, be so considered and adjudged by every competent mechanic.
>
> The only way in which Mr. Hunt is able to account for so singular a decision of the examining officer is that his specifications may have been mistaken for

those of Mr. Milus of the City of New York, who has made and I am informed has applied for a patent for a decanter stopper *precisely* similar to Messrs. Kinseys. The notice of interference claims was probably intended for Mr. Milus.

Clark had failed to advise the Patent Office that he was empowered to act as attorney for Hunt and so he supplemented this letter with one dated June 2, 1852, in which he stated that on April 12, 1852, Hunt had appointed him to represent him as counsel.

In answer to Clark's letter, the Commissioner of Patents wrote, on June 17, 1852, that Walter Hunt had not definitely established the date of his invention, and that therefore he could not claim priority. Hunt was thoroughly incensed at what he considered unjust treatment.

Deciding to "speak plainly" to the commissioner, himself, on July 3, 1852, he wrote:

> Yours of the 17th ult. addressed to my attorney, Edward Clark, Esquire, has come to hand and its contents been duly considered.
>
> I find that the only new feature of any note contained in this last communication is the suggestion that I have lost the benefit if any should arise from the fate of the invention. If this is the result of my neglect in citing Messrs. Kinsey to the examination of witnesses, the same rule I should suppose would apply equally to them for the same neglect.
>
> It is my determination to avoid all uncourteous language and even to refrain from expressing the strong sentiments which I cannot help but feel, but still I deem it my duty to speak plainly in a case when in connection with this I have so much at stake involving also the rights and interests of inventors generally and I hope therefore the Office will accord to me a patent hearing when it shall be considered that I have devoted thirty years of my life to the construction of novel machinery of my own invention for which over thirty patents have been granted in this country and in Europe, and that I have at the same time made the patent laws—especially of our own country—my text book and study, and have had the honor of associating with and enjoying the confidence of many of the profoundest elementary and practical mechanics in this country and in Europe. To persons of this character as many as I could conveniently consult I have submitted my claim together with that supposed to interfere with it, and in every instance they have agreed with me as to the non-interference between the plans in question.
>
> This much I have taken the liberty of pleading in *self-defense* against the official charge of "ill-timed action on my part under the circumstances." I did not expect the Office to give in the first instance reasons for its decision, but I did suppose—and I still hope not vainly—that any reasons which I could present tending to show that no interference really exists, would be carefully considered, and that I should, so far as sound, have the benefit of them. I have entire confidence in the justice of my claims and will still hope that upon

consideration the novelty and merit of my invention will be recognized and the patent granted to me as applied for.

But spurning the most favorable construction of your letters to be the correct one, and taking it for granted that I have by reason of not examining witnesses as to priority of invention lost all claim to further hearing in the matter, then it follows that I have not only lost an invention worth some thousands of dollars, but I have lost in addition over one thousand dollars worth of machinery and exquisitively wrought moulds constructed exclusively for the manufacture of the decanter-stoppers in question—the further use of which would subject me to a prosecution by the preferred applicant who would rapidly avail himself of my plan as better and cheaper by at least fifty per cent than his own. This is a most important feature in the comparative merits of these *supposed conflicting inventions*. As evidence of this fact I will take the liberty of quoting the assertion of Mr. Milus of this city made to me personally a few days ago since, namely, that he could not afford to sell his stoppers (which are identical with the Messrs. Kinsey's) short of $9. per gross by the quantity, whereas I am now selling mine at $36. a gross or $3. a dozen. And this difference in price as Mr. Milus avers inevitably results from the dissimilarity in the mechanical principles of the two devices. In mine the *cylinder center shaft* and supporting *arms* are *case entire* and form only one piece. The Messrs. Kinsey's cannot be so cast because their plan of construction and operation requires it to be made and operated in *separate* and *distinct parts*.

In conclusion, I do most *earnestly* and *respectfully request* that the Office will take into consideration the facts above hinted at, and such as have been previously suggested and give them their due weight in the final action in this case.

In this letter Hunt not only exhibits his anger but does not hesitate to stoop to a little hyperbole. He states that he was the recipient of over thirty patents in this country and Europe. Actually, according to count, he only received twenty-one patents, but he may have counted reissues as additional patents. No English patents were obtained in his name, but were taken out in the name of other individuals. Possibly, the reissues and the English patents would bring the number of patents he received to more than thirty.

Hunt further stated that he had devoted over thirty years of his life to the construction of novel machinery, which implies that he began prior to 1822. This again may be true, but the earliest known patent awarded in the name of Walter Hunt was his joint patent of June 26, 1826, which he received in connection with Willis Hoskins on the spinning and flax machine. It is possible that he was engaged in building novel machinery prior to the award of the patent and that he was merely telling the simple truth.

Walter further states that the invention was worth thousands of dollars to him. This may have been the case, especially as he states that he expended a thousand dollars for the purchase of molds and machinery.

For his safety pin he received only $100. He gave away a half interest in his sewing machine for nothing, and transferred the remaining half for a return of his interests in a nail machine and the pill box machinery. Other inventions likewise brought him notoriously poor returns. In this case Hunt may have been a little too optimistic—but he always was, until too late.

On the same day he wrote the Commissioner of Patents, Hunt revoked the power of attorney granted Edward Clark. One factor that may have influenced the change in lawyers was that Clark was so busy fighting the many sewing machine cases that he could not afford to spend the time successfully to prosecute Hunt's patent application. Hunt appointed John J. Greenough to represent him. Possibly the situation demanded representation in Washington, and Greenough, an experienced patent attorney, could better handle the situation than Clark.

Greenough was one of the editors of the *American Polytechnic Journal*, and was well versed in patent lore and law. His connection with the Patent Office, official and otherwise, was of more than sixteen years' standing.

Interestingly enough, John J. Greenough was the same Greenough who had also invented a sewing machine. It is an ironic commentary that the inventor of the first lock-stitch sewing machine should appoint as his attorney the man who had received the first sewing machine patent.

Despite the controversy and the interference suit, neither claimant to the bottle-stopper invention made a spectacular effort to prove priority or the merit of their claims. In making his decision, the patent commissioner based his opinion upon an affidavit signed by W. S. Morsell, May 1, 1852, before Peter Bell, Justice of the Peace, in Cincinnati, Ohio, in which he swore that he remembered seeing the Kinseys' improved self-acting bottle-stopper on the 15th day of October, 1851.

Priority of claim having been established to the satisfaction of Patents Commissioner Thomas Eubanks, he rendered his decision in favor of the Kinseys on October 1, 1852.

But Hunt had no intention of abandoning his invention, because he felt that there was no similarity between his own and the Kinseys' bottle-stoppers. The next known step undertaken in Hunt's behalf on the subject was a letter sent to the commissioner of patents from Charles Grafton Page* of Page & Company, Washington, D.C., on October 21.

Page's letter again described in detail the differences between the Kinsey bottle-stopper and Hunt's. Being on the ground and familiar with the technicalities of the Patent Office, Page was able to present his case in person and show

---

Page had been associated with John J. Greenough, and had been one of the editors of the American Polytechnic Journal *before he became one of the partners in the above-named patent law firm. Page was subsequently employed in the Patent Office from May 10, 1861, to May 5, 1868.*

UNITED STATES PATENT OFFICE.

WALTER HUNT, OF NEW YORK, N. Y., ASSIGNOR TO CHARLES T. KIPP.

IMPROVEMENT IN BOTTLE-STOPPERS.

Specification forming part of Letters Patent No. **9,527.** dated January 4, 1853.

To all whom it may concern:

Be it known that I, WALTER HUNT, of the city, county, and State of New York, have invented a new and useful plan of a Decanter-Stopper, which I designate as the "Swivel-Cap Decanter-Stopper," of which the following is a full and exact description.

Said stopper is composed of two parts or pieces—viz:, a tube combining in one piece two flanges or annular disks with a central vertical shaft having radiating arms at its base, which extend horizontally and unite with the inner periphery of said tube a little below the upper flange or lip of the same, as shown in the elevated cut section, Fig. 3, and the top view, Fig. 2, in the annexed drawings, where similar letters refer to the same parts throughout.

A indicates the tube; B, the upper or lip flange; C, the bottom flange; D, the shaft; E, the spokes or supporting-arms; F, the cap. The other portion of said stopper is a funnel-shaped cap, F, having a central perforation sufficiently large to allow it to fall down over the shaft E, as shown in Fig. 1, cut section, Fig. 3, and entire view, Fig. 4, which exhibits the stopper opened as in the act of discharging. The cap having been placed upon the shaft while the tube is in the lathe, the orifice at its apex is partially closed by means of a burnish in the hands of the turner, to prevent it from coming off over the ball on the summit of the shaft, and at the same time allow the requisite play when the stopper is in a horizontal position for the cap to slide forward, and consequently separate from the lip-flange B, as shown in Fig. 4, thereby producing an opening sufficiently large for the requisite discharge from the bottle in which it is inserted; and, again, when raised to a vertical position (as shown in Fig. 1 inserted in the neck of the decanter) it falls back and closes the opening effectually by its own gravity, in which two

positions it operates as a self opening and closing stopper, combining at the same time one or more important advantages over any other plan in use—viz., a perpendicular discharge from the tube—thereby effectually obviating the unpleasant and wasteful results of other plans of pouring aside or over the glass or receiving-vessel. In addition, this plan combines the extremest simplicity without a single objection.

I am aware that there have been other plans of self-acting stoppers recently introduced. I allude to the bivalves hinged at the top, which, in short, is nothing more than the valve of the treacle-cup duplicated, and its application to rum instead of molasses. There are also other plans of recent date, which have sprung up since mine were commenced, constructed upon the principle of puppet-valves, all of which have the same objection of producing an uncertain, scattering, or over discharge, and are constructed upon principles widely different from my above-described plan, and to which I make no claim in this application; but

What I do claim, and desire to secure by Letters Patent in my above-described invention, is—

The combination of the circular cap F and the central shaft, E, upon which said cap is suspended, so as to allow of its having three principal motions—viz., the swivel, pendulous, and sliding motions—by means of which, without regard to which side of the stopper is upward, (when it is placed horizontally, or nearly so,) the under portion of the cap swings off from the flange C, thereby producing a downward opening between the two for the requisite discharge of the liquids contained.

WALTER HUNT.

Witnesses:
A. DONALDSON,
E. M. DUNHAM.

W. Hunt,

Bottle Stopper,

Nº 9,527,   *Patented Jan. 4, 1853.*

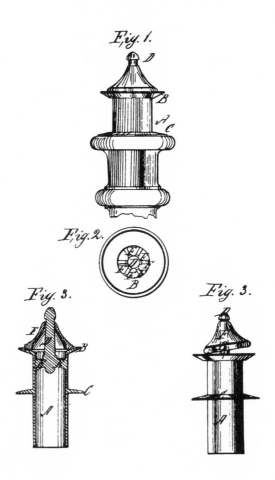

Fig. 1.

Fig. 2.

Fig. 3.   Fig. 3.

the dissimilarity between the two patents, even though both were for improvements in bottle stoppers. This letter evidently served part of its purpose, because on January 4, 1853, the Patent Office granted Walter Hunt U. S. Patent No. 9,527, allowing him:

> The combination of the circular cap and central shaft upon which said cap is suspended, so as to allow of its having three principal motions—viz., the swivel, pendulous, and sliding motions....

The letter did not entirely, however, have the desired effect: on November 16, 1852, the Patent Office awarded U.S. Patent No. 9,407 on an improvement in a bottle stopper to Edward Kinsey and D. Kinsey.

Chapter 23

As it was expected that the bottle stopper patent would be granted sooner or later, Hunt's friends visited him on New Year's Day 1853 to congratulate him. As was customary, discussion of the sewing machine occupied most of the conversation.

"I can't understand why Howe doesn't confine his lawsuits solely to manufacturers who are infringing upon his patent," George Washington Hunt stated.

"According to section fourteen of the Patent Act of July 4, 1836," Chapin explained, "patentees and their assignees are authorized to bring actions to recover damages for making, using or selling the thing whereof the exclusive right is secured by patent."

"But why should they sue those who use the machines?" Caroline Van Buren, Hunt's daughter inquired.

"If you bring suit against the ultimate users of the machines," Kipp answered, "you may stop other people from buying them. You might frighten them sufficiently so that they won't buy. That will affect the business and sales of the infringers."

"And when you stop people from buying these machines," Chapin added, "you are forcing the infringers to either go out of business or capitulate."

George Washington Hunt spoke to his father. "Why don't you try and get a patent? I understand Howe is reaping a fortune. It's too bad that you're not getting anything for your efforts."

"If you get a patent, then you too can collect royalties," Caroline suggested hopefully.

Hunt fidgeted. He disliked the constant harping on his failure to profit from the sewing machine, yet he seldom attempted to change the tenor of the conversation. He replied quietly, "I am not interested in the royalties. What I am concerned with is the recognition I deserve. That's all that I want."

"Didn't you say that Mr. Howe had acknowledged the priority of your invention?" asked Polly Hunt, who had hesitated before entering the conversation.

"Others have also admitted it," Walter Hunt replied. "But there are always strings attached. Howe will not make a public statement. What I want to prove is that my sewing machine actually worked. I should get this recognition. I deserve it."

"But you can't live on glory," Polly protested. "If you are entitled to money for your invention, there is no reason why you shouldn't get your full share of it."

"I am fifty-eight years old now," Walter Hunt said calmly. "It's about time I received my due recognition."

"And some day you'll have it, Father," Caroline said consolingly.

Regardless of Hunt's hopes, the sewing machine was a dead issue as far as Arrowsmith was concerned. It didn't make any difference to him whether Hunt or anyone else received credit for its invention. He felt Howe was so firmly entrenched and backed by unlimited capital that it was foolhardy to attempt to oppose him. Arrowsmith gave no thoughts to his early attempts to introduce the machine. The chapter was closed. He realized that recognition was not negotiable at banks. Why then try to revive a dead issue?

But Edward Clark, attorney for Singer, one of the so-called infringers, was interested. He reasoned that whoever acquired the rights to Hunt's early machine would hold a good argument against Howe's claims.

He contacted Arrowsmith in January 1853 and gave him $250, of which $150 was for the remains of the sewing machine built by Adoniram Hunt and $100 for relinquishing all his title, rights and patent rights.

Arrowsmith was very happy to receive this sum. At least it offset some of his investment and could now be considered clear profit as he had considered the matter dormant for the previous seventeen years.

Howe's attorneys, Rufus Choate, J. D. Bell and Joel Giles, drew up a bill of complaint on February 3, 1853, against John Wooldridge, George W. Keene and Abner S. Moore for using the Singer's Sewing Machine. The defendants were being sued, but in reality they were merely pawns in a much greater battle.

Ambrose Latting Jordan, Charles M. Keller and A. B. Ely were hired by the defendants and on February 14, 1853, they began taking testimony. Polly Hunt and Caroline M. Van Buren were called upon for their depositions. On February 23, additional depositions were given by Walter Hunt, John R. Chapin, and Jay N. Perkins, a manufacturer of machines. The following day, Tylee W. Lafetra, who had given work to Walter Hunt, Frances Augusta Roe, Walter's daughter, wife of Townsend Roe, Garrett D. Adriance, a machine manufacturer, Helen Merrill, a draftsman, and George A. Arrowsmith were summoned.

Arrowsmith's testimony was taken before Joseph Bridgham, United States Commissioner of the Southern District of New York. Arrowsmith stated that the said machine was frequently worked in the presence of others who were brought there to examine it, and no particular means were adopted to keep it secret. [And] that the two machines above mentioned worked well and sewed good seams though occasionally when they were not correctly adjusted the stitches were not so perfect.

I cannot describe it better than by saying that sometimes the seams were good and well made and sometimes imperfect; by the imperfection I mean that sometimes the thread was straight on the side next to the shuttle with loops of the needle thread wound loosely around it, and when the seam was well made the thread was well drawn up so as to make a firm strong and regular stitch on both sides. I remember that when Walter Hunt worked the machine after he had it fully completed it usually worked well though it appeared to require some care and skill in adjusting it and he appeared to understand it perfectly. The machine which Walter Hunt originally made and also the first one made by Adoniram F. Hunt, I considered too small and rather deficient in strength and power for the general purpose of sewing and my object in employing said Adoniram was to have him construct said machine with more solidity and strength—I considered the principle of the machine perfect and it was perfect.

Both Arrowsmith and Walter Hunt identified Hunt's old sewing machine and affixed their signatures on identifying tags.

The depositions were forwarded to Boston for the lawsuit. The machine was likewise dispatched but there was a little delay in its arrival.

On March 13, 1853, Edward Clark wrote to Hunt:

The battle against Judge Sprague will, I have no doubt, commence tomorrow. Our counsel feel pretty confident of success. There is no evidence at all except that of Carlock, Gardiner, and Cochran, to show imperfection in your original machine, and its subsequent abandonment. It seems to me that the proof of your invention is irresistibly strong. I am now most apprehensive that they will abandon the attempt to deny that you invented and made the machine, such as we present it to the Court, and will endeavor to make the Court believe that Singer infringes somehow on Howe's combination and arrangement. This strikes me will be up-hill work.

The *Boston Daily Evening Transcript* of March 14, 1853 (page 2, column 5) commented upon the case: "A sewing machine patent case is on hearing before the U.S. Circuit Court (Judge Sprague). The lawyers are working button-holes in the pockets of the contestants." A preliminary injunction was obtained; it was recorded [in the same newspaper] thus:

MARCH 22, 1853, Tuesday—The Sewing Machine Case in the Circuit Court yesterday in equity suit of Elias Howe, Jr. vs John Wooldridge et al. The court decreed a preliminary injunction against the use or sale of Singer's Straight

Needle Perpendicular Action Sewing Machines by defendants, requiring them to give bonds to account for the use of the machines hereafter in case of verdict for plaintiff.

The decision of the court was also published in the *Scientific American* of April 2, 1853:

In U.S. Circuit Court, Boston, Monday, March 21, 1853 in a suite for equity, plaintiff Elias Howe, Jr. def–John Wooldridge et al, the court granted a preliminary injunction against the use, sale and manufacture of Singer's Sewing Machines, and the defendants were required to give bond to account for the use of the machines in case of a verdict for the plaintiff in the future trial at law.

Elias Howe, Jr., was quick to capitalize upon the court's decision and advertised in the *New York Daily Tribune*:

I have recently obtained an injunction against Singers machine (so called) of which a certified copy from the records of the United States Court may be seen at my office and have now a suit pending against the Two Needle Machines (so called) for infringing my original patent. And all persons, making, selling or using any of the Sewing Machines now known to the public, with out a license from me, will be prosecuted to the fullest extent of the law.

ELIAS HOWE, JR. Patentee.

There was much talk about the sewing machine. It ranked high in news value in periodicals which did not feature cartoons, gossip and scandal. It was still a topic of conversation when the Crystal Palace Exposition opened on Thursday, July 14, 1853, at New York City despite the excitement in the city when General Franklin Pierce, president of the United States, Jefferson Davis, secretary of war, James Guthrie, secretary of the treasury and Caleb Cushing, attorney general, visited the displays.

In reply to Howe's advertisement, or by coincidence, Singer moved swiftly. The following day he advertised [in the *New York Daily Tribune*] (July 13, 1853, page 4, column 1) that the price of his sewing machines had been reduced from $125 to $100. The price reduction was no panacea. The anticipated sales, evidently, were not as great as expected. To allay the fears of prospective buyers of lawsuits, Singer advertised in the same paper on July 26, 1853.

Howe is publishing the falsehood that he obtained an injunction against the Singer Sewing Machine. The fact is, there is not or never has been any suit between us and said Howe, except one which we commenced against him for alleging that we infringed upon his rights, which suit is still pending ... [and] We also aver and stand ready to prove, that until after the invention of the sewing machine by I. M. Singer, Howe never made a machine which any one would buy or could use.

The I. M. Singer Company renewed its attacks on Howe in an advertisement in the *Daily Tribune*, August 4, 1853. This heated salvo in a long-continued battle of printers' ink venom and mud-slinging was resorted to by both sides. They bought newspaper space to spew their hatred. Singer's notice read:

SEWING MACHINES. Elias Howe, Jr., of Massachusetts, is advertising that the United States Court has decided that he was the originator of the Sewing Machine. In truth, no Court has ever decided any such thing. Two patents were granted for Sewing Machines several years before Howe had any application, and the Needle and Shuttle Machine was invented, made, used and the rights to a patent sold by Walter Hunt of this city, twelve years before the date of Howe's patent. Witnesses in ample number know these facts which are utterly fatal to Howe's pretensions. The public ought by this time to be satisfied that Howe's advertisements are designed simply to deter timid and credulous persons from buying such machines as will answer their purposes. It is utterly untrue that we are restrained by injunction or otherwise from selling Singer's Sewing Machines and in fact, we are selling them rapidly, with perfect right to do so, at our offices in New York, Boston, Philadelphia, Baltimore, and Cincinnati. They are the best machines ever made, the public have long since decided. Price $100.
I. M. Singer & Co.

These advertisements angered Howe. To stop the Singer Company from having further denunciatory notices printed, and to make newspapers impose censorship over further copy, Howe brought suit against the *New York Daily Tribune* for publishing this "libel." I. M. Singer & Company countered by bringing suit against Howe for libel. They advertised in the *Daily Tribune* of August 9, 1853:

SEWING MACHINES and libel suits. Elias Howe, Jr. of Massachusetts, advertises a libel suit by him against the publishers of the *Tribune*, and threatens the press generally. We presume the public care little about such controversies, but will state that we have commenced an action at law against Howe for publishing the libelous article headed, "Caution—the Original Sewing Machine, etc." We request all editors to scrutinize any advertisements presented by said Howe, and keep them within the limits of propriety. The public may rest assured that the suit we have commenced against Howe is a real and bona fide action. The best, and only perfect Sewing Machine, always for sale at No. 323 Broadway.
I. M. Singer & Co.

The pot was certainly called the kettle black, and if nothing else was accomplished, both sides of the acrimonious controversy were daily furnishing some pretty peppery reading for an amused populace.

On the 16th, Singer's ad in the *Tribune* said: "It is an easy matter to write and get printed deceptive statements about suits and injunctions."

On the 18th, the company offered: "The first original sewing machine operating with needle and shuttle was made, used and sold by Walter Hunt, of New York."

On the 19th, they warned: "No other person can have a valid patent on that combination or any part of it."

The controversy created furore in the sewing machine field. Customers and dealers were afraid to buy sewing machines. They were afraid they might be prosecuted for infringement. Even the press was disturbed and the scientific journals were hard put to announce their opinions. Prospective customers eagerly awaited the outcome of the court decisions.

The *Scientific American*, the trade journal for inventors and those with a scientific bent, could not restrain its feelings in the conflict and in the issue of August 20, 1853, they commented upon the situation:

> We certainly do not think that Mr. Howe was justified in suing the "Tribune" for libel, but neither was it right for that paper to admit the advertisement of Singer containing, as it did, such pointed and offensive language.

The magazine condemned the slow, antiquated method of the courts in dealing with patent cases and concluded:

> Among the many new inventions which are still wanting to benefit mankind, we recommend inventors to try their genius and skill in improving our United States Courts in patent trials.

On September 8, 1853, Howe placed this notice in the *Tribune*:

> All persons making, selling or using Singer Sewing Machines, having a needle or needles with an eye near the point, are hereby cautioned against infringing my Original Patent, granted September 10, 1846, as all infringers will be held responsible according to law.

The newspaper columns carried much advertising copy from both Howe and Singer, who continued their representations that each owned the original sewing machine and that the other was an infringer. Although Singer consistently argued that Walter Hunt was the original inventor, Hunt himself took no part in the hectic battle of the prints until September 19, 1853, when an advertisement appeared above his signature in the *Tribune* contradicting one of Howe's statements. It read:

SEWING MACHINE: CARD TO THE PUBLIC.

I perceive that Elias Howe, Jr. is advertising himself as patentee of the Original Sewing Machine, and claiming that all who use machines having a needle or needles with an eye near the point, are responsible to him. These statements I contradict. Howe was not even the original patentee. John J. Greenough and George R. Corliss, each had a patent on a sewing machine before Howe obtained his patent as the records of the Patent Office show. Howe was not the original and first inventor of the machine on which he obtained his patent. He did not invent the needle with the eye near the point. He was not the original inventor of the combination of the eye pointed needle and the shuttle, making the interlocked stitch with two threads, now in common use. These things which form the essential basis of all sewing machines were first invented by me, and were combined in good operative Sewing Machines which were used and extensively exhibited, both in New York and Baltimore more than ten years before Howe's patent was granted.

By law, no other person than myself could, or can have a valid patent upon the eye pointed needle and shuttle, or any combination of them. The proof of these facts is abundant and conclusive. I have taken measures, as soon as adverse circumstances would permit, to enforce my rights by applying for a patent for my original invention. I am by law entitled to it, and in due course, no doubt, will get it. In that case Howe's license will be no protection against my just claims; and I shall then ask and insist upon a just compensation from all who use my invention. All who feel an interest in this subject can, by calling on me receive the most satisfactory evidence that I was the first and original inventor of the Sewing Machine.

Walter Hunt, No. 115 Charles Street, N.Y.

The controversy in the daily newspapers carried over to the magazines. The most august and respected of the trade publications was the *Scientific American*. On October 1, 1853, they devoted almost half of their editorial page to the "sewing machine controversy." They claimed impartiality and paternally announced how ever-ready they were to give every man his just need of praise. They accused Hunt of entering the newspaper battle as a handle to the dispute between Singer and Howe, either for the purpose of frightening or befooling others.

The *Scientific American* was owned by Munn & Company, which had previously acted as attorneys for Elias Howe, Jr. They did not like Hunt's statement printed in the *Tribune*. In it he had laid claim to the invention of the sewing machine which used an eye-pointed needle and shuttle. The editorial hinted that it was most peculiar, if Walter Hunt actually had invented the machine as he claimed, that he had not obtained a patent when he had "found means to obtain patents, and to induce others to purchase inventions of far less importance and value."

All in all, in the opinion of the *Scientific American* editorial writer, it had "an ugly appearance" for Hunt to try to set up a claim for a seventeen-year-old invention and in the midst of a fight. (The *Scientific American* editorial in full will be found in the Appendix, pages 297–299.)

The magazine made no mention of Hunt's own struggle and the national events and coincidences which conspired to prevent his getting a patent on his machine years ago. They merely prophesied he would never get it, because the commissioner of patents was too well versed in patents and inventions to give it to him. Their own purpose in taking a hand, they blandly asserted, was purely altruistic, wanting an end put to the sewing machine strife "in order that the ear of the public may not be used as a kettle drum on which to beat the loudest tones for personal purposes."

So much for publicity in 1853, which apparently was not the golden era of "public relations counsel," known better in modern parlance as "press agents." (One cannot help but wonder if Walter Hunt would not have been better off, and much of industrial history changed, if his affairs had been in the hands of a press agent.)

Court actions and lawsuits were merrily going on, keeping pace with the fanfare blared in the newspapers and magazines. Walter Hunt determined to battle to the finish. Defiantly, he flouted his editorial advisers and went ahead and applied for a patent to cover his lock-stitch sewing machine invention of 1834.

Following the due course or procedure, since it was recognized that his application conflicted with Howe's patent and with other improvements on sewing machines on file in the Patent Office, interference hearings were scheduled for the early part of 1854.

To offset his critics and to establish the validity of his claim, Hunt placed another advertisement in the *Tribune*. It was published on December 9, 1853.

SEWING MACHINES—CARD TO THE PUBLIC.

The Hon. Commissioner of Patents of the United States has adjudged that my application for letters patent for a sewing machine, which was originally invented, constructed and put in operation by me, as early as the year 1834, interferes with all the patents and applications for patents upon Sewing Machines containing the combination of the eye-pointed needle, and the shuttle making the interlocked stitch. All the parties to this matter of Interference are called upon by notice from the Patent Office to prove the date of their inventions. Numerous and most respectable witnesses who saw my Sewing Machine I am already apprized of. But it is desirable to prove its good and successful operation by as many as possible. Any persons who, between the years of 1833 and 1840, saw my Sewing Machine, or saw such a machine in the possession of my late brother, A. F. Hunt, or to whom it was exhibited or specimens of its work shown by Mr. George A. Arrowsmith, will confer a great favor upon me, and will forward a righteous cause, by informing me of their knowledge upon the subject. A powerful combination is interested in defeating my just claims, but with the testimony I have, the truth must prevail. I would wish it to prevail overwhelmingly. Address Walter Hunt, No. 530 Hudson Street, N.Y.

Neither Hunt's sudden activity nor the pending patent interference case put a damper on Howe's determination to win. The *Tribune* continued to print his advertisement, warning and threatening infringers.

And Howe lived up to his threats in case after case. In the suit he brought against Orson Underwood et al. in the Circuit Court of the United States, Massachusetts District, George A. Arrowsmith made a deposition. It was taken by Richard E. Stillwell, a commissioner, in the Southern District of New York, on December 20, 1853, in Stillwell's office in the new City Hall.

More than fifty pages of testimony were taken, explaining Arrowsmith's connection with Walter Hunt at the time the sewing machine was invented. Hundreds of pertinent questions dealing with all angles and phases of the invention were asked and answered.

But this suit, like others, was not to settle the validity of the claims of either Elias Howe, Jr., or Walter Hunt. The issue was solely the infringement of patent and was decided on that basis.

Judge Sprague rendered his decision in a ten thousand word report on February 22, 1854. "This is an application for a preliminary injunction, by Elias Howe, Jr., and another, to restrain the defendants, Orson Underwood and others, from using a sewing machine, which, the complainants allege, is an infringement of their patent." Judge Sprague then discussed the Hunt claim:

> The great fact of this machine having been laid aside, as it was, is not accounted for, and is entirely inconsistent with the idea that it was a perfected or valuable machine at that time. The whole testimony leaves upon my mind no doubt, that however Mr. Hunt had advanced with his machine, it was never perfected, in the sense of the patent law; that it was only an experiment, and ended in experiment, and was laid aside as an unsuccessful experiment, until the introduction of Mr. Howe's machine.

He stated there was no doubt of the infringement of the Singer machine upon Howe's claims and patent.

> The weight of testimony, however, as a matter of opinion, is strongly preponderating in favor of the plaintiffs; and from the examination which the court has been able to give to this subject, aided by the evidence, and by the knowledge and experience of counsel, I am unable to arrive at any other conclusion, than that which the experts for the complainants have expressed. The result is, that the plaintiff's patent is valid, and the defendants' machine is an infringement. An injunction is granted.

Judge Sprague rendered the decision that there was no doubt whatever of the infringement of the Singer Machine, in use by Underwood, upon Howe's claims and patents. Howe himself announced the decision in an advertisement in the *Tribune* of February 28, 1854. It read in part:

CAUTION—SEWING MACHINES—Last Wednesday the injunction from the United States Court in Boston, PROHIBITING THE USE OF THE SINGER MACHINES, and have now a suit pending against him here, which is soon to be tried, and, without doubt will result in like manner. The old bugbear of Walter Hunt was, as heretofore, the defense relied upon, the insufficiency and fallacy of which will be manifest by an examination of the full and clear decision of Judge Sprague in the case, printed copies of which will be ready for free distribution in a few days at my office.

It was a long and expensive advertisement; in his jubilation Howe cared nothing for that. In included, among other things, after listing the concerns to which he had granted licenses, the statement, "It is immaterial whether machines use one or two needles, with the eye near the point; without a license they are infringements."

Much attention had been directed to sewing machines. The controversy had opened a new field and inventors filed patent applications for improvements.

A group of Hunt's friends were discussing the situation.

"There is no doubt but what you invented the first sewing machine," John Richardson said sympathetically. "If you had only the sense to apply for a patent, you might have made a million dollars by now."

Hunt consoled himself. "If I had obtained the patent then, it would have expired by now, and the invention would now be common property."

"Well, you'll certainly have to hand it to the new crop of inventors. They put the finishing touches on it," Richardson added.

Kipp rose to Hunt's defense. "You know the old story of Columbus and the egg. Once the way is shown, it is easy for others to follow suit."

"Yes," Richardson argued, "but all these people not only followed, they improved."

"And I'll bet that Walter Hunt can still beat them all. I'll bet that he can still outclass all of them. I'll put my money on him anytime," Kipp stated heartily.

Hunt joined the conversation. "Richardson," he said slowly, "I know that you are talking in good faith. You just said that others put the finishing touches to the sewing machine. I disagree with you. I'll show you that I can still put the finishing touches to the sewing machine."

Richardson apologized, "I didn't mean, Mr. Hunt, that you couldn't."

"Listen, Richardson, once an invention has been announced improvements will always be made. Just as there already are hundreds of patents on the sewing machine, so will there be hundreds and possibly thousands of more patents. Inventions generate new inventions."

"Hunt," Kipp interrupted, "did I hear you say a minute ago that you can still put finishing touches on the sewing machine?"

Hunt paused briefly. Richardson and Kipp looked at him questioningly.

"There is one great disadvantage to the sewing machines now in use," Hunt

UNITED STATES PATENT OFFICE.

WALTER HUNT, OF NEW YORK, N. Y.

IMPROVEMENT IN SEWING-MACHINES.

Specification forming part of Letters Patent No. **11,161**, dated June 27, 1854.

To all whom it may concern:

Be it known that I, WALTER HUNT, of the city, county, and State of New York, have invented certain new and useful Improvements in Sewing-Machines, of which the following is a full and exact description.

Said improvements consist in the manner of feeding in of the cloth and regulating the length of the stitch solely by the vibrating motion of the needle; in a rotary table or platform, upon which the cloth is placed for sewing; in guides and gages for controlling the line of the seam.

The subjoined drawings exhibit a machine constructed on said improved plan, the same letters of reference indicating the same parts throughout.

Figure 1 is a sectional side elevation, Fig. 2 a top, and Fig. 3 an open front end elevation, of the machine and its parts in their order of connection and arrangement. Figs. 4, 5 are enlarged side and front views of the needle and stock detached. Figs. 6 and 7 are front elevations of the same, connected with the slide. Figs. 9 and 10 exhibit the position of the shuttle-slide and carrier in connection with the shuttle when the motion is given either way. Figs. 9 and 10 also show two positions of the needle.

The following is a minute description of the construction, arrangement, and operation of said machine, the drawings of which are about the full size of the smallest working model. Fig. 11 is a side view of the cam-wheel, and Fig. 12 a front view of the same.

The driving or cam wheel A, Fig. 11, is discous in its form and about one inch thick. Upon its periphery is a projecting pin or continuous cam, B, Fig. 2, which crosses the rim of the wheel twice at opposite sides of the periphery, leaving nearly one-half of the pin projecting radially in a straight line from opposite sides of the rim. This continuous cam B traverses in a notch cut in the upper end of a vertical limb, C, (shown in Fig. 3,) which forms a part of the rock-shaft D, which is thereby moved forth and back at each revolution of the cam-wheel A. At the opposite end of D is an elevated limb, E, (see Fig. 1,) which extends upward and enters into a longitudinal slot in the under corner of the slide-race F in Figs. 3 and 8, and fits into a gap in the slide G at H, thus giving motion to the shuttle K by means of the shuttle-carrier I, the ends of which alternately enter cavities J J

in and near the ends of K at each vibration of the carrier, the rear ends of which are tripped and thrown back by coming in contact with the back of the needle-guide L (see Figs. 8 and 3) at each vibration, so that one of the ends of I is at all times connected with K. The slide-race F is laterally connected with the shuttle-race M, which together are horizontally supported at their ends in the frame directly under the table O. (See Fig. 3.) Through said frame or case of the machine there is an opening, P, in Fig. 1, corresponding with those of the shuttle and slide races, for the purpose of inserting and withdrawing G, the slide, and K, the shuttle, which are disengaged by dropping the end of the rock-shaft D, which has a bearing, near E, on a bridge, Q, the end of which is let down or raised and secured by means of a pendulous hook, R, which engages and disengages the upper end of the limb E from the gap H in the slide G.

Having described the instrumentalities which give motion to the shuttle, I will next consider those which operate the needle.

Upon one face of the wheel A is an elevated fin or groove, S, Figs. 11 and 12, which, in effect, is a continuous compound eccentric and concentric cam, on or in which traverses the limb T, Fig. 1, which is connected with or forms the lower end of the needle-arm U, which is here a lever of the first order, having its fulcrum at V, which fulcrum has a slight horizontal movement, (in order to disengage its front end from the needle-slide at W,) and is fixed by the prop q.

At the extreme front end of the arm X is a vertical tube, open in front, in which plays the needle-slide a, directly over the center of the table O. Lengthwise in said needle-slide a, Figs. 6 and 7, about two-thirds upward from its bottom end, is cut a small groove, in which the needle-stock b (containing the needle c) is inserted and suspended upon the pivot d, Figs. 4 and 6, which passes through said slide and through near the upper end of b, upon the extreme upper end of which a slight spring, e, (secured in the upper portion of said groove,) is made to bear with sufficient force to throw out the lower end or point of the needle from a straight line as far as may be required for taking the longest stitches, which is regulated by a set-screw, f, bearing against the opposite surface of a.

Immediately below the point of the needle, and in a line with the same, is placed the gage-finger g, Figs. 1 and 3, which is secured and regulated by the set-screw h in the arm X. The office of said finger is to hold down the cloth or other material in sewing, it having a central slot through which the needle passes while the machine is in operation.

Upon the under surface of the table O a sliding cap, i, is placed, and connected centrally to said table by a rivet-washer, j, or hub, in Fig. 2, which forms an axis upon which O may revolve back and forth at pleasure. The cap i is made to slide horizontally and fasten by means of flanges upon the top of the pedestal at the outer end of the frame Y, directly over the shuttle-race, as before mentioned.

Through the center of the hub j is a perforation in which is placed a button, l, supported upon an upward-acting spring, m, which is secured to the under surface of i. This spring-button presses the cloth up against the finger g, and prevents it from moving when the needle is withdrawn, but is depressed as it enters and allows it to move the cloth forward the distance of the length of stitch required. The lateral or sidewise movement of the needle which makes the feed is produced by means of a hopper-shaped groove, n, (see Figs. 9 and 10,) cut vertically or nearly so in the face of the needle-guide L. The needle having passed through the slot in the finger g, the cloth and the spring-button l, in a partially-inclined position, now enters the groove in the needle-guide L, which is partially inclined the opposite way from the inclination of the needle. Consequently, as it descends down the inclined groove, it assumes a vertical position, and consequently, having pierced the cloth to its center of the line to be sewed, draws it forward in the direction and to the extent of its lateral movement, to fix the length of the stitch, and as the needle is withdrawn it rises vertically, the cloth being held by the spring-button l against the finger g sufficiently firm to prevent its being moved by the needle-spring e, which, however, throws the needle out in the inclined position as it raises its point above the cloth the proper distance for the next stitch.

Upon the arm X is placed my tension-forceps o, Figs. 1 and 2, suspended upon the pin p, through the bite of which at r the threads from the spool s' is passed, thence through t', and thence through guide-holes in the cap of the needle at t, thence down in front of said slide and through the eye of the needle at d'. The forceps are operated by means of the connecting-link u, which extends from the same to the needle-arm U, having the pins v and w as connecting-joints with the same, and by means of which any required tension may be given to the needle-thread.

The shuttle K is double-pointed and made of sheet metal, with portions of the same bent inward, forming bearings x x, (see Fig. 8,) in which the ends of the bobbin-spindle y are held with any required tension.

From underneath the back end of the arm X extends a movable gage, Z, having set-screws e' e', the outer end of which may be fixed upon the table O at any required point, operating as a gage against which the edge of the cloth may be placed while sewing, and the course of the seam thereby regulated. There is also a sliding gage, a', which traverses in a groove, b, cut across the face of O, having a stud-pin, c', upon which the cloth, &c., may be placed for the purpose of stitching circles, curves, &c.

Mode of operation: The needle being threaded from the spool through the forceps, as before directed, and the filled bobbin inserted in the shuttle, with end of the thread protruded about two inches through the shuttle-eye, the shuttle is taken in the right hand and the slide G in the left. The back end of the carrier I is inserted in the rear cavity, J. I and K, being thus held, are inserted together into the slide and shuttle races. The bridge Q, being down, is now raised, (so that E enters into the gap H,) and is secured by the hook R. The cloth to be worked is now introduced (guided by the hand or otherwise) between g and j, (the needle being raised for the purpose.) The machine is now put in motion by means of the crank j', by hand or other power, as may be preferred.

I claim—

The rotary table-top, in combination with the guides and ways underneath the same, all arranged and operating in the manner and for the purposes set forth.

WALTER HUNT.

Witnesses:
    JOHN RICHARDSON,
    T. CAMPBELL.

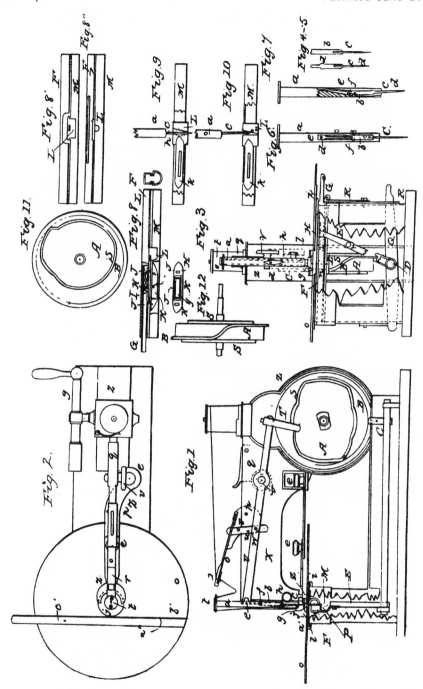

replied. "Practically all of the models made by the different companies can sew, but they all possess a serious fault which makes it difficult for the inexperienced operator. The cloth is fed to the vibrating needle by pushing. A motion that is too fast or too slow causes an irregularity of spaces and often machines jam. I will rectify this."

"What do you intend to do?"

"Experiment," was the laconic reply.

True to his word, Hunt went to his shop and analyzed the situation. Although about eighteen years passed since his original invention, it was not difficult for him to reconstruct the principles of the machines. He devised a rotating circular top which permitted the cloth to be fed at an even rate.

Several months later when his labor was completed, Hunt showed the improvement to both Kipp and Richardson.

"I knew you could do it." Kipp said excitedly.

"What are you going to do with it?" Richardson asked.

"I'll get a patent on it. They won't be able to take this one away from me."

On April 2, 1853, Hunt applied to the Patent Office for a patent. His application had nothing to do with the pending Hunt-Howe sewing machine controversy. It covered only the one improvement. By coincidence, on April 2, the *Scientific American* published the outcome of the Howe-Wooldridge case.

Inasmuch as the Patent Office was filled with applications for inventions and improvements on parts, it was only natural that there would be some delay in the patent grant and that an interference suit would first be held. After a lapse of time, Hunt received a letter to the effect that his application interfered with those of James Seymour of New York City and William Johnson of Granville, Hampden County, Massachusetts, for whom William P. Elliot of Washington, D.C., was attorney.

The hearing scheduled for November 4, 1853, was not to Hunt's liking and on October 21, 1853, he wrote the Commissioner of Patents requesting a delay of thirty days as Dr. Sewall Gleason, an important witness would not be able to testify. On October 26, 1853, the Patent Office notified Hunt, through Page & Company, of Washington, that his request for a postponement would be granted and that interference proceedings would be held the first Monday in December.

Page communicated with the examiner and explained that there might be a problem in the grant of the patent as the claims embraced too much.

"Make the necessary restrictions, Mr. Hunt," Page advised. "It is better to receive a modest patent than to have it held up for years in expensive litigation with no guarantee whatsoever of the result."

The reasoning was sound and Hunt agreed to limit his claim. On November 25, 1853, Charles G. Page wrote to Charles Mason, the Commissioner of Patents, on behalf of Walter Hunt:

I hereby restrict and modify my claims in the sewing machine as follows; I disclaim the general feature or principle of feeding by the needle and confine my claim to my particular mode of feeding, to wit: I claim sustaining both ends of the needle whilst moving the cloth, to effect and feed, by means of an inclined guide made adjustable and placed under the shuttle side of the cloth.

The scheduled interference proceedings were held and Hunt's application was scrutinized closely. Every word and phrase in the technical document was closely studied.

"There is no reason why this patent application should not be granted," the examiner reported. "Your claims do not conflict with other patents or with applications on file, however, there are a few minor changes which must be made."

The patent application was returned to Hunt who made the necessary corrections and returned it on April 8, 1854, to the Patent Office. Ten days later, Hunt sent another letter in which he made additional revisions.

On June 14, 1854, the Patent Office advised Hunt officially that he would be granted a patent if he would make further minor changes. Hunt did not object and on June 27, 1854, he was awarded U.S. Patent No. 11,161.

"I knew you could do it," Kipp exclaimed excitedly when Hunt showed him the patent.

Polly Hunt was proud that the patent had been awarded. It was Walter Hunt's boast to the world that he was still able to invent and improve upon the best sewing machines. The new patent gave Hunt still further recognition in the industry.

"This patent should bring in some money," Richardson prophesied.

But Hunt was too busy with other things to turn all his attention to the amassing of money.

There was little interest in the improvement. The ownership of rights to manufacture sewing machines was still at issue. This had to be decided first, before improvements could be considered.

Howe seemed to be winning the fight. He won decisions against Phelps, Bradford and Wooldridge.

But still the infringers refused to capitulate. Howe brought suit against Underwood.

Since no court declared Howe's patent invalid because of Hunt's prior invention, the defendants turned to another source. Perhaps Howe's patent could be invalidated by citing other patents. The I.M. Singer Company acquired John J. Greenough's patent of February 27, 1842, the first patent on a sewing machine in the United States, antedating Howe's patent by more than four and a half years.

The value of the industry was too great to overlook any detail. Every effort to stifle Howe's dominance of the market was a necessity.

Chapter 24

Controversy over financial matters embroiled Hunt's household. His family constantly fought and argued with him. And his friends did the same.

"You're crazy not to demand your rights," Kipp counseled. "You are entitled to a patent on your sewing machine and you're a fool if you don't get one."

"Ignore all those court proceedings," Chapin advised. "They don't affect you. The value of your rights has never been tested in court. You never brought suit. You were only a witness. And your recent application for a patent on your improved machine has nothing whatsoever to do with your original machine."

"You can get a patent, and the recognition you deserve." Kipp continued, "I don't understand why you don't do something. I'm sure I wouldn't let an opportunity slip by if I was involved."

"You could have had a patent if you had applied for one. The judges decided that. It's not too late now." Polly Hunt pointed out. "Why don't you apply now? Send them your application now and get your patent."

"You're letting thousands of dollars slip through your fingers because you don't demand your rights," Caroline added.

"You owe it to your family to do so," said Chapin.

"Why don't you do it, Hunt?" Kipp inquired.

"I haven't the time or the money," Hunt said with finality.

"You know you don't need money," Chapin argued. "You told me so yourself. Didn't you say that John P. Bowker would bear all the expenses?"

"But what about Arrowsmith?" inquired George W. Hunt, joining the conversation. "Doesn't he own the patent rights?"

"Arrowsmith has nothing to do with them," said Hunt angrily, "He owns nothing. I bought back all the rights."

"Then why don't you fight for your patent?" Polly interrupted. "You don't need Bowker. Why is he so interested in it all of a sudden?"

"Because if the Patent Office awards a patent," Chapin explained, "Bowker wants a half interest in the patent with a free license to I. M. Singer reserved."

"That's asking a lot," George said.

"In case the patent isn't granted, will you have to put up any money?" Caroline asked.

"No," Hunt replied emphatically.

"Then you might as well do it." Polly urged. "You're not getting anything now—not even recognition. You have nothing to lose and everything to gain."

After further argument and advice, Hunt finally agreed to file his application. He prepared the necessary papers and mailed them on April 2, 1853, to the Patent Office.

But eighteen years had passed since his original invention of the sewing machine. Eighteen unproductive years!

Upon receipt of his application, the Patent Office notified Hunt that it conflicted with eleven others and that interference proceedings would be held to determine the validity of his varied claims. This might result in a long delay before any final action would be taken. Hunt was displeased by this situation and naturally felt dejected. But he said philosophically, "At least now we can settle this bugaboo once and for all."

Elias Howe naturally welcomed the delay. He had no desire to see the Patent Office grant Hunt a patent which might antedate his patent. Howe's attorney, J. Giles, filed a protest with the Commissioner of Patents on November 3, 1853, against the Hunt application, stating,

> a patent, which if granted will supersede the patent to me, September 10, 1846, for an Improvement in Sewing Machines ... the claims of said Hunt, substantially as set forth in said advertisement ... having been twice presented, and investigated before the United States Circuit Court holden in Boston, as a defense in an action at law, and a suit in equity, and well pronounced by the verdict of the jury and the decision of the court to be of no avail against my said patent and a final decree and judgement was rendered in favor of my said patent notwithstanding such defense.

Priority of invention alone was not to be the sole and determining factor, and as legal points would also be at issue, Samuel Cooper was engaged to fight for Hunt's application.

On February 24, 1854, Cooper served notice on all those whose claims conflicted that on February 28, 1854,

> at the office of R. E. Stillwell, United States Commissioner, Clerk's Office, U.S. Court, and before him or some other competent authority, I shall proceed to take testimony of the following named persons, viz; Eleazer Johnson, William Wood, Caroline M. Van Buren, Alexander M. Alling, G. D. Adriance and George A. Arrowsmith.

The necessity for taking the depositions was to establish that Hunt's machine had been invented in 1834-1835 and, if possible, to show that it was practical and operative.

The small chamber of the commissioner's office was crowded when Commissioner John Whilson began the proceedings. The first witness, William Wood, was "sworn to testify the truth, the whole truth and nothing but the truth." The formality completed, the deposition began.

"Where do you reside and what is your business?"
"I reside at Westport, Connecticut, and am a cotton manufacturer."
"What is the extent of your business, large or small?"
"Large."
"Have you ever had any trade, and if so, what?"
"Machinist."
"How long did you work at that trade?"
"I began at the age of fifteen, and I have worked at it more or less ever since."
"Have you ever taken out any letters patent for your own inventions?"
"I have taken out three."
"Are you acquainted with Walter Hunt of the City of New York; if so, when and where did you first become acquainted with him?"
"I am acquainted with him. I became acquainted with him in 1834. I became acquainted with him in the City of New York."
"Did you engage with Mr. Hunt, and, if so, what?"
"I did engage with him as a machinist."
"How long did you work under that engagement?"
"About six months."
"At the time you first went to Mr. Hunt's shop had he a sewing machine there?"
"He had one partly finished."
"Where was this shop?"
"It was at the Globe Stove factory in Amos Street."
"How near was that machine to be finished?"
"It was not finished."
"Was it finished while you were there?"
"It was and put in operation."
"Who worked on it beside Mr. Hunt?"
"I worked upon it and Mr. Hunt's brother, Adoniram F. Hunt."

Wood was asked seventy-nine questions to which he replied. His examination was adjourned until March 2, when he was reexamined and cross-examined by attorneys for the plaintiffs and defendants.

Queried as to the reason why Hunt's machine was not patented, Wood stated,

"He [Hunt] told me that he had sold it to Mr. Arrowsmith on conditions that he should take out letters patent for it and give him an interest therein, that Mr. Arrowsmith had failed to do so, although he had often requested him to do so."

"What were Mr. Hunt's pecuniary circumstances at that time?"

"Not very good. He told me that he was poor and merely made out to live."

"What examination, if any, did you make of the work you saw done by Hunt's machine yourself?"

"I examined it frequently myself and so did everyone that came there; it was a new thing, and every person who saw it examined it very closely."

Wood's testimony was corroborated on March 1, 1864, by Alexander M. Alling of 202 Eighth Avenue, "keeper of a public house." He stated,

I was employed in manufacturing matches and the other frictions. I was employed in manufacturing shoes; that is the trade I was brought up in.

Alling declared he had seen Hunt's sewing machine in operation in 1834-1835 and that it utilized two threads and made a loop stitch. The eye of the needle was near the point, he swore, and the machine employed a shuttle and worked satisfactorily.

"Did you communicate your knowledge of the machine to any of your friends?"

"I did to an intimate friend engaged in manufacturing clothes as a tailor; this was Mr. Munn of Newark, New Jersey. I carried specimens of the sewing, three or four pieces, and showed them to him."

"Why did you exhibit those specimens to Mr. Munn?"

"I was so strongly impressed with the operation of the machine and the sewing, that I supposed he might turn it to great advantage in his business."

On the following day, March 2, 1854, Culver Randel, a pianoforte manufacturer, was examined. He stated,

Between 1834 and 1835, I saw Mr. Hunt building a sewing machine.... I examined the work, it was evenly done and appeared strong.

Randel stated that he had been familiar with the Globe Stove Shop and had frequently seen Hunt work on various parts of the machine. He stated he had owned the building and Hunt had "hired" it.

Caroline M. Van Buren, Walter Hunt's daughter, was cross-examined on March 3, 1854. She testified that she had seen her father's sewing machine about 1834 in the office of the Globe Stove Manufactory, New York. She described its operation in simple nontechnical language and said that the stitches were strong and even.

The examination continued.

"Did he [Hunt] ever say anything to you about doing work with it?"

"Yes sir. When I was between fourteen and fifteen, he wished me to engage in corset making and use his machine for doing the stitching."

"Did you assent to that purpose, and, if not, why not?"

"I did not; because my friends advised me not to, because it took work out of sewing girls' hands."

"Was this the last time your father spoke to you of his machine?"

"No sir. He spoke to me a great many times."

"From conversations between your father and yourself, and in your family generally, did you form any opinion of what your father's intentions were in regard to that machine, during the period of time of which you have been testifying, and, if so, what opinion?"

"We all thought that he intended to go on and build them as soon as he could conveniently."

"Did you think so yourself from what your father said to you?"

"Yes sir, he would have built one for me if I would have used it."

"How were your father's circumstances during that space of time?"

"Like all inventors, he just made enough to live on."

Real fireworks occurred March 16, 1854, when William D. Carlock and George A. Arrowsmith appeared at the commissioner's office.

William Carlock stated that he lived in Williamsburg, Kings County, and was a manufacturer of plumbs and bores. He said he knew both Arrowsmith and Hunt and that he had known both since 1831 and that he and others had seen the machine in operation and that others had also seen it work. Carlock stated that he went to Boston as a witness for Howe in the Bradford lawsuit. He admitted that he had kept a sample of the work done on Hunt's sewing machine for sixteen years, but that he had thrown it away six weeks ago.

Carlock did not explain why the sample was so intriguing that he had kept it for sixteen years nor why after the Bradford trials it had suddenly become so valueless that he threw it away prior to the start of the Patent Office litigation case.

Carlock's lack of enthusiasm was the first intimation the prosecution had that Hunt's so-called friends were no longer cooperative.

If the lawyers were surprised at the sudden change of attitude, they did not show it, and if the testimony was different that they expected, they had yet to hear Arrowsmith.

Arrowsmith stated he was sixty years of age, and resided in Middlesex County, New Jersey, and was a blacksmith by profession.

While the battle was being waged in the Patent Office, an equally intensive campaign was being conducted in the daily newspapers. The first of a series
of advertisements appeared in the *New York Daily Times* (page 4, column 6) on
March 16, 1854:

Sewing Machines—Caution to the Public—All persons making, using or selling Sewing Machines wherein the eye-pointed needle is employed, are hereby
notified that unless they procure a license from the undersigned, they will be
proceeded against legally for infringement of the original patent granted to
John J. Greenough, Esq., on the 27th day of February 1842. That patent was
the first ever granted, and is the only patent covering the grooved and the eye-
pointed needle in the Sewing Machine. In this, and in other respects, we claim
that all Sewing Machines now in use infringe upon the Greenough patent.
That patent has been assigned to us, and we intend to enforce it against the
entire Boston combination now endeavoring to crush us, and to disturb and
oppress the industrious citizens of New York.
I. M. SINGER & CO.,
No. 323 Broadway.

The following day, March 17, 1854, I. M. Singer inserted another advertisement in the *New York Times*.

SEWING MACHINES—THE BATTLE OF THE SEWING MACHINES has fairly
begun. Elias Howe, Jr. of Boston, and Walter Hunt, of New York, are contest-
ing before the United States Patent Office which has the prior right to the
combination of the needle and shuttle in Sewing Machines. The prior right of
Mr. Hunt is proved by numerous and most respectable witnesses. If he succeeds
in the contest, we have his license to use his invention. In the meantime, however, the only machine that can be bought with entire safety is SINGER'S SIN-
GLE-THREADED SEWING MACHINE, which is secured by the original patent
granted to Morey & Johnson, on the 6th of February, 1849. These machines, as
recently improved are, for all purposes, the most perfect ever produced.

Four days later, Howe responded in an advertisement which appeared
March 21, 1854, in the *New York Tribune*:

J. J. Greenough never obtained a patent which in the most remote degree covered the eye-pointed needle. Those who know from whence the reports proceed
that he did so need no denial of their truth; but those who do not, are informed
that such reports are entirely false and without foundation in truth.
A certified copy of said patent is at all times open for the inspection of those
interested at my office, and if any person will therein point out an eye-pointed
needle, or any claim to, or specification, or drawing of the same, I will forfeit
$1,000.—$500. to go to such person and $500. to some charitable institution in

this city as the Mayor may designate. I entertain too high an estimate of Mr. Greenough's integrity and talents to believe that he countenances the imposition now attempted upon the public by those persons having control of said patents.

To further their claim the I.M. Singer Company retorted with the following advertisement in the *New York Times* on March 30, 1854:

SEWING MACHINES—Who invented the combination of the needle and shuttle to make the interlocking stitch? We say Walter Hunt, of New York. He is applying for a patent for it, and the Commissioner of Patents will soon decide upon his claims. To the original Morey & Johnson Patent, which we own, there is not, and never has been any objection. We only have the right to sell these admirable machines.

A further blast appeared on April 13, 1854, when the I. M. Singer Company countered with the following advertisement:

Forbearance sometimes ceases to be a virtue. Especially in this maxim true in reference to Elias Howe, Jr. and his Boston confederates, who are attempting to make the industrious public pay a tribute to Howe for an invention which notoriously belongs to Walter Hunt of New York, and for which Mr. Hunt now has an application pending for a patent.

A vehement denunciation was made by Elias Howe, Jr., in an advertisement which appeared May 1, 1854, in the *New York Daily Tribune*:

The Boston Conspirators of whom I. M. Singer & Co., have so much to say are those who know and respect law and justice, and of course are denounced by all PIRATES AND OUTLAWS.

The following day the *Tribune* carried a warning from Singer.

The whole combination of Howe's licenses are infringing in various ways on our patent rights, and no good sewing machine can be made without violating our patents. We have commenced prosecuting all infringers. Let the public beware of touching the spurious Boston Machines.

In the same issue, Howe's advertisement stated that

the most reliable source of information as to my claims to the Sewing Machine, may be found in the able opinion lately given by Judge Sprague.

The public was intensely interested in the case even though no scandal newspapers fanned the flames.

Back at the Patent Office, J. Giles of 4 Court Street, Boston, Massachusetts, submitted on April 27, 1854 a twenty page refutation of Singer's position. He contended that Howe's patent was a matter of record and *prima facie* proof of his priority of invention, and that the burden of proof was required to be submitted by Hunt, whom he claimed had not definitely proven that he had invented a machine, nor had he been able to produce the actual machine as evidence.

Such a machine, if constructed, Giles contended, was incomplete. He further argued that there was a similar nomenclature and that the witnesses who testified they had seen Hunt's machine in operation were aided in describing it because of their association with the Howe machine which was on the market.

Giles also asserted that

Hunt made an experimental sewing machine, somewhat like Howe's patented in 1846, but it was never completed and never did anything of practical utility, and was sold to Arrowsmith without reserve, before it was in a patentable condition, and was abandoned and forgotten for many years until evidence of it was hunted up by infringers for a defense against Howe's patent.

Giles filed six reasons for his appeal, three of which presented the pertinent facts at issue:

one, because the said commissioner in arriving at his said decision stated that in cases of interference he had jurisdiction, and actually exercised jurisdiction over the question of abandonment or dedication to the public use. Second, because the honorable commissioner in arriving at said decision decided that the sale by Hunt of his invention (as distinguished from the sale of a practical machine or machines embracing said invention, and for practical use for the purpose) and with the intention of procuring a patent therefor for the benefit of the grantee or assignee, was such a sale as is contemplated in the seventh section of the statute of 1836 and the seventh section of the statute of 1839; and being more than two years before application for letters-patent is an absolute bar to the grant thereof [and third] because the honorable commissioner in arriving at his said decision decided that a sale by said Hunt of his invention to Arrowsmith was tantamount to giving his consent that any person or all the world might use the same.

Giles contended further that Hunt had shown no model, drawing or description of his machine or the one made by his brother and that no evidence of priority was shown.

Sam Cooper found the prosecution of Hunt's claim required a greater knowledge of patent law than he possessed. The case was too intricate for him alone to handle. It was necessary to obtain the aid of someone located in Washington in close contact with the Patent Office and also familiar with patent office detail and procedure.

He noticed a professional advertisement in the *Scientific American*:

W. P. N. Fitzgerald, Counselor at Law, has recently resigned the office of principal Examiner of Patents, which he has held for many years, is ready to assist, professionally, in the preparation and trial of patent causes before the U.S. Courts in any of the States, and before the Supreme Court of the United States. He also acts as Counsel in cases before the Patent Office, and on appeals therefrom, but does not prepare applications for Patents. Office corner E and 8th Sts., Washington, D.C.

Fitzgerald was peculiarly fitted to serve as counsel for the merits of all the machines concerned were at his fingertips. By an odd coincidence, it was Fitzgerald who was the Examiner of Patents in 1846 when Howe applied for his own sewing machine patent. In his report to the Secretary of the Treasury about the Howe sewing machine, Fitzgerald wrote:

It is proper here to remark that several patents have heretofore been granted for sewing machines, but none of them operate in a similar manner, nor produce a similar result. The inventor has not followed the footsteps of his predecessors, but has struck out a track of his own; it would be difficult, by any means heretofore known, to sew as fast or as well as can be done by this machine.

Fitzgerald assumed command of the case. He was the man to fight Hunt's battle—hot-headed, but keen and clever, conversant with every line of patent law, and afraid of nothing and no one. He assembled all the facts in the case and studied them carefully. He perused the testimony at the various trials in equity in the Circuit Courts.

What stirred him most was a discrepancy offered by Arrowsmith before the patent office hearing compared with his previous testimony and depositions in previous cases.

Fitzgerald submitted these contradictory depositions together with a ninety-seven page brief closely written on legal-size paper which completely covered every possible angle on the subject.

Fitzgerald gave many reasons why Hunt was entitled to a patent and he denied Howe's objections and claims. His opening and chief argument was:

The question here is not whether Howe's patent is invalid, but whether a patent shall be granted to Hunt—not whether Howe has since Hunt's invention made such improvements in sewing machines as justly entitle him to a patent, but whether the invention previously made by Hunt is patentable. Whether Hunt would have been entitled to a patent in 1835, or 1836, before Howe entered upon consideration of the subject. And, if so, whether anything has since intervened depriving him of that right.

Necessity's Child

Using his knowledge as an examiner of patents, Fitzgerald supported his contention by quoting the decisions of learned judges in previous patent controversies. He proved conclusively that Hunt had invented a sewing machine in 1834 and that it operated, even though its operation may not have been absolutely perfect. He contended:

> If Hunt had applied for a patent in 1836 the Commissioner of Patents would not have, and under the patent law could not have with propriety enquired whether he had constructed a perfect working machine, or whether he had done sewing on it for the market. At once, and without the possibility of a refusal, Hunt would have been granted letters patent.
>
> Mr. Howe's machine in the Patent Office will not produce a seam at all—and never would since it was filed in the office produce a good seam. I myself remember that when I examined it preparatory to granting a patent for it, it would not work perfectly. There were defects in almost every seam—and soon it ceased to sew at all.
>
> Even if Hunt had presented a model of some of the principle features, falling short of an entire sewing machine, he would also have been considered an inventor and would now have his patent.
>
> I do not mean that the machine Hunt built, though it was complete, was so perfect as to be incapable of improvements. There was scarcely ever in the world an invention so perfect as this—or if the invention were thus perfect no man could build the machine thus perfect, until he had built many, and had much experience.

Fitzgerald totally refused to accept Howe as the inventor of the sewing machine! He maintained that if Howe had not obtained a patent in 1846, Hunt would have been credited with the invention of the lock-stitch sewing machine.

Fitzgerald credited Howe only with an improvement in sewing machines, not a basic invention. He illustrated his point:

> The Patent Office was not sufficiently stupid to confound the repairing or adjusting of a strikingly new machine with the invention of it—and when the machinist, now employed to repair models in the patent office, shall reach Mr. Howe's model, and put it in order, it is presumed that neither Mr. Howe nor the Commissioner of Patents will consider the machinist the inventor. The fact that the machine of Mr. Hunt could be put in such order as to sew a perfect seam, at all, proves that the invention was complete—proves it incontestably.

To substantiate Hunt's claim, Fitzgerald quoted the decision of Judge Sprague in the case of *Howe v. Underwood*.

> Now that Mr. Hunt made an ingenious machine there is no doubt. He advanced so far that he made a machine that to a certain extent would sew.

He commented upon the judge's decision and said;

> He mentions it sewing up canvas into several tubes, the seams being so perfect that when the canvas was made impervious to air, the seams were so perfect that the tubes were used for conducting air! Did any machine ever make a better seam than is required for air tubes?

Although Fitzgerald maintained that the work of the Hunt machine was perfect at times, he showed that perfection was not requisite to a patent and illustrated the point by reference to Howe's machine.

> Your honor will probably be surprised to find that Howe has never made a perfect machine. It is notorious that his machine did not operate successfully until others made improvements upon it, and that others made the first successful machines. We should never have heard of Howe's machine if others had not made it practical, and we hear of him and his patent now only through the lawsuits he is everywhere instituting against all who have succeeded in getting up successful machines.

Fitzgerald did not question the Patent Office's award of a patent to Howe. Neither did he demand that it be canceled. He avoided both points of contention and skillfully showed that Hunt was also entitled to a patent on his invention of the sewing machine because of the proven and undisputed evidence of priority. He maintained that Hunt had never abandoned his machine and that Howe's contention of abandonment was impertinence in view of the facts. Fitzgerald furthermore challenged Howe's assertion and promised,

> When Hunt's patent is obtained, we will give Mr. Howe an opportunity to test this question of abandonment before a tribunal having jurisdiction and before which witnesses will be obliged to appear.

Maintaining that the function of the Patent Office was to grant or deny patents and was without the power to judge questions of abandonment, Fitzgerald continued:

> But, as I have remarked, the Honorable Commissioner has no jurisdiction of the question of abandonment, but only of questions of novelty, patentability and priority. The Commissioner is not a court, but has conferred upon him certain limited quasi judicial powers to be exercised in particular specified cases, and reaching to certain specified questions. As his powers are limited specifically—and as there was obviously no intention of embarrassing him with the general powers of a court, his jurisdiction cannot be extended by implication, but according to the universal rule in such cases, is confined strictly within the limits prescribed by statute, and then his decisions are only *prima facie* evidence

of the right to adjudicate—the same parties having a right to re-contest them before Courts of Law or Equity. He is not to reach after jurisdiction like a court of denier resort—but to shrink from it like all tribunals of limited jurisdiction.

Fitzgerald concluded his brief by attacking the integrity and honesty of those testifying in behalf of Howe. As the bitter brunt of his target, he questioned the reliability of two of his own witnesses whose testimony seemed decidedly contrary to that which they had previously given in other courts. The special victims of his anger were none other than George A. Arrowsmith and William Carlock.

Fitzgerald minced no words in calling a spade a spade. He had no consideration of personal feelings when he launched into his denunciatory attack. Arrowsmith was the first to feel his sting. The embittered lawyer began his attack:

I beg you will compare this affidavit [February 24, 1853, *Howe v. Wooldridge*] with the deposition given by him in this case, and observe the miserable shuffling when cross examined with reference to it—and see if you ever witnessed a piece of perjury so perfectly bare faced and palpable. After reading these papers nothing will be left uncertain but the time and the price of the subornation. The impudence of offering such a deposition as the one filed in this case in the face of those previously filed is past endurance. The affidavit of February 1853 not only shows the perjury of that filed in this case, but by the answers of Arrowsmith to questions on cross examination no. 20 and no. 33, we claim we have made this affidavit evidence for Hunt and claim the benefit of it. But [it is] useless to waste words upon a witness whose perjury is proved out of his own mouth. He may safely be left with the Grand Jury where I understand an indictment for perjury is now preparing against him or is already found. Your honor will readily see to what straits the Howe party are driven, and what they are willing to resort to, by comparing Arrowsmith's several affidavits and depositions.

You will further find by examining the testimony in the case in which the pretended opinion of Judge Sprague was given, Howe vs. Underwood, that this Howe offered Hunt a thousand dollars to withhold his testimony in the case. The money was refused and the fact came to light, but where it has been received, it is, of course, denied—but the perjury is not the less palpable, but I will waste no more time on Arrowsmith. We called him as our witness knowing what he had previously sworn to, but discovered before we examined him that the miserable thing had been bought, and delivered him over to his purchasers.

But, let us turn our attention to Carlock. We have no former affidavits to convict him. He was brought into the traces too early—but he is equally worthy of reliance with his worthy companion and former partner. This man swears that he had in his possession several specimens of the sewing of the machine of '35 and that all were defective. Now, if they were defective, if produced in court they would have been an important confirmation of his testimony before Judge Sprague. But where were they? In answer to 3rd Cross Question, he says he kept them until "within three years," that is, he parted with them since 1851. No explanation why he had kept them upwards of sixteen years and then parted with them. But some light may be thrown upon the subject that in 1852, he was a witness for Howe to prove that Hunt's machine would not sew a good seam according to his statement.

In Int. 12 Direct, and by putting the two answers together you will perceive that the specimens disappeared about the same time! Did they disappear because they would have confirmed his statements, or because they would have given the lie to them? If he had had a single specimen that would have confirmed his statement, would it not have been forthcoming? Those specimens were bought up cheaper than Hunt could be bought. Sixteen years is too long to keep specimens and then let them disappear so strangely—a tale hangs thereby!

Fitzgerald did not provide any actual instances of bribery or payments of money to Arrowsmith or Carlock. Minor sums, however, were paid to them for their services as witnesses in previous lawsuits. Although the following sums were paid to Arrowsmith, Fitzgerald did not introduce the list into the testimony.

June 9, 1852 Arrowsmith, Carlock and Gardner, witness fees	10.00
June 23, 1852 Arrowsmith, time and expenses	50.00
July 3, 1852 Arrowsmith, time and expenses	5.00
July 7, 1852 Arrowsmith, time and expenses	100.00
July 13, 1852 Arrowsmith and Carlock, board during trial	44.00
Aug. 9, 1852 Arrowsmith, time and services	50.00
Aug. 12, 1852 Arrowsmith, fare to Boston	4.00
Oct. 13, 1852 Arrowsmith, time	8.00
June 11, 1853 Arrowsmith, witness, deposition	40.00
July 1, 1853 Arrowsmith, time and expenses	40.50
Oct. 29, 1853 Arrowsmith, time and expenses	12.00

Nor did Fitzgerald introduce the small payments which Arrowsmith may have received for services rendered. He did not wish to confound the issue with minor points. His plan was to be deliberate and stress his denunciation in no unmistakable language.

But Fitzgerald's impassioned arguments and pleas had not been able to break the evil charm of misfortune which ruled Hunt almost since the cradle. His arguments and briefs of the case were carefully weighed by Honorable Charles Mason, Commissioner of Patents, who ruled on May 24, 1854, that the interference was dissolved.

The decision of the Commissioner of Patents, which was reprinted in the *Scientific American* of June 10, 1854 was that

He [Hunt] contrived a machine by which he actually affected his purpose of sewing cloth with considerable success. Upon a careful consideration of the testimony I am disposed to think that he had then carried his invention to the point of patentability.

I understand from the evidence that Hunt actually made a working machine thus even going farther than was absolutely necessary to entitle himself to a patent had he then applied for it.

The papers in the case show that Howe obtained a patent for substantially the same invention in 1846. The presumption is that since that time the invention had been in public use or sale.

I am therefore of the opinion that Hunt is not entitled to a patent and the interference will accordingly be dissolved.

The decision was both pleasing and displeasing to Hunt. He was sorry that he had not been granted a patent but was pleased that his invention was recognized and would have been entitled to a patent had he applied. Noncompliance with the technical rules of procedure of the Patent Office barred him from obtaining a patent. He lost, but it was not a complete loss, and he won, but it was not a complete moral victory.

The expense of the trial, $1,124.99, was borne by John P. Bowker, Jr., of Dorchester, Massachusetts. For underwriting it, Bowker was to receive a half-interest in the patent when granted with a free license to I. M. Singer reserved.

The commissioner's decision did not end the sewing machine controversy and did little to clarify it. It still flared as a live issue in the newspapers.

On the May 29, 1854, the I.M. Singer Company advertised in the *Times*:

Sewing Machine—Important Intelligence. Hon. Charles Mason, Commissioner of Patents has just decided that the NEEDLE AND SHUTTLE SEWING MACHINE was invented and made to operate by Walter Hunt, in 1834, about 12 years before the patent of Elias Howe, Jr. This able and conclusive decision, showing that Howe patented an old invention to which he had no right, will be published in a few days, and copies supplied to the public gratuitously. The credit will now be given to the inventor, and the rights of the public be vindicated. A certified copy of this important document, under the seal of the Patent Office, may be seen by applying to I. M. Singer & Co.

Elias Howe, Jr., responded in the *Times* on June 1, 1854, with this refutation:

Caution—Sewing Machine—None but the most abandoned liar would put forth the statement that I have been defeated by Walter Hunt, at the Patent

Office, or that the Patent Commissioner has given any decision "showing that I patented an old invention, to which I have no right."

THE FACTS ARE THESE

The Commissioner of Patents has refused to grant a patent to Walter Hunt, alias I. M. Singer & Co., their shiffling advertisements to the contrary notwithstanding.

Printed copies of said decision will be distributed free at my office in a few days.

All persons using the Singer's Machine (so called) without a license from me will be prosecuted to the full extent of the law.

Elias Howe, Jr.

May 30, 1854.   No. 305 Broadway, N.Y.

But the Singer Company was not pleased. They denied the assertion. They made their position clear in an advertisement in the *Times* of June 3, 1854.

SEWING MACHINES—The Decision of Hon. Charles Mason, Commissioner of Patents, shows that Elias Howe, Jr., in the year 1846 became the "Patentee of the original Sewing Machine," invented by Walter Hunt in 1834. The invention being old, the law declares Howe's patent void. The invention is public property. Printed copies of this important decision may be had gratis at the office of I. M. Singer & Co.

Elias Howe declared his wrath in a lengthy, expensive and detailed advertisement published in the *Times* on June 13, 1854:

SEWING MACHINES

CAUTION—All persons making, using or selling Sewing Machines not made or sold by the following licensees, will consult their interest by examining the recent decision of the United States Court, stopping the use of Singer's Sewing Machines (so called) in Massachusetts. Printed copies may be had free at my office, or by mail, by forwarding a postage stamp. Also copies of the recent decision of the Commissioner of Patents *refusing a patent* to Walter Hunt. My claims will be legally enforced against all persons making, selling, or using Sewing Machines by whatever name called, having one or more needles with the eye near the point, for the purpose of passing a loop of thread through the article to be sewed, unless purchased of my licensees, viz:

    Wheeler, Wilson & Co . . . . New York.
    Grover, Baker & Co . . . . New York.
    A. Bartholf. . . . . New York.
    American Magnetic Sewing Machine Co. . . New York.
    Dorcas Sewing Machine Co. . . . . New York.
    J. B. Nichols . . . . Boston, Mass.
    J. W. Bean . . . . Boston, Mass.
    Hood, Battel & Co . . . . Worcester, Mass.

N. Hunt . . . . Boston, Mass.

Messrs. Wooldridge, Keen & Moore . . . . . Lynn, Mass.

Charles A. Durgin has no longer a license to make, use, or sell SEWING MACHINES under any patent. It has been revoked and surrendered. No persons will be licensed who infringes the patents of other licensees, and an advance payment of $1,000. on account will be invariably required of those taking a license.

Elias Howe, Jr.

Patentee of the original Sewing Machine,

No. 35 Hanover St., Boston, and No. 305 Broadway, N.Y.

May 1, 1854

The I.M. Singer Company replied the next day with their daily installment of vitriol and rancor.

SEWING MACHINES—THE COMBINATION of Needle and Shuttle in Sewing Machines has been declared public property. The decision of the Hon. Charles Mason, Commissioner of Patents, proves that this invention was made by Walter Hunt, in 1834, and that it has been given to the public. The extortions of Elias Howe, Jr., and his associates are now at an end. Copies of this decision can be had gratis at any of the offices of I. M. Singer & Co.

These bitter advertisements were merely part of the battle of printer's ink that had been waged with increased fervor and venom from the moment Elias Howe, Jr., claimed a royalty on all sewing machines manufactured or in use in the United States.

Even though the Commissioner of Patents had decided that Hunt was not entitled to a patent, the issue was not conclusively decided. Hunt's attorney appealed the decision on the grounds that the commissioner had exceeded his jurisdiction.

The case was again tried in the Circuit Court of the District of Columbia in February 1855 before Judge James S. Morsell. The principles involved in this case were threefold; one, the jurisdiction of the commissioner under the act of March 3, 1839; two, a determination of what constituted "public use"; and three, the question of abandonment.

The litigation between those connected with the machine industry was a lengthy and costly procedure. Furthermore it undermined the confidence of the public. Despite public apathy, many patents had been granted to newcomers who jumped on the bandwagon. But machines which incorporated the improvements could not be manufactured, because each patentee insisted upon royalties from those who used their devices. The improvements were not aids, they were impediments. As matters stood, all of them hampered the manufacture of better machines.

It was a situation that probably has had little equal in the United States or any other country. Plans were devised to remedy the confusion. They offered little result. New laws, not new machines, were needed. In the meantime the only thing possible was to accede on compromise with the man, or men, who held the whip hand.

Orlando B. Potter, of the Grover & Baker Company, sponsored a reciprocity and cooperative arrangement which found ready acceptance. He obtained the support and cooperation of numerous manufacturers who agreed to pool interests and form a combination. The manufacturers agreed to pay a license fee of $15.00 for each machine they manufactured, the administration of the patents to be controlled by the combination.

Howe was to receive $5.00 of each $15.00, the $10.00 balance being set aside until $10,000 was accumulated as a fund for the expense of future lawsuits in the interest of the combination. After this sum was reached, the royalty fees were apportioned as one-third to Howe, one-third to I. M. Singer, one-sixth to Wheeler and Wilson and one-sixth to the Grover & Baker Company.

In 1860, the $15.00 fee was reduced to $7.00; in 1863 to $5.00; and in 1870 to $3.00.

And meanwhile one final chapter was written in regard to Walter Hunt's interest:

> Appeal from the decision of the Commissioner of Patents for refusing to grant Letters Patent to Walter Hunt for his invention of a new and useful machine or mechanical apparatus for sewing and stitching cloth, leather, etc. by means of which a new plan of an interlocked stitch is produced.
>
> Decision Jas. S. Morsell, Assistant Judge, Circuit Court of the District of Columbia, February 10, 1855:
>
> I, James S. Morsell, Assistant Judge of the Circuit Court of the District of Columbia certify to the Hon. Charles Mason, Commissioner of Patents, that I have considered the reasons of appeal filed by the applicant in this cause, and the grounds of the decision of the said commissioner upon the points involved in the said reasons, and have heard and considered the arguments submitted by counsel: Whereupon I do decide and adjudge that the said decision of the said Commissioner of Patents, upon the said points involved in the said reasons of appeal, be, and the same is, hereby affirmed. [6/27/1854 pat. agreement April 3, 1857. Received May 14, recorded July 7, 1857 in Liber 4, page 259 Transfer of Patents.]

And once again Walter Hunt lost. For after hearing the lengthy argument for the appeal—six reasons were given—Judge Morsell decided that Hunt was not entitled to a patent as the law prior to 1839 was that,

> If the inventor sold to any one who might choose to buy, although it was only a single specimen of his invention, and sold for profit on it as an

invention, such a sale would be a "public use," and the unlimited nature of the object with which a knowledge of the invention was imparted would prevent him from resuming his exclusive right by a subsequent patent.

This decision established the point that an absolute sale of all the inventor's interest for a valuable consideration, and the public exhibition by the purchaser of a machine embodying the invention many years before the filing of the application is conclusive evidence of a public use with the consent of the inventor. And that he cannot again acquire a right to a patent by a repurchase of the invention.

Although the agreement did much to simplify matters, sewing machine controversies still existed. No circuit court would have considered itself open for business and doing its duty without its quota of sewing machine infringement cases on the calendar. In all of them, Howe took honors as a champion litigant.*

Walter Hunt was not essentially a fighter. He was stubborn and could cling to an idea, once formed, especially if he considered that justice was being flouted. But he was not fond of strife.

In time when the sewing machine battledore and shuttlecock bade fair to go on, he tired of it.

At least, Hunt grew utterly weary of inaction and of waiting for things to happen. There was too much more of the world's work still to be done. Other fields interested him.

The decision dimmed Walter Hunt's interest in the sewing machine. He gave his attention to other things.

---

*New York Court of Appeals, Cases and Briefs 536-1878, *149 pages—Albany, N.Y.*

Chapter 25

Before Hunt's controversy had been decided by the Commissioner of Patents, Jonathan Chapin visited him in his hotel room in Boston.

"I don't think we will win the case," Chapin said resignedly. "Everyone says Elias Howe has too much influence."

"Regardless of whether we beat him," Hunt replied, "I have another iron in the fire. I thought of something which will make me a fortune."

Chapin snapped to attention, cupped his hand behind his ear and wrinkled his forehead. "What now?"

"Who are the main buyers of sewing machines?" Hunt asked.

"I suppose," Chapin hedged, "you want me to say the dress trade and manufacturers of shirts and collars."

"I've come up with something new which will develop a new industry, and will help the poor and make me rich! Here, read this."

He handed Chapin two pages of yellow paper covered with notations in red ink.

Chapin adjusted his spectacles on the tip of his nose and began to read.

Attempts have been made at various times to manufacture shirt collars of paper, but they have never been extensively introduced; nor has anything beneficial or lasting resulted therefrom, on account of the fragile nature of the material, which rendered it liable to be easily broken and defaced, while it was liable to be quickly soiled and to be entirely destroyed if exposed to either rain or perspiration.

"What's this, an essay?" Chapin inquired.

"It's a copy of my patent application that I made on January 28, 1854." Chapin continued to read:

The object of my present invention is to produce a shirt collar that shall not be easily broken, while it shall have sufficient elasticity to bend to the motions

233

of the head, that shall possess the beauty and whiteness of the most carefully-dressed linen collar, and at the same time shall preserve itself unsoiled for a much greater length of time, and shall cost originally less than the washing and dressing of a linen collar; and my invention consists in making the collar of a fabric composed of both paper and cloth, and in subsequently polishing the same by enameling or burnishing, or in any suitable and efficient manner.

"Sounds interesting," Chapin commented.

"Go on, continue reading!"

Chapin moved closer to the flickering gas jet so that the light shone over his left shoulder. He continued reading;

My invention further consists in covering the collars made of the above material with a thin pellicle of transparent colorless varnish, whereby they are rendered proof against injury from either rain or perspiration, and when soiled may be wiped off with a damp cloth or sponge, and restored to nearly their original whiteness.

"Sounds like a good idea," Chapin agreed, "but the chances are that it won't be any good."

"Why not?"

"Because papers collars are vulgar. They are frowned upon by society."

"Society!" Hunt interrupted, "I'm not interested in society. I've created a new collar. Not for society. It's for the poor man. For people like you and me."

"But will people take to paper collars?" Chapin asked.

"Why not? Right now the poor are using collars made from the paper inter-lining used on ribbon spools." Hunt explained. "But those cheap collars are hor-rible. They don't fit, they don't wear, and they look terrible. I've invented a process that is completely different and much better. My collars look clean and neat. They will do away with the stigma of paper and men will be glad to buy a better collar at a lower price."

"Any prospects of selling the idea?"

"I've spoken to Sam Cooper. He's the patent agency man who has that small office at 39 State Street that I told you about. He and John Murdock wit-nessed my patent application. Cooper says he knows somebody who finances new ideas," Hunt explained.

"Just a bit of advice, Mr. Hunt. Don't sell it to them for chicken-feed," Chapin cautioned.

A few days later, Hunt went to Cooper's office. Cooper introduced him to John W. Ridgway, a money broker and real estate operator residing in Boston.

"The idea looks pretty good." Ridgway enthused. "And it won't cost much money to manufacture them. Have you got your patent yet?"

"Not yet." Hunt replied. "I sent the application to the Patent Office. Here is a copy I made."

Ridgway looked at it and began to read.

Thin white cotton muslin is coated upon both sides with a very thin white paper, a layer of paste, glue, or other suitable sizing being interposed between them. For the purpose of rendering the material more tough and pliable and less easily broken when bent, I mix with the sizing with which the cloth and paper are united a portion of saccharine matter, varying in quantity according to the circumstances. The fabric thus produced is then polished by passing it through calendering-rollers, by an agate burnisher, by covering the fabric with a coating of enamel, or by other suitable means. The collars are then stamped or cut out, and may be made either in one piece or in two pieces, the separate portions being afterward glued or pasted together, and if found desirable the collars may be pressed between heated forms to give them the exact shape of the neck. The collar thus formed is then provided with the requisite button-holes or other means for securing it to the shirt, and is ready for the last process, which consists in covering the cotton with a thin coating of transparent, colorless, water-proof varnish for the purpose of protecting it from the effects of moisture, and also of preserving it for a much longer time from being soiled. The varnish which I prefer for this purpose is composed of bleached shellac, as it is transparent, colorless and resists humidity much longer than any other which I have tried. This varnish may be applied to the fabric either in the sheet or after the collar is made, as may be found preferable.

"Cooper says the Patent Office should grant a patent on it," Ridgway stated. "The application seems all right to me. I don't see any reason why these paper collars can't be made. How much do you want for the patent?"

"It should be worth a couple of—" Hunt stopped and reflected. "It's hard to estimate its real value."

"If you'll assign a half-interest in the patent," Ridgway proposed, "I'll give you my personal check for four thousand dollars."

"It's a deal," Hunt snapped. The offer was so large that it almost took his breath away.

On June 28, 1854, Hunt assigned the patent to Ridgway. It was witnessed by George C. Varney and John Vail, the tailor. Hunt made out the bill of sale.

Within a month on July 25, 1854, Hunt received U.S. Patent No. 11,376 on a polished and varnished fabric equally adapted to shirt-bosoms, wristbands and collars.

A small quantity of the collars were manufactured. The reaction to them was not anticipated. Washerwomen protested that the fabric collars would deprive them of laundry income and would throw thousands of them out of work. Society, unwilling to see linen collars copied by the poorer classes, frowned upon the idea. They maintained that if a man could not afford the upkeep of linen collars, he had no right to adopt the style with an inferior product. Despite these objections, the sales of paper collars gradually increased.

UNITED STATES PATENT OFFICE.

WALTER HUNT, OF NEW YORK, N. Y.

IMPROVEMENT IN SHIRT-COLLARS.

Specification forming part of Letters Patent No. **11,376,** dated July 25, 1854.

To all whom it may concern:

Be it known that I, WALTER HUNT, of the city, county, and State of New York, have invented a new and useful Method of Making the Collars and Bosoms of Shirts, of which the following is a full, clear, and accurate description.

Attempts have been made at various times to manufacture shirt-collars of paper, but they have never been extensively introduced; nor has anything beneficial or lasting resulted therefrom, on account of the fragile nature of the material, which rendered it liable to be easily broken and defaced, while it was liable to be quickly soiled and to be entirely destroyed if exposed to either rain or perspiration.

The object of my present invention is to produce a shirt-collar that shall not be easily broken, while it shall have sufficient elasticity to bend to the motions of the head, that shall possess the beauty and whiteness of the most carefully-dressed linen collar, and at the same time shall preserve itself unsoiled for a much greater length of time, and shall cost originally less than the washing and dressing of a linen collar; and my invention consists in making the collars of a fabric composed of both paper and cloth, and in subsequently polishing the same by enameling or burnishing, or in any suitable and efficient manner.

My invention further consists in covering the collars made of the above material with a thin pellicle of transparent colorless varnish, whereby they are rendered proof against injury from either rain or perspiration, and when soiled may be wiped off with a damp cloth or sponge and restored to nearly their original whiteness.

To enable others skilled in the art to which this most nearly pertains to make use of my invention, I will proceed to describe the method which I have adopted of carrying it out.

Thin white cotton muslin is coated upon both sides with a very thin white paper, a layer of paste, glue, or other suitable sizing being interposed between them. For the purpose of rendering the material more tough and pliable and less easily broken when bent, I mix with the sizing with which the cloth and paper are united a portion of saccharine matter, varying in quantity according to the circumstances. The fabric thus produced is then polished by passing it through calendering-rollers, by an agate burnisher, by covering the fabric with a coating of enamel, or by other suitable means. The collars are then stamped or cut out, and may be made either in one piece or in two pieces, the separate portions being afterward glued or pasted together, and if found desirable the collars may be pressed between heated forms to give them the exact shape of the neck. The collar thus formed is then provided with the requisite button-holes or other means for securing it to the shirt, and is ready for the last process, which consists in covering the cotton with a thin coating of transparent, colorless, water-proof varnish for the purpose of protecting it from the effects of moisture, and also of preserving it for a much longer time from being soiled. The varnish which I prefer for this purpose is composed of bleached shellac, as it is transparent, colorless, and resists humidity much longer than any other which I have tried. This varnish may be applied to the fabric either in the sheet or after the collar is made, as may be found preferable.

I will enumerate some of the advantages which a collar prepared as above possesses. Its smooth surface renders it exceedingly pleasant to the face; second, it may be worn many times longer than an ordinary laundry-dressed linen collar without being soiled, and when it is so soiled it may be wiped over with a moist sponge or cloth and be made almost as white as when first made; third, it is not injured by exposure either to rain or to perspiration, as is a starched linen collar, and may even be immersed for a considerable time in water without being materially affected thereby; fourth, it may be made and sold at a price that will not equal the cost of washing and dressing an ordinary linen collar.

I have heretofore spoken of my invention as particularly applicable to shirt-collars; but it is evident that it is equally adapted to shirt-bosoms and wristbands.

I do not claim making collars of paper, neither do I claim the peculiar fabric which I make use of, nor the enameling and polishing of such fabric, nor do I claim making paper or cloth water-proof by means of varnish; but

What I do claim as my invention, and desire to secure by Letters Patent as a new article of manufacture, is—

The above-described shirt-collar, made of the fabric set forth, and polished and varnished in the manner and for the purpose specified.

WALTER HUNT.

Witnesses:

SAM. COOPER,
JNO. MURDOCK.

The linen collar industry severely felt the competition. Laundries decried the loss of revenue. They developed devious tactics to stop the increasing sales. They spread a rumor campaign. They claimed that paper collars were covered with a poisonous coating which constituted a menace to health. Fictitious and isolated instances of infections and disease were attributed to them. The fear campaign spread. Opposition to them increased. Sales dropped. It was a difficult situation for a new product to combat.

This unexpected reaction worried Ridgway and he doubted the sagacity of his investment. His enthusiasm waned and he lost interest. Other pending deals which might prove more profitable attracted him. He was a promoter, not a pioneer. He was anxious to salvage his original investment. Hunt could fend for himself.

Elsewhere the sewing machine lawsuits were decided by the Boston courts. The verdict did not please Hunt. He was dejected when he returned to New York City. He wore one of his paper collars and carried a small quantity of them to give to his friends. They created some interest and attention wherever they were shown but no one was willing to invest in their promotion.

Finally Edward E. Valentine and M. Howland Hall of the firm of E. H. Valentine and Company, manufacturers, of 408 Broadway, New York City, heard about Hunt and his paper collars.

"We are interested in securing the rights to your patent," Valentine told Hunt.

"I only own a half-interest," Hunt replied. "I sold half of my rights to John W. Ridgway of Boston."

"We will give you three thousand dollars for your half-interest," Valentine offered. "And, we'll offer Ridgway the same amount for his."

"I accept, and I'll contact Ridgway. I presume he'll also accept your offer."

Ridgway, who had concluded that the deal was a bad investment, jumped at the opportunity to salvage what he could. The offer appealed to him.

The deal was closed February 28, 1855, when Valentine and Hall paid Hunt and Ridgway three thousand dollars each for their half-interests. Cyrus J. Bunker, a member of the Valentine company, witnessed the assignment of the patent rights. The necessary transfer papers were drawn up by Horace M. Ruggles, a lawyer, who also witnessed the signatures.

Hunt's brief contact with collars proved both profitable and satisfactory. Seven thousand dollars for an invention conceived and executed in one day. He was pleased with his sudden windfall and felt like a millionaire.

The public gradually withdrew its opposition and accepted the invention and he decided to cash in on it.

The more Hunt thought about how a near calamity turned into a windfall, he envisioned other improvements which might similarly produce the same success.

Two months later, on September 25, 1854, Hunt filed a caveat with the Patent Office on an improved collar, one layer of which consisted of a fabric. On July 25, 1855, one year to the day of the grant of the first paper collar patent, Hunt submitted the completed application. It was witnessed by B. S. Cooper and W. D. Wisner, and affirmed before Joseph Breck, Commissioner of Deeds.

The application was rejected by the Commissioner of Patents who wrote on August 18, 1855, that:

> Your application for letters patent for alleged improvements in Fabrics for Shirt Bosoms, etc. has been examined and found to present no patentable novelty in view of your patent dated July 25, 1854 for a similar fabric. The substitution of a sheet of cloth or muslin for a sheet of paper in which consists the only difference between your application and your patent, is not patentable, and as two patents cannot issue for the same invention, your application is necessarily rejected.

In an endeavor to have the Commissioner reverse his decision, Hunt appointed Zenas C. Robbins, a patent attorney, to represent him in prosecuting his patent claim. Robbins had considerable experience. He was also the inventor of steam boilers, churns and carriage brakes, and knew patent office procedure.

On August 25, 1855, Hunt appeared before William H. Dusenberry, a Commissioner of Deeds, and "made solemn oath according to law that he still verily believes himself to be the original and first inventor of the within-described improved fabric for shirt collars and that he does not know or believe that the same was ever known or used; and that he is a citizen of the United States."

Robbins resubmitted the application with a few minor modifications. In accordance with patent law, Hunt was required to file a new affidavit.

The application, affidavit and necessary papers were resubmitted to the Patent Office by Robbins on September 6, 1855, who wrote,

> I hereby return the specification of Walter Hunt's invention for improved shirt-collar fabric with oath renewed, and respectfully request a reconsideration of the case on the amended claim herewith submitted.
>
> You will perceive that the claim is laid to a new article of manufacturing adapted to a new and specified purpose. The invention consists not merely in uniting two or more thicknesses of cloth by suitable size or parts but in a fabric thus prepared, and also finished in quantities, so as to require no further manipulation but cutting out the parts and uniting them together, previous to wearing, whereby collars can be made at a much less cost than by any method heretofore known. The invention by this means can furnish a desirable article, for the market at a cost which will be economical to the purchaser.

I believe this restricted claim will not be found subject to the objection offered by the office in rejecting the original claims. Hence, I trust you will see sufficient distinctive novelty in the new manufacture to afford protection to the inventor by letters patent.

A few days later, the Patent Office advised that the patent would not be granted.

But this did not satisfy Hunt. On October 13, 1855, Hunt applied for still another collar patent. This application was witnessed by Benson S. Cooper and Charles A. Griffin. Hunt appeared before William B. Aitken, Commissioner of Deeds, who verified his signature.

This application, unlike the previous one which was rejected, was also handled by Zena C. Robbins. It encountered little opposition from the examiners and was found acceptable by the Patent Office on January 1, 1856, which awarded Hunt U.S. Patent No. 14,019 on

shaping and uniting the several perfectly flat parts of the collar, that the sides thereof will fit about the face as easily and gracefully as collars which are made in the usual manner, and which have been starched and ironed by hand in such a manner as to curve and stretch the outer layer of the collars.

Hunt's reputation in the collar industry was enhanced by the grant of his second patent in this field. Sales opposition dwindled and sales resistance diminished. Merchants found that collars were acceptable. People were now willing to buy them and wear them. Time had worked in his favor. As the demand for collars increased, so did those interested in profiting in the new industry.

A syndicate of businessmen approached Hunt. "We'll give you four thousand dollars for the patent."

"I'll take it." Hunt replied without hesitation.

Concluding the verbal agreement, Hunt assigned his patent on January 12, 1856. A half-interest was acquired by Daniel G. Rollins for $2,000 and a half-interest jointly by Walter Seely and George C. Close for $2,000.

Hunt was deliriously happy. His two patents had brought him [$11,000], a fortune. But this was only a pittance compared to what the manufacturers would earn later.

Valentine and Hall, who had acquired the earlier patent rights from Hunt and Ridgway, began manufacturing collars in the third story of a building at 408 Broadway, New York City. The $6000 they paid for the rights made a big dent in their working capital. To carry on, they were obliged to borrow $2000 from William G. West. As security they placed the patent with him as collateral.

Hall sold his interest in the patent to Frederick E. Radcliff in the fancy goods business. Then Valentine and Radcliff sold their interests to Norman Cutter, who later resold it to E. H. Valentine & Company. John Schuyler and Abraham Mead later came into possession of the patent, which they assigned

UNITED STATES PATENT OFFICE.

WALTER HUNT, OF NEW YORK, N. Y.

SHIRT-COLLAR.

Specification of Letters Patent No. 14,019, dated January 1, 1856.

To all whom it may concern:

Be it known that I, WALTER HUNT, of the city, county, and State of New York, have invented a new and useful Improvement in the Manufacture of Shirt-Collars; and I do hereby declare that the following is a full and exact description thereof, reference being had to the accompanying drawings, making a part of this specification, Figure 1 being a view of one of my improved collars made to open in front; Fig. 2, a view of a collar made to open behind, and Fig. 3 a transverse section in the line *a a* of Fig. 1.

I make an article of sham shirt collars, of some white glazed cheap material. This material may be two united thicknesses of thin cotton cloth, properly bleached, sized, and calendered; or the said collars may be made of paper properly prepared; or of any other suitable material.

My invention consists in so shaping and uniting the several perfectly flat parts of the collar, that the sides thereof will fit about the face as easily and gracefully as collars which are made in the usual manner, and which have been starched and ironed by hand in such a manner as to curve and stretch the outer layer of the collars. The sides *b, b,* of the collar, and the neck band *d,* may be cut out by machinery in large numbers, and at the same time holes may be formed in the said parts for the reception of the eyelets *e, e,* or their equivalents. Only the extremities of the lower edge of each side piece *b,* of my improved collar must be se-[35] cured to the neck band *d,* and this allows the intermediate portions of said sides *b, b,* to play freely upon the polished surface of the band *d;* which arrangement causes the said exposed portions of my improved collar [40] to fit easily and gracefully about the face of the wearer. Sham shirt collars can be got up so cheaply on this plan that they can be sold for about the same price that a laundress would charge for washing and doing [45] up a more expensive collar. These collars are intended for travelers, who may be so situated that they have not time to have their collars washed and done up, and who do not wish to incur the expense of purchas-[50] ing fine linen collars.

What I claim as my invention and desire to secure by Letters Patent, in the manufacture of shirt collars, or sham shirt collars, is— [55]

Uniting only the extremities of the lower edges of the side pieces *b, b,* to the neck band *d,* by means of any suitable fastenings, for the purpose of enabling a flat sided collar to fit easily and gracefully about the face, sub-[60] stantially as herein set forth.

The above specification of my improved shirt collar, signed, and witnessed this 13th day of October A. D. 1855.

WALTER HUNT.

Witnesses:
BENSON S. COOPER,
CHARLES A. GRIFFIN.

---

to Smith and Graham, who in turn assigned it on March 4, 1858, to William E. Lockwood of Philadelphia for $2,200.

Lockwood undertook manufacturing collars in the Keystone Mills, near Fairmount. Six months later, he discontinued manufacturing them as the supply exceeded the demand. To offset the unfounded prejudice held by many against the collars and to promote their sale Lockwood began a judicious advertising campaign in which he stressed that new fresh collars could be purchased for less than the cost of washing linen ones, and that they could be worn longer.

W. Hunt.
Collar.

Nº 14019.

Patented Jan.1. 1856.

Fig.3

Fig.1

a

b

a

d

b

b

Fig.2

b

e

d

e

b

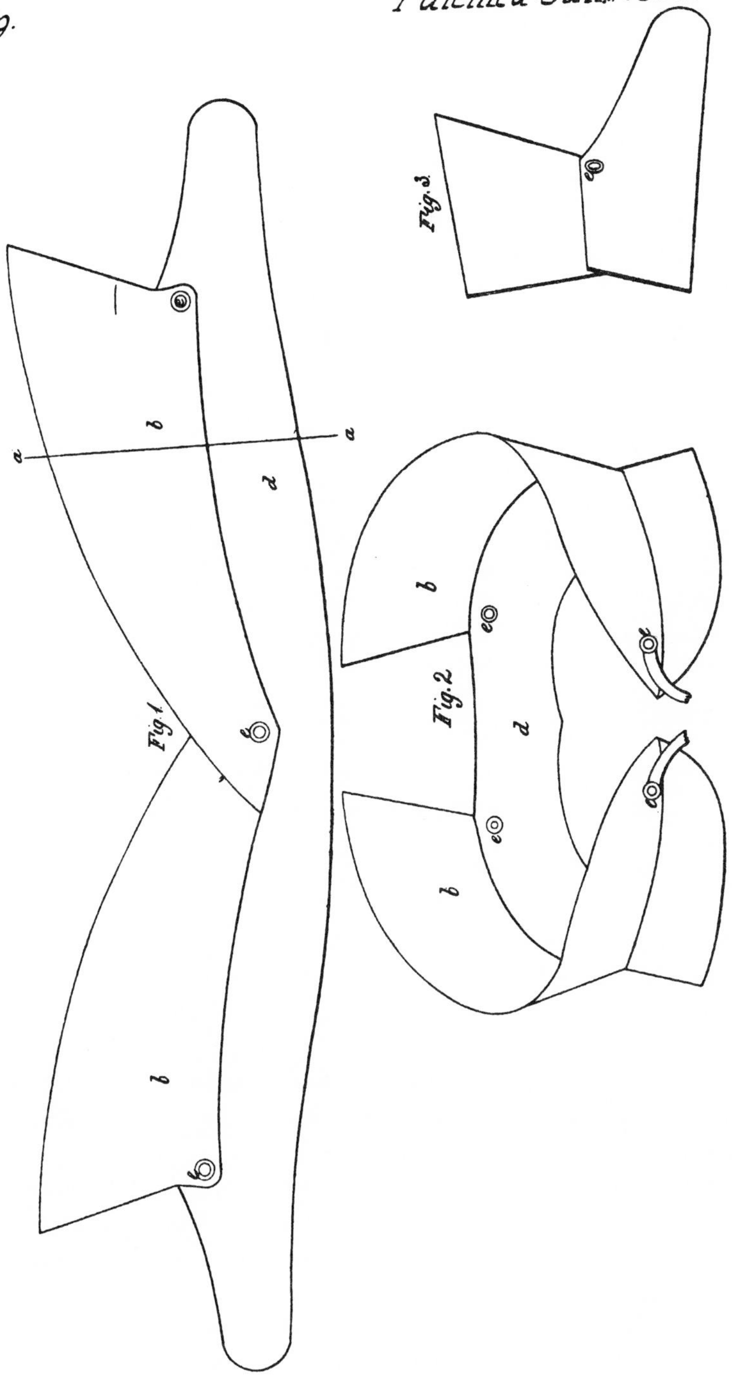

He stressed the cleanliness angle and also showed that the quality of paper collars was equal to that of linen.

The advertisement stimulated sales. The opposition to collars gradually melted away and demand for the collars increased. Lockwood disposed of his surplus collars, re-opened his factory and found that the demand was greater than his production. He moved to a larger factory, a five-story building at 255, 257 and 259 South Third Street, Philadelphia with 47 feet of frontage and 187 feet deep.

The demand for paper collars increased year by year. In 1864, about 500,000,000 collars were produced valued at $10,000,000. As the Civil War curtailed the production and transportation of cotton, the demand for paper collars increased. Blockade runners bootlegged them to the South where they found as ready an acceptance as in the North.

Hunt's patent was a basic one. Other inventors joined the bandwagon. William E. Lockwood, Solomon S. Gray and Andrew A. Evans also obtained patents on improvements.

Bootleg manufacturers made collars without regard to patent rights and paid no royalties. Infringers ransacked the lucrative field. Lawsuits and counter lawsuits to protect the patentees from infringers threatened to clog the courts. The industry was in turmoil.

Eventually, the legitimately licensed manufacturers realized that the pirates would have to be curbed and that a profitable industry was being ruined by competition. Protection of patents and pooling of interests, they reasoned, would result in mutually satisfactory arrangements. Consequently, twelve competing firms, more or less at loggerheads with each other, decided to combine. In 1866, they organized the Union Paper Collar Company, a three-million dollar corporation.

The Union Paper Collar Company acquired Lockwood's interest in paper collars. Other manufacturers also joined the combine. Some of the companies in the combine were the Albany Paper Collar Company, in Albany, the Springfield Collar Company, Springfield, Massachusetts, the Reversible Paper Collar Company of Boston, the Ne Plus Ultra Collar Company, in Biddeford, Maine, and the Lockwood Manufacturing Company, of Philadelphia. All agreed to purchase license stamps and labels from the Union Paper Collar Company which they placed on every package. Each manufacturer in the combine agreed to pay a royalty on every collar they produced.

Paper collar patents proved to be very valuable and the utmost effort was made to protect them. Lockwood, however, never lost his interest in paper collars. He hired Henry Howson, a patent attorney, to study the patent situation. He maintained that Hunt's patent number 11,376 of July 25, 1854, embraced more than he had claimed. They requested the Patent Office to grant a reissue covering the broader claims. The Patent Office favorably considered the request and on November 29, 1864, reissue No. 1,828 was awarded to William E. Lockwood.

Still more attention was focused on its intricate points and on February 7, 1865, reissue No. 1,867 was granted. On April 4, 1865, two additional reissues were granted which bore the numbers 1,926 and 1,927. The latter reissue was in turn surrendered and reissued in two divisions, number 2,306 and number 2,307.

Walter Hunt's patents were of too great a value not to squeeze every possible ounce of value from them. While checking the patents, the reissues and the patent rejections, Lockwood and Howson stumbled upon something which elated them. They found that Walter Hunt had made an application for a patent on July 25, 1855, which was rejected by the Patent Office on August 18, 1855. They approached the Hunt family to obtain control of the rejected patent application.

An agreement was made with the Hunt family who assigned the patent application and rights, if any, to Lockwood. Fortified by this agreement, Howson sent the following letter to the Commissioner of Patents on April 20, 1869.

This application (preceded by a caveat filed Sept. 25, 1854) was rejected August 10th, 1855 in reference to Walter Hunt's patent dated July 25, 1854.

On Sept. 5, 1855, the original claims were abandoned and an amended claim introduced. The application was however rejected Sept. 7, 1855 on grounds which I think the Office will now consider totally unjustifiable. I have therefore to request that the application be submitted to a reexamination with the view of determining whether the late Walter Hunt and his assignees had or had not been wronged by this action of the Office.

If the Office decides in the affirmative there can be no other course to pursue than to grant a patent on the application as amended Sept. 1855 to the present assignee on whose behalf I make this request and who has furnished me with the enclosed power of attorney to act in the case.

It is contended that the Office did err in refusing the patent and that the moment the office discovers this error it is its duty to issue the patent.

Although fourteen years had elapsed since the original application was submitted, the Patent Office reexamined the application and the claims which had been made. They recognized that they had made an error and bravely reversed their decision. On May 4, 1869, U.S. Patent No. 89,768 was granted to Walter Hunt of New York, assignor by mesne assignments to William E. Lockwood of Philadelphia.

It allowed the claim on a

fabric for making shirt-collars, composed of two or more thicknesses of muslin, cambric or other suitable cloth, united and finished by the web or quantity, substantially as herein described, whereby the necessity of sewing or stitching

UNITED STATES PATENT OFFICE.

WM. E. LOCKWOOD, OF PHILADELPHIA, PENNSYLVANIA, ASSIGNEE, BY MESNE ASSIGNMENTS, OF WALTER HUNT.

IMPROVEMENT IN SHIRT-COLLARS.

Specification forming part of Letters Patent No. 11,376, dated July 25, 1854 ; Reissue No. **1,828,** dated November 29, 1864.

DIVISION B.

To all whom it may concern:

Be it known that I, WILLIAM E. LOCKWOOD, of Philadelphia, Pennsylvania, am the owner of certain Letters Patent for an Improvement in Shirt-Collars, granted to WALTER HUNT on the 25th day of July, 1854, that I deem the said patent inoperative and invalid by reason of a defective specification, and that the following is a full, clear, and exact description of part of the said invention, which consists of a shirt-collar composed of paper and muslin or its equivalent, so combined and so polished or burnished that the collar shall not be readily torn or broken at the parts subjected to the greatest strain, shall be sufficiently elastic, shall have the whiteness and brilliancy of the most carefully dressed linen collar, for which the improved collar forms a cheap substitute.

To enable others skilled in the art to which this invention most nearly appertains to make use of the said invention, I will now proceed to describe the manner of constructing the same.

White paper properly prepared presents a more smooth and glossy surface, and one which is less liable to attract dust and dirt and absorb perspiration and other moisture, than the most carefully starched and ironed linen. With a full knowledge of this fact the said WALTER HUNT determined to apply this smooth and polished white paper to the manufacture of shirt-collars, shirt-bosoms, and other articles of wearing-apparel, with the view of substituting the cheaper paper article for the more expensive one of linen, and of saving the time occupied and wear and tear which takes place in washing, starching, and ironing ordinary linen collars. The fragile nature of paper, its liability to crack and to tear at the button-holes, rendered it necessary to stiffen and make it more tough and elastic by combining it with textile fabrics or submitting it to other stiffening or strengthening processes. The said HUNT took sheets of thin white paper, and by means of paste, glue, or other appropriate sizing, secured one sheet of paper to one side and the other to the opposite side of thin white cotton, muslin, or other textile fabric or fibrous material not readily torn. The fabric was then polished and rendered more stiff and elastic by subjecting it to the action of calender-rollers, rubbing it with an agate burnisher, or other suitable means. The collars or other articles of wearing-apparel were then cut or stamped out, and were made in one piece or in two or more pieces, the separate portions being afterward glued or pasted together and finally provided with suitable button-holes.

Among the advantages which the improved collars present are the following: First, they have a smooth, glossy, and pure white surface; second, they can be worn much longer than ordinary laundry-dressed linen collars; third, they may be made and sold at a price less than the cost of washing, starching, and dressing linen collars.

I have heretofore alluded to the invention as particularly applicable to shirt-collars; but it is evident that it is equally well adapted to shirt-bosoms, wristbands, &c.

I claim as the invention of the said WALTER HUNT and desire to secure by Letters Patent as a new manufacture—

A shirt-collar composed of paper and muslin or its equivalent, and polished or burnished, substantially as and for the purpose described.

In testimony whereof I have signed my name to this specification before two subscribing witnesses.

WILLIAM E. LOCKWOOD.

Witnesses:
HENRY HOWSON,
JOHN WHITE.

UNITED STATES PATENT OFFICE.

WM. E. LOCKWOOD, OF PHILADELPHIA, PENNSYLVANIA, ASSIGNEE, BY MESNE ASSIGNMENTS, OF WALTER HUNT.

IMPROVEMENT IN SHIRT-COLLARS.

Specification forming part of Letters Patent No. 11,376, dated July 25, 1854; Reissue No. **1,867,** dated February 7, 1865.

DIVISION C.

To all whom it may concern:

Be it known that I, WILLIAM E. LOCKWOOD, of Philadelphia, Pennsylvania, am the owner of certain Letters Patent for an Improvement in Shirt-Collars, granted to WALTER HUNT on the 25th day of July, 1854; that I deem the said patent inoperative and invalid by reason of a defective specification; and that the following is a full, clear, and exact description of that part of the said invention which consists of a shirt-collar in which white paper is used to imitate starched linen, and which has the desired shape imparted to it by formers applied under pressure.

The said WALTER HUNT made collars of stiff white paper, and polished or enameled the surface by calender-rolls, by rubbing with an agate burnisher, or by other suitable means, the collar being shaped by formers applied under pressure. Deeming the paper itself too fragile and liable to tear, especially at the button-holes, he took sheets of thin white paper, and by means of paste, glue, or other appropriate sizing secured one to one side and the other to the opposite side of thin white cotton muslin. The fabric thus composed had

a smooth and polished or enameled surface imparted to it by passing it between calender-rollers or by other suitable means. The collars or other articles of wearing-apparel were then cut or stamped out from this fabric and provided with suitable button-holes. In order that they might be made to conform to the shape of the wearer's neck, the paper collars were finally pressed between forms of appropriate shape.

It is evident that the invention is adapted to shirt-bosoms, wristbands, &c.

I claim as the invention of the said WALTER HUNT and as a new manufacture—

A shirt-collar in which white paper is used to imitate starched linen, and which is made of the desired shape by dies or formers applied under pressure.

In testimony whereof I have signed my name to this specification before two subscribing witnesses.

WILLIAM E. LOCKWOOD.

Witnesses:
 HENRY HOWSON,
 JOHN WHITE.

---

the collars, and of subsequent washing, starching, and ironing is dispensed with.

Lockwood contacted the Patent Office and, on July 13, 1869, obtained reissue No. 3,552 of this patent.

The reversal of the Patent Office commissioners and the re-issue of the patent caused George Hunt to review their past decisions. He appealed to the Patent Office to extend the life of U.S. Patent No. 11,376 granted July 25, 1854.

UNITED STATES PATENT OFFICE.

WM. E. LOCKWOOD, OF PHILADELPHIA, PENNSYLVANIA, ASSIGNEE, BY MESNE ASSIGNMENTS, OF WALTER HUNT.

IMPROVEMENT IN SHIRT-COLLARS.

Specification forming part of Letters Patent No. 11,376, dated July 25, 185:; Reissue No. **1,926,** dated April 4, 1865.

DIVISION A.

To all whom it may concern:

Be it known that I, WILLIAM E. LOCKWOOD, of Philadelphia, Pennsylvania, am the owner of certain Letters Patent for an Improvement in Shirt-Collars, granted to WALTER HUNT on the 25th day of July, 1854; that I deem the said patent inoperative and invalid by reason of a defective specification; and I do hereby declare that the following is a full, clear, and exact description of that part of said invention, which consists in so indenting shirt-collars, made of a fabric composed of paper and muslin, or an equivalent fabric, that the indentation will represent the stitches of an ordinary dressed linen collar.

The said WALTER HUNT made shirt-collars of white paper, strengthened and stiffened by the interposition of muslin secured to two sheets of the paper, the fabric thus composed being polished by passing it through calendering-rollers, or by other suitable means, the collars to be afterward shaped, if desired, by dies or formers applied under pressure, to adapt them to the wearer's neck. The collars thus formed were provided with the requisite button-holes, and indentations were made near the edge of the collar, to represent the row or rows of stitches of an ordinary dressed linen collar.

It is evident that the invention is adapted to shirt-bosoms, wristbands, &c.

I claim as the invention of the said WALTER HUNT, and desire to secure by Letters Patent—

So indenting shirt-collars made of a fabric composed of paper and muslin, or an equivalent fabric, that the indentations will represent the stitches of an ordinary dressed linen collar.

In testimony whereof I have signed my name to this specification before two subscribing witnesses.

WILLIAM E. LOCKWOOD.

Witnesses:
    HENRY HOWSON,
    JOHN WHITE.

They listened to his request and advised him fourteen years had elapsed since it was originally issued, its life had expired and that it was in public domain. Instead of dropping the matter, Hunt appealed to Congress to extend the life of the patent. His request was referred to committee.

The fair-minded Patent Office acted promptly. On March 31, 1870, the Commissioner of Patents decided

in the matter of the application of Polly Hunt, administratrix, and George W. Hunt, administrator of Walter Hunt, deceased, for the extension, in pursuance of an act of Congress for their relief.

UNITED STATES PATENT OFFICE.

WM. E. LOCKWOOD, OF PHILADELPHIA, PENNSYLVANIA, ASSIGNEE, BY MESNE ASSIGNMENTS, OF WALTER HUNT.

IMPROVEMENT IN SHIRT-COLLARS.

Specification forming part of Letters Patent No. 11,376, dated July 25, 1854; Reissue No. **1,927,** dated April 4, 1865.

DIVISION D.

To all whom it may concern:

Be it known that I, WILLIAM E. LOCKWOOD, of Philadelphia, Pennsylvania, am the owner of certain Letters Patent for an Improvement in Shirt-Collars, granted to WALTER HUNT on the 25th day of July, 1854; that I deem the said patent inoperative and invalid by reason of a defective specification; and I do hereby declare that the following is a full, clear, and exact description of that part of the said invention which consists of a shirt-collar made of a fabric composed of paper and muslin, or an equivalent fabric having a smooth white surface covered with a transparent varnish, for the purpose specified.

The said WALTER HUNT made shirt-collars of white paper, strengthened and stiffened by the interposition of muslin secured to two sheets of the paper. The fabric thus composed was subsequently polished by calendering-rolls, or by other suitable means, the collars to be subsequently shaped, if desired, by dies or formers applied, under pressure, to give them the shape of the wearer's neck. The collar thus formed was provided with the requisite button-holes, after which it was covered with a thin coating of transparent colorless water-proof varnish, for the purpose of protecting it from the effects of moisture, and also of preserving it from being soiled. The varnish which the said WALTER HUNT preferred was composed of bleached shellac, it being transparent, colorless, and capable of resisting humidity longer than any other varnish which he, the said HUNT, had tried. The varnish may be applied to the fabric either in the sheet or after the collar is made, as may be found preferable.

It is evident that the invention is adapted to shirt-bosoms, wrist-bands, &c.

I claim as the invention of the said WALTER HUNT, and as a new manufacture—

A shirt-collar made of a fabric composed of paper and muslin, or an equivalent fabric having a smooth white surface coated with transparent varnish, for the purpose specified

In testimony whereof I have signed my name to this specification before two subscribing witnesses.

WILLIAM E. LOCKWOOD.

Witnesses:
HENRY HOWSON,
JOHN WHITE.

Senator Waitman Thomas Willey, chairman of the Committee of Patents and the Patent Office, reviewed the appeal and sided with Walter Hunt's executors. His report was published in *Senate Reports No. 203* (40th Congress–3rd Session).

Vol.1.

Senator Willey reports favorably as to the petitioner's prayer to be allowed a rehearing before the Commissioner of Patents on their application for an extension of patents for improvements in manufacturing paper collars.

UNITED STATES PATENT OFFICE.

THE UNION PAPER COLLAR COMPANY, OF NEW YORK, N. Y., ASSIGNEES, BY MESNE ASSIGNMENTS, OF WALTER HUNT.

IMPROVEMENT IN SHIRT-COLLARS.

Specification forming part of Letters Patent No. 11,376, dated July 25, 1854; Reissue No. 1,927, dated April 4, 1865; Reissue No. **2,307**, dated July 10, 1866.

DIVISION B.

To all whom it may concern:

Be it known that WALTER HUNT, of the city, county, and State of New York, did invent certain new and useful Improvements in Shirt-Collars; and I do hereby declare that the following is a full, clear, and exact description of the same.

The invention of the said HUNT consisted of a shirt-collar composed of paper and muslin, or its equivalent, so combined and so polished or burnished that the collar shall not be readily torn or broken at the parts subjected to the greatest strain, shall be sufficiently elastic, shall have the whiteness and brilliancy of the carefully-dressed linen collar, for which the improved collar forms a cheap substitute.

White paper properly prepared presents a more smooth and glossy surface, and one which is less liable to attract dust and dirt and absorb perspiration and other moisture, than the most carefully-starched linen. With a full knowledge of this fact the said WALTER HUNT determined to apply this smooth and polished white paper to the manufacture of shirt-collars, shirt-bosoms, and other articles of wearing-apparel, with the view of substituting the cheaper paper article for the more expensive one of linen, and of saving the time occupied and wear and tear which takes place in washing, starching, and ironing the ordinary linen.

The fragile nature of paper, its liability to crack and to tear at the button-holes, rendered it necessary to stiffen it and make it more tough and elastic by combining it with textile fabrics or submitting it to other stiffening or strengthening processes. The said HUNT took sheets of thin white paper, and by means of paste, glue, or other appropriate sizing secured one sheet of paper to one side and the other to the opposite side of thin white cotton, muslin, or other textile fabric or fibrous material not readily torn. The fabric was then polished and rendered more stiff and elastic by subjecting it to the action of calender-rollers, rubbing it with an agate burnisher or other suitable means. The collars or other articles of wearing-apparel were then cut or stamped out, and were made in one piece or in two or more pieces, the separate portions being afterward glued or pasted together, and finally provided with suitable button-holes. The collar thus formed was covered with a thin coating of transparent, colorless, water-proof varnish, for the purpose of protecting it from the effects of moisture, and also of preserving it from being soiled.

The varnish may be applied to the fabric either in the sheet or after the collar is made, as may be found preferable, and the varnish which he preferred for this purpose was composed of bleached shellac.

Among the advantages which the improved collars present are the following:

First, they have a smooth, glossy, and pure white surface.

Second, they can be worn much longer than ordinary laundry-dressed linen collars.

Third, they may be made and sold at a price less than the cost of washing, starching, and dressing linen collars.

The invention has been alluded to as particularly applicable to shirt-collars, but it is evident that it is equally well adapted to shirt-bosoms, wristbands, &c.

What is claimed as the invention of the said WALTER HUNT, and desired to be secured under this patent as a new article of manufacture, is—

A shirt-collar, bosom, or wristband made of a fabric composed of paper and muslin, or an equivalent fabric, having a smooth white surface coated with transparent varnish, for the purpose specified.

UNION PAPER COLLAR COMPANY,
By JAMES A. WOODBURY, *President.*
Witnesses:
   A. B. STOUGHTON,
   JOHN S HOLLINGSHEAD.

Exhibit K.

Showing Eight styles of Collars, as manufactured under the Patent of Walter Hunt, between the years 1855 and 1858.

B

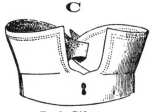

No. 1—Button.

Nine Sizes.

C

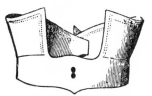

No. 3—D'Orsay.

Two Sizes.

D

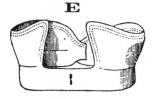

No. 4—Sharp Loop.

One Size.

E

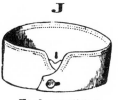

Tipp'd Loop.

F

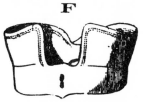

No. 7—Round Loop.

One Size.

G

No. 6—Narrow Loop.

One Size.

H

Back Fastening to Nos. 3, 4, 6 and 7.

I

No. 2—Byron A.

Nine Sizes.

J

No. 8.—English A.

Three Sizes.

Congress acted favorably upon the committee report and a special act of Congress (Stat.L.) was passed March 15, 1870 "for the relief of Polly Hunt, Administratrix, and George W. Hunt, Administrator, of the estate of Walter Hunt, deceased."

Empowered to hear the extension application, Acting Commissioner Silas Henry Hodges reviewed the case on March 31, 1870:

POLLY HUNT AND G. W. HUNT, ADMINISTRATRIX
AND ADMINISTRATOR OF ESTATE OF WALTER HUNT.
Extension.
March 31.

In the matter of the application of Polly Hunt, administratrix, and George W. Hunt, administrator of Walter Hunt, deceased, for the extension, in pursuance of an act of Congress for their relief, approved 15th March, 1870, of the patent for an IMPROVEMENT IN PAPER COLLARS, granted to their intestate 25th July, 1854, and reissued to William E. Lockwood, his assignee, in five divisions, numbered and dated respectively No. 1828, 29th November, 1864; No. 1867, 7th February, 1865; No. 1926, 4th April 1865; No. 2306, 10th July, 1866; and No. 2307, 10th July, 1866.

HODGES, Acting Commissioner:

On the day appointed for hearing this case the remonstrants moved for an order for taking further testimony, which was denied. Upon a careful consideration of the act under which this proceeding is held, it seems not to authorize the reception of any evidence except that which has already been introduced.

The application which is to be heard is evidently the one filed in 1868. The expressions "to rehear," and to rehear "as if no hearing thereof had ever occurred," are inconsistent with the supposition of a new application being contemplated. The statute, therefore, authorizes the Commissioner to rehear and determine the application heretofore made to his predecessor upon the evidence, in the same manner and with the same effect as if no hearing thereof had occurred. It does not prescribe the publication of new notices, nor any of the preliminaries usual in this class of cases. The rehearing is to be, not upon evidence, but upon *the* evidence, confirming the supposition that some particular testimony was intended. This could be no other than that which is on file. The whole provision seems to point to this construction.

The circumstances which occasioned the enactment led to the same conclusion. The evil which Congress undertook to remedy was not any defect in the publication of notices, the filing of the application, the taking of testimony, or anything to be done previous to the hearing, but in the failure to obtain the hearing itself. It gave the applicants all the relief they needed when it gave them a fresh opportunity to have their petition considered anew by the Commissioner. It does not appear that any further interposition on the part of the legislature was called for, or was intended.

It is urged that the hearing shall be, in the language of the statute, "in the same manner and with the same effect as if it were an original application." If it had been said that the *proceedings* shall be in the same manner there would have been great force in the argument. In that case new notices would have been necessary, and a new report from the examiner as well as other steps, none of which are now pretended to be requisite. It is the *hearing*, and the *hearing* only, that is to be in the same manner. The hearing only is provided for, that being all in fact that was wanted.

Upon the principal hearing the application was strenuously opposed, mainly upon the ground that the supposed invention in controversy was destitute of novelty at the time when the original patentee devised it. Passing over, for the present, the different branches which are specified in the reissued grants, the definition of the invention which was embodied in the original becomes material in determining this question. It was restricted to a shirt collar composed of "thin white cotton muslin, coated upon both sides with a very thin paper," and "polished and varnished" in the manner described in the specification.

To show that this was wanting in novelty, a number of witnesses were introduced. The most important incident of which they speak is that which is testified by Brown, House & Holdridge. According to them, Brown purchased a few dozen collars in New York or Boston, in 1854 or 1855, which were composed of cloth lined with muslin, or, as Holdridge says, "the muslin was inside the paper." They were not purchased for resale or for use, but in order to determine, upon examination, whether it was advisable to engage in making them for sale, Brown being employed in selling collars. He testifies that they "made or tried to make a few," but all agree that the project was given up as an unpromising one, after tearing up, in the investigation, all the collars that had been purchased. This is all that seems to be known of the circumstances. The whole affair can be regarded in no other light than as a crude and abandoned experiment, which resulted in nothing practical, which had been all but forgotten, and would never have been brought to remembrance had it not been for the success which attended Hunt's endeavors. The paper collar now in such extensive use would never have been known had it depended upon what these witnesses have narrated.

The rest of the remonstrant's testimony on this point requires but little notice. It tends to show, either the use of what are usually denominated paper collars in foreign countries, or that of collars consisting entirely of paper in this. Neither of these circumstances, if ever so well established, would have the slightest bearing upon the validity of the patent. There is also a large body of depositions taken in a chancery suit now pending between the owners of the reissued patents and others, among whom are some of the remonstrants, and a copy of these depositions was put into this case upon the former hearing. It was objected to as being taken in a case to which the applicants were not parties, as well as because the witnesses themselves should have been produced, because the copy was not duly authenticated, and for other reasons. Even if the objection had been overruled on the former hearing, the

UNITED STATES PATENT OFFICE.

WALTER HUNT, OF NEW YORK, N. Y., ASSIGNOR, BY MESNE ASSIGNMENTS, TO WILLIAM E. LOCKWOOD, OF PHILADELPHIA, PENNSYLVANIA.

IMPROVEMENT IN COMPOUND FABRICS FOR THE PRODUCTION OF SHIRT-COLLARS.

Specification forming part of Letters Patent No. **89,768,** dated May 4, 1869.

To all whom it may concern:

Be it known that I, WALTER HUNT, of the city, county, and State of New York, have invented a new and useful Improvement in the Production of a Fabric for Making Shirt-Collars, Bosoms, Waistbands, &c.; and I do hereby declare that the following is a full and exact description thereof.

The nature of my invention consists in combining and uniting two or more thicknesses of muslin or linen cambric in the piece by means of starch or other equivalent sizing, and ironing, mangling, or otherwise polishing and finishing the same, suitable for cutting out and making up into shirt-collars, &c., without requiring any further laundry-work in completing them for sale or use, instead of cutting them out from the plain muslin, making up, and then performing the laundry-work in separate pieces, as in the usual manner.

The mode of uniting and forming the fabric may be done by a process similar to that of making pasteboard, viz., by sizing each thickness of cloth with a brush or otherwise, laying one upon the other upon a smooth table, and pressing them together by means of a roller, and when sufficiently dry polished by means of a press, polishing-calender, mangle, or smoothing-irons, or other similar process.

The most advantageous process, however, in forming said fabric is that of passing the pieces of cambric to be united separately through the sizing or starching vats, then uniting the ends and passing the whole together through a rolling-press, so graduated as to remove the superfluous starch and unite the whole into one sheet or piece, which, after being suspended and sufficiently dried, may be ironed or polished in the manner above described or otherwise.

Admitting that the same materials are used in making collars by my process that are used in making them in the ordinary way, it will be obvious that my plan of first preparing and finishing the fabric in the piece, as above described, of any required quantity, will greatly facilitate the work of the manufacture, inasmuch as the uniting and ironing or polishing in the larger pieces, which may be cut out into collars with greater advantage by machinery than can possibly be done from the plain cloth, and ironed separately in the usual way. Consequently this invention will be found peculiarly advantageous to the extensive manufacturer of said articles.

I am aware that two or more thicknesses of muslin or linen have been united and made into a fabric for envelopes, book-covers, playing-cards, and other like purposes; and I am also aware that a cloth and paper fabric, water-proofed or enameled, has been used for making water-proof shirt-collars, &c., as described in my patent for the same, dated the 25th of July, 1854, neither of which above-named fabrics do I claim in this application, inasmuch as neither of them were intended or suitable for the purposes to which my herein-claimed collar fabric is peculiarly adapted. As, for instance, from this fabric collars can be cut out, the edges turned in, and stitched by machinery, ready for use, without requiring any laundry-work whatever until they are worn and require washing, &c., for which they are as well adapted as any other hand-made collars, which is not the case with the said fabric composed of cloth and paper, while the ordinary envelope-fabric is entirely unsuitable for said purposes.

As a further evidence of the patentability of this invention, so far as novelty is concerned, I believe it will be granted that a prepared muslin or linen fabric cannot be found in any market or establishment, (my own excepted,) which is suitable to be cut out and worked into shirt-collars, ready for use, without requiring any additional laundry-work in their completion. Granting this to be the fact, and that the fabric thus prepared is suitable and facilitates the manufacture of the articles in question, as before stated, the validity of my claims will be readily apparent.

Independent of the adaptation of this fabric to stitched collars of the finest and most expensive kind, a cheaper muslin fabric can be made on this plan, which will be well adapted to the manufacture of a cheaper seamless collar, united by means of eyelets, &c., as described in my application for a patent for

2   **89,768**

the same, which application bears even date herewith, and which collar, when worn and soiled, can be stitched or seamed to advantage, and then washed and ironed as usual.

What I claim as my invention, and desire to secure by Letters Patent as a new article of manufacture, is—

A fabric for making shirt-collars, composed of two or more thicknesses of muslin, cambric, or other suitable cloth, united and finished by the web or quantity, substantially as herein described, whereby the necessity of sewing or stitching the collars, and of subsequent washing, starching, and ironing is dispensed with.

WALTER HUNT.

Witnesses:
B. S. COOPER,
W. D. WISNER.

---

applicants have a perfect right to renew it, as they now do, and the depositions are excluded.

On the other hand, it is shown on behalf of the applicants, that when the deceased inventor, Hunt, obtained his patent, there was no such article known in market as his composite collar. There was not even such a manufacture as that of imitation collars in existence. Immediately afterward he set up an establishment for fabricating those which he had invented; and it was not long before they were produced upon a scale that seemed all but fabulous for its dimensions. It may be said that he made the market; if so, it was because the usefulness of what he had devised became manifest to the world and created the demand. The advent of the late war is said to have contributed to increase the sale, but that was because it demonstrated the especial advantages attendant upon the use of the new commodity.

Taking into consideration, therefrom, the undeniable fact that when Hunt commenced his enterprise, there was no such thing known as a manufactory of imitation collars, and that the vast production of these now witnessed in this country dates from his invention, there is no room for questioning that it was new and entitled to a patent. We may go further and form a decided conclusion as to its value and importance to the public. Looking at the immense extent to which the business has attained, there can be no reasonable doubt but that the deceased inventor conferred such a benefit upon the community as entitled him to an ample remuneration. It does not seem to be pretended that he ever obtained it, or that his failure was owing to any want of diligence on his part.

The reissued patent No. 1828, dated 29th November, 1864, follows the original very closely. It sets up no title to anything which is not clearly described in the latter. The claims are indeed nearly identical; the difference consisting almost entirely in this substitution of the word "burnished" in the renewed grant for the word "varnished" in the other. By extending this patent the representatives of the deceased will have, for a prolonged term, substantially the same exclusive privilege which he obtained.

The next reissue is for giving shape, by means of dies or formers, to paper collars in general, not to the composite collars. When the patent was allowed it was on the supposition that it was for shaping a composite collar by the means

United States Patent Office.

WILLIAM E. LOCKWOOD, OF PHILADELPHIA, PENNSYLVANIA, ASSIGNEE, BY MESNE ASSIGNMENTS, OF WALTER HUNT.

Letters Patent No. 89,768, dated May 4, 1869; reissue No. 3,552, dated July 13, 1869.

IMPROVEMENT IN COMPOUND FABRICS FOR THE PRODUCTION OF SHIRT-COLLARS.

The Schedule referred to in these Letters Patent and making part of the same.

To all whom it may concern:

Be it known that WALTER HUNT, deceased, late of the city, county, and State of New York, did invent a new and useful Compound Fabric for the Production of Shirt-Collars, Bosoms, Wristbands, &c.; and that I, WILLIAM E. LOCKWOOD, of Philadelphia, Pennsylvania, assignee, by mesne assignment, of the said WALTER HUNT, do hereby declare the following to be a full, clear, and exact description of the said invention, which consists of a fabric composed of cotton or linen cloth, as a facing, so secured by cementing, sizing, pasting, starching, or otherwise, to a backing consisting of one or more thicknesses of cotton, or other equivalent material or fabric, that seamless shirt-collars, bosoms, wristbands, &c., may be made from the said compound fabric, without requiring any further laundry-work in completing them for sale or use, instead of cutting them out from the plain material, making up, and then performing the laundry-work in separate pieces, as in the usual manner.

The mode of uniting and forming the fabric may be by a process similar to that of making pasteboard, namely, by sizing each thickness with a brush or otherwise, laying one upon the other upon a smooth table, and pressing them together by means of a roller, and when sufficiently dry, polishing the compound fabric by means of a press, polishing-calender, mangle smoothing-iron, or other similar process.

The most advantageous process, however, in forming said fabric, is that of passing the pieces of cotton, or other equivalent material, or fabric, or linen cloth to be united, separately through a sizing or starching-vat, and then uniting the ends, and passing the whole through a roller-press, so graduated as to remove the superfluous starch, and unite the whole into one sheet or piece, which, after being suspended and sufficiently dried, may be ironed or polished in the manner above described, or otherwise.

When the same materials are used in making collars by said process that are used in making them in the ordinary way, it will be obvious that the said WALTER HUNT's plan of first preparing and finishing the fabric in the piece, as above described, of any required quantity, will greatly facilitate the work of the manufacture, inasmuch as the uniting and ironing or polishing is done in the larger pieces, which may be cut out into collars with greater advantage by machinery, than can be possibly done from the plain cloth, and ironed separately in the usual way; consequently, this invention will be found peculiarly advantageous in the extensive manufacture of said article.

The said WALTER HUNT was aware that two or more thicknesses of muslin or linen had been united and made into a fabric for envelopes, book-covers, playing-cards, and other like purposes, and he was also aware that a cloth-lined paper fabric, water-proof or enamelled, such as described in his patent for the same, dated July 25, 1854, had been used for making water-proof shirt-collars, &c., neither of which fabrics did the said WALTER HUNT claim, nor do I now claim in this application, inasmuch as neither of them was intended or suitable for the purposes to which the above-described collar-fabric is peculiarly adapted.

For instance, from the improved fabric can be made collars, &c., having a facing of textile fabric, whereas the fabric patented by WALTER HUNT, July 25, 1854, has a paper surface.

Again, from a compound fabric made with a textile facing and a backing of the same, the collars may be cut out, the edges turned in, and stitched by machinery, ready for use, without requiring any laundry-work whatever, until they are worn and require washing, &c., for which they are as well adapted as any hand-made collar.

Independent of the adaptation of this fabric to stitched collars of the finest and most expensive kind, a cheaper fabric can be made with a facing of muslin and backing of the same, or equivalent material or fabric, the compound fabric thus produced being well adapted for the manufacture of a cheaper seamless collar, united by means of eyelets, &c., as described in the patent granted to the said HUNT, January 1, 1856.

I claim as the invention of the said WALTER HUNT, and desire to secure by Letters Patent, as a new article of manufacture—

1. A fabric whereof to make shirt-collars, wristbands, bosoms, &c., the said fabric consisting of cotton or linen cloth as a facing, secured to a backing of the same material, or equivalent material or fabric, by cementing, sizing, pasting, starching, or otherwise, all prepared substantially as set forth.

2. Also, as new articles of manufacture, shirt-collars, bosoms, wristbands, &c., made from the above-described compound fabric.

In testimony whereof, I have signed my name to this specification, before two subscribing witnesses.

WILLIAM E. LOCKWOOD.

Witnesses:
H. HOWSON,
JOHN WHITE.

described, as will be seen by looking into the decision. How the alteration in the language came to be made is not material. It is sufficient that no such broad claim was warranted by anything contained in the original application, and the instrument is void. In other respects it is open to the same remarks as the remaining three patents.

The last three embrace, each of them, the composite fabric already mentioned, but only when it has been subjected to a special treatment. In one it must be indented so as to represent the stitches of an ordinary linen collar; in another it must have its surface covered with enamel; and in the other, a smooth white surface coated with transparent varnish. It is unnecessary to inquire whether these several modifications were novelties at the time. Even if they had been entitled to a patent, that alone would not justify prolonging a monopoly in them. They should confer substantial advantages on the community, and have something more than mere patentability to entitle them to such a recognition. The use of varnish for purposes analogous to those described in the last-mentioned grant, for instance, was universal. Admitting, then, that it was new to varnish a composite collar, can it be pretended for a moment that this new application of a familiar process involved such a remarkable exercise of the inventive faculty, or was productive of such great benefit to the world, as to justify the extraordinary favor on account of it for which the applicants are seeking? There is not the least foundation for such a supposition. To give it plausibility there should have been the most satisfactory proof that the ascertained value of the invention was such as to sustain the claim. The evidence on this point, however, is eminently defective. The applicants do indeed declare what their belief is as to the comparative value and importance of each of the improvements specified in the several reissues. But they do not furnish the slightest circumstance on which they found their estimate, or any criterion by which to test its correctness. There is not a particle of evidence, in fact, which tends to show that either of those improvements is, in itself, of any value whatever. The estimate furnished is a matter of the merest conjecture, and should not receive the least attention.

It should be remarked, in connection with this, that the deceased inventor was not only experienced in taking out patents, but, in obtaining that which is before us, he had the aid of able counsel. No one knew better than he what he could legitimately claim, and there can be no reasonable doubt but that he specified all that he supposed he was entitled to. Yet he expressly disclaimed most of the very improvements set up in the last reissues, and his judgment was thereby clearly pronounced against their patentability. Those reissues are none of his production. They owe their origin to a vicious practice which has been severely rebuked in the highest judicial tribunal in the nation, and may justly be regarded with suspicion and repugnance.

The patent No. 1828, dated 29th November, 1864, is extended as prayed for; the prayer of the petitioners is refused as to the rest.

Reissue No. 1,828 was extended seven years from the date, July 25, 1868.

After the reissue extension was granted, reissue No. 1,828 was surrendered and reissued again as reissue 5,109 on October 22, 1872, to expire July 25, 1875.

This extension was important, as it prolonged the life of Hunt's patent seven years, and kept the monopoly of manufacture in the hands of the Union Paper Collar Company. In a suit in the United States Circuit Court, Eastern District of Pennsylvania, before Judge William McKennan, Judge of the Third Circuit, it was ruled in the case of the Union Paper Collar Company against Henry J. White that:

> It is true that paper and muslin, or linen cloth, were before united, and used as a fabric for maps, etc., but this was not analogous to the use to which Hunt adapted them, nor was it in anywise suggestive of his invention. He was the first to discover the adaptability of this material to a use not cognate to any to which it had before been applied, and by appropriate manipulation, to give it a successful and practical form. He, thus, [not] only supplied the public with a new article of manufacture, but he demonstrated unknown susceptibilities of the material, out of which it was made. This is something more than the mere application of an old thing to a new purpose. It is the production of a new device by giving a new form to an old substance, and, by suitable manipulation, making its peculiar properties available for a use to which it had not before been applied, thereby distinguishing it from all other fabrics of the class to which it belongs. This seems to me to involve an exercise of an inventive faculty, and, in view of the great practical benefits resulting from it, to invest the product with special patentable merit.
>
> The patent in controversy is the seventh reissue of Hunt's original patent. This multiplication of reissues, of itself, suggestive of a purpose to cover intervening improvements, and some phrases in the specification of the last reissue may, not without semblance of reason, be treated as having that significance.

In all of the patent lawsuits, the importance and validity of Hunt's patents were maintained. An attempt was made to have the patent renewed for another seven years. The patent was also of great value to the Hunt family. Walter Hunt had died on June 8, 1859.

George W. Hunt of Jersey City, New Jersey, made an agreement with the Union Paper Collar Company on April 17, 1875, by which they agreed to pay him $1,000 on signing the contract, $1,000 in thirty days, $1,000 sixty days and $2,000 in sixty days after a patent renewal was obtained. They also agreed to give $150 every month and $100 a month and traveling expenses for time spent in Washington entreating for the extension. He was also to receive $50,000 par value of the stock of the Union Paper Collar Company and 10 percent of all royalties collected.

Chapter 26

Though the financial rewards came too late, Hunt was satisfied with the glory his inventions had brought him. Publicity as the inventor of the sewing machine and creator of the idea of saleable paper collars brought Hunt great prestige. Those who had looked upon him as a poor mechanic suddenly changed their opinion. They hailed him as an unsung genius.

The ephemeral glory did not encourage him. To him, the thrill of creation was greater than financial returns.

His recent successes brought inventors with problems from near and far to seek his advice. Generally he charged small fees for his services but to those with limited incomes he gave assistance gratuitously. This gesture coupled with the fact he was willing to submerge his own identity and work on the ideas of others became known the trade and he was often called upon to "ghost" inventions for others.

His uncanny ability to iron out the quirks and put finishing touches on complicated machinery proved a great asset and his fame as a consultant spread. His success also reached the ears of financiers and capitalists who made it a point to visit him to find whether he had any other inventions which they could acquire. His shop was filled with activity. The old days of looking for buyers for his inventions were gone.

John W. Martin, grandson of Brigadier General Walter Martin, for whom the town of Martinsburg, New York, had been named, was one of the many who beat a path to Hunt's door.

"With all your inventions," Martin said, "it's a wonder you're not one of the richest men in America."

"There is more to life than money," Hunt answered.

"I agree with you, Mr. Hunt," Martin replied, "except for one point. I maintain that if something has value, no matter how much or how little, it is bad business to sell it for less than it is worth."

"I guess that's good logic," Hunt said abstractly.

"I'll tell you what I'll do, Mr. Hunt," Martin explained. "you have a few patents which have not brought you in any money as yet, and I know that you are working on several others. It is almost impossible for one man, no matter how talented he may be, to be both an inventor and a business man at the same time. Both require a full day's work."

"I have found that out," said Hunt.

"I'll tell you what I'll do," Martin repeated. "I would like to make some real money for you and myself. Let us go into partnership. You be the inventor, and I'll be the business man. I'll put up the money to open an office to handle the business details of your inventions. And I'll put my son George in charge of that office. After expenses are deducted, then we can split the profits equally."

"The proposition doesn't appeal," Hunt said conclusively. "I don't need a partner on the ideas that I have finished, but I could use one on the plans I'm now working on. They will require money to complete. I'll need some new tools, new supplies, and those things, as you know, cost money."

"How much will you require?"

After negotiations had progressed several days, Martin made an appealing offer. "I'll advance you twenty-two hundred dollars which you said you will need for your experiments. You can repay this to me from the profits which will accrue to you from our partnership."

"Under these conditions, I accept," Hunt agreed.

"But," Martin countered, "as a protection and guarantee, I want you to assign lien to me on those patents and inventions. The rights will be returned to you when the loan is repaid and then we can split the profits."

Other conditions of the arrangement were mutually agreed upon and on the April 9, 1857, Walter Hunt, John W. Martin and George G. Martin signed a partnership agreement which was witnessed by John C. Field and E. L. Shute.

To offset this assignment, Hunt and Martin signed another contract which reconveyed the interest and right in the machine when Hunt repaid the loan. This contract was witnessed by John C. Field and George G. Martin, both of whom witnessed the original assignment.

Hunt assigned his interest in his patented rotary tabletop sewing machine to John W. Martin on April 3, 1857, a few days before the contract went into effect. Martin forwarded the assignment to the Patent Office where it was received on May 14th. The transfer was recorded July 7, 1857, in the *Transfer of Patent Records* (Liber 4, page 259), the acknowledgement of entry and transfer being signed by Charles Mason, Commissioner of Patents.

Hunt also conveyed the rights to his lock-stitch sewing machine which he invented in 1834 to Martin which was an asset of more or less doubtful value as the Commissioner of Patents had already decided that no patent would be granted on it.

Another of Hunt's inventions included under the Martin agreement was the safety lamp. An application for a patent on this lamp was made by Hunt on December 29, 1856, and was witnessed by Charles E. Patterson, conveyancer, 10 Centre Street, and Shubael E. Swain, lawyer, 11 Chambers Street, New York City.

In less than nine months, Hunt became dissatisfied with Martin's promised performance. The harmony that had bound them disappeared and Hunt had become embittered and Martin had become dissatisfied.

On January 28, 1858, Hunt wrote to the Commissioner of Patents:

That the said contract has been violated in every particular by the said Martins and that the said John W. Martin is now secretly endeavoring to dispose of the said inventions thus obtained notwithstanding the fact that no actual sale of the same has ever been made by the said Hunt to the said Martins.

That said assignments then made were not intended to be final, nor did the said Hunt at the time of executing the same believe that he was at the time selling the same, but only transferring them to be held as collateral security.

Said Walter Hunt therefore protests against any further assignments of the said rights to other parties, by John W. Martin, Geo. G. Martin or their legal representatives, agents, or assignees by record on the books of the Patent Office, the same having been obtained from him by false means and in an unfair and illegal manner.

It did not take Hunt long to realize that no further income would be received from Martin and that he would have to continue working as before.

Chapter 27

"You're sixty years old, Walter," said Polly. "I see no reason why you have to work so hard. I think that at our ages we should take it easy. Let's move to Jersey City and be near George and Francis. We can rent a nice house there for much less than we pay here. And, furthermore, we've already lived here four years. I've had enough of 552 Hudson Street."

"What? Move to Jersey City—the wilderness?"

But Polly had her way, and they moved to Jersey City. Hunt, however, still maintained his shop in New York City.

Commuting was an arduous burden and Hunt's hours became more irregular than they had been. Instead of taking it easy, he was working harder and longer.

"Why are you away so much?" Polly said angrily. "You didn't come home for dinner last night until ten o'clock."

"I don't work with a clock in my hands. If I am not home for dinner at the usual time, eat without me. If I don't come home, then I am staying in the city at Caroline's house."

"What are you so busy about now?"

"Tomorrow I'll take you to the city. We'll go to my shop and I'll show you. It'll make you happy."

The next day, Polly accompanied Walter. They crossed the Hudson River on the ferry boat and when the boat docked they walked to Bleecker Street.

"This is not the way to your shop," Polly said. "Where are we going?"

"Close your eyes and promise you won't open them until I tell you."

"I promise."

They turned the corner, walked a few steps and stopped in from of 69 Bank Street.

"Now you can look."

Polly stared at a small two-story brick building, the lower floor of which was fitted with a latticed window. From the upper floor a large gaily colored wooden sign in the shape of a mortar and pestle swayed in the breeze.

"Now let's step inside," Hunt said as he opened the front door latch with a large brass key.

Bewildered, Polly didn't say a word. They entered a small room containing cane chairs and a multicolored circular hooked rug. In the rear, a small glass showcase stood on top of a long rectangular table. The rear wall of the room was lined with shelves containing bottles, empty and filled, and small cartons neatly stacked. A three-sectional divider screened off a doorway.

"I don't understand," Polly said in amazement.

"Well, you will. Just read that large painted sign on the wall."

"The Life Preserver, or Hunt's Restorative Cordial," Polly read aloud. "It relieves pain, restores and sustains vital energy."

"Keep on reading!" Hunt urged.

Wherever it is used it is believed to be the most important family medicine in existence—as a remedy for Bowel Complaints in their worst forms; for Ague and Chills, Colds, Coughs, Sore Throat, Croup, Cramps, Cholics; Want of Rest, Sleep or Food; for Nervousness, Delirium Tremens, Over Exertion, or Exposure to heat or cold; Faintness, or Feneral Debility, or Physical Prostration for any cause whatever.

This cordial is unequaled. Every family should be supplied with it, and none should travel without it. Observe the proud testimonials in the public prints and the enclosed wrapper, which please preserve and read with care.

"That's an enlarged copy of what is printed on the label," Hunt exclaimed pointing to the blue ink type on the yellow paper label. "Had the label copyrighted, too. Entered according to the Act of Congress, August 25th in the year 1857, in the Clerk's Office of the District Court of the Southern District of New York."

"Is this—" Polly faltered.

"Yes."

They looked tenderly at each other. Neither one spoke until Walter gulped. "Yes. This is the old remedy. It's the one which Walter Junior would have featured had he opened his drug store and not been called to his Maker in heaven."

"Walter," said Polly with deep feeling. She could say no more.

"Come, and I'll show you the rest of the place."

Hunt pushed aside the three-section red screen blocking the entrance to the adjoining room littered with milk cans, brandy casks, tin boilers, empty bottles, corks, funnels, a large brass mortar and pestle, cord and odds and ends.

"Even if you are still making the cordial, I still can't understand why your hours are so irregular." Polly protested. "You don't have to stay in the store at nights."

"I'll show you, follow me." Hunt answered.

They climbed the narrow rickety stairs at the end of the room. The upper floor was divided into two rooms. One contained a foot lathe, some drills, and a varied assortment of tools. The other contained a portable upright engine boiler with shafting and pulleys and a small portable forge. A pine table and four rows of shelving were littered with papers.

"Now, I think I understand." said Polly.

"I have a few things here," Hunt answered, "which are going to keep me busy."

"You are working entirely too hard," Polly protested.

"Here's a miniature suit of submarine armor," Hunt pointed out, "I'm working on it now. A man can descend from a boat, go down in the water and remain submerged for a long time."

"But how will he breathe?"

"The boat pumps air down to him through an India rubber hose."

Polly wasn't too impressed. She picked up a polished brass fitting. "What's this?"

"It's a new kind of lamp I'm working on."

"And look," Polly exclaimed in surprise. "Here's your velocipede. I thought you had given up the idea. I didn't know that you're still working on it."

"It's almost finished now."

"And you're still working on the pressure machine to form adamantine candles! And the window-lock! And the medicated vapor bath!" said Polly scolding. "Work! Work! Work! It's about time that you take a rest."

"When I finish them—"

"When you finish them," Polly interrupted, "you'll have another bunch that you'll have to finish. Then another bunch, and then another bunch."

Walter Hunt smiled and made no effort to reply.

"You don't have to do all these things," Polly said angrily. "Why don't you drop everything and just advertise the Restorative Cordial so that people will go to apothecary stores to buy it?"

"Maybe you're right," Hunt agreed. "I'll think about it."

Although business conditions in the city were bad, Hunt realized that the only way to increase sales was to advertise. He walked to the office of the *New York Herald*, owned by James Gordon Bennett, and placed an advertisement in the "miscellaneous" section.

And that afternoon, Friday, October 13, 1857, the panic hit. Runs on the banks had assumed such large proportions that eighteen banks suspended payment. New York was in turmoil.

The following morning, on October 14, 1857, the advertisement appeared (page 8, column 6).

"Look here, friend, hardscrapple," said an old lucky one to a Wall Street victim, whose face was about the length of a bunch of stalks, "do you go straight up to

208 Broadway, first floor and room upstairs, and get a bottle of Professor Hunt's Restorative Cordial; it will cheer you up and shorten your face about a foot!"

The day this advertisement appeared, all the banks in New York City except the Chemical National Bank suspended specie payment. The runs on the commercial banks spread to the savings banks. They invoked the specific notice of withdrawal clause and paid out only ten percent for necessities. Instead of paying out in gold as was their custom, they paid out in banknotes of the institutions. Money on collateral loans was unobtainable. Premiums of sixty percent were charged on loans.

Thousands of men were thrown out of work and panic gripped the city. Money was too scarce and too elusive a commodity for people to afford the Restorative Cordial. Months and months passed before conditions became normal again.

"You see," Walter Hunt explained, "no one can predict the future. No one can tell what unexpected turn of events will alter a person's life."

Plans for the further promotion of Professor Hunt's Restorative Cordial were set aside awaiting a more propitious time.

Chapter 28

"No one can foretell what unexpected turn of events will alter a person's life," Walter Hunt told Polly while she was arranging the cordial bottles on the shelf. "Life is completely unpredictable."

"Now what's the trouble?" Polly asked.

"That contraption I was toying with, that automatic steam table to keep food warm in restaurants. Well, by chance, I met a man who claims to have considerable influence with tavern keepers and will be able to sell them and make a lot of money for me."

"Do you think he can?"

"Certainly but my model has to be perfected first. Not much though. Just a couple of rough edges need to be smoothed. Then I suppose a full-size machine must be built. Meeting him may not be of much importance, but it just goes to show how queerly little things in life turn out. Really it doesn't matter much anymore because I relinquished my rights to [K---] who obtained a patent on it."

The tinkling of the doorbell interrupted his further explanation.

"It's either a customer or a bill collector," Hunt joked, "and now, luckily, I'm not afraid to meet either of them."

"Better go downstairs and see who it is."

Hunt descended the stairs into his shop. He saw a well-dressed man holding a bottle of the Restorative Cordial in his hands and reading its label.

"Good morning," Hunt said cheerfully.

The man replaced the bottle on the counter and turned to face Hunt.

"Well, if it isn't Mr. Clark!" said Hunt surprised. "I never expected to see you here. From the distance I thought you was a customer. It's about twelve years since I last saw you. Are you still with Singer?"

Clark nodded.

"If you came in for a bottle of the Life Preserver," said Hunt, "I'll give you one with my compliments."

"Is it any good?" Clark asked.

For a moment Hunt was taken back. Then he realized that the remark was made facetiously.

"It really is good, Mr. Clark. I've made the cordial off and on for about twenty-five years. It's never killed anyone and it has helped many. Previously, I've given most of it away. But now I'm actively engaged in selling it."

"How's it going?"

"Business is slow, but steady. A good thing that selling doesn't take up much of my time and I can work inside my shop on other inventions."

"That's fine," Clark commented.

"Did you come here to get a bottle of the Life Preserver?" Hunt asked.

"No, I really came to see you about your sewing machine."

"About the sewing machine?" said Hunt surprised. "What about it?"

"I've got a proposition for you." Mr. Clark spoke briefly and Hunt made numerous notations on a small pad.

"That's fine, Hunt. I'll drop in soon again," said Clark, concluding the interview.

"Polly!" Walter called, after Clark had closed the door. "Come downstairs a moment."

Polly carefully walked down the narrow stairs leaning against the wall to avoid misstepping.

"Do you know who was just here?" Hunt asked excitedly.

"Of course not."

"That was Mr. Clark of the Singer Company. He came to see me about the sewing machine."

"Now, what's the trouble?"

"Trouble? Trouble?" Walter said gleefully. "Why, it's turned out to be a gold mine."

"For Mr. Howe. For Mr. Singer and the others," Polly retorted. Then she felt sorry for her caustic retort.

"No. For us! Mr. Clark just agreed to give me a hundred dollars a month—"

"You mean to work for him?"

"A hundred dollars a month from May 10, 1858, to September 10, 1860, and then ten thousand dollars—"

"Walter Hunt, have you gone crazy?"

"And then when they get a patent, I'll get an additional forty thousand dollars."

"Walter, have you gone crazy," she repeated.

"No, I'm serious."

"I don't understand," Polly said perplexed. "Why after all this time? What's the reason for this sudden generosity? I'm sure the offer is not made from the goodness of his heart..."

"A patent is good for fourteen years," Hunt explained. "Howe's patent has already been in force twelve years. It will expire in two years. Naturally, he will apply to have it renewed. For another seven years. When he does, all the other sewing machine manufacturers will object to the extension. And if it is not renewed, then, with no valid patent in force, Mr. Clark wants me to make another application for a patent and thus establish my priority. Whoever gets there first if Howe's extension isn't granted will be the patent holder."

"It sounds too good to be true. I can hardly believe it."

On May 3, 1858, Edward Clark brought Hunt a contract to confirm their oral agreement. Hunt read section five.

> If a valid patent shall be obtained which can be sustained at law ... fifty thousand dollars to be paid in five equal installments of ten thousand dollars each.

The words seemed to blur before his eyes. He held the contract firmly and appeared to be nonchalant but his hands trembled. He reread the paragraph. It was there. In black and white. "Really I don't know why. Maybe to void Howe's patent. Maybe to give me the credit I should have had. Maybe they are starting on some other system. Really I don't know. In any event, if it is granted, it will be to their advantage and mine also."

He continued to read. Section six stated,

> If the said applications for a patent or for a legislative grant in the nature of a patent shall not be made as herein provided, or being made shall be withdrawn in their discretion, then and in that case ... shall and will pay ... the sum of ten thousand dollars within one year from and after the tenth day of September in the year 1860.

Walter Hunt was jubilant and eagerly affixed his signature to the contract. The date was May 3, 1858.

Virtually assured of one hundred dollars a month until September 10, 1860, and of ten thousand dollars, if not five times that amount in the not too distant future, Hunt's ever-resilient hope was revived. Optimism replaced pessimism. Deprivation was a thing of the past. Now, he was longer a slave striving to make a living. He could do with a free mind what he wanted, when he wanted. He could even explore in experimental fields which before had seemed far away and impossible. He would no longer be obliged to do everything himself. He could engage assistants to do the minor tasks or carry out his plans and designs. He could contract debts without worrying how payments could be made. At last, the expense of experimentation would no longer be his prime problem.

With the hundred dollars monthly—a not inconsiderable sum—he apportioned an amount sufficient for the support of his family and household. The balance he put aside for his experiments. Bigger and better things now seemed to be within his reach. Dreams were shaping themselves into reality.

The contract brought about a change in Hunt's perspective. He viewed the future with optimism.

Others, however, felt differently. They predicted that the mild depression plaguing the nation would ultimately develop into a serious one. Money became tight and people hoarded their savings. Only necessities were purchased.

The first hundred dollars received from Mr. Clark saved Hunt from being too deeply affected by the depression, but Polly took a gayer look at things and felt he should look prosperous.

"You'd make a better impression on people by appearing well groomed," she lectured. "And furthermore, you're working too hard. You should stop inventing and pay more attention to your appearance. You pay no attention to yourself. You don't care about your health or your clothes. People will begin to feel sorry for you. Look at your heels."

"What's the matter with them?"

"They're all worn down on one side. I'll get you a new pair of shoes for Christmas."

"There's nothing the matter with my shoes. Well, maybe the heels are worn down on one side, but that's nothing. I can fix them in a minute."

"How?"

Hunt took a paring knife and reached into a drawer where he had large scraps of leather. He cut several circular discs the same size, placed one on top of the other and fastened them together by a center screw. With his pliers he tore off his worn down heel and replaced it with his circular discs. He trimmed them and applied a little blacking to the outside circumference. Then he added another screw nearer the outside.

Polly watched in silence. She knew better than to interrupt him while he was working. In a comparatively short time, he handed her his shoe with the new heel.

"Now, that problem is solved."

"It was no problem," Polly replied. "You just put on a new heel." She looked at it carefully. "It looks all right. Now fix the other heel and your shoes will be as good as new."

"Don't you see anything?" he asked. "Anything different?"

"Of course not, just a new heel."

"A new heel? It's new in more ways than one. When you wear down one side of the heel, all you have to do is to unscrew the outside screw, revolve the heel, and you'll have a fresh surface at the place where the heel was worn down."

"That's a good idea," Polly said jubilantly, "You ought to get a patent on it."

"I'll think it over."

Five days after Christmas, on December 30, 1858, Walter Hunt appeared before Andrew De Lacy and attorney Horace Andrews to make his affirmation of invention and application for a patent.

Then, Hunt contacted George W. Keene of George W. Keene and Sons, manufacturers of boots, shoes and gaiters, whose factory was in Lynn, Massachusetts. Keene acquired the rights to the invention in Massachusetts on January 8, 1859, "for and in consideration of one dollar." An assignment was made which was witnessed by William H. Bishop and Andrew De Lacy who witnessed the patent application.

Thus the legal complications were concluded, no other record of the purchase price has been found.

On January 29, 1859, the patent application and the assignment were forwarded to the Patent Office with a letter by Hunt authorizing

> C. C. Browne (in connection with Charles M. Keller as counsel) to act as his attorney in presenting this application, altering or withdrawing the same as the case may require and to receive the patent when granted.

Keller notified Hunt that the application for a patent was rejected by the Patent Office on February 14, 1859, as it was anticipated by another patent.

"I'll look up the references they cited," Walter Hunt answered. "There is evidently some mistake somewhere. I'm certain that there is no valid reason for the rejection of my application and that there is no conflict, either real or imaginary. I'm certain that a rewording of the claim will overcome any objection."

Keller wrote to the Patent Office on May 9, 1859, to have them return the patent application. They did so and on May 19 Hunt amended his claim and a new affirmation was made before Horace Andrews.

Hunt delivered the revised application to Keller, who wrote a three page letter to the Patent Office stating in part:

> The specification has been amended and is herewith returned with the amendment, which not only disclaims all that has been referred to in the official letter as bearing any resemblance to Mr. Hunt's invention, but points out clearly the essential differences between the things disclaimed and the features claimed as new by Mr. Hunt.

His freedom from debt pressure had not made Hunt relax completely. It enabled him to forget only the problem of making ends meet and gave him more time for his inventive problems.

Punctually he would leave his home at Hackensack Junction, New Jersey, take the stagecoach to Hackensack and board the Northern Railroad of New Jersey train to Jersey City which arrived at 7:30 A.M. in time to take the ferry scheduled to arrive in New York City at 7:40 A.M.

Returning home he usually left the city at 5:50 P.M. and arrived at Hackensack Junction at 6:37 P.M., but often he did not return until nine, ten or eleven o'clock, usually with a bundle of papers which he studied for hours before retiring.

"You're spending altogether too much time at work," Polly protested. "Things are different now. You don't have to!"

Walter Hunt smiled. He was busy, very busy, but happy.

"You can't burn the candle at both ends and at the middle too." Polly lectured.

But Walter Hunt paid no attention to Polly. There was still work to be done and he intended to do it.

Nothing could make him slow up, no protests, no scoldings. He rushed to his shop on Saturday, June 4, 1859, absent-mindedly forgetting his spring coat. He was late.

A cold wave and high wind ushered in the day, a continuation of unseasonable weather, which, before it got through, had destroyed thousands of dollars worth of crops and made the city shiver.

Hunt was not prepared for the change in climate. He developed a slight cold, a running nose and a forceful sneeze.

Two days later on Monday, June 6, 1859, there was no improvement. In fact his condition seemed to grow worse and Polly refused to let him leave the house.

"Listen to me," Polly scolded. "You are going to stay in bed."

"I am sixty-three years old, and I've never had to stay in bed in the daytime before, and I'm not going to start now. I'm too busy. I've got a job to do."

Tuesday morning, despite his fever and cold, Walter made his usual trip to work. He went into his shop and started to work. He was putting the finishing touches on a diver's apparatus when he began to feel dizzy. The shop alternately seemed hot and cold. Hunt knew his temperature had gone up. In the late afternoon, he closed his shop and went home. He felt weak. His vitality snapped. He went to bed refusing to eat supper.

"Tomorrow you must stay home," Polly said sympathetically. "You need a rest."

"A rest?" Walter laughed. "I'll be all right by tomorrow morning. I've worked hard all my life and I'll continue working hard. A rest is good for the shiftless, but not for me."

On Wednesday morning Hunt felt a little rested. He went to his shop. He worked hard all day Wednesday, pausing only long enough to eat the lunch which he had brought from home. As the lights in the adjoining offices and buildings were being extinguished, Hunt kept on working. He wanted to make up the time he had missed the previous afternoon. He kept on working. He did not go out for dinner. Neither did he send a telegram to Polly stating he would not be home for dinner.

Polly was anxious and nervous because he did not come home but her fears were slightly allayed as she realized that Walter often stayed at their daughter Caroline's house when he worked late or was absorbed with some difficult problem.

Thursday morning came. Walter Hunt had not returned. His bed was undisturbed. More indignant than fearful, yet genuinely alarmed, Polly Hunt rushed to his shop in New York. She intended to tell him he had no right to work so hard and that there was no necessity of overdoing it.

From the street, she peered into the shop window. Polly breathed a sigh of relief. There was Walter Hunt asleep at his desk, his head resting on his folded arms. His blue pencil was in his hand and his shabby green eye-shade was still tied about his head.

The tinkling of the glass chimes over the door did not awaken him as she entered the shop. She spoke to him but he did not answer. She adjusted her quaint poke bonnet and tiptoed to his desk. She laid her hand on his shoulder—and, alone, faced the great tragedy of her life. Her husband did not move. Walter Hunt was dead.

In the newspaper obituaries Hunt's death was attributed to pneumonia.

NEW YORK HERALD
Thursday, June 9, 1859
DEATHS
On Wednesday morning, June 8, of pneumonia. Walter Hunt, age 63 years. The relatives and friends of the family are requested to attend the funeral, without further invitation, from the residence of his daughter, Mrs. Caroline M. Van Buren, No. 16 Morton Street, this (Friday) morning at ten o'clock [page 5, column 4].

NEW YORK TRIBUNE
Friday June 10, 1859
HUNT: in this city on Wednesday morning, June 8, of pneumonia, Walter Hunt, aged 63 years.

On Monday, June 13, 1859, the *New York Tribune* gave Walter Hunt a certain meed of praise and recognition in a brief obituary:

DEATH OF A DISTINGUISHED INVENTOR.
Among our recent notices of deaths, we find that of Walter Hunt. For more than forty years, he has been known as an experimenter in the arts. Whether in mechanical movements, chemistry, electricity or metallic compositions, he was always at home: and, probably in all, he has tried more experiments than any other inventor. He originated the sewing machine, spinning flax by machinery, the first nail machine, the first machine for cutting brads by one operation, placing plugs in leather for soles of boots and shoes, a method of constructing

docks by concrete, preparing a paper pulp so as to form boxes by one operation, the vapor baths, the ball known as the Minie ball for the rifle, and
many improvements in firearms, printing by rollers instead of balls, and so
many other things our space will not admit of details. Walter Hunt like most
inventors devoted his life to his friends rather than to himself; was liberal to a
fault, and none knew but to love him; he struggled with that master, the dollar,
all his life, in hopes of mastering. Yet his numberless experiments kept him
always poor. Notwithstanding, his life of exertion has benefitted the world; he
dies, as most inventors do, at the very moment he anticipated success. He,
however, lived to the ripe age of 63 years, in full vigor until the last four days
of his life.

The Lewis County *Republican* of Wednesday, June 22, 1859, published at
Martinsburg, New York, devoted only a few lines to Hunt's accomplishments.

Walter Hunt, a well known inventor, and former resident of Martinsburg, died
in New York last week. He made and patented many useful machines, and it is
claimed he was the original inventor of the sewing machine. He spent large
sums in conducting his experiments and died poor.

The *Scientific American*, which bore no great love for Hunt, published an
article "Death of a Prominent Inventor" in its July 2, 1859 issue. It was written
by J. L. Kingsley, a friend and neighbor who had known Hunt for many years.

Walter Hunt, who has been an originator for about fifty years, has been at
last relieved from that shell of earth, and has passed to the future, where the
annoyances of human strife can no longer torment the head or heart. From
early childhood he exhibited signs which told that his destiny was that he
should be a teacher, an almoner to the grieved ones, rather than a servant of
self. His earliest practical workings were in mechanical movements, the breech-
loading cannon being one; from this he, after much experiment, succeeded in
making the breech-loading many-chambered pistol, usually known as the
"revolver" at this day, and upon which others, by dint of perseverance have
reaped the reward which justly belonged to him. The experiments in endeavors
to control the lightning-flash of electricity so far back as 1833, as a motive
power, were as nearly successful as the then known circumstances would admit,
and to this day have been slightly advanced. At about the same time, on the
very spot where the Sun office now stands, he experimented with a very crude
machine for spinning flax, with such success that by imitations and innovations
it has in other hands become one of the most valuable machines in that department of treating fabrics.

    That he was the first inventor of the sewing machine there is no doubt, inas-
much as in a contest with Howe, during the term of Judge Mason as Commissioner of Patents, he opened an interference against Howe, but unfortunately
he had sold the invention to a Mr. Arrowsmith, therefore, the Commissioner

decided as follows, in substance, viz: "Walter Hunt was the original and first inventor of the sewing machine, but inasmuch as he had sold all his right, title and interest, and neither himself or his relatives had prosecuted the business to the advantage of the public, the community had not been benefited, and that Howe by persevering had made it valuable, and therefore must be sustained!"

While I have not space to describe it, it is certain that his machine for forging wrought-nails has never yet been superseded, although many patents have been subsequently granted in hopes of so doing. His machine for cutting brads from one sheet metal was exhibited at the American Institute Fair in 1835 at Niblo's Garden simultaneously with his machine for punching leather and filling the holes with wire plugs, so that the leather should support the metal, thus producing an iron and metal surface for a durable sole of a shoe or boot. Prior to this time he had experimented in preparing concrete blocks for the purpose of making docks, etc, which would be permanently lasting, and one of his latest griefs (as expressed to the writer), that more than twenty years ago he explained this plan of building docks to Peter Cooper, who but a few months ago put it before the public with a view that it would appear to have emanated from himself. Another effort was the molding paper-boxes directly from the pulp, by having a female mold into which a corresponding male-punch or piston would so nearly fit as to form the boxes at one operation, thus making a box per second. The vapor bath was, as a medical instrument, extremely valuable at the time he introduced it.

The hollow rifle-ball having a conical shape with a sharp point, and the charge within the ball, was a beautiful chemical and mechanical discovery, yet it met no favor until Minie, in France, had adopted it to use, and in consequence he received the credit which belonged to Walter Hunt. Not content with his former experiments in fire-arms, he to the very last hour continued to exercise his brain in relation to this class of instruments. The latest and probably the best of his improvements in this line was to arrange a new priming which would always be safe, it being water-proof and arranged in sticks, so that as the hammer came down to discharge the piece it would cut off a little piece, and the final closing of the hammer would cause the little piece to explode, thus igniting the powder or the charge in the ball, which would cause the displacement of the ball so that it would go to its intended destination. He also had an invention for reducing tobacco stems to a pulp, after which they could be rolled into sheets like paper, and thus formed into the most elegant segars. It was in his early days that he suggested the roller as a substitute for the old-fashioned balls for inking the form on the hand printing-presses, this being before power-presses had come into use. He was successful in preparing a paper-pulp which, when rolled on to or combined with the coarsest cotton, would appear like the finest linen for collars, bosoms, etc. His several medicines, of which his life-invigorating cordial is one, have proved extremely valuable.

Although what the writer has here enumerated are scarce a tithe of his inventions, which covered every branch of mechanical art, chemistry, and science, yet fearing to become tedious, I will be content that there is sufficient for the present occasion and purposes.

Walter Hunt, like most inventors, devoted his life more to his friends than himself; the writer had frequently seen him give his last cent to the poor when he knew not where the next was to be found for himself; and the succoring of families in distress was his most holy thought; it was thus that all who knew, knew but to love him, no friend in need could want when he was supplied. In early life he became a free and accepted Mason, which undoubtedly contributed to his disposition to be philanthropic. He struggled with that monster, the dollar, all his life, in hopes of mastering it, but his almost numberless experiments kept him always comparatively poor. At the time of his death he was engaged in experiments which seemed to promise a rich reward for his past labors, but his long and ardent devotion, by night as well as day, resulted in an attack of pneumonia, which in four days closed his earthly existence at the age of sixty-three years, thus parting the spirit from the house of clay that it might be wafted to the realms of bliss.

Below Kingsley's communication, the *Scientific American*, which was owned and printed by Munn & Company (who had at one time acted as attorneys for Elias Howe, Jr.), added:

Our correspondent, takes the unqualified position that Walter Hunt was the original inventor of the sewing-machine. When this assertion appeared in the "Tribune," Mr. Howe denied the fact, and quoted from the decision of Judge Sprague to sustain his position.

Walter Hunt died intestate and on July 12, 1859, his widow and his son applied to the surrogate to be appointed administrators and executors of his estate. Ten days later, two appraisers, David R. Jaques and William F. Proctor called to prepare an inventory of his estate.

They itemized and recorded his belongings. "One small diamond pin $2.25; one diamond for cutting glass $3.50; six cane seat chairs $1.20; one brass chemists scales and weights $3.00."

"One brass chemists scales and weights." Polly, who had stifled her grief, burst into tears as she heard the entry. "One brass chemists scales and weights!" Her first gift to her husband. She ran out of the room.

The appraisers continued. "One galvanic battery, fifty cents; one suit submarine armor, fifty cents; one empty brandy cask, fifty cents; one T square, ten cents."

The assets amounted to $521.83.

"How about his patent interests?" Proctor asked.

"The boot and heel patent," said George.

"Let's put it down for two hundred," Jaques suggested.

"The Restorative Cordial copyright," George added.

"Call it five hundred dollars," Proctor announced.

"I guess we've listed everything," Jaques said, "the whole thing totals $1,221.83."

"We'll file the inventory with the Surrogate."

Chapter 29

The death of Walter Hunt on June 8, 1859, did not end the litigation dealing with his inventions nor the consideration of his patents pending decision by the Patent Office.

Thirteen days after Hunt's death, in ironic confirmation of his ability, the Hunt family received U.S. Patent No. 24,517 dated June 21, 1859, on an "improvement in the construction and mode of attaching boot heels," a metallic boot heel which could be rotated to provide a fresh surface. By rotating the circular heel, worn sections could be replaced by a fresh surface, making it unnecessary to discard heels because they were run-down on one side.

George W. Hunt notified the Keene factory that the patent had been awarded and on October 9, 1859, an agreement was reached whereby full rights to it were transferred to Keene.

Income from the reversible heel accrued to the family estate. Hunt did not live long enough to personally profit from its invention.

UNITED STATES PATENT OFFICE.

WALTER HUNT, OF NEW YORK, N. Y.

HEEL FOR BOOTS AND SHOES.

Specification of Letters Patent No. 24,517, dated June 21, 1859.

To all whom it may concern:

Be it known that I, WALTER HUNT, of the city, county, and State of New York, have invented a new and useful Method of
5 Constructing and Attaching the Heels of Boots and Shoes: and I do hereby declare that the following is a full, clear, and exact description thereof, reference being had to the accompanying drawings, making part of
10 this specification, in which—

Figure 1, is a perspective view; Fig. 2, a side elevation of the counter, sole, and heel seat; Fig. 3 a vertical section of the improved heel; Fig. 4 a plan view of the shell
15 of the heel; Fig. 5 a view of the plate of metal of which the shell of the heel is formed; Fig. 6, a bottom view of the top lift of the heel; and Fig. 7, a section thereof.

The same letters indicate like parts in all
20 the figures.

My invention relates to the method of forming and attaching heels to boots and shoes, and my said invention consists in making the external form of the heel of a
25 metallic shell with an inner flange at the upper edge to fit over the usual heel seat of the boot or shoe, and between that and the counter or back portion of the upper leather, so that when pushed on from behind and
30 fastened by a screw or screws, or other equivalent means, passing through the heel and into the heel seat or vice versa, the said heel will be firmly secured and held in place. And my said invention also consists in com-
35 bining with the said shell and upper flange the making of the said heel shell with a flange at the lower edge to inclose a core of wood or other suitable substance which fills up the inside of the said shell and forms a
40 support or rest for the heel seat. And my said invention also consists in combining with the heel shell a rotating top lift secured by a central screw, or equivalent therefor, so that it can be turned on the central
45 screw, or equivalent, as it wears to equalize the wear thereof.

In the accompanying drawings (a) represents the heel shell which I prefer to make of sheet metal. I take a piece of sheet metal
50 cut to the required form, such as represented at Fig. 5, which is the form required for a heel such as represented in the accompanying drawings, and by suitable dies and swages, or other suitable means, I put it into
55 the form represented in Figs. 1, 3, and 4, with a flange (b) at the lower edge extend-

ing inward, but the upper flange (c) I do not form until afterward. The two ends I connect by a clip joint as at (d) or by any other suitable means. To the inside of this 60 shell I fit a core (e) of wood, or other suitable material, taking care to give such a shape to the upper surface of the said core as to fit and form a rest for the under surface of the leather heel seat (f) of the boot 65 or shoe. The upper flange (c) is then to be bent in or formed by suitable means. This flange only extends along the back and sides of the heel, the shell being cut away along the upper edge forward of this flange, as at 70 (g), to fit the outer sole (h).

The heel shell being thus formed and filled in with a suitable core is to be pushed onto the heel seat from behind, the flange (c) fitting between the heel seat (f) and the 75 counter (i): the said heel seat being thereby embraced between the flange (c) and the upper surface of the core (e). The ends of the flange (c) and the part (g) of the shell are fitted to the rear end of the outer sole 80 (h) so as to make a neat finish. The whole is then secured in place by one or more screws (k, l, l,) which pass through the core and take into the leather of the heel seat. To give a better wearing surface I secure a 85 top life (m), as it is termed, to the under side of the heel, and this may be a plate of chilled cast iron, or other metal, or leather or other suitable substance, the outer edge of which is shaped to conform to the outer sur- 90 face, of the shell, and to fit against the under surface of the flange (b) and then to be secured in place by the screws (k, l, l) or other equivalents, by which, the heel is secured to the heel seat. If the lower part of 95 the heel instead of being of the horse shoe form be made circular the top lift can then be made in the form represented which is a circular plate that can be turned on the screw (k) as a center to equalize the wear. 100 And in that case if other screws (l, l,) be used as additional means of fastening, the top lift can be made with a series of holes to admit of shifting it.

I prefer to make the top lift of chilled 105 cast iron as being cheap and durable, but it will be obvious that other substances may be used instead, such as brass or other metals, or leather, or vulcanized india rubber or gutta percha. 110

Instead of making the heel shell of sheet metal, which I prefer, it may be cast of the

form required, but in that case if the cord be made of wood or other solid substance shaped before being put into the shell the upper flange (*c*) is to be made separate and
5 then secured to the shell in any suitable manner. The shell may however be cast with both flanges in which case the core may be made in sections to admit of being inserted, or it may be made of some suitable
10 substance or composition which can be put in and shaped while plastic, and then indurated, such as vulcanizable india rubber or gutta percha put in while in the green or plastic state and then vulcanized.
15 The outer surface of the metallic heel may be polished, if a metallic surface be required, as for military boots, or it may be lacquered in imitation of leather and ornamented in any desirable manner. In some
20 instances, as for ladies' shoes, instead of a metallic top lift I propose to use leather attached by nails or other suitable means to the core inside of the heel shell.
From the foregoing description of the
25 mode of construction which I prefer, and the specified variations which I have contemplated, the skilful mechanic will be enabled to vary the mode of application of my said invention to suit all styles of shoes and
30 boots according to fashion; and to make many changes in the mode of application without departing from the method of construction and attachment which I have invented.
35 I am aware that it has been proposed to make the heel of a boot of a metallic shell to be attached to the leather, but in such case the metallic shell was not provided with a flange projecting inward to fit over the
40 usual heel seat of the sole, and between that and the counter or back portion of the upper, and therefore deficient both in the means of attachment, and in the finish, there being no means of preventing the heel from
45 being stripped or torn off except the screws, while on my improved plan the heel is held by the flange, and the only purpose of the

screws or nails is to prevent the heel from being pushed back. Nor have such metallic heel shells, prior to my invention, been pro- 50 vided with an inward projecting flange combined with the upper flange to hold in and protect the inclosed core, and at the same time to give strength to the shell, although such shells have been made with a 55 flange inside to fit against and form a seat for the under surface of the heel sole. And I am also aware that it has been proposed to use a rotating metallic top lift for the heels of boots, but not under a combination 60 such as I have invented and herein described. And therefore I wish it to be distinctly understood that I do not claim broadly as of my invention a metallic shell, nor a rotating metallic top lift for the heels 65 of boots and shoes.
What I claim as my invention, and desire to secure by Letters Patent is—
1. Making the external form of the heels of boots and shoes of a metallic shell with 70 an inner flange at the upper edge to fit over the usual heel seat of the sole, and between that and the counter or back portion of the upper, substantially as described, and to be provided with an inner core, and the whole 75 to be secured to the heel seat, substantially as described.
2. I also claim in combination with the shell and upper flange and inner core substantially such as described, making the said 80 shell with an inner flange at the lower edge, substantially as, and for the purpose, specified.
3. And I also claim in combination with a heel constructed substantially as above de- 85 scribed, and consisting of the shell with the upper and lower flanges and the inclosed core the employment of a rotating top lift, substantially as, and for the purpose, specified.

WALTER HUNT.

Witnesses:
    HORACE ANDREWS,
    ANDREW DE LACY.

W. Hunt,

Boot Heel.

No. 24,517.

Patented June 21. 1859.

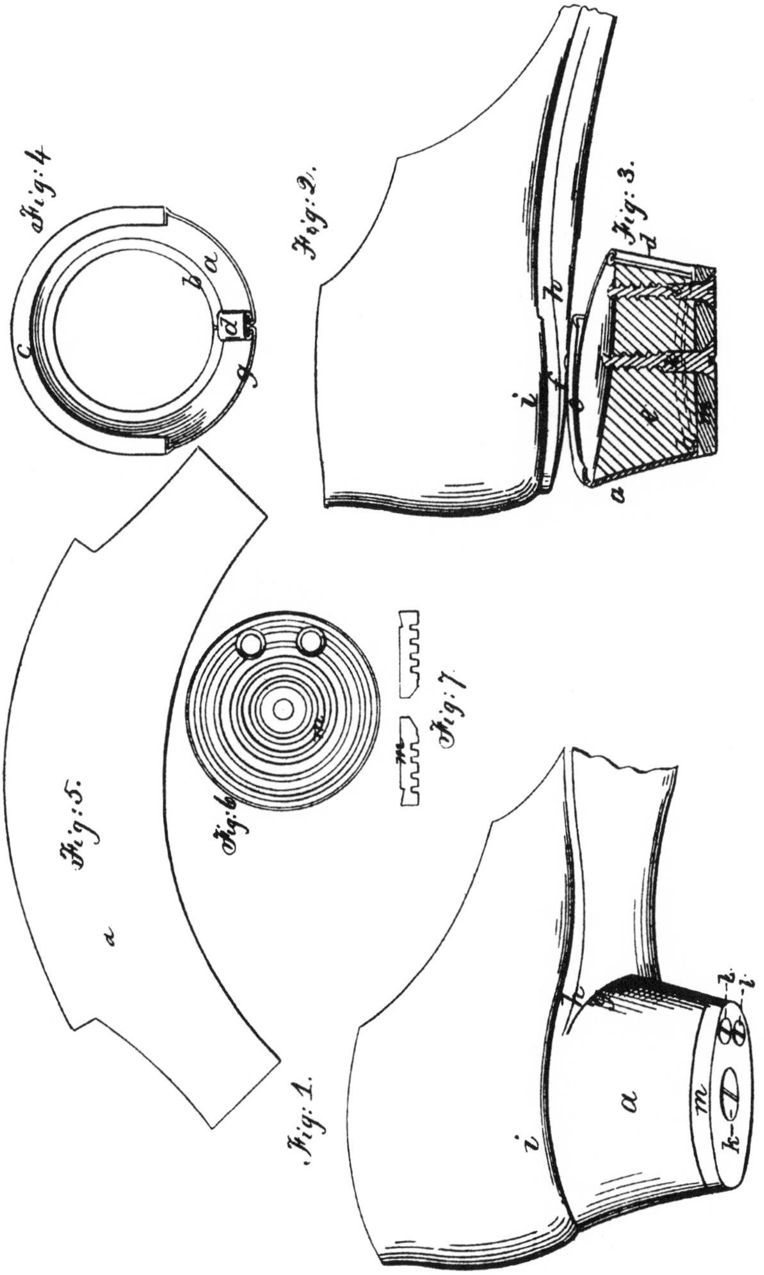

Fig: 4.

Fig: 2.

Fig: 3.

Fig: 5.

Fig: 6.

Fig: 7.

Fig: 1.

Witnesses
Wm H Bishop
Andrew De Lacy.

Walter Hunt

N. PETERS, PHOTO-LITHOGRAPHER, WASHINGTON, D. C.

Chapter 30

Still another patent had been awarded Walter Hunt and was received by his family after his death. It covered his safety lamp.

The fuel used in most lamps was highly volatile. Lard oil, whale oil, pine oil, and rectified spirits of turpentine were used in place of the costly sperm oil. Then camphene was used. Although camphene had many advantages, it likewise had its disadvantages. When exposed to a temperature of 180° camphene expanded one-ninth of its volume. Gas formed in the lamp reservoirs, ignited and exploded. Fires and accidents were numerous.

Hunt realized that the spontaneous explosions were due to a greater passage of oil than was necessary and that a safety device to regulate the flow of oil and gas would eliminate most of the accidents. He worked diligently and perfected a lamp with many safety features.

On December 29, 1856, Hunt appeared before Commissioner Charles E. Patterson and affirmed that he

invented a new and useful improvement in preventing the explosion of lamps and filling cans for Spirit-gas or burning fluid or the accidental ignition or escape of fluid therefrom.

On February 1857, the Patent Office wrote Hunt,

Upon examination of the specification and claims of your application for improvements in safety gas lamps it is apprehended that your cut offs L.L. are apt to act off so far the capillary tubes of the wick as to absolutely prevent the ascension of the fluid. You are therefore requested to send enough burning fluid to try by experiment the working of your service.

Shubael E. Swain, lawyer

In compliance with the request from the Patent Office, Hunt submitted a sample of a burning fluid suited for his lamp. The fluids for sale on the market varied. Uniformity was unknown and no set standards were used. Three parts of oil to one of turpentine was the formula used by one dealer, seven parts of oil to one part of turpentine was the formula of another manufacturer, yet others added resin. Generally, the mixtures consisted of any kind of hard grease blended with oil to the consistency of a soft paste.

Two months passed. No further communication was received from the Patent Office regarding the status of the lamp patent application.

On April 9, 1857, Hunt signed a partnership agreement with the Martins. It lasted only a few months.

Hunt wrote to the Commissioner of Patents on January 28, 1858, that the assignment made to Martin was only as a lien and that the arrangement was only temporary.

Cognizant of the dispute, Martin wrote to the Commissioner of Patents as follows;

> You will please recognize J. J. Greenough, a counselor at law as our attorney in the prosecution of the application of Walter Hunt for letters patent for safety lamp and filler assigned to us now before the Patent Office and permit neither the inventor or any other party except our above named attorney to have access to the papers, model or drawing.

(This was the same Greenough who had received the first patent in the United States on a sewing machine, had acted for Hunt as attorney in the prosecution of his fountain pen application, and had represented Buchtel in the gun interference case.)

Greenough, noticing a slight variance between the submitted model and the patent application, sent Hunt the papers for correction and amendment. But Hunt had died on June 8, 1859 and the executors of his estate turned them over to Charles S. Newell, an attorney at 77 Nassau Street.

Newell refused to return the papers to Greenough or the Martins. On July 18, 1860, Martin wrote to the Commissioner of Patents:

> On the 15th April 1857, Walter Hunt assigned to myself and my son George G. Martin a safety lamp patent for which he had applied some months previous. On taking up the lamp by the Examiner at my request he found that the specifications did not conform to the model and by mistake sent the specifications for correction to Walter Hunt instead of myself.
>
> Mr. Hunt died about a year since without returning the paper and during his life term as I have lately discovered left among these papers, this, with a lawyer in town by the name of Newell who refuses to give it up until he receives pay for some law business that he alleges he performed for this Hunt.
>
> I ask to inquire in what way I can, or the Department, reach this paper in the Lawyers hands.

UNITED STATES PATENT OFFICE.

WALTER HUNT, OF NEW YORK, N. Y., ASSIGNOR TO JNO. W. MARTIN AND GEO. G. MARTIN, OF BROOKLYN, NEW YORK.

LAMP.

Specification of Letters Patent No. 32,402, dated May 21, 1861.

To all whom it may concern:

Be it known that I, WALTER HUNT, of the city, county, and State of New York, have invented certain new and useful Im-
5 provements in Lamps for Burning Fluid, &c.; and I hereby declare that the following is a full and accurate description thereof, reference being had to the accompanying drawings, and to the letters of ref-
10 erence marked thereon, in which—

Figures 1 and 2 are elevated cut sections of the filler and lamp, here shown, as in the process of filling the latter, in which A is a tubular cut-off valve, inclosing a portion of the up-
15 per end of the filler vent-tube B, which is closed at its upper extremity, upon which rests the coiled spring, c, which is now compressed between it and the stop or cap of A, by the upward pressure of B, near the upper
20 end of which are side vent-holes a, corresponding with others in A, at b. About one third of the lower portion of B is inclosed by, and supported centrally in, the filling tube, C, by means of the two perforated col-
25 lars, E, a face view of which is seen in Fig. 3. Upon the bottom end of B, is fixed a conical piston valve, d, somewhat less than the caliber of C, but suitably large to close its contracted end, which forms a valve-seat there-
30 for, effectually making an internal tap-and-faucet for the filler, which tap is forced up when C, is pressed into the lamp-tube F, as here shown in the process of filling, and again closed when drawn out by the down-
35 ward pressure of the spring, c. The upper end of the filler-tube, C, is fitted centrally into the top of the filling-can, Fig. 1, by a screw, or otherwise, at D, through which orifice the filler can be supplied in the ordinary
40 manner or a tube, &c., as used in my lamps, as hereinafter described, may be inserted in the top of my filler, through which it may be supplied from cans or casks of the retailers of fluid, &c., which cans are provided
45 with filling tubes similar to those in my filling cans as above described, in which case the escape or accidental ignition of the fluid from the cask, or filling-can, would be rendered impossible, either in the hands of
50 the seller, or user, as scales would be substituted, for measures, by the dealers in burning fluid, &c.

The improvements in my plans of lamps may be attached to the common lamp, as shown in Figs. 2, 6 and 9, letter H. Fig. 6 55 gives a vertical cut section of the entire mechanism of the said lamp-top, as herein claimed, in which the cap, H and the tube, F, are cast in one piece. I is a discous, conical valve fixed centrally upon the vent- 60 tube, G, which forms the vent-tube of the lamp, while in the process of being filled, having its bottom end closed, near by which, are side vent-holes, f. This end of G is inclosed in the thimble g, the bottom rim or 65 flange of which, forms a diaphragm or bottom of the tube, F, upon which bottom rests the coiled spring K, the upper end of which bears against the conical valve, I, which valve has its seat at J, Fig. 2, somewhat 70 below which the tube F, is pierced with side openings k, through which the fluid from the filler flows into the lamp as indicated by the arrows i and k. When the lamp and filler are connected by the intro- 75 duction and pressure of the tube C, into the recipient lamp-tube F, the vent tubes, B and G, are united by a conical male and female junction, indicated by l, Figs. 2, 5, and 6, thus forming one entire vent-tube from 2 80 to 1, as before described, while the tubes C, and F, being thus united constitute one continuous filling tube from 1 to 2, the valve I, being forced below the orifices k, and the recipient vent-holes, f, below the thimble, g, 85 allows the escape of the air up through G and B and out at a (as before stated) the escape of which ceases as soon as the fluid in the lamp rises to the vent-holes, f, in the lower end of G, above which the lamp can- 90 not be filled, except by intended misuse.

The above description explains the construction and mode of operation, so far as the supplying of the lamp and filling-can is concerned. 95

Figs. 5 and 6 are elevated cut sections of the mechanism claimed, in both my lamp and filling-can, which are here shown as closed before the process of filling. Figs. 7 and 8 give a profile view of the same. 100

Fig. 10 is a face view of the lamp-top H, with the escutcheon M, placed over the tube F, and Fig. 11 with it removed aside, for the purpose of filling the lamp.

What I claim in the above described invention and desire to secure by Letters Patent is—

The combination and arrangement of the
5 filling tubes C, and F, valves d and I and with the vent‑tubes B, and G, the same being constructed, arranged, and operated, substantially in the manner, and for the purposes above specified.

WALTER HUNT.

Witnesses:
   CHAS. E. PATTERSON,
   SHUBAEL E. SWAIN.

No action was received from any source and, on August 6, 1860, Martin sent the Commissioner of Patents another letter.

In 1856 or 1857 Mr. Walter Hunt of this City made an application to the then Comm. of Patents for Letters in a case concerning lamps or to prevent the explosion of lamps.

After the application was made, I purchased his entire interest in it, and the same was duly assigned to me, and the assignment recorded in the department according to law. After the assignment was thus made and recorded this specification was improperly or through mistake returned to Hunt by the department for correction or alteration. Mr. Hunt omitted to return the specification until he became deceased and his Atty. who has possession of his papers, refuses to give up or return the specification unless he is paid some $300 which he says Hunt owes him.

Now I am advised, that it is in your power to compel this man to return the specification, and it is important to me, that you should do so. The facts set forth in the form of a petition to one of the judges of the Supreme Court of the U.S. showing that the paper was returned to Hunt through mistake or oversight of the department, he will, no doubt, grant an order of injunction requiring him to return the said paper or to stand committed until he does so.

You will oblige me by taking such action in the premises as may be necessary to obtain the specification.

A settlement was made between the Martins and the Hunt executors on November 24, 1860.

In the transfer of patents Y5-431
Nov. 24, 1860. Rec. Dec. 18, 1860
Polly Hunt, George Washington Hunt and J. W. Martin and Geo. G. Martin
That the parties of the first part in consideration of the sum of $1 to them in hand paid, by parties of the second part [convey to the parties of the second part all] rights, title and interest of, in and to the safety lamp and filler for burning fluids with all models, and specifications relating thereto and also the cylindrical priming for firearms and all the rights, title and interest[.]
Second Party—All and singular their right, title and interest of in and to any and all sewing machines in which the said Walter Hunt had or might have had any interest whatsoever, and the breech loading and other fire arms, and any

W. Hunt,

Lamp.

No. 32.402.

Patented May 21. 1861.

Fig. 7.

Fig. 8.

Fig. 12.

Fig. 5.

Fig. 6.

Fig. 11.

Fig. 3.

Fig. 4.

Fig. 10.

Fig. 1.

Fig. 2.

Fig. 9.

other inventions referred to in the said recited agreement, except those conferred in the first article of this agreement.

Release each other from claims.

After expenses have been paid and $2,800 advance to Walter Hunt has been paid, one equal half part of all profits which they may derive from said safety lamp and filler during the continuance of their patent for the same.

The patent papers were returned to the Martins, who made the necessary amendments.

Inasmuch as Walter Hunt was the inventor and the applicant for the patent, the Patent Office wrote the Martins on March 7, 1861, advising that the assignee must show they possess entire right to amend.

On March 11, 1861, the Martins wrote,

Yours of the 7th was received and contents noted. In reply we would refer you to the assignment to us from Walter Hunt recorded in the Patent Office, July 16, 1857, in Liber M Page 211 of Transfers of Patents. Said assignment is dated April 9, 1857.

Four years and three months had passed since the date of the original application. The Patent Office had neither accepted nor rejected the claim. The delay irked the Martins, and they appointed Charles Mason to represent them and expedite the application.

Charles Mason had been the Commissioner of Patents and had rendered the decision that Hunt had not been entitled to the sewing machine patent. Now, Mason was fighting for the grant of the Hunt lamp patent.

On April 3, 1861, John W. Martin and George G. Martin as assignees of Walter Hunt wrote the Commissioner of Patents,

We hereby authorize and empower Charles Mason to act as our Attorney and Agent in the matter of the application for a patent for a "safety lamp and filler for burning fluid" to alter and amend the specifications to receive the patent when granted and to do all that we would do if we were personally present and acting in the premises.

John P. Townsend and G. M. Bucklin acted as witness.

Twelve days later, on April 15, 1861, the Patent Office sent a letter to the Martins at their former place of business at 191 Broadway which was forwarded to their new address, 14 Pine Street. It stated that Hunt's assignment was insufficient in law and that the issuance of the patent was necessarily withheld. For the same reason,

your authority to recognize cannot be granted, under section 10 of the act of July 4, 1836, and that the authority is granted to the executors.

The Martins advised the Patent Office that an agreement had been reached with the executors, and that their assignment had been recorded.

Satisfied that the claims of the Martins were legal, the Patent Office awarded Walter Hunt U.S. Patent No. 32,402 on May 21, 1861, which was assigned to Jno. W. Martin and Geo. G. Martin.

On June 11, 1861, the Martins assigned this patent to Isaac Seymour.

As everything has been settled amicably with the Martins, the Hunt executors directed their attention to other fields. They attempted to collect from Singer the money due the estate as stipulated in Hunt's contract with him.

Chapter 31

ON THE PETITION OF ELIAS HOWE, Jr. of Brooklyn, N.Y., praying for the extension of a patent granted to him on the 10th of September 1846, for an improvement in sewing machines for seven years from the expiration of said patent, which takes place on the tenth day of September 1860.

It is ordered that the said petition be heard at the Patent Office on Monday the thirteenth of August next at 12 o'clock M. and all persons are notified to appear and show cause, if any they have, why said petition ought not to be granted.

Persons opposing the extension are required to file in the Patent Office their objections, specially set forth in writing, at least twenty days before the day of hearing; all testimony filed by either party to be used at the said hearing, must be taken and transmitted in accordance with the rules of the office, which will be furnished on application.

The testimony in the case will be closed on the third of August. Depositions and other papers relied upon as testimony, must be filed in the office on or before the morning of that day, the arguments, if any, within ten days thereafter.

Ordered also, that the notice be published in the "Constitution," Washington, D.C., and the "Daily News," N.Y. once a week for three weeks, the first of said publications to be at least sixty days before the thirteenth of August next, the day of hearing.

PHILIP F. THOMAS
COMMISSIONER OF PATENTS

Mrs. Hunt and her daughter, Frances Augusta Roe, visited Edward Clark to see whether he could resurrect Hunt's original patent application. They were told that if they persisted and offered any objection to the extension of Howe's patent that Singer would consider his contract with Walter Hunt void and would discontinue making any monthly payments.

They conveyed the decision to George who was so angry that he excitedly rushed to Edward Clark to protest.

"Now is the time to file my father's patent claim," George insisted. "If you don't file at once, heaven knows what will happen."

But Mr. Clark and the powerful sewing machine combine were not taking orders from the Hunt family. They had their own plans and had no intention of doing anything which would interfere with them.

Other sewing machine manufacturers, however, had decided collectively to act on their own behalf to forestall Howe's renewal and prosecute their own cases. George B. Sloate, Williams & Orvis, and others hired Samuel Blatchford of Blatchford, Seward and Griswold, noted attorneys at 31 Nassau Street, New York City, to oppose the extension.

(Blatchford was an able lawyer, who later became Judge of the United States District Court and finally an Associate Justice of the Supreme Court of the United States.)

Howe was represented by George Gifford, who was assisted by Charles M. Keller and Causeten C. Browne, who had helped Hunt obtain his patent on the revolving heel.

The case was scheduled for trial Monday, July 23, 1860, but George Gifford requested postponement until the following day to take further testimony.

Fourteen years had passed since Howe obtained his patent and twenty-six years since Hunt had invented his sewing machine.

Practically everyone who had any knowledge of the early sewing machines was called in the proceedings to testify and comment upon the character of those concerned.

The testimony was voluminous and when it was printed it filled 228 pages. George Gifford's argument against disposal of the counter claims consisted of 80 printed pages. He advanced six reasons against Hunt's machine.

Commissioner Philip Francis Thomas very carefully weighed both sides of the controversy. He decided that Howe was entitled to a seven-year renewal. Accordingly Howe's patent of September 10, 1846, which expired September 10, 1860, was renewed to September 10, 1867. After its grant, a reissue was requested, and on March 19, 1861, reissue No. 1,154 was granted.

This decision ended the sewing machine controversy. Howe had emerged victorious and his opponents could not change the monopolistic situation. Hunt's chances of finally obtaining a patent on his machine had been conclusively blasted. His rights and interests to his sewing machine were worthless and useless.

While the controversy was under Patent Office consideration, Hunt's family had been regularly collecting the $100 monthly checks on the tenth of each month. The final $100 check was due on September 10 at which time the additional $10,000 payment was also to have been made.

But on that date, coincidentally, the Patent Commissioner's decision was announced.

When George W. Hunt called for the final installment of the monthly hundred dollars and the ten thousand dollar payment, he received a very cold reception. He did not get either check. He was told he would not get any further payments, he should tear up the contract. The patent decision had terminated everything.

Before the Commissioner of Patents had decided to grant the renewal to Howe for an additional seven years, Orlando B. Potter of the Grover and Baker Company prepared against an unfavorable decision. He sponsored a cooperative and reciprocity arrangement among the manufacturers. He reasoned that it would be better and cheaper to pay a license fee for the right to manufacture than be embroiled in time-consuming expensive litigation. Reluctantly, it was accepted.

An amicable agreement was reached to form a combination, the manufacturers to pay a license fee of $15.00 for each sewing machine they produced, the pooled patent rights to be controlled by the combination. Howe was to receive $5.00, the $10.00 balance being set aside until $10,000 was accumulated as a fund for the expense of future lawsuits in the interest of the combination. When this sum was obtained, the royalty fees were to be apportioned, one-third to Howe, one-third to I. M. Singer, one-sixth to Wheeler and Wilson and one-sixth to the Grover and Baker Co.

In 1860, the $15.00 fee was reduced to $7.00; in 1863 to $5.00; and in 1870 to $3.00.

The agreement did away with the chaos. The big companies found that it was more profitable to mutually control the industry than to fight each other for mastery until nothing remained but bones.

George Hunt was not happy with the verdict or the unification plan. He consulted many people seeking advice. His first step was to insist that I. M. Singer & Co. pay the Hunt estate, the amount agreed upon under the contract. But they were adamant and he received no satisfaction. As constant requests for payment were ignored, he decided to bring the matter to court.

On January 25, 1861, the Hunt estate brought suit against the Singer organization in the Marine Court of the City of New York which had jurisdiction of cases under $500.00.

A summons was issued January 25, 1861, to Edward Clark returnable January 28, 1861. C. W. Sandford was the attorney for the plaintiffs. John C. Perry represented the defendants.

The case was tried before Judge Arba K. Maynard on March 11, 1861, but was adjourned for trial. On the 18th of March, the judge decided that the Hunts were entitled to collect the sum of $163.46 of which amount $60.46 was for costs, $100.00 the amount of the last installment under the contract and $3.00 interest.

The following day, a transcript was issued against the property of the defendants who on March 29, 1861, appealed the decision of Judge Maynard to the General Term of the Marine Court. The case was scheduled and was argued October 31, 1861, on which date the decision of Judge Maynard was affirmed. The case was reviewed by the two judges of the General Term who sustained the verdict and awarded costs of $12.79 for the hearing.

The two judgments were not to the liking of the Singers. They wholeheartedly maintained that Hunt's contract with John W. Martin of April 9, 1857, barred his claims against them despite the fact that it was shown they knew of the existence of that contract and had considered it valueless. With full knowledge of it, they had paid all the $100 installments which fell due before the date when Howe's patent had been extended.

George Hunt insisted that the purpose of the agreement was to prevent any opposition from Hunt for the Howe extension of patent and that it was a deliberate plot to shelve Walter Hunt's claims. In order that this argument could be made useless, and in conformity with a provision of the contract, the defendants applied to the Hunt family on May 15, 1861, to sign a paper for an application for a patent.

On the 20th of May, the papers were returned properly executed and on June 3, 1861, they made an application for a patent on Hunt's sewing machine invention of 1834, which application was promptly rejected.

With this threat disposed of, the defendants appealed the two decisions of the Marine Court to the General Term of the Court of Common Pleas on November 18, 1861, filing their application two days before the twenty-one day statute appeal limitation.*

The laws of the court required the approval of one of the justices of the Marine Court or of the judges of the Court of Common Pleas for the grant of an appeal. Decision to appeal was granted and on November 20, 1861, notice of the appeal was sent to the Clerk's Office of the Marine Court.

The case in the Court of Common Pleas was scheduled for trial on December 18, 1861. The suit was tried before Judge Henry Hilton with J. Van Ness Lyle representing the appellants and Charles W. Sandford representing the respondents.

On May 19, 1862, Judge Henry Hilton ruled:

Here, it was shown that the defendants knew of the Martin contract prior to December 1859, and regarded it as worthless, that they were unwilling, not only to advance a small sum to procure its cancellation, but in addition, continued to pay the monthly installment to Hunt for many months thereafter, and until

*4 pages (very last) C. W. Sandford, *Facts and Points for Plaintiffs and Respondents*, 20 pages (points for appellants), 140 pages—*Papers on Appeal*.

Howe procured an extension of his patent, when the interests derived under their agreement with Hunt became positively valueless to anyone.

Having, as I think it may fairly be inferred from the evidence, by means of their controlling Hunt's invention, made a satisfactory arrangement with Howe and silenced any opposition to his claim for an extension on the part of those who might represent Hunt's claim to having been the original inventor of the sewing machine, they now desire to rescind and annul their contract when it is impossible to place the plaintiffs in the condition they would have been prior to the extension of Howe's patent having been procured; and, after the defendants have acquired and realized, in all probability, all the benefit they ever expected to gain by their contract with Hunt.

A plainer illustration of the propriety of the rule stated could not be found.

Judgment affirmed.

A brief notice of the confirmed judgment appeared in the *New York Daily Tribune* of May 20, 1862, and the *New York Times* of May 21, 1862.

On the nineteenth of June, the judgment was filed in the Court of Common Pleas, plus court costs, but the Singer interests were still unconvinced. They filed another appeal.

The appeal was filed on June 21, 1862, in the Court of Common Pleas. The case was put on the calendar to await its turn. Singer shifted attorneys. George Gifford, the attorney for Howe's patent extension who had been called in to help, was replaced on September 22, 1863, by Abraham Underhill, a lawyer at 4 New Street. Before the case came to court, Underhill was removed and Charles H. Glover and William R. Darling of the firm of Glover and Darling were substituted on March 9, 1864.

On April 5-6, 1865, the case was tried before Judge Charles Patrick Daly. Trial by jury was waived.

The plaintiffs demanded

the said sum of $10,000.00 with interest thereon from the 10th day of September 1861, and the costs of this suit.

The defendants denied

that there is any sum of money or anything due or owing from them to the said plaintiffs under said agreement or contract... [and requested] that the said plaintiffs' complaint be dismissed with costs.

In his decision, Judge Daly reviewed the facts of the case and stated,

My conclusions upon this state or facts are:
(1) That as the monthly payments were to be made up to the termination of

Howe's patent on the 10th of September 1860, that that must be regarded as the time under the agreement within which the defendants were to determine whether they would or would not apply for a patent or for a legislative grant in the nature of a patent.

(2) That if they did not apply within that time or if having applied they should conclude to withdraw the application before the 10th of September 1860, that then they were to pay Hunt or his legal representatives the sum of $10,000.

(3) That if the defendants meant in good faith to make the application contemplated by the agreement, it was essential that it should have been made before September 10, 1860, and before Howe obtained a renewal of his patent.

(4) That the defendants intentionally deferred making the application until Howe had secured the extension of his patent, that they would not themselves oppose the renewal of Howe's patent, and that they prevented the legal representatives of Hunt from doing so at the peril of forfeiting all claim thereafter under the agreement.

(5) That this was wholly inconsistent with any design on their part to apply in good faith for a patent under the agreement, that it was, and was meant to be prejudicial to the success of any such application and that it was done with the view of assisting Howe in the accomplishment of his object and in consequence of an understanding or agreement with Howe to that effect.

(6) That Clark's statements to Mrs. Hunt that Martin's ownership of the interest which Hunt had in his invention had prevented Clark from doing anything was a mere pretext, and his statement that that was the reason why he would not pay the last installment of $100. was untrue, the real reason being that Howe had then secured a renewal of his patent, and that object being accomplished the defendants meant, if they could, to get rid of any further obligation under the contract with Hunt.

(7) That the agreement between Hunt and the Martins presented no obstacles to the defendants applying for a patent under their agreement with Hunt if they meant in good faith to do so, that Clark attached no importance to the agreement whatever, that he knew all about it for eight months before Howe obtained an extension of his patent and yet continued to perform the agreement entered into with Hunt by making the monthly payments until Howe had secured the extension.

(8) That the question whether the prior agreement with Martin and son did or did not discharge the defendants from their liability under their contract with Hunt was tried between the plaintiffs and the defendants in the suit in the Marine Court and decided against the defendants, that that question is therefore res adjudicata and is conclusively settled between them the decision and judgment of the Marine Court having been finally affirmed upon appeal.

(9) That the long delay of three years from the time of the making of the agreement with Hunt, until the application for a patent by the defendants during which the defendants made no effort to revive Hunt's claims, while Hunt and his legal representatives were prevented by the agreement from making any was prejudicial to the success of the application.

(10) That the application which the defendants made for a patent on the third of June 1861 was not made with the intent or expectation of obtaining one, but for the sole purpose of evading if they could the payment of $10,000.

(11) And my final conclusion is that the plaintiffs are entitled to recover from the defendants the $10,000 with interest from the 10th day of September 1861.

On April 25, 1866, Judge Daly of the Special Term of Court of Common Pleas, New York City, ruled that Hunt's family was entitled to recover $13,237.49, an allowance of $663.87 and $177.00 in costs, a total of $14,078.36 and $89.00 costs of the General Term of the Court of Common Pleas.

The $14,078.36 judgment was recorded April 25, 1866, but the defendants were not disposed to pay it. They appealed the decision, and declined to pay the award.

One week earlier, the Singer interests changed their attorneys. They appointed E. H. and C. B. Stoughton to replace Glover and Darling. The new attorneys brought the case before the Court of Appeals.

The Singer interests naturally were dissatisfied with the verdict of the courts. They maintained that the Marine Court was wrong, that the appeal to the Marine Court was wrong, that the Court of Common Pleas was wrong, and that the appeal to them was also wrong!

Despite the fact that in the eight years in which the case had been in litigation the Singers had lost every decision, they would not agree with the decisions of the courts. An appeal, win or lose, would delay judgment for two or three years.

In the meantime, the Howe patent renewal had expired. On September 10, 1867, the patent became public property and no longer had any monetary value. It had netted Howe about $2,000,000 in royalties. Less than a month later, Howe died at Brooklyn, New York, on October 3, 1867.

Two years passed uneventfully. No legal action was taken. At last the suit against the Singer interests was placed on the calendar for May 10, 1869, before Judge John Riker Brady of the Court of Appeals.

The plaintiff's brief was a folio printed by William C. Bryant & Co., Printers, Nassau Street, New York City. They requested that the court's judgment be affirmed.

At a General Term of the Court of Common Pleas, May 3, 1869, N.Y.C., Presiding Judge Hon. C. P. Daly—John R. Brady—and George C. Barrett

This cause having been submitted upon the case made therein and the written arguments of E. W. Stoughton, Esq. of counsel for the appellants and C. W. Sandford, Esq., of counsel for the respondents, and due deliberation being thereupon had. It is ordered that the judgment of the Special Term herein be affirmed with costs.

Nathan L. Jarvis, Jr. Clerk

Judge Brady reviewed the case and stated in his decision that

> the judgment must be affirmed without adding one word to the findings of fact
> and conclusions of law made by Judge Daly at Special Term.

The judgment was satisfied January 13, 1870, and the long overdue award was finally received by the Hunt family.

Although the sewing machine matter had finally reached a conclusion, the Hunt heirs were still embroiled in litigation. The paper collar invention again came to the fore. The decision of the Patent Examiners was not to their liking and they appealed to their elected officials for a reversal or reexamination of their interests.

Their appeal finally reached Congress and on March 15, 1870, a law was enacted which empowered the Commissioner of Patents to rehear and determine the application of Polly Hunt, administratrix, and George W. Hunt, administrator, for the extension of certain reissues of the patent for the manufacture of paper collars issued on the 25th of July. (See Chapter 25, bottom of page 242 on.)

"Don't be so glum, mother," George consoled. "You've finally won. You should be happy. You've won after eleven years, eleven long years."

Polly Hunt sat motionless, her hands tightly gripping the sides of the straight-back wicker rocker. Through the portieres, the setting sun cast a glowing color on her ashen face. Her skin was flabby with deeply imbedded wrinkles. Old age spots dotted it. Despondency was etched in every line.

"I've won? I've won?" Polly repeated slowly in a voice trembling with emotion. "What have I won? Money?" She paused a few seconds before continuing. "No, George, I've lost. I've lost the finest husband a woman could have. I've lost him to an unappreciative world."

Oblivious to almost everything, Polly generally stared through the window most of the time. Days, weeks and months had slipped by. The court victory did little, if anything, to cheer her. It emphasized the years of unjust treatment she felt she had received.

In the early afternoon on August 24, 1870, Polly Anne, Caroline, Frances and George who had been called stood at her bedside, but she did not recognize them. In a faint whisper, she kept calling, "Walter, Walter!" She was confused, her vision was blurred and her breathing was heavy. After one of her lengthy seizures, she gasped for breath, then lapsed into unconsciousness. Mercifully within a few minutes, she breathed her last.

The funeral service was brief.

She was buried alongside her husband in a little plot in Green-Wood Cemetery, Brooklyn, New York.

The earthly struggles of Walter and Polly Hunt for recognition were over. Their moment of triumph was short-lived and came too late.

The grand Elias Howe, Jr., monument at right and Walter Hunt's six-foot shaft at left are a hundred feet apart in Green-Wood Cemetery, Brooklyn, New York.

Even Elias Howe, Jr., on whom fame conferred its laurels had gone to meet his Maker.

The sewing machine fight was a thing of the past.

Twenty years later on March 16, 1890, Elias Howe's remains were reinterred at Green-Wood (also: Greenwood) Cemetery. The new grave was marked by a lofty monument surmounted by a hugh bronze bust. The memorial towers high and casts its shadow three plots away on a small granite shaft in a simple plot beneath which Walter Hunt sleeps his last sleep.

As in life, so in death, does the shadow of Elias Howe, Jr., fall on Walter Hunt.

THE END.

Appendix.
Scientific American
(October 1, 1853) Editorial

Sewing Machine Controversy

There never was a useful invention of any importance brought before the public to which there was not more than one who laid claim to be the inventor. As it has been, so will it be, for human nature is the same in every age, and every country. In the performance of our duty to inventors and the public, we have endeavored in all controverted patent cases to be impartial in examining the claims of each inventor, and in giving every one his just meed of praise. Such a course is never satisfactory to those who claim too much, but it is the only honest course—the one we humbly endeavor always to pursue. It is but a few years since there was not a single sewing machine in our country—not one—now there are some thousands of them, and their value and importance are becoming better known every day. The first sewing machine brought to our notice, was the one of E. Howe Jr., of Cambridge, Mass.—It was very favorably noticed in the Commissioner of Patents' Report of 1846, but although this sewing machine was noticed in the Scientific American a short time after the patent was issued, we never saw one of them in operation until 1849. The chief merit of Howe's machine consists in being the first which sewed the lock stitch—that is, using two threads, one on a needle and the other on a shuttle. In 1848 the sewing machine of Johnson & Morey, of Boston, was exhibited in this city, but it made only a running stitch and was far inferior to Howe's. Since that time Singer's and Wilson's sewing machines have become very prominent, all using the lock stitch of Howe, but employing somewhat different devices to make it. The claim for making the lock stitch is the grand subject of controversy, for no sewing machine, excepting one using two needles making a shoemakers' stitch, is of any use without it. The claims set up to overthrow those of Howe, as to the originality of the lock stitch, are those of Walter Hunt, of this city. In a patent trial which took

297

place at Boston, and noticed by us in our last volume, evidence in support of Hunt's claims were presented, but the trial terminated in favor of Howe. There has been a sharp controversy for some time between Singer and Howe, the former using the asserted claims of Hunt to strengthen his position before the public, and as a handle to the dispute, W. Hunt—either for the purpose of frightening or befooling others—presented himself before the public in the following card, which was published in the "New York Tribune" of the 19th inst.:—

"To the Public.—I perceive that Elias Howe, Jr., is advertising himself as patentee of the Original Sewing Machine, and claiming that all who use machines having a needle or needles with an eye near the point, are responsible to him. These statements I contradict. Howe was not even the original patentee; John G. Greenough and George R. Corliss, each had a patent on a Sewing Machine before Howe obtained his patent, as the records of the Patent Office show. Howe was not the original and first inventor of the machine on which he obtained his patent. He did not invent the needle with the eye near the point. He was not the original inventor of the combination of the eye-pointed needle and the shuttle, making the interlocked stitch with two threads, now in common use. These things, which form the essential basis of all Sewing Machines, were first invented by me, and were combined in good operative Sewing Machines which were used and extensively exhibited, both in New York and Baltimore, more than ten years before Howe's patent was granted.

"By law no other person than myself could, or can, have a valid patent upon the eye-pointed needle and shuttle, or any combination of them. The proof of these facts is abundant and conclusive. I have taken measures as soon as adverse circumstances would permit, to enforce my rights by applying for a patent for my original invention. I am by law entitled to it, and in due course no doubt will get it. In that case, Howe's license will be no protection against my just claims; and I shall then ask, and insist upon, a just compensation from all who use my invention. All who feel an interest in this subject can, by calling on me, receive the most satisfactory evidence that I was the first and original inventor of the Sewing Machine.

Walter Hunt."

We publish this card in full, because it presents topics of great importance to patentees,—We take a positive position in opposition to the claims and assumptions set up in this card, and will give our reasons for so doing. Mr. Hunt *may* have invented what he claims, but at this date, when the value of such machines have been brought into public notice by others, and seven years after Howe obtained his patent, it has rather an ugly appearance to set up ten years' prior claims to the lock stitch and eye-pointed needle. Since the time when it is asserted he invented his machine, he found means to obtain patents, and to induce others to purchase inventions of far less importance and value; how came this one to be neglected? We are opposed to such rusty claims, especially by one so well versed in patents and inventions. The Commissioner of patents, we believe, will never grant them; he is too good a lawyer to do so. If it can be proven that sewing machines, embracing the lock stitch and the eye-pointed needle, were on exhibition and in use in 1843 and no patent applied for, and that the inventor suffered Howe's patent to be uncontested for two years, then, as we understand the law, the invention for which he sets up his claims will become public property. This setting up of new claims for 17 year old private unclaimed inventions, is something we condemn heart and soul, especially when those claims are set up by persons who deal in inventions. This is a case wherein the importance of the *seire facias*, as an amendment to our patent law, comes prominently into view; and we hope that it will be added at our next session of Congress. We want to see the means provided by law to settle such controversies with dispatch, in order that the ear of the public may not be used as a kettle drum on which to beat the loudest tones for personal purposes.

Appendix.
Walter Hunt's Patents

Walter Hunt received the following U.S. Letters Patent:

1826, June 26   *Machine for Spinning Flax and Hemp.* Joint inventor, Willis Hoskins. This machine revolutionized flax spinning.

1827, July 30   *Coach Alarm.* An alarm gong used as a warning signal.

1829, February 19   *Knife Sharpener.* Two series of concentric discs which revolved and supplied an ever fresh sharpening surface.

1829, June 11   *Self Supplying Twister.* For use in making rope.

1833, April 22   *Castor Globe.* To more easily move heavy furniture.

1834, February 8   *Globe Heating Stove.* It was designed for anthracite coal and radiated heat equally in all directions.

1836, January 6   *Saw for Felling Trees.* Awarded a diploma by the American Institute.

1838, March 21   *Flexible Spring.* A flat spiral spring attachment used in belts, suspenders, pantaloons, etc.

1838, October 3   *Ice Boat.* Joint inventor, Jacob Townsend. A portable attachment for vessels which served to clear their paths and break up ice cakes.

1839, November 12   *Nail and Machine for Making Same.* An improved method of manufacturing nails, brads, tacks, etc.

1840, November 13   *Nail Machine for Cutting Nails, Brads, &c.* A new method.

1843, August 17   *Sole of Boot and Shoes (Hob Nails).* Circular threaded pegs inserted into the outer sole served as hob nails. The heads were flattened so as to prevent them from falling out, and the outer sole was then attached to the inner sole.

1843, October 12	*Method of Feeding Nail and Tack Plates, &c, into Machines for Cutting.* This machine introduced a new principle and proved very successful.
1845, May 29	*Inkstand.* A floater was inserted in the inkwell which tended to keep the ink from evaporating and supplied the pen with sufficient ink.
1845, October 7	*Inkstand.* An inkwell with a clapper springtop which prevented ink from spilling in case the inkwell tipped. It also enabled pen points and quill points to be kept clear of sediment.
1845, December 11	*Inkstand.* This inkwell introduced the pressure spring principle. A downward pressure of the pen on a floater supplied the pen with as much ink as desired. When the pen was withdrawn, the inkwell automatically closed.
1847, January 13	*Fountain-Pen.* The forerunner of the modern fountain pen.
1848, August 10	*Improved Method of Attaching a Ball to a Wooden Cartridge.* A wooden cartridge enclosing a lead ball designed for the Hunt breech-loading gun.
1848, August 10	*Loaded Ball.* A metal cartridge provided with a percussion point.
1849, April 10	*Dress-Pin.* This patent covered the safety pin in common use today.
1849, August 21	*Combined Piston-Breech and Firing-Cock Repeating-Gun.* A gun designed for breech loading, instead of muzzle loading, containing a load of cartridges available for instant use.
1853, January 4	*Improvement in Bottle-Stoppers.* A device which regulated the amount of fluid which could be poured from a bottle with each tilt of the bottle.
1854, June 27	*Improvement in Sewing-Machines.* An improved sewing machine.
1854, July 25	*Improvement in Shirt-Collars.* This invention introduced the successful paper collar and their method of manufacture.
1856, January 1	*Shirt-Collar.* A new method of cutting and forming collars.
1859, June 21	*Heel for Boots and Shoes.* A circular heel-plate was inserted in the heels of shoes, which when worn down on one side could be revolved so that a fresh surface would appear.
1861, May 21	*Lamp.* A nonexplosive lamp utilizing two individual wicks.
1869, May 4	*Improvement in Compound Fabrics for the Production of Shirt-Collars.* A new method of manufacturing and producing shirt fronts, collars and cuffs.

This is the model made by Hunt of the fountain pen sent with the original patent application.

Walter Hunt was not only the recipient of these patents, but the inventor of many other devices and improvements for which he did not apply for patents. Among the latter were the invention of a sewing machine in 1834; a japanned warming table for which the American Institute awarded him a silver medal in 1846; an "Antipodean Apparatus" (a device which enabled one to walk on the ceiling in an inverted position like a fly) which was used as a circus attraction by Richard Sands, the famous performer; a medicinal compound featured as a restorative cordial; medicated vapor baths; adamantine candles formed by pressure; pill boxes and hat bodies formed from pulp; galvanic rollers; and molded stone for buildings; there were many others.

Bibliography

This listing was completed in 1935 by the author and is here reprinted almost verbatim from "Walter Hunt, American Inventor" (Clinton N. Hunt, 1935)

Walter Hunt was the subject of many magazine articles. A few of the many articles may be found in the *Atlantic Magazine* (May 1867), *Atlantic Monthly* (May 1867), *Belgravia* (June 1870), *Chamber's Journal* (Sept. 21, 1895), *Concrete Age* (vol. 26–4), *Galaxy* (vol. 4), *Hobbies* (June 1935), *Invention* (Jan. 7, 1899), *Journal of Society of Arts* (vol. 11.358), *Living Age* (August 31, 1867), *Masonic Outlook* (Nov. 1934), *Mechanic's Magazine* (1834), *Machinery* (March 1898), *Practical Magazine* (1875), *Scientific American* (August 20, 1853; July 8, 1854; July 2, 1859; August 16, 1902; Jan. 23, 1904; March 16, 1912; May 3, 1913; Sept. 4, 1920, *Sewing Machine Advance* (July 1879), *Sewing Machine News* (Sept. 1880, Nov. 1880, Oct. 1883), *Sewing Machine Times* (Feb. 10, 1893; Jan. 25, 1906; April 25, 1907; August 25, 1919), *Sewing Machine World* (June 1875), *Smithsonian Institution Bulletin* 3056, *Young People's Weekly* (Jan. 22, 1901).

Walter Hunt also received newspaper notices: *Brooklyn Daily Eagle* (April 9, 1899; August 1, 1920; April 8, 1934), *Buffalo Commercial* (Oct. 2, 1895), *Buffalo Times* (Oct. 11, 1895), *New York American* (Jan. 29, 1912), *New York Journal* (August 2, 1920), *New York Sun* (Feb. 26, 1916; Sept. 13, 1915), *New York Tribune* (May 2, 1920), *New York World* (May 29, 1902; May 10, 1908; Aug. 1, 1920; April 26, 1927; Oct. 1, 1921; Dec. 8, 1929), *Philadelphia Times* (Sept. 15, 1895); etc.

References to Walter Hunt and his inventions may be found in the following encyclopedias: *Chamber's Encyclopedia, Champlin's Young Folk's Cyclopedia of Common Things, Compton's Pictured Encyclopedia, Encyclopedia Americana, Encyclopædia Britannica, National Eneyclopedia of American Biography, Nelson's Encyclopedia, New International Encyclopedia.*

Additional references pertaining to Walter Hunt and his inventions may also be found in J. Battey *Manual of the Sewing Machine*, Bishop's *History of American Manufactures*, A. F. Collins *A Bird's Eye View of Invention*, R. C. Cook *Sewing Machines*, A. Daul *Das Buch von der Amer. Nahmaschine*, C. Depew *One Hundred Years of American Commerce*, W. H. Doolittle *Inventions in the Century*, C. R. Gibson *Wonders of Modern*

Manufacturing, U. Green *The Sewing Machine*, Haydn's *Dictionary of Dates*, H. Howe *Adventures and Achievements of Americans*, G. Iles *Leading American Inventors*, J. N. Kane *Famous First Facts*, E. H. Knight *American Mechanical Dictionary*, Meyer's *Konversation Lexicon*, W. A. and A. M. Mowry *American Inventions and Inventors*, J. Parton *Triumphs of Enterprise*, F. A. Talbot *All About Inventions and Discovery*, J. C. Wait *Calendar of Invention and Discovery*.

Index

The inventions of Walter Hunt are indicated by •

A. Bartholf (NYC) 229
Abbott, Dr. Alexander 67
Adams, John 20
Adams, President John Quincy 9, 29, 50
Adelphi Hotel (NYC) 77
Adriance, Garrett D. 201, 216
Aimee, Mademoiselle 192
Aitken, William B. 239
•alarm gong 30–31, 42, 43, 44, 45, 48
Albany (N.Y.) 10, 11, 12, 59
Albany Evening Journal 79
Albany Paper Collar Company 242
Albertson, William 14, 16, 17
Alexander, G. C. 138
Alexander, I. 138
Alling, Alexander M. 184, 216, 218
almshouses 45, 68, 91
alum 39
American Institute 66, 91, 106, 111, 120,
    147, 161; Fair 80, 94, 273
*American Magazine of Useful and Enter-
    taining Knowledge* 172
American Magnetic Sewing Machine Co.
    (NYC) 229
American Polytechnic Journal 196
Amos Street (NYC) 53, 72, 178, 180, 217;
    (#103) 54, 66; (#111) 52, 54; (#112) 54
Anatomy (Cheselden) 32
Andrews, Horace 269
Angevera, S. E. 50
aniseed 32
Annual Journal of the American Institute 94
antimacassar 69
•antipodean walker 187–192
apples 36

Arrowsmith, Augustus T. 130, 131, 136, 148
Arrowsmith, George A. 62, 72, 73, 74, 75,
    76, 77, 78, 79, 80, 88, 89, 90, 92, 106,
    107, 130, 142, 143, 145, 146, 147, 151, 152,
    153, 154, 155, 156, 158, 165, 166, 172, 177,
    178, 179, 181, 184, 185, 201, 202, 207,
    208, 215, 216, 218, 219, 222, 223, 226,
    227, 272
Art of Love (Ovid) 32
asafœtida 32
Ashland, William K. 184
Astor, John Jacob 48
Asylum Street (NYC) 53; (#22) 53
Auburn (N.Y.) 10
auction 21
Austin Sisters 192
•automatic steam table 265

Bachelder, J. 175
Baillie, James S. 68
Baldwin, George E. 67
Ball, Joshua D. 178, 179, 184, 186
•ball caster 55–56
Baltimore 90
Bank of the United States 91
Bank Street: (#69) 260
banks 10, 18
Barclay Street 14; (#65) 14, 16
barge 12
Barnes, Erastus 26
Barnum, P. T. 191
Barnum's American Museum 191
Barrett, George C. 293
Bartholf, A. (NYC) 229

307

Batchellor, C. 3
Bean, Benjamin W. 173
Bean, J. W. (Boston) 229
beans 36
beaver hats 18, 44
Beaver Street 77
Bedford Street: (#62) 53, 54, 57, 59; (#63) 54
beef 35
beeswax 39
Bell, J. D. 201
Bell, Peter 196
Bennett, James Gordon 81, 263
Bennett, S. O. 104
Bible 40
Bishop, William H. 269
black crepe 21
blacksmiths 38, 219
Blackwell's Island 68
Blatchford, Samuel 288; Blatchford, Seward and Griswold (law firm) 288
Bleecker Street 120, 178; (#182) 66; (#256) 115
Bliss, George W. 186
Bliss, Signor 192
blockade runners 242
Blodgett, S. C. 175, 186
Bloomer, Elisha 148
bombazines 17, 25
Booneville (N.Y.) 11
borax 32
Boston (Mass.) 76, 79, 175, 230
Boston Daily Evening Transcript 202
The Botanic Garden 32
Botany (Lee) 32
•bottle stopper 192–199
Bowery: (#37) 188
Bowery Theater (NYC) 41
Bowker, John P., Jr. 215, 228
Boyd, Maria 46
Boyd, Samuel 46
Bradford, William 183, 186
Bradish, Charles 4
Bradish, James S. 177
Bradshaw, J. A. 175
Brady, John Riker 293
brass foundry 47
Breck, Joseph 238
brewery 47
Bridgham, Joseph 201
Broad Street 21; (#8) 89

Broadway 17, 77; (#111) 17; (#112) 14; (#179) 192; (#191) 285; (#201) 183; (#208) 264; (#256) 62; (#286) 17; (#287) 17; (#305) 229, 230; (#321) 17; (#323) 204, 220; (#407) 18; (#408) 239; West Broadway (#105) 68
Brooklyn (N.Y.) 10, 76, 88, 287, 293, 294
Browne, Causeten C. 269, 288
Bryant, William C., & Co. 293
Buchel, Christian W. 158, 161, 172
Bucklin, G. M. 285
Buffalo (N.Y.) 10
Bunker, Cyrus J. 237
Burgundy pitch 32
Burke, Commissioner Edmund 149, 153, 156, 158, 170
Burlingame, Anson 174
Burns, Robert 32
butter 36

cabinet and chair makers 21
Cambridge (Mass.) 173
camphene 280
camphor 32, 39
Canandaigua (N.Y.) 10, 28
candles 39
Canton Iron Works 90
capital 9, 10, 23, 45, 58, 73, 77, 89, 93, 106, 166, 173, 175, 188, 201
capitalists 173
carbonic gas 27
Carlock, William D. 184, 219, 226, 227
Carthage (Ill.) 130
cashmere shawls 17
Castle Clinton 28
Castle Garden 39
castor oil 32
Cedar Street 14
Centre Street: (#10) 259
Cerro Gordo (Mexico) 152
Chambers Street: (#11) 259; (#61) 193
Champlain Canal 59
chandlers 16, 21, 47
Chapin, Jonathan 115, 127, 130, 136, 138, 139, 143, 148, 149, 150, 155, 167, 168, 170, 200, 201, 215, 233, 234
Charles E. Muzzy & Company 17
Charles Street: (#115) 206
Chatham Street 22
Chatham Street Chapel 76

Chatham Theater 41
Chelsea 46, 47
Chemical National Bank 264
Cherry Street: (#68) 73
chickens 35, 36
Chillicothe (Ohio) 92, 177
chimney sweeps 38
China 130
Chippendale furniture 55
Choate, The Hon. Rufus 184, 186, 201
cholera epidemic (1834) 75, 76
Christopher Street 53
cigar *see* segar
Cincinnati (Ohio) 193, 196
cinnamon 32
cistern 37, 53
city directories 53, 66
City Hall (NYC) 21, 47
City Hotel (NYC) 14
city water 37
Civil War 242
Clark, Edward 193, 194, 196, 201, 202,
    265, 266, 267, 268, 287, 288, 289, 292
Clark, Joseph 122, 123
Clay, Secretary of State Henry 9, 50, 130
Close, George C. 239
clothing (descriptions) 18, 19
coaches 43; coachmen 43
Cochran, John W. 182
Cochran and Affroms (clothing store) 17
Coke, Sir Edward 77
Cole, George 184
Cole, M. I. 193
Cole, Phineas 23
collar industry 237, 239, 242; *see also*
    paper collars
Columbia College 46
"Comin' Thru the Rye" 39
Commerce (steamboat) 12
Commerce Street 53
Commissioner of Patents 104, 149, 155,
    156, 158, 193, 194, 213, 216, 224, 227,
    228, 229, 230, 231, 233, 238, 246, 247,
    250, 258, 259, 280, 281, 283, 285, 287,
    289, 294
Common Council 20–21, 46, 47, 48
Conant, J. S. 175
Congress 91, 142
Connecticut 10
consumption 115
contracts 23

cook 40
Cooper, Benson S. 238, 239
Cooper, George 66
Cooper, James Fenimore 38
Cooper, Peter 273
Cooper, Samuel 216, 222, 234
Corl, Abraham 101
Corliss, George Henry 173
Corliss, George R. 206
corn 13, 36
Cornelia Street 53
corsets 76
Cortland Street 13
Court Street: (#4) 222
Crystal Palace Exposition 203
curriers 21
Cutter, Norman 239

Daly, Charles Patrick 291, 293
Daniel (Biblical) 82
Darling, William R. 291, 293
Davenport, Thomas 77
Davis, Jefferson 203
Day, Benjamin Henry 69
Dayan, Charles 23, 28
de Bois, Jacob 131
"debtor's oath" 174
Declaration of Independence 20
De Lacy, Andrew 269
Delancey Street: (#252) 122
Democrat 4
De Witt, John 120
Dey Street 14
Dictionary of Terms Employed in Medicine
    32
Diseases of Children (Underwood) 32
distillery 47
•diver's apparatus 263, 270
Dixon, C. P. 164
Dodge, Dr. Jonathan 67, 111, 115
Doig, Andrew Wheeler 8, 9, 23
domestics 40
Donaldson, Alexander 192
Dorcas Sewing Machine Co. (NYC) 229
Dorchester (Mass.) 228
Doyle, James E. 66, 67
Doyle and Patterson 66, 67
dragon's blood 32
•dress pin 161–171
dressing 47

Drury Lane Theater 191
dry goods merchants 21
Duane Market 35
Duane Street: (#48-50) 153
Duncan, John 172
Dunham, E. M. 193
Dunlap's Hotel (NYC) 181, 182
Durgin, Charles A. 230
Dusenberry, William H. 238
Dutch Reformed Church (NYC) 153

E. H. Valentine & Company (NYC) 237,
239
ear trumpet 17
earthenware dealers 21
East River 88
The Economy of Human Life 32
Edinburgh Encyclopedia 172
eels 5, 6
Eighth Avenue 46; (#202) 218
Eighth Avenue Theater 192
electric motor 77
Elements of Arithmetic 25
Eli Hart & Company (NYC) 91
Elliot, William P. 213
Ellis, Charles Edward (Commissioner of
Deeds) 23
Elmendorf, Edmund, Jr. 124, 152
Ely, Albert Brewster 176, 177, 179, 184,
185, 186, 201
Emerson, William 182
England 78, 173, 174
Eubanks, Thomas 193, 196
Europe 25
Evans, Andrew A. 242

Federalist Party 4
Felton, Mrs. 54
Ferry Street 21
Field, John C. 258
fire (1835) 88–89, 93
Fire Engine Company No. 33 (NYC) 73
fire engines 38, 88
•firearm, breech-loading repeater 144–148,
151, 158, 161, 162, 163–166
•firearm cartridge: (metallic) 151–156, 159,
160, 161; (wooden) 154–158, 160, 161
firemen 39, 84, 88
Fisher, George 173, 175, 176, 186

Fitzgerald, W. P. N. 223, 224, 225, 226,
227
Five Points riot 78
flatrunner 26
flax 2, 3; flax mill 1, 7
flax machine 3, 4, 42, 48
•flax spinner 1–9, 10, 11, 20, 21, 22
flute 38
Folger, Benjamin H. 58, 59, 60, 62, 66;
Folger and Lamb (law firm) 58
•forest saw *see* saw for felling trees
forge 47
foundries 58
•fountain pen 138–141, 148, 149, 150
France 78
Frankfort Street 22
Franklin House (NYC) 14
Franklin Market (NYC) 35
Freemasons 27, 274; Master Mason 27
Front Street: (#26) 58
Fulton Market (NYC) 35
Fulton Street 14, 120; (#135) 182
furnace 47
furriers 21

Gadwin House (NYC) 14
•galvanic current machine 98
Gardiner, Smith 181
gas lamps/lights 27, 39
General Theological Seminary (NYC) 46
General Trades Union of New York 76
Geneva (N.Y.) 10
George W. Keene and Sons (manufactur-
ers) 269, 276
Germany 78
"ghost" inventions 257
Gifford, George 288, 291
Giles, Joel 179, 186, 201, 216, 222
A Glance of New York (Green) 41
Glasgow (Scotland) 172
Gleason, Dr. Sewall 213
•Globe Stove 57–68; Globe Stove Com-
pany 73, 217, 218; *see also* Hunt's Patent
Globe Stove Factory
Glover, Charles H. 291, 293
Glover, Thomas James 136, 138, 139
glue 47
Gold Street 161; (#42) 120, 123, 145, 167,
178; (#60) 119
Goodyear, Charles 94

Gould, Commissioner D. 178, 179, 182
Gouverneur Street 73
Graham, Mr. 119
Graves, Lyman 27
Gray, Solomon S. 242
Great Masonic Hall (NYC) 45
Green, Asa 41
green tea 36
Green-Wood [also, Greenwood] Cemetery
    (Brooklyn, N.Y.) 294, 295
Greenough, John James 158, 172, 196, 206,
    214, 220, 281
Greenwich (N.Y.) 173
Greenwich Street 14, 43
Greenwood, John, Jr. 191
Greenwood Cemetery 294, 295
Griffin, Charles A. 239
Grim, Charles E. 152
grindstone 48, 49
Grover, Baker & Co. (NYC) 229, 231,
    289
gum albumin 32
gum aloes 32
gum myrrh 32
Guthrie, James 203

Hackensack Junction (N.J.) 269, 270
hackney coaches 13, 14, 34
Hall, Asa 43, 44
Hall, M. Howland 237, 239
Hammond Street: (#56) 82, 93
Hampton (Conn.) 170
handcart 14
handyman 40
Hankins, J. 189
Hanover Street: (#35) 230
Harlem 82
Harris, Townsend 67
Hart, Eli, & Company (NYC) 91
Harvard University 174
Hassler, Ferdinand 25
Hatch, Cheney 186
Hebrew language 46
•heel for boots, shoes 268, 269, 276–279
Henry, B. Tyler 164
Highit, Mr. 60
Hilton, Henry 290
Hodges, Silas Henry 250
Hoe, Peter 27
Hoe, R., & Company 120

hogsheads 37
Hone, The Hon. Philip 30
Hood, Battel & Co. (Worcester, Mass.)
    229
horizontal spinner 3
Hoskins, Willis 1, 2, 3, 4, 7, 8, 9, 10, 11, 21,
    22, 23, 28, 31, 195
House, Jared 23
Howard's Hotel (NYC) 89
Howe, Amasa 173, 174, 182
Howe, Elias, Jr. 173, 174, 175, 176, 177,
    178, 182, 183, 184, 186, 193, 200, 201,
    202, 203, 204, 205, 206, 207, 208, 214,
    216, 219, 220, 221, 224, 228, 229, 230,
    233, 267, 272, 274, 287, 288, 289, 290,
    292, 293, 295
Howe v. Underwood 224
Howson, Henry 242, 243
Hudson (N.Y.) 10
Hudson River 16, 28, 34, 47, 59
Hudson Street 178; (#530) 207; (#535)
    187; (#552) 260
Hunt, Adoniram F. (son) 57, 59, 62, 74,
    75, 76, 78, 79, 80, 81, 82, 83, 84, 88, 89,
    90, 92, 177, 178, 179, 180, 184, 185, 201,
    202, 207, 217
Hunt, Albinos (brother) 57
Hunt, Almira (sister) 5, 57
Hunt, Angelina (sister) 57
Hunt, Caroline M. (daughter) 7, 9, 24, 25,
    32, 38, 49, 70, 71, 72, 76, 142, 182, 185,
    200, 201, 215, 216, 218, 271, 294
Hunt, Elizabeth (sister) 57
Hunt, Enos (brother) 57
Hunt, Frances Augusta (daughter) 53,
    142, 201, 287, 294
Hunt, George Washington (son) 29, 32,
    39, 70, 139, 141, 142, 144, 145, 146, 149,
    151, 152, 200, 215, 245, 246, 250, 256,
    276, 283, 288, 289, 290, 294
Hunt, Hannah (sister) 5, 57
Hunt, Harry (brother) 57
Hunt, Hiram (brother) 4, 5, 6, 57
Hunt, Levisa (sister) 57
Hunt, N. (Boston) 230
Hunt, Philo (brother) 57
Hunt, Polly (wife) 5, 6, 7, 8, 9, 10, 16, 21,
    24, 25, 28, 29, 31, 32, 35, 37, 38, 40, 41,
    42, 44, 46, 47, 48, 49, 50, 53, 54, 55, 57,
    69, 70, 71, 72, 84, 87, 93, 94, 96, 100,
    104, 105, 106, 107, 111, 115, 119, 139, 142,

153, 182, 200, 201, 214, 215, 246, 250, 260, 262, 263, 265, 268, 270, 271, 274, 283, 287, 292

Hunt, Polly Anne (daughter) 7, 9, 24, 27, 29, 30, 32, 72, 142, 294

Hunt, Rachel (mother) 5, 6, 57

Hunt, Sherman (father) 5, 6, 57, 107

Hunt, Sherman, Jr. (brother) 57

Hunt, Walter: absent mindedness 7; as "artist" 66; birthday 9; copybook maxims 25, 26; death of 27; deposition in Howe-Phelps lawsuit 178–179; grief at loss of son 119; illness (consumption) 270–271; impressions of New York City 13–19; on inventing 68; move to New York City 31–38; obituaries 271–274; physical description 1, 13, 93; Quaker-pacifist views concerning war 139, 141–143; reaction to court decision (Howe-Bradford lawsuit) 187; real estate 82–84; school-days 26; sewing 69; stubbornness 5

Hunt, Walter, Jr. (son) 7, 9, 25, 26, 27, 29, 32, 39, 49, 70, 71, 72, 84, 115, 153, 262

Hunt's Patent Globe Stove Factory 178

•"Hunt's Restorative Cordial" *see* "The Life Preserver"

hurdy-gurdies 39

"Hurrah for the Bonnets of Blue" 39

Hydraulic Flour Mills (Chillicote, Oh.) 92

I Spy (game) 24

I.M. Singer Company 204, 214, 220, 221, 228, 229, 230, 265, 266, 293

ice 13, 99

•ice-breaker 99–105

immigrants 83

•improvement to sewing machine (rotary tabletop) 209–214

•improvement to shirt collars: paper 233–237; fabric 238–242

India rubber 94

Indian corn 36

Indians 6

industrial revolution 172

influenza 28, 115

ink 47

•inkstands (inkwells) 127–137, 148

Irish diapers 17

J. B. Nichols (Boston) 229

J. G. Pierson and Brothers (nail dealers) 58

J. W. Bean (Boston) 229

Jackson, President Andrew 78

Jacob Street 21, 37

Jacob's Well (NYC) 37

Jaiapa (Mexico) 152

Japan 67

Jaques, David R. 274

Jarvis, Nathan L., Jr. 293

Java 36

Jefferson, Thomas 20

Jennings, Lewis 161

Jersey City (N.J.) 256, 260, 269

Jersey shore 16

Johnson, Eleazer 216

Johnson, Joel 90, 185

Johnson, John P. 27

Johnson, Joseph B. 175

Johnson, William 213

Jones Street 167; (#45) 120

Jordan, Ambrose Latting 186, 201

Journal of Arts, Sciences and Manufacturers and Repertory of Patent Inventions 153

Journal of the American Institute 86

Journal of the Franklin Institute 50, 52, 63, 111, 156

Juniper berries 32

katydids 20

Keene, George W. 201, 269; Keene, George W., and Sons 269, 276

Keller, Charles M. 153, 155, 201, 269, 288

Kent, John M. 155

Keystone Mills (collar manufacturer) 240

Kidder, Levi 53, 55, 60, 62, 98, 100, 101

Kilby, John 59

King, S. 3

Kingsley, J. L. 272, 274

Kinsey, D. 193, 194, 195, 196, 199

Kinsey, Edward 193, 194, 195, 196, 199

Kipp, Charles T. 187, 188, 190, 192, 193, 200, 209, 213, 214, 215; Kipp and Brown (NYC) 44

Knapp's Springs (NYC) 37

•knife sharpener 48–52, 99, 100

Knox, John M. 170

Knox, Ziba 3, 4, 8, 28

Lackawanna Coal Office (NYC) 62
Lady Clinton (barge) 12
Lafetra, Tylee W. 201
Lake Ontario 79
Lansingburgh (N.Y.) 10
Last of the Mohicans (Cooper) 38
"The Last Rose of Summer" 39
Laurens Street: (#156) 153
Lawrence, Richard 78
lease/leasing 47, 54
Lectures (Blair) 32
Lee, J. E. 79
Leroux, Pierre 121, 122, 123
Lerow, J. A. 175, 186; Lerow and Blodgett
    sewing machines 183
Lewis County (Martinsburg, N.Y.) *Repub-
    lican* 272
Leydon (N.Y.) 11
•"The Life Preserver" 262, 265, 266, 275
lime water 39
liquor 27
Little Green Street 169
livery stable 43, 47
lobster 38
Lockport (N.Y.) 10
Lockwood, William E. 240, 242, 243,
    245, 250; Lockwood Manufacturing
    Company 242
Lombardy poplars 17
London 153
Lord Byron 139
lottery 18
Loucks, A. 62
Loucks, Polly *see* Hunt, Polly
Loucks, Dr. William 7, 29, 32
Lowville (Lewis County, N.Y.) 1, 3, 8, 10,
    11, 21, 23, 24, 29, 32, 36, 37, 38, 41, 45,
    49, 53, 107, 177
Lyle, J. Van Ness 290
Lynn (Mass.) 269

McClelland, John 67
McCormick, John 188, 189, 191
Macdougal Street: (#141) 84
machinist 217
McKennan, Judge William 256
mackerel 38
Madresberger, Josef 78
magnesia 32
mahogany 60

maid 40
Mandarin capes 17
Manhattan (N.Y.) 52, 88
Manhattan Company (NYC) 37
Marines 89
markets 35, 37
Marseille quilts 17
Martin, George G. 258, 259, 281, 283,
    285, 286
Martin, John W. 257, 258, 259, 281, 283,
    285, 286, 290
Martin, Joseph P. 173, 175
Martin, Brigadier General Walter 257
Martinsburg (N.Y.) 36, 257
Mason, Charles 213, 227, 228, 229, 231,
    258, 272, 285
Masonic: hall 75; lodges 27
Maynard, Arba K. 289, 290
Mead, Abraham 239
mechanical designer 120
Mechanics Magazine 63, 85, 86
medical kit 32
•medicated vapor bath 263
Merchant's Bank (NYC) 45
Merchants Exchange (NYC) 17
merino 17
Merrill, C. 3
Merrill, Helen 201
Mexican-American War 142–143, 151, 152;
    opposition to 144
Mexican army 144, 151
Mexico 139, 142
Middlesex County (N.J.) 219
Midwest 92
midwife 29
Midwifery (Denman) 32
milkmen 38
Milus, Mr. 194, 195
Mohawk River 59
Montgomery Boarding House (NYC) 14
Montgomery Street 73
Moore, Abner S. 201
Moore, Bishop Benjamin 46
Moore, Professor Clement Clarke 46, 47,
    48, 80
Morey, Charles 175; Morey & Johnson 221
Morgan, William 28
Mormons 130
Morris, William L. 104
Morrison, Consider H., Jr. 27
Morrison, Lewis B. 96

Morsell, James S. 230, 231
Morsell, W. S. 196
mortar and pestle 32
Morton Street 53; (#16) 271
mosquitoes 20, 38
"The Mountain Maid" 39
mourning dresses 17
Munn & Company 206, 274
Murdock, John 234
musicians 38
muslin 16
mutton 35
mutton tallow 39
Muzzy, Charles E., & Company 17

N. Hunt (Boston) 230
Nagle, Cornelius 131
•nail-cutting machine 111–115
nail factory 47
•nail-feeding machine 120
•nail-making machine 106–111
Nassau Street 43, 167, 293; (#15) 152; (#23) 62; (#31) 288; (#77) 281; (#79) 148; (#82) 139; (#128) 96
Nathan, Emma 189
Nathan, J. J. 189
National Hotel (NYC) 14
Navy 89
Ne Plus Ultra Collar Company (Biddleford, Maine) 242
New Bedford (Mass.) 183
New Haven Arms Company 166
New Haven (Conn.) 94
New Street: (#4) 291
New York Amphitheater (NYC) 188, 191
New York City 9, 12, 24, 25, 29, 31, 34, 36, 37, 38, 41, 45, 48, 52, 62, 76, 78, 79, 82, 88, 89, 90, 91, 93, 100, 101, 158, 173, 175, 176, 177, 178, 182, 193, 206, 207, 229, 230, 239, 259, 260, 269, 288, 293
New York Clipper 191
New York Commercial 62
New York Courier and Examiner 89
New York Daily Times 220
New York Daily Tribune 183, 189, 203, 204, 205, 206, 207, 208, 220, 221, 291
New York Evening Post 22, 79, 84
New York Herald 80, 189, 191, 263, 271
New York Hospital (NYC) 45
New York Mirror 22, 28

New York Morning Herald 67, 81, 82
New York Patent Nail Company 119, 120, 121, 123
New York Sacred Music Society (NYC) 76
New York State Prison (NYC) 53
New York Times 220, 221, 291
New York Tribune 220, 271
Newark (N.J.) 76, 218
Newell, Charles S. 281
newspapers 18
Niblo's Bank Coffee House (NYC) 14, 39
Niblo's Garden (NYC) 92, 147, 273
Nichols, J. B. (Boston) 229
Nile (Berrien County, Mich.) 173
Niles Register 76
19th Street 46, 47, 48; West (#270) 177
noise 19
Northern Journal 107, 177
Northern Railroad of New Jersey 269
Norwich (Conn.) 166
notarization fee 9

Ohio 91
oil lamp 7
omnibuses 19, 38
organ grinders 38
Orient Lodge No. 150 Free and Accepted Masons (NYC) 27
Ostrum, Shepherd 47, 50
Ostrum, William F. 47
oxygen soap 18

Page, Charles Grafton 196, 213; Page & Company 196, 213
Palmer, Courtland C. 164
Panic of 1837 91, 92, 93
paper collars 257; demand for 242
Paris 25
Park Place House (NYC) 14
Park Theater (NYC) 41
Parsons, Sparhawk 123, 124
Patent Act (July 4, 1836) 200
patent application 9, 31, 50, 52, 56, 62, 85, 96, 104, 111, 115, 120, 124, 131, 136, 139, 148, 149, 152, 153, 155, 156, 161, 170, 192, 193, 196, 214, 233, 234, 235, 238, 239, 243, 259, 267, 269, 283, 285, 292
patent law 222, 223

patent rights 242
patents 9, 31, 50, 52, 53, 56, 62, 66, 67, 74, 75, 77, 78, 85, 90, 96, 104, 107, 115, 119, 123, 124, 127, 136, 149, 152, 170, 175, 176, 177, 183, 192, 193, 195, 200, 201, 205, 206, 207, 209, 213, 215, 216, 225, 228, 234, 239, 242, 245, 246, 256, 266, 267, 288, 293
Paterson (N.J.) strike (1835) 78
Patterson, Abijah 66
Patterson, Charles E. 259, 280
Pearl Street 21; (#124) 183
pencil 7
Pennsylvania 91
Perkins, Jay N. 201
Perote (Mexico) 152
Perry, John C. 289
Peruvian bark 32
pet banks 91
Phelps, Orson C. 176, 183
Philadelphia (Pa.) 76, 242
Phillips, John 68
Pierce, General Franklin 203
Pierson, J. G. 58, 60; J. G. Pierson and Brothers 58
pillboxes 32
Pine Street 43; (#14) 285; (#14½) 152
pineapples 27
Platonists 41
policeman 13, 14, 19, 84
Polk, President James Knox 142
"poor debtor's oath" 174
porters 13; charges 14
postmaster 149
potatoes 36
Potter, Orlando B. 231, 289
Poughkeepsie (N.Y.) 10, 76
Pratt, E. P. 177
Pray, Henry 96
press agents 207
•pressure machine (adamantine candles) 263
Proctor, William F. 274
public domain 246

Quakers 24, 25, 27, 39, 41, 139, 143, 144, 146, 179

R. Hoe & Company (printers) 120

Rabbeth, Jesse 170, 171
race violence (1834) 76
Radcliff, Frederick E. 239
railway locomotive 77
Randel, Culver 218
real estate 45, 47, 48, 52, 80, 82, 83, 84, 91, 93
red lead 6
Remsen (N.Y.) 11
resin 32
"Rest, Warrior Rest" 39
•"Restorative Cordial" see "The Life Preserver"
retail emporiums 21
Reversible Paper Collar Company (Boston) 242
Rhode Island 91
Richardson, Jonathan 169, 170, 209, 213
Richardson, William 170
Ridgway, John W. 234, 235, 237, 239
Rio Grande 142
Rivers Family 189
Rivington Street: (#257) 101
Robbins, Zenas C. 238, 239
Robbins & Lawrence Company 164
Rochester (N.Y.) 10, 78, 79
Rochester Daily Democrat 78, 79
Rodgers, James 173
Roe, Frances Augusta (daughter) 201, 287, 294; *see also* Hunt, Frances Augusta
Roe, Townsend 201
Rogers, Halsey 120
Rogers, John 149
Rollins, Daniel G. 239
rope 52
ropewalks 52
•rotary tabletop sewing machine 209–214, 258
royalties 200, 242
Ruggles, Horace M. 237
Ruggles, Robert B. 123
Ruggles, Sam 23
Ryder's Alley 120

Sacket's Harbor (N.Y.) 10
•safety lamp 259, 263, 280–286
•safety (dress) pin 161–171
Saint, Thomas 78
St. John's Day 45
Saint Nicholas 24

saltpeter 39
Sandford, Charles W. 289, 290
Sands, Richard 188, 190, 191
Sandy Hook (N.J.) 17
Santa Anna, General 151
Saratoga (N.Y.) 111
•saw for felling trees (forest saw) 80, 84–87
scale and weights 32
Schenectady (N.Y.) 10
Schuyler, John 239
Scientific American 184, 186, 203, 205, 206, 207, 213, 223, 228, 272, 274
Scioto Gazette 177
Scott, General Winfield 152
Seely, Walter 239
segar 11, 21, 146
Senate Reports No. 203 247
Sergeant, John 111
Sermon on the Mount 139
17th Street West: (#174) 167
sewage 15
"Sewing by Machinery" 78
•sewing machine 69–73, 74, 76, 77, 78, 80, 89, 90, 92, 130, 156, 172, 174, 175, 176, 179, 183, 185, 193, 196, 200, 201, 203, 205, 206, 207, 208, 214, 215, 216, 218, 219, 222, 224, 225, 233, 257, 258, 287, 288, 289, 290; *see also* sewing machine improvement
sewing machine controversy 172–186, 200–209, 215–232, 266, 267, 287–295; Howe-Bradford lawsuit 183–186; Howe-Phelps lawsuit 176–184
•sewing machine improvement (rotary tabletop) 209–214
Seymour, Captain George E. 12
Seymour, Isaac 286
Seymour, James 213
shad 38
ship chandleries 16, 21, 47
•shirt collar improvements: paper 233; fabric 238–242
shoe pegging machine 77
Shute, E. L. 258
Sickles, George C. 148
Sing Sing Prison 53
Singer, Isaac Merritt 193, 201, 203, 204, 205, 206, 215, 220, 222, 228, 231, 266, 286, 289; Singer, I.M., Company 204, 214, 220, 221, 228, 229, 230, 265, 266, 293

Singer Sewing Machine 201, 202–203, 204, 205
Sixth Avenue 47
skins and hides, preparing of 47
slaughter house 47
Sloate, George B. 288
Smith, E. 164
Smith, Frederick 182
Smith, Hiram 130
Smith, Horace 164
Smith, J. D. 22
Smith, Joseph 130
Smith, T. G. 66
Smith and Graham 240
Smith & Wesson 164
snake root 32
Society for the Encouragement of Faithful Domestic Servants (NYC) 40
soda water 13, 27
•soles for boots and shoes 121–126
soup kitchens 37
South Street 21
South Third Street: (#255) 242; (#257) 242; (#259) 242
speaking trumpets 16, 39, 88
specie payment 91
spinning and roping machine (Hoskins/Knox) 3, 4
•spiral self-supplying twister 52
•spiral springs for belts, pantaloons, etc. 93–97
spit boxes 12, 146
sponges 32
Sprague, Judge Peleg 184, 202, 208, 221, 224, 226, 227
Springfield Collar Company (Springfield, Mass.) 242
stagecoaches 11, 16, 19, 59
State Street: (#39) 234
Staten Island 17
steamboats 12, 13, 16
Stevens, Thomas S. 68
Stevenson, George 77
Stillwell, Richard E. 207, 216
Stock Exchange 46, 89
Stonington and Providence Railroad 164
Stoughton, C. B. 293
Stoughton, E. H. 293
Stranger's Guide to the Commercial Metropolis (Blunt) 14
straw-sellers 38

street singers 38
•street sweeping machine 62
Strong, George D. 111, 115
sugar 36
sulfur 32
The Sun 69
Supreme Court 184
Surgery (Cooper) 32
surgical instruments 32
Surveying (Gibson) 32
Suydam, Henry 17
Swain, Shubael E. 259, 280
sweet oil 32
syringes 32

table and piano covers 17
taffetas 17
tallow chandlery 47
tambour machine 172
Tammany Hall 22
Taney, Judge Roger Brooke 183
tanning 47
taverns 11, 16
Taylor, Henry 66
Taylor, Stephen 153
Taylor, Zachary 151
Tenth Street 17
Thames Street 14
Thimmonier, Barthelemy 78
Thomas, Philip Francis 287, 288
Thomas, William 174
Thompson, James 111, 120
Thompson, W. T. 120
Thornton, Captain 142
three R's 26
tooth powder 28
Torboss, Sarah Arnetta 142, 152, 153
Townsend, Jacob 98, 99, 100, 101, 104, 106
Townsend, John P. 285
Transfer of Patent Records 258
Trenton (N.Y.) 11
Trinity Church (NYC) 46
Troy (N.Y.) 10, 59
Turin (N.Y.) 11
turnips 36
turpentine 47
20th Street 47, 48
24th Street 46
•twine twister 52

Ullman, Daniel 66
umbrellas with whalebone frames 17
Underhill, Abraham 291
Underwood, Orson 207
Union Paper Collar Company 242, 256
United States Circuit Court 176
United States Congress 91, 142
United States Patent Office 9, 50, 52, 53, 62, 66, 67, 77, 85, 96, 97, 101, 104, 111, 115, 120, 124, 131, 136, 138, 148, 150, 152, 153, 154, 156, 157, 158, 160, 161, 170, 172, 173, 193, 194, 196, 199, 206, 207, 213, 214, 215, 216, 219, 220, 222, 224, 225, 228, 234, 235, 238, 239, 242, 243, 245, 246, 247, 258, 269, 276, 280, 281, 285, 286, 287, 288
United States Supreme Court 183
Utica (N.Y.) 10, 11, 76

Vade Mecum (Hooper) 32
Vail, John 235
Valentine, Edward 237, 239; Valentine, E. H., & Company 237, 239
Van Buren, Caroline M. (daughter) 182, 185, 200, 201, 216, 218, 271, 294; *see also* Hunt, Caroline
Van Buren, Martin 91
Vandervoort, P. L. 17
Vanduzer, S. 73
Van Pell, David 111
Van Stoutenburgh, Henry 68
Varney, George C. 235
varnish 47
Vauxhall (NYC) 39
velocipede 263
Vera Cruz (Mexico) 152
Vesey Street 14
View of Society and Manners in America (Darusmont) 54
vitriol 32, 47
Volcanic Arms Company (New Haven, Conn.) 166
Von Schmidt 160

wages 2, 76
wagon 26
Wall Street 17, 46, 88; (#20) 80, 82; (#26) 81
War of 1812 1

warning horns *see* alarm gong
Warren, Ohio 92, 177
washerwomen 235
Washington (D.C.) 75, 170, 196
Washington, George 29
Washington Market (NYC) 35
Washington Street 14; (#45) 34; (#46) 184
watchmen 83
Water Street 21; (#213) 66
water supply 37
Waterford (N.Y.) 59
Waterman, John 77
Watson, P. H. 170
Wesson, D. B. 164
West, William G. 239
West Broadway: (#105) 68
West Street 15, 16
Western Territory 92
Westport (Conn.) 85, 217
Wheeler, David Everett 62, 77, 96
Wheeler, Wilson & Co. (NYC) 229, 231, 289
Whilson, John 217
White, Henry J. 256
white beans 36
Whitin, M. D. 18
Whiting, William E. 183
Whittemore, Amos 77
whittling 2

Wilkes, Edmund 45, 46, 47
Willey, Senator Waitman Thomas 247
William C. Bryant & Co., Printers (NYC) 293
William Street: (#8) 58, 62
Williams & Orvis (sewing machine manufacturer) 288
Williamsburg (Kings County, N.Y.) 182, 219
Wilson, John C. 193
Winchester, O. F. 166
Winchester & Davis 166
Winchester Repeating Arms Company 166
•window-lock 263
Windsor (Vt.) 164
Wirt, Attorney General William 9, 50
Wisner, W. D. 238
Wood, Elias 3
Wood, William 216, 217
Woodbury, Justice Levi 184
Wooldridge, John 201, 202, 203; Wooldridge, Keen & Moore (Lynn, Mass.) 230
Worcester (Mass.) 186
working hours 2
Wounds (Bell) 32

Yorkville (N.Y.) 82